Building High Availability Windows Server™ 2003 Solutions

Microsoft Windows Server System Series

Books in the **Microsoft Windows Server System Series** are written and reviewed by the world's leading technical authorities on Microsoft Windows technologies, including principal members of Microsoft's Windows and Server Development Teams. The goal of the series is to provide reliable information that enables administrators, developers, and IT professionals to architect, build, deploy, and manage solutions using the Microsoft Windows Server System. The contents and code of each book are tested against, and comply with, commercially available code. This series should be an invaluable resource for any IT professional or student working in today's Windows environment.

For more information please go to www.awprofessional.com/msserverseries

Building High Availability Windows Server™ 2003 Solutions

Jeffrey R. Shapiro

Marcin Policht

⚔Addison-Wesley

**Upper Saddle River, NJ • Boston • Indianapolis
San Francisco • New York • Toronto • Montreal
London • Munich • Paris • Madrid • Capetown
Sydney • Tokyo • Singapore • Mexico City**

Library of Congress Catalog Number: 2004115104

ISBN 0-32-122878-2

This product is printed digitally on demand.

First printing, *December 2004*

This book is dedicated to all the victims of terrorism.

Contents

PART I   HIGH-PERFORMANCE WINDOWS COMPUTING

Chapter 5   **Preparing the Platform for a High-Performance Network** **97**

PART II   BUILDING HIGH AVAILABILITY WINDOWS SERVER 2003 SOLUTIONS

Chapter 9   High Availability, High-Performance SQL Server Solutions **245**

Acknowledgments

This was not an easy book to write. Writing aside, many long days, nights, and weekends over the past two years were spent focusing on little else than high availability, high-performance Windows Server 2003 solutions. For several very large and very complex networks, at three different organizations, I relied on a team of highly available individuals who are dedicated to high-performance computing. It took a large amount of team effort to put together the architecture and implementations to follow that are discussed in the chapters.

Much of my experience in high availability solutions in the past two years was spent at Broward County, Florida, Office of Information Technology (OIT). There, I worked to transform the county's Novell Netware Network into a highly sophisticated Windows Server solution. We started with architecture (which took almost two years to perfect) and then focused on clustering, load balancing, security, operations, and more for another six months. Every Windows XP client (and there were thousands of them) was then migrated off NetWare and onto the Windows Server network by the desktop migration team in record time.

I would like to thank the entire IT team at OIT, but special mention must go to several individuals. Philip Bardowell, director of Infrastructure Services, gave incredible support and was, with his life no doubt bonded to nationally recognized IT chief CIO Nicole Fontayne-Mack, willing to allow us to implement many of Microsoft's bleeding-edge technologies, which at the time many considered too new and too risky to contemplate on a network supporting thousands of users and more than 80 local government agencies. It became very clear to me from the get-go that Philip placed tremendous faith in me, and for that I will always be grateful. Martin Gicala, manager of Lan Technologies, provided unfailing support and had the ability to foster a productive environment with the right brand of humor. As commander of a gaggle of very stressed LAN engineers, Marty succeeds because he is always able to see the light that will come at the end of an eclipse when others only see darkness. The beacon on the team was Philippe Dufour; he provided unwavering support, confidence, and faith—not only in me, but also in the project as a whole. Few project managers can smell the Belgium Chocolate like Philippe.

Another individual who deserves special mention is the ubiquitous Jay Schroff, the most highly decorated MCSE on the planet. Jay spends so much time up in the data center you would think he is one of the server rack components. And then there is Kevin (also known as Norman) Carosella, Lori Yonkman, and James Calcanes, whizzes at server operations and at handling all the paperwork a major Windows Server rollout requires. Kevin has an amazing ability to find all the weapons of "mass confusion" when dealing with the large computer hardware vendors that can turn any project into a crying game. I also had a lot of help from the desktop team of Gayle Dimodica and Christopher Wilbanks who put together an amazing group policy strategy. And, of course, no high availability server implementation is possible without a solid network infrastructure. Throughout the process, I had help from the Data Communications team manager, Benjamin Sanchez, and network architecture expert Carlos Hernandez at my disposal. My hat goes off to Tim Clark; not only did he always stay cheerful while his NetWare network was ripped out from under him, but he also transformed from Netware CNE to Windows Server guru faster than you can spell DFS. You can say that for the DR team of Aixiang Liu, Derrick Ricketts, Hansrum Rarup, and Catalin Anghel as well.

There were many others at OIT that helped me tremendously; however, the individual I really enjoyed working with was Mike Cahill. Without Mike, I doubt I would have made it through the times of extreme technical challenges. I miss working with you, Mike. Keep up the good work.

Over the years, I have come to depend a lot on the character, heart, and soul of a special individual who is both a good friend and an outstanding technical resource. His name is Omar Martinez. We have worked together since 1998 and no other person is as knowledgeable about the client workspace as Omar.

And, certainly, Marcin Policht is a fine engineer and author whom I have depended on with previous books and I thank him for his co-authoring of several of the chapters in this book, including the works on load-balancing and Internet Information Server.

I know many good SQL Server wizards, but Steven Bowman qualifies as the Merlin of them all. If SQL Server is your meal ticket, then immediately turn to Steven's Chapter 9.

I would also like to thank my editorial team at Addison-Wesley. Special thanks go to my acquisitions editor, Jill Harry, for her support, expertise, and amazing project management during the storms (especially the four hurricanes that ravaged her publishing schedule for this book). Special thanks to Brenda Mulligan, editorial assistant—keeping the work flowing. Last words on editing always go to the team that makes sure the words come out right: Michael Thurston, project editor, and Sarah Cisco, copy editor.

And, of course, I would like to thank Keith Holcomb of Royal Palm Technology, Inc., and Debbie Ferencsik of Dell Computers for their support and confidence. The year 2004 is going to be fondly remembered by us all; for all the good (great projects) and the bad (four hurricanes) that it brought.

Jeffrey R. Shapiro

About the Authors

Jeffrey R. Shapiro has worked in Information Technology for nearly 15 years. He is an industry-celebrated author and has published more than a dozen books on IT, network administration, and software development. Jeffrey has written for numerous publications over the years as well. He also regularly speaks at events and frequently participates in training courses on Microsoft systems.

Jeffrey has specialized in Microsoft technologies since 1989. From 1992 to 1998, he was CTO for a leading software development company specializing in telephony solutions for business and was credited with designing the architecture for one of the first Windows-based computer telephony platforms.

In early 2003 Jeffrey was selected to lead the Novell NetWare to Windows Server 2003 migration project for Broward County, Florida. His mandate was to design the architecture for an Active Directory network that would replace the hundreds of servers and Novell Directory Services (NDS) required to support more than 80 agencies. He was also in charge of designing the architecture for three mission-critical, high availability, high-performance data centers supporting thousands of public servants in one of the largest population centers in the United States.

In late 2004 Jeffrey turned his attention almost exclusively to systems and software architecture. He recently formed Normal Data, Inc., a company that specializes in architecting software for enterprise information technology solutions www.codetimes.com. Jeffrey can be reached on the Web at jshapiro@codetimes.com.

Marcin Policht has diverse experience in areas of scripting and programming, as well as system engineering and administration of large-scale, high availability, Windows-based environments. He has shared his expertise as a technical trainer and as a writer, authoring a number of books and Web articles on subjects varying from WMI scripting to Active Directory management.

Preface

The year 2004 will long be remembered as the year that saw the beginning of a huge push by companies and government organizations to once and for all migrate to a Windows Server operating system underpinned by Active Directory and Windows Server 2003. What is also significant about this year is that it will be remembered as the year Microsoft finally ended all support for Windows NT 4.0, the grandfather of the current version of Windows Server that many IT professionals now regard as the Serengeti of the operating system jungle.

In 2004, many companies have finally made the move to ditch Novell NetWare. However, it is not simply enough to trade one operating system for another. Many IT shops going to Windows Server 2003 need to install and configure high availability, high-performance Windows Server 2003 systems that can service their needs day in, day out, 365 days a year. At the same time, they are also striving to lower the cost of installing, operating, and maintaining these systems and the overall cost of ownership (TCO). Windows Server 2003 delivers on all these points.

As companies migrate to the platform that is the *de facto* winner in the network and operating system wars, they face a huge learning curve and dilemma on how best to set up high-performance Windows Server networks for maximum availability and power. Their aspirations come down to one thing: service level—"How do we do it with Windows Server 2003?"

Companies that have made the decision to migrate to Windows Server 2003 ask how they can keep systems up 24/7 or how they can achieve three, four, and perhaps even five times the availability with Microsoft technology. Network administrators ask, "Do we cluster, do we load balance, do we do both, do we invest in hot standbys, replication…what works?" This book gives you the answers to those questions. It will also go further than just failover and fault tolerance and discuss monitoring and operations management and choosing the right technology to accompany Microsoft's high-performance and high availability offerings.

This is the book that caters to your needs. It is about achieving service level and keeping systems up 24/7 with the Windows Server 2003 platform. This book provides a clear and concise roadmap for how to go about using Microsoft Server 2003, (in some cases) with third-party add-ons, for scalability, uptime, performance, and management—and for how to avoid trouble at the same time.

Many administrators and engineers find it hard to make decisions about what they need to do. They hear that clustering and using load balancing is a black art—extremely difficult and prone to disaster. Up until today, their only resources for architecting a high availability solution has been rare and expensive consultants and overzealous consulting services engineers, particularly from hardware vendors. If you are turned to Microsoft technology to achieve your SLA, this book will be the foundation to turn to, to bring it all together.

Microsoft now offers a rich toolset for administration and monitoring, not only what is built into the server products, but also with collateral offerings such as Microsoft Operations Manager (MOM) and Systems Management Server. According to Gartner, Microsoft will own the systems administration market, and possibly surge ahead of IBM, in the coming years. Efforts in this area became very evident in 2003 and 2004 with the advent of new versions of MOM and Systems Management Server. We have thus devoted an entire chapter to monitoring and installing MOM as the essential operations platform for any high availability network.

The book is divided into two parts: Part I, "High-Performance Windows Computing," provides background for high availability, high performance, and service level, and covers theory, but also Active Directory architecture and implementation. Part II, "Building High Availability Windows Server 2003 Solutions," delves into the actual installation and architecture of systems for print, file, SQL Server, Exchange, and IIS, covers network load balancing clusters (NLB), and provides an introduction to MOM.

Chapter 1, "The World of High-Performance, High availability Windows Computing," covers service level, the meaning of high availability, downtime, failure, and more. We also define scale-out, availability, and high-performance computing (HPC).

In Chapter 2, "Choosing High-Performance Hardware," we talk hardware and cover choosing high-performance equipment, standards, CPUs, and memory.

Chapter 3, "Storage for Highly Available Systems," certainly covers storage for these systems, but it also talks about redundancy and offers a RAID Refresher, discussing RAID controllers, Network Attached Storage Solutions (NAS), Storage Area Networks (SANs), and IP-Based Storage Solutions.

In Chapter 4, "Highly Available Networking," we discuss backbone design, bandwidth, and what to look for in network interface cards, hubs, switches, and routers. We'll also look into layer two, three, and four switches and routers, routing in high availability architecture, and using hubs for failover interconnects. This chapter also introduces SAN topology, fibre channel, Point-to-Point Topology for storage area networks, FC-AL, Fabric, and zoning.

If you need to design the architecture for an Active Directory network, Chapter 5, "Preparing the Platform for a High-Performance Network," is for you. This chapter covers preparing the platform for a high-performance network and creating a design plan, design goals, design components, design decisions, design implications, and more. This chapter also covers Active Directory services and logical architecture, the forest plan for highly available systems. The latter part of the chapter covers Active Directory physical architecture, such as subnets, site links, and naming convention.

Chapter 6, "Building the Foundations for a Highly Available Architecture," covers building the foundations for a highly available architecture. This chapter also covers Windows Clustering 101, cluster models, quorum resources, quorum resource deployment scenarios, and more. We also go into the forest creation process, how to form clusters creating shared disk resources, and preparing the cluster network.

The first chapter in Part II, Chapter 7, "High-Performance Print-Server Solutions," looks into high-performance print-server cluster solutions. We will look at design specifications, installations, and clustering the spooler resource.

Like printing, every network needs file servers. Some networks need to have a highly available file-server solution. Chapter 8, "High-Performance File-Server Solutions," covers high-performance file-server solutions, scale-out versus scale-up, Configuring 2-Node clusters, disk replication solutions, and so on.

Chapter 9, "High Availability, High-Performance SQL Server Solutions," introduces scale-out versus scale-up with Microsoft SQL Server, failover for SQL Server, SQL Server cluster design, documenting the dependencies of the cluster, and so on. We look at the SQL Server Active/Active configurations, multiple instance solutions, N+1 configurations, and so on. We also cover noncluster redundancy solutions, such as replication, and show step-by-step how to cluster the Analysis Services (OLAP).

Chapter 10, "High Availability, High-Performance Exchange," covers scale-out versus scale-up with Microsoft Exchange, storage group architecture, exchange store considerations, transaction logs, the SMTP queue directory, Exchange permissions in the clustering architecture, and so on. The section titled "Getting Started with Exchange 2003 Clustering" covers installing the Exchange Virtual Server on the cluster nodes and how to cluster Exchange using replicated disk technology and Microsoft Cluster Services.

Chapter 11, "Load Balancing," deals with scale-out, Network Load Balancing (network load balancing) for high-performance solutions, sharing server load, what cannot be scaled, selecting NLB clustering, and more. We look into what constitutes a candidate for NLB, architecture for and designing the NLB cluster, setup and configuration of the NLB cluster, and so on.

In Chapter 12, "Internet Information Server," we turn to the Web and go into scale-out versus scale-up IIS, round-robin DNS load balancing, NLB for Internet

Information Server, planning and configuration, IIS Storage, NLB for FTP, and troubleshooting and maintaining the IIS NLB server cluster.

Chapter 13, "Looking for Trouble: Setting Up Performance Monitoring and Alerts," is all about operations management. The first half of this chapter delves into the Windows Server 2003 monitoring systems, the event viewer, system and performance monitoring objects, rate and throughput, the work queue, response time, and more. The second half covers MOM. We will cover the steps to take in a MOM rapid-deployment project. These steps involve verifying software and hardware requirements for MOM, the MOM service accounts, MOM database sizing, installing the First Management Server, importing MOM 2005 Management Packs, and so on. We also show you how you can trap alerts to the event logs and how MOM collects these and emails the alerts to operators and the event log.

Windows Server 2003 high availability and high-performance engineering is not an easy vocation. We hope this book will provide you with the kick-start you need to correctly implement your own high availability, high-performance systems. If there are issues you need clarification on, or you need some advice, we will certainly try to help. You may contact us at hpc@codetimes.com.

PART I

High-Performance Windows Computing

CHAPTER 1

The World of High-Performance, High Availability Windows Computing

Introduction

This chapter presents an overview of *high availability* (HA), *high-performance computing* (HPC), and in particular, how the Windows Server 2003 platform from Microsoft caters to this critical need.

We begin our sojourn into the subject matter by exploring the basics of service level, availability, the concepts of fail-over and redundancy, scalability and high-availability, and technology operations management. We explore the proactive management of computer systems for highly available purposes, as well as the reactive functions that need to be planned for as well, such as disaster recovery. We then consider high-performance architectures, hardware, and software.

The central theme and objective of this chapter is to provide a wide understanding of the subject matter that becomes much more complex and detailed in the chapters to follow. We introduce new terms, clarify some older ones, redefine some terms, and also set the scene to introduce what Microsoft's newest operating system brings to the operations management team and the network analysts and architects of our high-performance computing needs.

Before we embark on this journey, it is important to note that two publications have greatly influenced how we set about architecting mission-critical Microsoft systems—they are the *Microsoft Operations Framework* (MOF) and the *Microsoft Systems Architecture* (MSA).

MOF contains extensive information on operations architecting, operations planning, change management, security operations, service level, and so on. The MSA provides unparalleled coverage of networking architecture, storage and backup services, directory services, file and print services, clustering, distributed services, and more. Both publications are essential reading for any high-availability systems architect. The MSA also includes so-called Solution Accelerators that can help you plan, test, build, and operate the various systems you are architecting.

You can take several approaches to architecting systems. The approach used by the authors of this book is based on the Zachman framework. You can get to know the Zachman Framework at www. zachmanframework.com, the Web site for the Zachman Institute for Framework Advancement (ZIFA).

Service Level

An often misused term in LAN and server technologies management is *service level.* It is probably misused because there are many interpretations of what it means. For example, some managers and analysts like to use the term to refer to how "available" an individual computer system is or should be. This may be so in the world of legacy systems, where a system is more self-contained and not a collection of distributed and interconnected components, or in the telecom world to describe switches and PBX systems. Network and systems analysts are often asked to ensure that the system maintains a certain service level without really knowing what service level it can attain.

System

A system may be a single computer, multiple servers (and clusters of servers), and even multiple sites of servers. A system is not complete without a system administrator, either human or computer; it also needs operators. Other things that make it work include power, enclosures, racks, building, fire suppression, and so on.

The quest to meet service level and keep a computer system running 24×7 often leads to misdirected provisioning. It is better to avoid using service level to describe a computer system's availability; instead, it should be used to describe the amount of time in an operational period the service window, a service, or application is available to its users or subscribers.

Service level describes how available a service must be in the service window. It is not a system alone that must meet the service level requirement, but rather the service, possibly comprising of numerous systems and components, including human resources, that must be available.

When we assess or determine the service level of an application or service we need to first ask what the expected operations period is for that service. The *service level agreement* (SLA), which we discuss shortly, is the agreement, usually in writing, that the service is available for all or most of the required time during the operational period.

First, we need to determine what the operational period is. Is the service required for 12 hours of the day, 18 hours, or all the time? After the operational period has been established, we need to know how much time in the operational period the business or service user can tolerate service interruption. If the operational period is 12 hours, and during that time the service is required all of the time, then the service level needed is 100 percent. If the user or business owner can tolerate no more than, say, 45 minutes of service interruption in the required operational window, then the service level needed might be pegged at 90 percent, or 95 percent, and so forth.

After the service level has been determined and agreed to, the information technology specialist and the systems analyst can begin to craft a system comprised of hardware and software components that must be available for the agreed upon period in the SLA. This is known as *availability* and is discussed in the next section. Table 1.1 provides an example of some categories of service level required for a typical busy e-commerce site.

Table 1.1   Service Level Categories for an E-Commerce Site

Service Level Category	Service Level Required
Hours of Operation	■ The service must be available 24×7×365. ■ There shall be no downtime during planned maintenance of components. ■ The only permissible cessation of service is in the case of a severe security event, such as an attack on the servers or an invasion, to prevent damage to the systems.
Performance	■ The service must be able to accommodate at least 2500 concurrent connections with no degradation in the user experience. ■ Latency between posts and acknowledgments shall be no more than two seconds. ■ The system must handle approximately 25,000 transactions per hour.

TIP: When negotiating a service level agreement, consider all aspects of service availability, especially operations management, which always includes the management of human resources. Even the most highly available systems need operators because there is no such thing as a "fail-never" system.

This book is not the forum for discussing SLAs; however, a good reference for SLAs is the International Engineering Consortium (IEC), which is on the Web at www.iec.org.

Availability

The systems we develop to meet a certain business or operational need should be provisioned and engineered first and foremost with the required service level already agreed upon. You may disagree and counter that security of the system is the primary requirement, or data integrity, or cost. Yes, these issues are critical, and they are part of the objective.

A system's integrity, security, and manageability are vital, but they do not need to be considered *before* the service level has been determined. After all, a system's engineering considerations affect its availability potential. If the system can be hacked, made with cheap components, or is badly designed, it makes the system less available and, thus, not able to meet the service level requirements placed upon the applications the system is hosting.

Availability

Availability can be defined as the amount of time an application or service is available to a user in the service window. A *redundant array of hard disks* (RAID), for example, describes storage that remains available even when one, two, or even three of its hard disks simultaneously crash. This is not the same thing as reliability; although it goes without saying that you need to engage reliable components in your efforts.

If we talk about the availability of a system, for example Exchange, then we mean the percentage of time (in the operations window) that the service is running and able to send and receive email.

Various levels of availability exist. We can say a system is moderately available when it is comprised of components and technology that have potential to cause system failures or system downtime such that it impacts service level and breaks the SLA.

Certain small businesses, for example, can tolerate longer periods of downtime than larger businesses or service providers that have commitments to make. When only a few people need a print server in a normal business day—the service level being "available 9 to 5"—the loss of an hour or two in the service level of the day is not considered critical or business-threatening. However, if hundreds of users need the services of the print server in the same service window, then the loss of even 15 minutes of the service can have a disastrous impact on the business.

In the latter scenario, we understand that to meet the service level of continuous operation, a system needs to be built using a highly available architecture and high-performance components and technology. Earlier we stated that in the case of less-critical need, a single computer can serve as the print server; however, in the latter case, a high-end server cluster capable of immediate service recovery when a node fails is required to meet the service level.

Throughout the years, service availability of computer and software systems has been measured in terms of percentage of uptime (in service computers). The 9's model refers to percent available, of which 99.9999 (six nines) percent is the highest, and is often used to describe an email system or a database server without really knowing what the 9's refer to.

Availability is typically measured in *nines*. For example, a solution with an availability level of *three nines* is capable of supporting its intended function 99.9 percent of the time, which is equivalent to an annual downtime of 8.76 hours per year on a 24×7×365 (24 hours a day, seven days a week, 365 days a year) basis. Table 1.2 lists common availability levels that many organizations attempt to achieve.

Six nines (99.9999 percent) means that on an annual basis a system cannot be offline for more than 32 seconds each day (for every 24 hours of operation). Clearly, this is impossible to achieve in the 21st century. The average Windows 2003 Server is regularly restarted to update itself with security patches and updates.

A system engineered with three nines is more realistic and capable of meeting its service level commitment 99.9 percent of the time— this is equivalent to an annual downtime of 8.76 hours per year, on an SLA operations window of 24×7×365. Table 1.2 shows how percentages translate into actual downtime.

Before we get into practical application here, let's get a bit more scientific and return to the factors of the availability equation. Availability is really a function of two factors: the *Mean Time Between Failures* (MTBF) and the *Mean Time To Repair* (MTTR), which is the essence of reliability. Both means are typically measured in hours and, thus, you have the following equation:

$$\text{Availability} = \text{MTBF}/(\text{MTBF}+\text{MTTR}) = .9xxxxxx$$

Let's flesh this out some more. What we are talking about is the formula that calculates the probability of component failure. The MTBF is the average time interval, measured in thousands or tens of thousands of hours (also known as *power-on hours* or POH), that passes before the component fails. The MTBF is thus calculated with the following equation:

$$\text{MTBF} = (\text{elapsed time} - \text{total downtime})/\text{number of failures}$$

The MTTR is the average time (usually expressed in hours) that it takes to repair the component. So, if a system offers a MTBF of 60 (1,000 hours) and a MTTR of 4 hours, then we get back to the nines as follows:

$$60/(60+4) = .9375 \text{ or } 93.75\%$$

See Table 1.2 as your guide. How do you mitigate undesired or expected downtime? You design and build systems that are more reliable, and this means employing redundant and fault-tolerant hardware. In other words, when your hard disk has reached its one-millionth hour of operation and fails, the last thing you care about is the MTTR. As long as you have another hard disk to pick up the work, who's going to bother to repair the drive? These days it is really a case of "MTTS"—the mean time to shop for a new hard drive or fetch one from the store. More about redundant components in the next section.

NOTE: In the computer systems world, MTTR is often used to describe Mean Time To Restore.

Table 1.2   Availability Using the Nines Systems as a Guide

Availability (%)	Downtime in a Year (24×7×365) for 24-Hour Operation
99.9999	32 seconds
99.999	5 minutes, 15 seconds
99.99%	52 minutes, 36 seconds
99.95%	4 hours, 23 minutes
99.9%	8 hours, 46 minutes
99.5%	1 day, 19 hours, 48 minutes
99%	3 days, 15 hours, 40 minutes
95%	18.25 days
90%	36.5 days

Clearly, this is not attainable if you consider the need for regular patching, hardening against worms, viruses, and hackers, and, sometimes, defective hardware. While useful as a point of reference, the 9's formula is not the standard by which to determine availability or service level requirements. Besides, how many engineers put together a system and jot down every component's MTBF and MTTR to arrive at a magical formula for the whole system? When it comes to an SLA, most customers do not understand the 9's formula; so just promise them daily expected downtime when you author your SLA. Later in this chapter and throughout the book, we discuss availability goals for the various services we are engineering.

So, to briefly recap, we first need to determine the service level required when designing a system. Then we need to determine what availability we can expect from the system to meet the service level. We can agree to three levels: low availability, medium availability, and high availability. After we have determined service level and availability, we can begin crafting a system to meet both user's and owner's expectations.

High Availability, Downtime, and Failure

A high availability system is a system that meets the high availability requirements of an SLA. It can thus mean any technology, configuration, design, technique, or combination thereof that ensures the system meets the SLA.

Designing High Availability Systems

A *highly available* system is one that is designed to meet the service level requirements of an application or service. Such a system employs components from redundant power supply units to full-blown failover nodes to ensure system continuance in the event of failure.

We have talked a little about *downtime* that is planned. In other words, you know at 2 AM your servers need to be rebooted to finalize changes in the operating system and program that have occurred as a result of patching, updates, fixes, and service packs. In the world of mainframes, this is known as *initial program load* (IPL), and this is *planned downtime.*

Unplanned downtime is downtime that occurs because the server has failed or stopped responding as a result of a failure. The failure might be a software error, or it could be failure of one of the server's components. Unplanned downtime is just that; it is unplanned. You don't know when it will happen. It could happen in the early hours of the morning when the server is idle, or it could happen when the server is serving thousands of live users. (Murphy's Law dictates that unplanned downtime will occur when the server or system is at its busiest.) The quest for high availability and high-performance computing is to lessen or completely eliminate unplanned downtime. In the following chapters, we implement standards and practices that let you eliminate system downtime even when a server must be restarted. This can be done with clustering by first transferring all services to an active node, then patching, fixing, or rebuilding the passive server. After the *fixed* server is back online, services can be transferred back to the fixed server with only a fraction of service interruption as connections are transferred.

In the following chapters, we cover how to work with the components and services whose failures cause loss of service and downtime. The following list is an example of these services and components. Many of them are listed in the SLA with specific notes on how they will be addressed.

- **Planned administrative downtime:** This includes upgrades of hardware, new drivers, new firmware, patches, services packs, and new software applications that require hardware restart.
- **Server hardware failure:** This includes server components, such as memory chips, motherboards, daughterboards, onboard interfaces (such as network interface cards), power supplies, disks, disk controllers, CPUs, and fans (especially CPU fans).
- **Network component failure:** This includes routers, switches, hubs, cabling, and interface cards.
- **Software failure:** This includes memory leaks, viruses, file and data corruption, software bugs, and so on.
- **Site failure:** This includes power failures, flooding, fires, hurricanes, earthquakes, and terrorist attacks. A site may fail as a result of a local disaster (such as a flash flood) or a regional disaster, such as an earthquake.

Okay, so the first thing we need to do to prevent downtime is build a fail-over cluster; however, as shown later in this book, even a wide area network is part of the high-availability design. Clustering is actually an exercise in redundancy. A highly available computer system is essentially a computer system that can transfer services from one system, with minimum unavailability, to another system, thereby keeping the service running. We discuss the fail-over cluster more in this chapter, but we cover the subject extensively in Part II, "Building High Availability Windows Server 2003 Solutions."

But what good is all this redundancy if the site itself fails? Recently, a building housing a computer system for a large insurance company in southern Florida flooded, and all power to the building was lost. The system was down (affecting thousands of insureds) for nearly three hours. Our project was to relocate the system to a better site that could ensure availability. The computer system is now housed offsite, deep inside one of the many network operations centers owned by a big telecommunications company in Miami. The building it is in can withstand both local and regional disasters, the most powerful hurricanes, and it can operate on its own power even if all of Florida is dark.

Such a facility has become very affordable because many centers were built during the Internet boom years, and now they are running at a fraction of their capacity. A full rack in any of these facilities that comes with burstable bandwidth connection to the Internet costs no more than $1,000 a month.

High availability also describes *load balancing* (both hardware and software), which is the effort to balance the load on resources to reduce bottlenecks, which ultimately lead to service failure (the system might be up and running; it just can't answer all the requests). Load balancing implies scalability. Obviously, if a system or software cannot scale, then it becomes very difficult to provide load balancing across multiple hosts. Microsoft provides *network load balance clustering* (NLB), *component load balancing* (CLB), and *failover clustering*; however, if the software providing the services is not itself scalable or NLB cluster-aware, then it is of little use to host it with any of the provided cluster services on the Windows Server platform.

High availability also refers to hardware redundancy. Even if a system is not fail-over supported or scalable, you can still meet the high availability provisioning in hardware redundancy. The most visible components in a computer system for redundancy are disks, and here we have several technologies that provide mirroring and striping and combinations thereof that prevent or eliminate downtime incurred because of disk failure. We discuss hardware redundancy in more detail in Chapters 2, "Choosing High-Performance Hardware," and 3, "Storage for Highly Available Systems."

While on the subject of storage, nothing contributes more to the high availability of systems than the technology to consolidate storage. Both *network attached storage* (NAS) and a *storage area network* (SAN) play critical roles in the high-availability arena. Not only is shared and consolidated storage central in designing fail-over clustering, but the technology itself—transfer rates, serviceability, manageability, and more—contribute to the fundamental availability requirement. For this reason, we spend substantial time discussing storage in Chapter 3, "Storage for Highly Available Systems."

Memory, processors, IO, busses, and the like play key roles as well, especially when dealing with the subject of scaling up, multi-processing, threading, and so on. These components of a high-availability system require certain availability monitoring, performance monitoring, and analysis to meet the high-availability requirements. Chapter 13, "Looking for Trouble: Setting Up Performance Monitoring and Alerts," thus delves into operations management using tools like the Performance console and *Microsoft Operations Manager* (MOM), both Microsoft technologies.

Finally, we consider the non-system–based factors that affect availability, human capacity to operate and maintain systems, as well as design, and implement them accordingly. In Chapters 5 and 6 we touch on the subject of design and implementation. The chapters that follow are design-oriented, providing information in the form of examples.

No book on the subject of availability and high-performance computing would be complete without discussing the security question. To meet service level, we constantly need to ensure that our systems are not attacked. Attacks come in various forms—viruses, worms, Trojan horses, low-level and interactive intrusions, and so on. While this book is not the forum to discuss computer security, a vast subject on its own, we draw attention to the need to manage the security aspect from the service level, availability, and performance aspects as well as the human one.

Scale-Out Availability and Windows Server 2003

When we talk about scalability, we mean how a service or application can be *grown* to meet increasing performance demands specified in the SLA. When we talk about scalability for the computer systems described in this book, we mean how we can add computers to an existing cluster configuration; so the load of the hosts can be portioned out to the additional hosts to meet the SLA and provide the desired performance. We explore two scalability options: scaling-up and scaling-out.

The Windows Server 2003 platform is riding the wave of scale-out availability because Intel systems and the OS are particularly well-suited to scale-out architecture. Scaling-out uses the so-called cluster approach to availability, where systems either operate in parallel as distributed computing systems to handle additional load or as fail-over clusters that provide redundant services.

Scaling-out as a form of parallel processing, load balancing, or both involves systems and software that operate according to a divide-and-conquer solution where application data or processing logic is distributed across multiple computer nodes. Each node can be working on its own part of the overall data set, or each node can be sharing a common dataset. In the latter case, a front-end data integrity solution employs a system of transaction procedures, distributed processes, and data replication scenarios to ensure that data integrity is maintained.

A typical business-to-consumer Web site that enjoys high usage is a good example. Multiple Web servers are employed to distribute the connection and processing load. Connections are then made through middle-tier components to backend databases living on either one or many SQL Server databases. Replication and isolation techniques are employed to ensure that data integrity is maintained. We discuss data integrity and techniques such as replication and log shipping in more detail in Chapter 9, "High Availability, High-Performance SQL Server Solutions."

As mentioned earlier, to scale applications, the application needs to be scale-out–aware. You either simply employ Windows Server 2003 network load balancing, if the application is NLB-aware, or partition your processing logic across multiple servers in what is known as a *federation*. You can use numerous techniques—and Microsoft provides a number of accomplished programming interfaces that exploit common libraries, especially those found in the .NET Framework—that support program execution distributed over a number of *High-Performance Computing* (HPC) systems.

Clustering

As you will discover throughout this book, the term *clustering* can refer to more than one technique for availability. Scale-out clustering, which we just discussed, employs services provided by Windows Server 2003 to load balance and distribute processing across a number of nodes. Fail-over clustering, on the other hand, is a technique to ensure node availability. It is a form of redundancy.

An *Active/Passive cluster* is comprised of a node-pair in which one node stands idle while the active node does all the work. If the primary node fails, the application will fail-over to the passive node, which is activated. A small interruption of service is experienced; however, the application is restored with negligible failure in availability and the processing continues on the new primary node. The failed node is then recovered and either remains as a standby or the application is failed-back to return the system to the active-passive state it was in before the fail-over.

On the Windows Server 2003, Enterprise Edition and Datacenter Edition, you can have more than one active node in the cluster. It is, in fact, possible to have more than two active nodes in the cluster and leave one passive while the others handle the load. Active/Active-Passive (n+1) configurations are discussed in more detail in Chapter 5, "Preparing the Platform for a High-Performance Network."

NOTE: You cannot create a failover cluster using Windows Server 2003 Standard Edition.

Scale-Up Availability

Often programmers encounter applications that cannot easily scale-out, and the application's requirements are more suited to a scale-up solution. Scaling-up implies the addition of hardware components, particularly processors and memory, to fully exploit parallel and multi-processing techniques.

Scale-up solutions exploit the modern capabilities of processors, such as threading, hyper threading, locks, semaphores, and other atomic functions. Scale-up systems are typically easier to manage because you usually only need to deal with a single operating system state, a single data repository, and a distributed processing space. However, some applications benefit from a hybrid of both scale-out techniques and scale-up logic.

Such systems include highly available transaction processing systems in which sophisticated multithreaded applications are scaled-out across several fail-over or load balanced clusters. We deal with this in more detail in Chapter 5, 9, 11 and 12.

Scale-Out or Scale-Up?

By scale-up, we add resources to existing computer systems. When server response time begins to degrade because of increased workload or higher database requests or email inflow, the most common initial answer to an immediate performance problem is adding bigger, faster (more expensive) hardware.

These days, hardware vendors are doubling device performance every 18 to 24 months. Given the rapid, almost limitless, supply of new power to the system, this approach might seem the way to go; but there is one problem. Many associated problems exist with constant hardware upgrades.

First and foremost, the hardware has certain limitations. Given that hardware performance doubles every two years, and assuming you have the money to upgrade your hardware every two years, what do you do when you max out your new system after only 12 months? Suffer with poor performance for the next year? That is probably not an option, especially after that expensive upgrade.

Even though hardware vendors are making 8-processor, 16GB memory chips, and fiber-meshed SAN-connected computers, the problem of scalability still exists. Sooner or later, you have to wait for your hardware vendor of choice to release the next version of super hardware to catch up with your desired performance counters.

And it gets more complicated. When a system reaches a certain point, further scaling up becomes so expensive that the cost is not worth the reward. Even beyond the hardware and compatibility issues, you'll probably encounter problems with accessing software when you're trying to scale up past a certain point.

For example, take the /3GB /PAE switch in boot.ini on your Windows 2000 server. Here we have a problem where the OS cannot correctly use large amounts of memory (4GB and larger). Some software systems, such as database engines, have internal algorithms for handling transactions, locking, and multi-user and three-tier database issues. The architecture of these software systems has limits to its efficiency. These limits can hamper the ability to continue to scale upward. It's like a bell curve; sooner or later at the top of that curve, you'll need very expensive hardware upgrades to get even the smallest levels of increased performance. Scaling-out still means more hardware.

Share Everything Versus Share Nothing

Let's talk about more hardware, not bigger or better hardware. Scaling-out can provide an effective answer to the problems of the scale-up scenario. We design to not *share everything* but rather *share nothing*.

Essentially, share-nothing architecture means that each computer system of the cluster operates independently. Each system in the cluster maintains separate resources (CPU, memory, and disk storage that other systems cannot directly access). To address capacity issues by scaling-out, you add more hardware to the pool—not bigger hardware to a single entity.

Scaling-out can address the cost factor associated with scaling-up because adding several smaller systems is typically less expensive than upgrading a single large mainframe-class system or the cost and emotional pain of a total "forklift" upgrade to a new platform. When you scale-out, the size and speed of a single system does not limit total capacity. Shared-nothing architecture also foils the software bottleneck bug by providing architecture that supports a multiple multiuser concurrency mechanism. Because the workload is divided among the multiple servers, total software capacity and throughput increases.

Even though scaling out provides solutions to the *built-in* limitations in scale-up architecture, this method has inherent problems as well. First, the ceiling is only so high. Scaling-out requires additional administrative overhead, subject matter expertise, and of course money. The pitfalls can potentially be as great as the performance gains it offers. Even so, scaling-out might be a viable solution for database implementations that have reached the limits of your hardware scalability problems.

You have a great deal to consider, especially when you have a client who simply says, "Make sure it's always on."

High-Performance Computing

High-Performance Computing (HPC) must not be confused with High Availability, but it is an integral concept without which you do not have the ability to meet or maintain service level.

You can build high-performance computers or architecture alone or as part of server farms or computer federations. However, you may not meet the service level required by the business or process owners if your design is not highly available. Conversely, highly available design or implementation fails if the components used cannot produce a high-performance computing environment.

With the objective being high availability, you might take it for granted that the computer systems built to meet service level are high-performance. However, this is not always the case, nor always possible.

For example, a bunch of low-end SCSI disks, running at no more than 7200 RPM, in RAID-1 or RAID-5 configuration, certainly offer a high degree of availability, as opposed to a single disk that trashes the SLA when it fails. But can you say that they are HPC components? Not exactly. A SAN implementation, comprised of a *cage* of 15,000 RPM disks, in a RAID-5 configuration, transferring data across a fiber-channel network fabric, instead of SCSI, offers both high availability as well as higher performance. Of course, what is HPC to one business may be supercomputing to another. SANs, like all technology, also have diminishing points of returns, and we discuss some of these in Chapter 3.

The Need for High-Performance Computing

Let us dwell on the HPC subject a while longer. Technology drives business today; for the most part, it drives society. Most enterprises would simply cease to exist if they were denied access to their technology for more than a couple of days. To remain competitive, you not only need to be available all the time, but the throughput (IO) of your systems must be as high as possible.

HPC is critical for all businesses. If a service is slow and a small group of people take minutes longer to post data than they should, at the end of the year they may lose weeks of productivity. This loss certainly affects earnings and the bottom line.

Database servers catering to Web sites, for example, or data input and calculations, need to be processing at the best transaction rates possible. Web servers must be able to cater to thousands of connections, not just a few. File and print servers must not die of memory and processor starvation just because the staff decides to print out an urgent memo all at the same time.

High-Performance Computing for Everyone

Information Technology is a science. And in the study of science, we have laws and formulas that describe certain hypotheses. In HPC, there is a hypothesis that all businesses can bank on: The cost of a new technology remains significantly high for the time it is considered new technology. As soon as something better comes along, the cost of the now old technology rapidly plummets. Without getting into *return on investment* (ROI) and other factors that can justify being on the bleeding edge, for most enterprise needs, it is better and cheaper to get into a technology after the crest of its wave.

Now does that mean that the old technology is no longer useful to business just because something better made headlines this morning? On the contrary, with the pace of technical innovation today, the outmoded and outdated device is usually still at least a year or more ahead of its time. In other words, most businesses lag significantly behind in their ability to use a new technology.

The reason is obvious—knowledge transfer. The people who can most likely use a new technology will not gain the knowledge or ability to use it until knowledge transfer has taken place. For many technologies, this transfer does not take place for years.

In a recent astonishing discovery, Gartner reported that more than half of corporate America still operates Windows 98. Companies are so far behind in their adoption of newer, more sophisticated operating systems, like Windows XP and Windows Server 2003, that Microsoft had to recently extend support of its outdated operating systems for several more years. Similar statistics abound in the use of server operating systems. Thousands of businesses are still using Windows NT, and even though Windows Server 2003 has been around since early 2003, most businesses will not move to the platform until at least 2005.

So consider this: A new system or technology becomes accessible and available to a business or service at the time enough information and knowledge of the system has been transferred to educate its architects, designers, and operators in its use. By the time market penetration has been achieved, there is likely a new generation of the technology emerging, and thus the so-called *obsolete* system has plummeted in price.

For example, a few years ago, the cost of a SCSI SAN fabric was beyond the reach of most small businesses, which could only afford network attached storage (NAS). With today's fiber channel SANs, the older SCSI copper SAN fabrics have plummeted. As you will discover in Chapter 3, you can craft a basic SAN for a small business for less than it costs to take all your technical staff to lunch.

HPC components become affordable in the time it takes an architect to design a system. Servers are constantly dropping in price because new models are constantly popping onto Web sites. The bottom-of-the-line server that was top of the line six months ago, in all likelihood, is adequate for your HPC needs at probably one-fifth the price of the newest server.

Thus, HPC is for everyone. After you have architected your systems and determined your needs, you can easily come up with a budget that acquires the components which meet your needs.

Supercomputers in Every Closet

Today's operating systems are pushing the envelope in their ability to make the most of the hardware on which they are installed. This book is devoted to one such operating system that practically puts supercomputing ability in the hands of all businesses at a fraction of the budget imagined just a few years ago.

For no more than a few million dollars, it is quite possible to fully replace an aging Novell NetWare, GroupWise system comprised of the following: several hundred servers spread across 100 subsidiaries, with a high-performance, high-availability Active Directory implementation that can file and print on several SANS, and caters to 5,000 Exchange/Outlook users.

Before the year 2000, such an *outgrade* of a network OS was deemed too expensive and painful to consider. What makes it easier and more affordable today is the Windows Server 2003 operating system and Active Directory—the core technology we discuss in the chapters to follow.

This operating system is not only affordable, but it runs systems that, by most scientific definitions today, can be considered supercomputers.

Processing and Memory

High-performance computing depends on several components, and the two components we usually focus on first are *memory* and *processors*. Processors are becoming cheaper, more available, and more powerful all the time. One factor that is no longer an issue for most budgets is the size and amount of processors to install on a server. Most businesses typically buy a server today and fill it up with all the processors for which its motherboard has a place.

Moore's Law states that "transistor densities on a single chip will double every 18 months." This has held up very well until recently. Now densities are doubling at faster rates than were imagined by Gordon Moore, the former chairman of Intel (the largest microprocessor maker and Microsoft's longstanding partner). Future processors are becoming less dependent on the traditional constraints of superconductive metal, as we see in Chapter 2.

In 1988, a $5,000 16MHz 386 machine with 1MB of RAM and a 40MB hard disk was beyond the reach of most businesses. Today a 1.5GHz machine with more than 256MB of RAM and a 40GB hard disk can be easily purchased for less than $500.

The hardware for memory is also advancing at a tremendous pace, and the amount of memory one places on a system is also becoming less of an issue. If you have HPC needs and an SLA to meet, "fill 'er up" is not an unusual expression a salesperson hears when quoting the configuration of a new SQL Server cluster or Exchange cluster.

The Windows Server 2003 operating system also heralds the age of 64-bit computing, which from hereon catapults most businesses, large and small, into the world of manageable supercomputer applications. The 64-bit supercomputing highway has unbelievable promise. In Chapter 2 we look at what storage capacity means for our software needs.

High-Performance Components

Besides memory and processors, many other system components need to contribute to the high-performance computing initiative. No system, of course, can be without storage. Also, no high-performance or highly available system can be without shared storage and redundant storage solutions (RAID 1, 5, 10, and so on). Storage and a number of other critical components are discussed in the next few chapters.

The other components that comprise all HPC-HA systems include *power supply units* (PSU), disk and storage controllers, switches and switch fabrics, network reticulation (particularly fiber or optical networking media), network interface cards, bus adapters, and so on.

Microsoft and the Cornell Theory Center

This surge in both the interest in and need for high-performance computing and high availability has led to the formation of several standards and bodies that represent the desire to build high-performance systems. One institution at the forefront of HPC on the Windows Server platform is the *Cornell Theory Center* (CTC).

The Cornell Theory Center is a high-performance computing and interdisciplinary research center located on the Ithaca, New York campus of Cornell University. CTC has direct affiliations with more than 500 researchers at Cornell in a variety of scientific and mathematical disciplines. This network extends worldwide through its researchers, partners, and external collaborations. CTC provides excellent high-performance computing and information technology solutions to researchers in the areas of

- Computational finance
- Computational biology and genomics
- Computational materials science

According to the CTC, it "has been at the forefront of high-performance computing for a number of years." Like many advanced computing organizations, CTC had based much of its work on expensive proprietary UNIX implementations. Amid declining budgets, increasing reliance of researchers on a high-performance computing infrastructure, and increasing commoditization of computer and networking components, CTC embarked on a unique strategy in 1999—embracing Microsoft Windows-based high-performance computing.

"Since then, CTC has been successful in developing a world-class, Windows-based supercomputing center. CTC's largest system is its 256-processor 'Velocity II' cluster, which is among the fastest 100 supercomputers in the world."

While the chapters that lie ahead focus mostly on availability, the HPC element features extensively with each class of hardware and software that completes or compliments our service level initiatives.

Time-Out

This chapter covered some important concepts that set the scene for the chapters to follow. We defined a number of things: availabilty, performance, reliability, redundancy, failure, repair, uptime and downtime. We also covered sevice level and the service level agreement (SLA). Finally, we shone some light on the issue of high-performance computing and supercomputing.

Besides setting the scene for the chapters to follow, you can take away a number of ideas from this chapter. Today, with Windows Server 2003, it is not very difficult or expensive to craft a highly available, high-performance computer system. Place this supercomputer system at a disaster-resistant site, and you'll be able to meet the most stringent of SLAs. If you properly define downtime in your SLA and keep it out of the operations window for which you are promising service, then it is very likely that you can achieve at least four nines availability without breaking the bank.

CHAPTER 2

Choosing High-Performance Hardware

Introduction

Before you can begin to architect your mission-critical applications and your cluster or load-balanced solutions, you first need to address the hardware choices you are going to make. Architects tend to leave hardware selection strategy until the last minute of a high-availability project, and then they end up regretting the final implementation because the hardware is rushed.

High-availability systems, for any of the solutions we discuss in this book, begin with choosing the right high-performance components. Because we are talking about Windows Server solutions, we focus on hardware platforms that are compatible with Windows-Intel technology, as opposed to systems made for HA/HPC UNIX or Linux systems.

This chapter first explores servers and what you need to look for when choosing the so-called cluster-node or host. We then briefly mention disks and storage because Chapter 3, "Storage for Highly Available Systems," is devoted to the subject of storage, particularly storage area networks or SANs. Chapter 4, "Highly Available Networks," deals with networking, so we do not address the subject of switches, fabrics, and interfaces at this time. These critical items get special attention later in Chapter 4. What we investigate in this chapter are processors and memory. Chapter 7, "High-Performance Print-Server Solutions," and Chapter 8, "High-Performance File-Server Solutions," look at some differences between servers, blades, and appliances.

Standards, Vendors, and Common Sense

While you are free to experiment with any combination of hardware component, it's in your best interest to use components listed on Microsoft's *Hardware Compatibility List* (HCL), which you can find at www.microsoft.com/whdc/hcl/. This is especially important when it comes to high-availability systems because a single failure due to suspect components instantly erodes any perceived savings going with brands not carrying best-of-American-breed labels. The mission-critical nature of the application doesn't leave much room for experimenting, and well-known vendors' products that provide all the components in the chassis are your best bet.

Choosing compliance with the HCL ensures the vendors have tested their systems with Microsoft's test guidelines, which are comprehensive. Vendors that maintain their own certification labs—ensuring entire systems, not just parts, correctly talk to the operating system's hardware interface (the *hardware abstraction layer*, also known as HAL)—provide reliable components and recourse should something go horribly wrong. You also have accountability, which is important, even if several of the components in a single system are made in places like South Korea or Taiwan, which host companies that make great components but terrible systems.

When it comes to choosing servers, the operating systems and software are built to be brand- or manufacturer-independent; so going with Dell, HP/Compaq, or IBM is a matter of personal preference. By personal preference, we mean brands you are familiar with, have a good vendor relationship with, and have a strong HPC or high-availability cluster base.

Vendors

Any of the three aforementioned vendors (and there are others) have a huge investment in supporting Microsoft HA/HPC solutions. These vendors also have strong OEM relationships with the likes of EMC, APC, and others. Dell, for example, licenses parts from EMC, IBM, Brocade, Q-logic, and others, and performs extensive testing to ensure the components work well together to deliver robust and reliable, all-around solutions.

Familiarity with a product is an important consideration as previously mentioned in this chapter. Dell server configuration, installation, and operations are very different from the HP/Compaq lines. Configuring IBM's iron is dramatically different from the other player's iron as well. If your shop is well-stocked with line-of-business PowerEdge servers, then install PowerEdge servers from Dell for your cluster needs as well, and then host them on a Dell-supplied EMC SANs (which is discussed in Chapter 3). However, if your racks are stacked with HP ProLiants, then stick with ProLiants.

There are two reasons to mention this. One reason has to do with available skill sets as already mentioned. The other reason has to do with monitoring the equipment you are going to put in place. Dell's Open-Manage is optimized for Dell equipment, while HP's OpenView is optimized for HP servers. All vendors provide packages for systems management products, like *Microsoft Operations Manager* (MOM); so, in addition to supporting configuration *cultures*, you don't need the overhead of supporting management products for hardware from multiple vendors.

There are only two reasons to support multiple vendors in a rack or data center. First, you might be planning a complete server replacement effort, which replaces your racks with one brand or another over time. Second, some turnkey products only support servers from a single source. Computer telephony systems, for example, are typically built with OEM versions of the ProLiant line, and, thus, you have to live with them in your Dell or IBM data center.

Common Sense

When configuring HA/HPC systems, you typically focus on four server subsystems: the *Central Processing Unit* (CPU), memory, the I/O system (which includes the controllers and interfaces to storage and storage itself), and the network interface card. Each subsystem configuration needs to be carefully considered.

For example, it makes no sense to spend a ton of money on high-speed, high-capacity disks only to cut corners on CPUs, NICs, or memory. Each area needs to be configured to meet the overall HA/HPC objective. Not only do you want performance (and elimination of bottlenecks), but you want to eliminate single points of failure wherever possible. In other words, redundancy within a system is the point we are driving at.

Think a CPU cannot fail? It has happened. CPUs attract a lot of dust, generate a huge amount of heat, rely on complex and delicate circuitry, and are prone to manufacturing problems. In a recent data center rollout, one of the most important systems, the Veritas master media server, which is used to backup critical data, kept crashing. Upon investigating the Windows Server dumps, we found the fault to be in the CPU. Dell shipped a new CPU, and the server stopped crashing. Go figure, no alerts on the server itself pointed to the problem being in the CPU.

Choosing the CPU

Choosing a CPU or simply the processor is not very difficult these days. True, Microsoft's operating systems run with either AMD or Intel, but most HPC systems are fitted with Intel CPUs and are standard with Dells and Compaqs, which are so suited to Microsoft clusters. The processing power of the CPU continues to provide adequate processing bandwidth for the most complex, mission-critical applications of the day; so, choosing proven and debugged processors is a safe practice.

When investing in systems for complex applications you plan to cluster, it makes sense to provide as much facility for multiprocessing as you can. Support for multiprocessing is important; therefore, make the additional investment and purchase systems with at least two processors. If the application you are going to cluster is going to be huge (like a high-performance SQL Server application supporting thousands of concurrent connections, or a Microsoft Exchange implementation supporting thousands of mailboxes), then add all the processing power you can. Windows Server 2003 is built for multiprocessor architecture, and you will witness increase in performance by an order of magnitude going from one to two or four processors.

We discussed processor scalability in Chapter 1, "The World of High-Performance, High Availability Windows Computing," and we revisit the subject in Part II, "Building High Availability Windows Server 2003 Solutions." For the time being, however, it does not hurt to know as much as you can about processors for your Windows Server 2003 HA/HPC solutions.

The processor's clock speed and its inherent architecture are significant when it comes to how much performance is delivered to the application. A higher clock speed almost always provides better performance, but you might see better performance with two 800MHz processors than one 1.4MHz processor on your SQL Server or Exchange server.

The 64-bit Intel Itanium (IA-64) processors made their debut with the 64-bit versions of Windows Server 2003, but by this edition of the book (end of 2004), there is not much software out there, apart from the OS, that can take advantage of the 64-bit address space. While some IA-64 systems outperform your 32-bit systems, you do not obtain much bang for your buck, and in some cases, the 32-bit systems using two or four processors clock in better performance.

It goes without saying that unless you fully understand the requirements and capabilities of your application, you are unable to really make the right processor choice. Factors to consider are the multi-threaded architecture of the application, if you must have several applications running simultaneously on the same server. Your application may actually perform well on a two-way system, but going four-way or eight-way might not add much more performance and may in fact reduce performance if the application begins to consume larger amounts of memory.

You may not realize this, but your 32-bit processors have an inherent design bottleneck with respect to memory. The design of the bus can limit the access to memory, slowing down memory-intensive applications, even if you max out the system with RAM. You will not notice the bottleneck on your two-way system. However, you might record the memory jamming on quad-processor systems and higher. The faster 133MHz front-side bus that now comes standard with the 32-bit architecture has gone a long way to relieving the bottleneck, and your system only suffers under extremely high load with applications that gobble up every bit of memory available.

By the time you read this, just about every new system will ship standard with Pentium Xeon-based processors. In the cases where you have an option to save some pennies going *non-Xeon*, resist the urge. Xeon processors are equipped with a so-called Level 2 cache (256KB to 2MB), which provides a significant performance boost over the non-Xeon CPUs. The reason is obvious—the cache lets the processor maintain all data in cache and obviates the need to swap or fetch from external memory. It is unlikely you are building applications to take advantage of the Level 2 cache, but Microsoft's server applications definitely benefit from the Xeons.

The cost of Xeons is of course a trade off and, in some cases, two four-way (CPU) systems instead of four two-way systems is going to be cheaper if high performance is substantially more critical than availability.

See Chapter 6, "Building the Foundations for a Highly Available Architecture," on determining scale-out versus scale-up in your cluster design. Rack space is also an important consideration. Racks don't come cheap, and there is a substantial additional cost added to the data center operations bill every time a new rack gets rolled onto the raised floor.

One last word about the 64-bit. While they herald a new age of performance, the systems are considerably more costly than the 32-bit systems. However, if you are processing a sufficient level of transactions where you can use all the available 3GB of RAM per processor, the enhanced memory access, and the numeric capabilities, then if the software can handle it, by all means go with the 64-bit architecture.

Memory

We do not delve into memory much in this book because, for the most part, memory provisioning has not changed much. Most architects know memory keeps getting faster and cheaper, and the underlying technology is the same as it was several years ago and is unlikely to be much different in the next four years. Your systems are able to hold more memory. Too a large extent, this is correct reasoning, and in recent years, many companies specializing in system memory are putting more R&D into collateral systems (such as interfaces) that improve memory access rather than on the chips themselves.

You might find it more important to consider *how much* memory you will need rather than *how sophisticated* it is. Once again, vendors introduce systems with the best memory, and you have to decide how *much* you need, rather than the *type*.

For those architects who have a strict budget or need more memory in existing systems, you will need to know a little more about memory than you would care to. Many administrators like to go to places like www.4Allmemory.com, where you can save some bucks and get exactly what you need. All you have to do is enter a model number of your system and the Web site returns the memory best suited for your system. In fact, some vendors recommend you buy the basic RAM from them and then shop around for better deals. This helps them get you within your budget with room to shop for the same, but cheaper, memory elsewhere on the Web.

Most of the servers you will be considering for your clusters or server farms only take up to 4GB of memory on the main board, even though the operating system is designed to use all of an OS's memory access ability.

Like processors, you need to consider the application you are going to run on the box and what it's doing. The more transactions, threads, calculations, and so on the system is doing, the more memory you need. But just maxing out on memory is foolhardy if the application and the operating system are not going to use all you plan to purchase or install. A typical Exchange cluster node serving—say, 2,000 users—has lots of head room on a 4GB system.

If you are looking at availability more than performance, then sticking with 2 to 4GB of memory is a safe bet and will serve to keep a two-processor system under the $10K level while still performing well.

If you are building systems out of existing hardware or need to move memory from one system to another, or you just simply need to buy more, then the following short explanation of memory will be sufficient. Further investigation into the actual workings of memory chips is beyond the scope of this book.

DRAM

Dynamic Access RAM (DRAM) has been around for a number of years. A DRAM chip is really nothing more than a capacitor that holds an electronic charge that can be accessed for a certain amount of time (and only while you have power to the server). DRAM is a marvelous concept—the capacitor is thin enough to sit on or between silicon wafers, which is kind of like getting 20 people into a Mini Cooper, and then squeezing the Cooper onto a bicycle.

The inside of the DRAM circuitry is like an Excel spreadsheet. Data is stored in various memory cells, accessible dynamically and randomly, hence the name DRAM. Memory can be accessed on the chip in any order.

For HA/HPC systems, the time it takes to access the memory in the cell is what is critical. As mentioned earlier, slow memory on a machine with a fast processor detracts from the ability of the processor. You can liken it to going fishing with a very expensive fishing rod and going cheap on the fishing line, which simply snaps every time you get a bite.

Standard DRAM has what is known as *fast page mode DRAM technology*, which typically lets the processor fetch memory with access times somewhere between 40 and 60 nanoseconds (10^{-9}ns). This was sufficient for the processors of the day, the old 66-100MHz CPUs that seemed so advanced at the time. These may have been HPC CPUs back then; but today, they are useless for any critical HA application.

DRAM with EDO

DRAM did not change much while processor capability improved over the years. The chips themselves were made faster to cope with the demands of the new processors. One improvement over the basic DRAM chip was the DRAM EDO chip. EDO stands for *extended data out* and means that the chip *lines up* the data the processor will most likely require after its first bite of memory apple.

The boost from EDO did not last long because technology whizzed ahead and the memory makers had to dig deeper into R&D pockets. There was a pause around the 400MHz era, but CPUs have been placing significant demands on RAM technology in recent years.

Synchronous DRAM

The advent of *Synchronous DRAM* (SDRAM) provided a significant performance boost. The chips practically doubled the access throughput by opening pages simultaneously. The data path was also widened to 128 bits, which improved throughput significantly. Today, SDRAM is practically useless for new architectures due to the limitations of SDRAM bandwidth and latency.

Nowadays, the demands on SQL Server, Exchange, and Windows Server 2003 require faster memory for program storage and data access. *RAM latency* is the amount of time required for the system to initiate and request memory. The *RAM bandwidth* is how much data can be read from or written to the RAM. SDRAM cannot satisfy modern high-performance computing requirements.

Still, new improvements in memory engineering are keeping the SDRAM standard alive. SDRAM latency has actually dropped over the years since the advent of the Pentium II and Pentium III computer (remember SQL Server 6.0 on a Windows NT 4.0 server). Manufacturers can subdivide the RAM into smaller sections, which allows memory requests to be queued in parallel.

A number of motherboard manufacturers have reengineered their hardware to achieve better transfer rates and bandwidth. *Advanced Micro Devices, Inc.* (AMD) and *VIA Technologies* (VIA) have been working on a technology called *Double Data Rate RAM*, or DDR RAM. DDR RAM doubles the memory bandwidth of traditional SDRAM, which has been re-engineered to perform two memory accesses for each tick of the memory bus clock. This technique effectively doubles the rate at which queued memory can be fetched.

DDR SDRAM is currently available in two standards. The first standard, PC1600 DDR SDRAM, is designed for a 100MHz memory bus. This means the bus is effectively doubled to a 200MHz memory bus, and thus the data bandwidth is increased to about 1600MB/sec. PC2100 DDR SDRAM, which is designed for a 133MHz memory bus, is the second standard. This doubles the 133MHz bus to 266MHz, providing a bandwidth that offers in the region of 2100MB/sec maximum bandwidth. A variation of this doubling technique is RAMBUS memory, which is discussed next.

Direct Rambus DRAM (RDRAM)

As processors demand grew, Rambus, Inc.—a company specializing in memory design out of Los Altos, California—came to the rescue with a high-speed memory interface that boosted DRAM performance by an order of magnitude. In fact, they were able to squeeze almost 1.5GB/sec out of the chips representing nearly twice the output of the SDRAM. While the output was a giant step in memory technology, interfaces and circuitry architecture was not in step with the access advancement. Thus, the chips were able to cater to the 700–800MHz CPU era but were not as popular as you might expect.

Memory makers like Rambus had to focus on cache technology, interfaces, error correction technology (ECC), and bus speeds to keep up with the new CPU bandwidth and data integrity requirements that began to emerge in the new millennium. Ironically, memory makers returned to the drawing boards and improved the architecture of DRAM considerably.

A technology to watch for is Rambus' XDR DRAM technology, which focuses on enhanced interfaces to standard DRAM memory cores. Rambus is seeing adoption of XDR architecture that they say will provide "quantum leaps" in memory bandwidth. More important is that XDR allows for less IC circuitry, which translates into small components.

If you have ever looked into a 32 or 64GB system to investigate the bee-hive of memory enclosed in the chassis, you know that footprint and component size is a big factor in architecting HPC systems. Faster memory that requires less IC space means prices soften while access speeds and RAM size increase by orders of magnitude.

Time-Out

You can easily make the analogy of a good marriage when it comes to processors and memory. Choices these days are relatively simple for new systems, the vendors are very quick to retire models as soon as the new CPUs stabilize (many still remember the day Intel recalled its best CPU from all over the world due to a floating point operation flaw). Thus, you are unlikely to have more than a few choices in processor speed. The big decisions and calculations you need to make center on the number of processors in each system and the amount of memory.

If you have calculated that you are going with a quad system, it would be absurd to consider anything less than 4GB of RAM. If your software requires a four-way, then it will likely choke on a gig or two of RAM. The decisions are not too difficult to make. If you can afford to drop four big ones onto the motherboard, then filling her up to the max with memory is not likely to break the budget.

It's worthwhile to fully understand the implications of faster memory and what one CPU can deliver over another. When it comes to SQL Server, Exchange, or Internet Information Server, you'll typically be looking for components that provide fast access to data. If you are look-ing at systems that need to host compilers, graphics editing systems, application servers, and the like, then you'll be looking for systems where data manipulation (in memory) is more important than data access.

The next subsystem to cover is the I/O system and the storage hard disks. Storage takes up more time and consideration and debate than any other subsystem. This is the reason we devote all of Chapter 3 to the subject.

CHAPTER 3

Storage for Highly Available Systems

Introduction

Of all the resources that constitute any computing environment, data is considered the most valuable, difficult to maintain, and costly to re-create. This becomes especially evident in light of political and social changes resulting, for example, in more stringent regulatory requirements, such as SEC 17a-3 and 4 in the financial sector, *Health Insurance Portability and Accountability Act* (HIPAA) in the healthcare industry, or the Sarbanes-Oxley Act of 2002 across all publicly traded companies. While such changes primarily affect backup and archival strategy, another aspect of data management that becomes more prominent is its availability; and there are more potential causes for downtime than ever. Besides natural disasters, old-fashioned human error, or simple, accidental component failure, there is an abundance of viruses and worms springing up after every newly discovered vulnerability, terrorist threat, and increased complexity of computing environment, introducing more chances for incompatibility clashes.

It is impossible to discuss data availability without focusing on primary storage technologies. While secondary storage, most commonly taking the form of backup tapes, offers some remediation in case of failures, it has several disadvantages. First of all, the time necessary to perform a restore can be significant and contributes to overall downtime. In addition, few system administrators pay sufficient attention to backup verification and testing. This means your best recourse in the quest for highly available storage is to follow the same principle that applies to other parts of the computing environment—eliminate single points of failure wherever possible. Your final decision, however, is still a difficult one because redundancy is inversely proportionate to cost, which tends to be the deciding factor behind implementing engineering designs. Other concerns also need to be taken into consideration, such as flexibility of storage allocation, ease of management, or consolidation capabilities. The purpose of this chapter is to present an overview of hardware- and software-based storage technologies supported on the Windows Server 2003 platform and help you determine which ones are most suitable for your high-availability needs.

Redundancy and Availability of Storage

In general, availability of storage can be improved by adding redundant components to the path between the data user and data source. While this might sound like oversimplification, an overwhelming variety of possible solutions exist. Duplication can happen on many different levels (from multiple disks attached to the same controller to geographically distributed, independently operated, intelligent storage) and can take many different forms (from simple, software-based replication mechanisms requiring manual failover to synchronous, fully automated, implemented in hardware, fault-tolerant systems). Additionally, duplication needs to be complemented with virtualization. Virtualization is one of the results of (and arguments for) a layered approach to storage management. Just as the well-known OSI model, it makes developing and modifying services operating on a particular level fairly easy. It accomplishes this by hiding complexity implemented on one level from others, exposing only those features that are relevant from the other level's perspective. This way, a user requesting a file does not have to be concerned about its location in terms of disk sectors. Instead, this is handled by lower level services, translating file name into disk geometry parameters and initiating a fetch procedure performed by the disk's circuitry. Other examples falling into the area of fault tolerance are bad sector remapping (invisible from the operating system point of view), volume creation and management (not relevant from the file system point of view), or Hierarchical Storage Management and Distributed File System (hiding the location of the file system from the end user and applications). Actual implementation is typically a part of the operating system or the primary or third-party vendor extension to it; it can also function as a hardware or firmware component. Our discussion covers solutions that fall into each of these categories—some complementing, others competing against each other. Obviously, each and any of these solutions has advantages and disadvantages that make them worth considering depending on your individual requirements.

Storage-related functionality supported by the Windows Server 2003 platform reflects Microsoft's intention of satisfying the diverse needs of its customers. All multi-purpose operating systems, which follow their Windows 2000 predecessors (Windows Server 2003 Standard, Enterprise, DataCenter, and Small Business Server editions) contain new and improved storage-related features, and the platform itself has been extended to include a function-focused operating system—Windows Storage Server 2003.

Before we start looking closer into storage availability in Windows Server 2003, let's go through a quick overview of underlying operating system architectural components relevant to our discussion. At the very core of the storage functionality lies its driver model. Its modular, multi-layered design remained mostly unchanged from the Windows 2000 Server release. Kernel mode components are responsible primarily for virtualizing hardware resources to software operating in the user mode and include the following:

- **Bus drivers:** Provide the ability to communicate between upper-level drivers (such as port drivers and minidrivers), class drivers (listed next), and system buses (such as PCI, SCSI, USB, or IEEE 1394), allowing functionality, such as enumeration of all Plug and Play devices connected to them.
- **Port drivers:** Implement features particular to subcategories of devices. More specifically, Windows Server 2003 comes with port drivers that existed on Windows 2000 platform (such as IDEPort or SCSIPort—intended for SCSI-2 and older devices) and a new Storport driver, supporting features specific to SCSI-3 and Fibre Channel devices.
- **Miniport drivers:** Expose these characteristics of individual devices, which have not been included in the port drivers. They are typically developed by third-party vendors that manufacture the hardware.

- **Class drivers:** Cover functionality that is common across a range of similar devices, which belong to the same category, such as disk, tape, or CD-ROM.
- **File System software:** Implements file system functionality, which provides representation of the disk data in the form of files and folders, including their properties (for example, permissions or ownership in case of NTFS). Windows supports a number of file systems, such as FAT32, NTFS, CDFS, or UDFS.

  Choice of the file system is important from the reliability perspective. NTFS offers significant advantages in this area. It is a journaling file system, keeping track of the changes to file system metadata, which can be used in a manner similar to a database transaction log to recover metadata (although not the actual data files) to a consistent state (it is also used to optimize such activities as backup, indexing, or replication). Other fault-tolerant features of NTFS include bad disk cluster and sector remapping. There are also significant performance and functionality benefits resulting, for example, in more efficient common maintenance operations, such as CHKDSK or defragmentation.
- **Volume Management, Partition Management, and Mount Management software:** The first manage *volumes*, which are, in essence, various combinations of logical divisions of physical disks, called *partitions* (managed by the second). Mount Manager takes care of mounting and dismounting volumes, and all associated activities, such as assigning drive letters to basic disks or keeping track of mount points. Mount Manager bases its actions on information provided by Volume Managers. Windows Server 2003 supports two of them—older FtDisk and newer *Logical Disk Manager* (LDM) , which is a limited version of Volume Manager licensed by Microsoft from VERITAS (also supported by Windows Server 2003).

The presence of two volume managers is related to the fact that Microsoft, starting with the release of Windows 2000 Server, in addition to *basic disks*, provided support for *dynamic disks*. While it is not necessary for us to get into the details and differences between them, here is some useful information to help you throughout our discussion in this chapter. Basic disks, which are managed by FtDisk, store information about the disk partitions in the structure called *partition table* on the disk, while the mount information (volumes can be mounted to drive letters or directories) resides in the Windows registry, and are recognized by all versions of Windows.

GPT and MBR Basic Disks

Basic disks are no longer that "basic" with the advent of 64-bit computing. On 32-bit systems, basic disks use a traditional partitioning scheme called MBR (which is derived from *Master Boot Record*—a small area on the disk where a single copy of the partition table supporting up to four partitions is located). On Itanium-based computers, basic disks take the form of GPT disks (an acronym derived from the term *Globally Unique Identifier Partition Table*, which denotes a new type of partition table allowing up to 128 partitions, having duplicate entries for redundancy, and containing Cyclic Redundancy Check values, which help ensure metadata integrity).

Because dynamic disks are managed by the Logical Disk Manager, they can be accessed only by Windows 2000 and later (they are not supported on laptops or removable media disks, such as USB hard drives). Disk configuration data (including mount information) resides in a *LDM database*, which is replicated across all disks in the same system (32-bit systems use this for the final cylinder on each disk, whereas 64-bit systems have a dedicated Microsoft Reserved Partition near the beginning of each disk). This not only provides redundancy, but it also makes it easier to move multi-disk configurations between computers. In addition, starting with Windows Server 2003, only dynamic disks support software-based fault-tolerant volumes (Windows 2000 did not allow creation of such volumes, but it provided access to the ones upgraded from Windows NT 4.0 systems). We cover the topic of fault-tolerant disk volumes in more details in the section "RAID Refresher."

User mode components communicate typically with kernel mode components through the Windows Management Instrumentation interface. In general, they can be divided into several categories, out of which the most relevant are hardware and software providers, including writers (such as Volume Shadow Copy Service, Virtual Disk Service, Removable Storage Manager, or Hierarchical Storage Management) and requestors, from both Microsoft and third-party software vendors.

FtDisk-Based Fault Tolerant Volumes Support in Windows Server 2003

Remember that support for FtDisk-based fault-tolerant volumes, created in Windows NT 4.0 Server, has been removed in Windows Server 2003. This means such volumes should be first backed up and removed before upgrading the operating system to Windows Server 2003.

In case you do not take proper precautions, you can still mount FtDisk volumes on a Windows Server 2003 with the FtOnline utility included with Windows Server 2003 source files (part of the Windows Server 2003 Support Tools, located in the Support\Tools folder on the installation CD). However, this is only a temporary measure because the mount does not persist between reboots and yields read-only access to the volume (which still allows you to copy your valuable data to another volume).

Now that we understand the architectural design of storage in Windows Server 2003, let's take a brief look at the I/O path, starting with an end user or an application requesting data and ending with fetching it from the disk (or retrieving it from cache) and sending it back to the client. Every portion of this path constitutes a potential point of failure (and, on the other hand, opportunity for increasing resiliency).

In this chapter, we are concerned primarily with what happens to client's request after it reaches a storage system (network-specific technologies are presented in Chapter 4, "Highly Available Networks;" Active Directory-related dependencies are covered in Chapters 5, "Preparing the Platform for a High-Performance Network," and 6, "Building the Foundations for a Highly Available Architecture;" and namespace virtualization methods, such as Distributed File System, are discussed in Chapter 8, "High-Performance File-Server Solutions"). Such system serves as an interface to raw disks providing storage virtualization and redundancy. In general, there are four different technologies that provide such capabilities, differing the way storage devices are attached and accessed—directly attached storage, network attached storage, storage attached networks, and IP-based storage. They are covered later in this chapter, in the sections "Server Attached Storage Solutions," "Network Attached Storage Solutions (NAS)," "Storage Area Networks (SAN)," and "IP-Based Storage Solutions," respectively.

Before we get there, let's first analyze technology common for all storage technologies, known as *Redundant Array of Inexpensive* (or *Independent*—depending on interpretation) *Disks*, or simply RAID.

RAID Refresher

Typically, at the far end of the storage I/O path, you find one or more physical disks (note that the concept of RAID can be applied to other types of I/O devices, such as tape drives or solid state disks). With a single disk only, our options in terms of increasing performance or reliability are limited. But what if we could combine the power and capacity of several of them? Using multiple disk devices to store redundant data that can be used to retrieve original content in case of a hardware failure seems to be the most intuitive approach to increasing storage availability. This is the basic idea behind RAID.

Obviously, there is still a question about how redundant data can be derived and how it can be stored. This is where a variety of RAID categories come into play, each with a distinct level of performance, cost, and data protection. This diversification is further magnified by the fact that RAID can be implemented in both software and hardware. For example, the most common levels of RAID have been included into Windows Server operating systems since their inception.

This duality of RAID implementations complicates some of the most basic storage vocabulary, such as *disks*, *partitions*, and *volumes*. The term *disk* typically refers to a physical hard disk device and sometimes is equated with the term *drive*. Note, however, that drives presented to the operating system through the *Hardware Abstraction Layer* (HAL) do not have to correspond to physical disks. As a matter of fact, it is fairly common to combine multiple disks using the RAID capabilities of disk controllers. As a result, a single disk displayed in the Disk Management MMC snap-in might consist of two hardware-mirrored disks or a multi-disk array located in a storage enclosure. In essence, you should keep in mind that what you see through disk utilities running within boundaries of the operating system might not represent underlying hardware, but instead its virtualized view. This means that we should look into defining disks, partitions, and volumes separately from hardware and software.

On the hardware level, there is little confusion about what constitutes a disk because the term describes a physical device. A partition, in turn, is a logical division of a disk, consisting of a number of contiguous disk sectors. Combining partitions from the same disk or different disks results in the creation of a volume (typically, such volumes are based on some type of RAID configuration). If partitions or volumes are created on the hardware level, they appear as separate disks on the software level. This means you can further subdivide them into software-based partitions and volumes, using operating system software (such as Windows Server 2003 Disk Management MMC snap-in or DISKPART utility). Such volumes frequently can be implemented as RAID configurations. It is possible to combine hardware- and software-based RAID, although you should use caution when engineering such solutions to make sure you take into consideration the performance implications of each and take advantage of synergies between them.

While in general, there are seven basic RAID levels—numbered from 0 to 6 and a few hybrids (RAID 10, 01, 30, 03, 50, 05, 15, and 51)—only a few of them (RAID 1, RAID 5, and RAID 10) have gained widespread popularity. We cover them in detail in the following subsections. However, for the sake of completeness, we are also providing short descriptions of the remaining types.

RAID 0 is the only level that is not fault-tolerant. Known also as stripeset without parity, it consists of a number of disks (at minimum two) onto which data is written in stripes. Content of the I/O buffer during a data write is divided into basic units of I/O (size typically ranges from 512 bytes to 8MB), with each unit being written to a separate disk in a round-robin fashion (first unit to the first disk, second unit to the second disk, and so forth; after the last disk is reached, the writing process starts from the first disk again). This can provide significant performance advantages during writes and reads (providing that hardware supports writing to and reading from multiple disks simultaneously), but it does not provide data redundancy. As a matter of fact, your data is effectively more vulnerable because a single disk failure yields an entire RAID 0 set unusable. RAID 0 is supported by Windows Server 2003 Logical Disk Manager in configurations with up to 32 disks. Due to its lack of redundancy, striping should be used for non-critical data only that requires excellent write performance. It is perfect for audio and video streaming or storing temporary data.

RAID 2 is obsolete because the functionality on which it was based (computing error correction code to verify data integrity) is included in the firmware of contemporary disk drives.

RAID 3 introduces the new concept of parity data. Just like RAID 0, it uses striping, which distributes data blocks across all data drives. However, for each stripe, it also performs additional calculations, which results in redundant data stored on a separate, dedicated disk. This data can be used to retrieve original content in case any of the disks participating in the RAID 3 array fails. Because the stripe size is small, each write operation (and, consequently, each read operation) involves all disks in the array. This improves write performance because each stripe's parity information can be obtained without additional reads. RAID 3 is known as striping with a dedicated parity disk. This level is not implemented in Windows Server 2003 Logical Disk Manager, but it is available in some hardware-based RAID implementations.

RAID 4 also uses dedicated parity disk and striping. Its distinguishing feature is larger stripe size, which means write operations do not necessarily involve every disk in the array. While this improves the efficiency of reads, the performance of writes suffers because data might need to be read from some of the disks to calculate parity information (which was not the case with RAID 3). In addition, because every write operation involves recording parity information, the dedicated parity disk becomes the bottleneck from the performance perspective. This level is also not available in Windows Server 2003 Logical Disk Manager.

RAID 6, known as block-level striping with dual distributed parity, constitutes improvement over lower levels because it protects against data loss in case two disks fail (while previously discussed RAID levels allow for a single disk failure without data loss only). This is accomplished by performing two independent parity calculations on each data stripe according to two distinct algorithms and then writing the result of each to separate disks. Its write performance is slightly worse than RAID 5 because of additional parity calculations; however, the speed of reads is approximately the same. Duplicate parity information requires another disk (compared to RAID 5 whose parity data is spread across all disks in the array). Due to its relatively high cost and low probability of two drives in the array failing simultaneously, this type of configuration is fairly rare—it also is not available in software-based RAID implementations.

RAID 30 is an example of a hybrid type combining two basic RAID levels—RAID 3 and RAID 0. By combining design principles applied to basic levels, the hybrid takes advantage of their individual strengths.

The implementation involves grouping all disks into several subsets (typically equal in size) and applying the first basic level to each subset. Next, the other basic level is applied to virtual disks created in the first step. RAID 30 involves striping across two or more RAID 3 arrays (each consisting of three or more disks), which means this level requires six or more disks. RAID 30, similarly to RAID 6, can handle failure of more than one disk without data loss as long as failed disks are not part of the same RAID 3 sub-array. While RAID 30 is not included in Windows Server 2003, you can create your own implementation of it by combining hardware-based RAID 3 (assuming your disk controller supports it) with Logical Disk Manager-based RAID 0, striping hardware RAID 3 volumes.

RAID 50 is another hybrid type that combines RAID 0 and RAID 5. It is similar to RAID 30; although, because it is based on RAID 5, it does not use dedicated parity drives (instead, it writes parity information independently across each RAID 5 array). Like RAID 30, it requires at least six disks, and it can gracefully handle failures of more than one disk (provided these disks are not part of the same RAID 5 subarray). Just as with RAID 30, it is not included in Windows Server 2003; however, you can combine the hardware-based RAID 5 implementation with Logical Disk Manager-based RAID 0, striping hardware RAID 5 volumes.

RAID 1

This type is also known as *mirrorset*, which best reflects its approach to providing data redundancy. RAID 1 consists of two drives. Each write operation is duplicated, so the same data is written to both. In case of any single disk failure, its exact replica is available on the remaining one. This is the only fault-tolerant configuration available with two disks. Its main drawback is its low rate of disk space utilization (only 50% of the total space is available for data), although with prices of storage constantly declining, this is becoming less relevant.

RAID 1 can be created in both hardware or software on the Windows Server 2003 platform. The hardware implementation uses two physical disks. To implement software-based RAID 1 in Windows Server 2003, you need to have two separate disks available through the Disk Management MMC snap-in, which can (but does not have to, as explained before) correspond to physical disks. One of the drives contains a partition to be mirrored, the other must have unallocated space equal to or larger than the size of the first partition. This is the only type of software-based fault tolerance suitable for system and boot volumes.

You can introduce an additional level of redundancy by attaching the second drive to a separate controller, which prevents downtime in case of a controller failure (this solution is known as *duplexing*).

Performance of the mirrorset is good during read operations as long as seek and reads can be performed against either drive. Writes, however, are much faster than RAID configurations relying on calculating and recording parity for redundancy. Failure of a single disk does not affect the speed of reads or writes (it equates to reading from and writing to a single disk); however, performance is impacted when a "broken" mirror needs to be recreated.

RAID 1 is most suitable for write-intensive applications. It also serves as a great location for Windows system and swap files. In database environments, RAID 1 tends to be used for transaction logs because its sequential write performance (as well as sequential read performance) is better than any other RAID configuration.

Remote Mirorring

Commonly, mirroring is handled either by the operating system components or disk controller circuitry. Both of these methods suffer from severe distance limitations. There are, however, more advanced technologies (both software- and hardware-based), which provide long distance replication functionality with mechanisms (such as checkpoints). This ensures the integrity of replicated content at remote end, or both local and remote ends (in case of bidirectional replication), and synchronous or asynchronous capabilities. Synchronous replication considers a write as complete only when it is verified to be completed on both local and remote devices. This approach sacrifices performance in favor of integrity (because typically an application that performs the write needs to wait for acknowledgement of successful completion of the operation). Asynchronous replication allows the write at the remote end to be postponed (for example, if the remote device is not immediately available) without affecting completion of the local write operation. This approach is used if the application response time on the local end is the top priority. There are also hybrid solutions, which operate synchronously unless a delay threshold is reached, in which case remote write requests are queued.

There are several remote mirroring products on the market supported on the Windows Server 2003 platform, such as LEGATO's RepliStor and Co-StandbyServer or Volume Replicator and Storage Replicator from VERITAS. We also pay particular attention to the technology from NSI Software, Double-Take, and GeoCluster, in Chapter 10, "High Availability, High-Performance Exchange."

RAID 5

This type is known as striping with distributed parity. The concept of striping with parity was already explained when discussing the principles of RAID 3, 4, and 6. The main difference of RAID 5 is the fact that parity data is not stored on a dedicated disk, but spread across all disks participating in the array. RAID 5 also protects against single disk failure.

RAID 5 is supported in both hardware and software on the Windows Server 2003 platform. While both implementations require at least three disks, the software-based one has an upper limit of 32 disks (hardware limitations are dependent on controller capabilities). To create a RAID 5 array in Windows Server 2003, you need multiple areas of unassigned disk space (not belonging to any existing volumes or partitions) of roughly the same size. It is not possible to use software-based RAID 5 to host a system or boot partitions (although this is not an issue when using the hardware-based configuration).

Disk space utilization in RAID 5 is better than RAID 1, and it improves with the larger number of disks involved. The formula specifying the amount of available space is simply (n-1)/n* 100% (parity information occupies space no larger than the size of a single drive participating in the array).

Performance of RAID 5 depends on underlying hardware. It provides fast seek and read time comparable to RAID 0 (because no parity information is required, unless the array operates with a failed disk) in implementations where multiple disks can be accessed at the same time (which depends on the hardware capabilities). Write operations are slower because parity information needs to be calculated and written to a disk.

RAID 5 operates best in situations involving frequent reads but limited writes. In database environments, it is ideal for *On Line Analytical Processing* (OLAP) purposes.

RAID 10

This is the hybrid type that combines RAID 0 and RAID 1, which means data is written in stripes across pairs of disks, configured as mirrors. The setup requires at least four disks (two striped mirrors); however, it can gracefully handle a failure of more than one disk, as long as they are not part of the same mirror set (you can lose a single disk from each mirrored pair across the RAID 0 stripe without impact on system availability). However, failure of two disks within the same mirror renders the entire array unusable.

The benefit of this configuration is combination of superior RAID 0 performance with redundancy provided by RAID 1. Reads and writes are very fast, just as with basic RAID 0 (because RAID 1 does not introduce any delay—on the contrary, it can further improve seek and read speed). The main drawback is cost, resulting from inefficient disk space utilization, which is 50% (the same as RAID 1).

The software-based implementation of RAID 10 in Windows Server 2003 is not available (unless you are using third-party products, such as the full-featured version of VERITAS Logical Volume Manager), but you can combine RAID 1 implemented in hardware with RAID 0 implemented in software.

Note that it is possible to reverse the sequence of applying basic RAID levels when setting up a hybrid RAID. Let's assume we have six physical disks. You could create two RAID 0 arrays with three drives in each and then combine resulting virtual disks into a mirror. We can call the end result RAID 0 + 1. Alternatively, you could also create three RAID 1 pairs with two physical disks in each and then include each mirror set in a RAID 0 stripe, resulting in RAID 1 + 0 (or RAID 10). While both RAID 0 + 1 and RAID 10 have the same number of disks, level of tolerance, and usable disk space, there is a difference between them. If you implemented RAID 1 in hardware rather than software, then rebuilding a mirror (in case of a single disk failure) has no direct impact on operating system performance (although I/O operations are likely to be slower due to higher utilization of the disk controller). On the other hand, re-creating a replica of a drive places much more significant burden on the main processor and memory in the case of software mirroring.

RAID Controllers

In general, RAID can be implemented in the server operating system software (this can be a built-in component, such as Windows Sever 2003 Logical Disk Manager or a third-party product, such as VERITAS Logical Volume Manager), or in hardware. In the latter case, RAID functionality is built into a controller, implemented either as a *host bus adapter* installed on the server to which disk devices are attached, or as circuitry residing in an external storage subsystem hosting disk devices.

The overwhelming majority of RAID controllers are SCSI-based (although IDE/ATA controllers are also common). There is a number of SCSI standards, ranging from the oldest SCSI-1 to the latest SCSI-3 (including Ultra 3 and Ultra 320); however, coverage of this topic goes beyond the scope of this book. It is sufficient to state that SCSI standards differ in terms of the bus width (8 or 16 bits), maximum length (between 6 and 25 meters), speed (between 5 and 320Mbps), and number of SCSI identifiers (8 or 16). The last of these characteristics determines the number of devices that can be connected to the SCSI bus because for SCSI devices to communicate, each one requires a unique address. In addition, if a device attached to the bus is a controller (rather than a disk or tape device), then you can further extend the addressing scheme by using *Logical Unit Numbers* (or simply LUNs), which identify devices attached to the controller.

Still, a SCSI bus is relatively limited considering the demands of today's enterprise computing. Technologies such as Fibre Channel or iSCSI help bypass existing distance, speed, and device addressability restrictions, providing support for distances measured in tens of kilometers, gigabit data transfer rates, and a much larger number of addressable devices. We discuss this in more detail in the sections "Storage Area Networks (SANs)" and "IP-Based Storage Solutions" later in this chapter.

While software-based RAID has its benefits, it cannot really compete with high-availability solutions implemented with RAID controllers when it comes to performance, functionality, and management capabilities. However, when deciding which solution is best suited to your environment, you should consider the following criteria:

- **Price:** This is the primary reason behind selecting software-based solutions. Logical Disk Manager, which supports RAID 0, RAID 1, and RAID 5 functionality, is the integral component of the Windows Server 2003 operating system (and its predecessors), included at no additional charge. On the other hand, the cost of RAID controllers vary dramatically, depending on their feature set (for example, the number of RAID levels supported), hardware sub-components (for example, the size of cache memory), and manageability.
- **Performance:** In hardware-based configurations, the majority of the work involved in maintaining fault tolerance (such as parity calculations) or recovering from disk failures (rebuilding a broken

mirror or regenerating a RAID 5 array) is handled through circuitry and firmware present on RAID controllers instead of by the operating system. This offloads processing from main system resources, such as processor, memory, and I/O bus. For example, outputting data to a RAID 5 array involves multiple reads and writes as well as parity calculation. In case of write-intensive applications, performance hit can be so substantial that use of software-based RAID 5 becomes questionable.

- **Supported RAID levels:** Windows Server 2003 Logical Disk Manager supports only RAID 0, RAID 1, and RAID 5. VERITAS Logical Volume Manager adds support for RAID 10. Capabilities of RAID controllers vary depending on model and price but cover all possible levels.
- **Hardware requirements:** Software-based configurations support practically any combination of disks and controllers. This does provide fault tolerance and virtualization but without performance benefits. Hardware RAID is much more restrictive in this aspect.
- **Additional hardware redundancy and performance enhancements:** Hardware-based RAID frequently includes such features as standby disks, independent power supplies and batteries, or sizeable cache memory.
- **RAID configuration persistence:** Software-based RAID records array configuration information in the Logical Disk Manager database, a copy of which exists on every dynamic disk on a Windows Server 2003 system. This makes moving disks between computers relatively easy (an actual move involves merging an LDM database with the one present on a new system because Windows Server 2003 natively supports only a single disk group). Keep in mind, however, that moving disks between servers should be limited to data volumes only—system and boot volumes do not handle such changes gracefully. The ability to move hardware-based multi-disk configurations between RAID controllers is dependent on the level of their compatibility.
- **Support for fault tolerant Windows Server 2003 system and boot volumes:** RAID 1 is the only type of software-based configuration that can host system and boot volumes. There is no such restriction with hardware-based RAID.

■ **Recovery (RAID regeneration) procedure:** While the operating system continues working normally after a single drive failure in both hardware and software-based configurations, in case of the former, recovery can be invoked automatically (subject to configuration) as soon as a replacement disk is installed in the system (even this might not be necessary if a standby spare is available). With software-based RAID, you need to use a Disk Management MMC snap-in to either break the mirror and then re-create it (in case of RAID 1) or regenerate the stripeset with parity (in case of RAID 5) using a sufficient amount of unassigned space on another dynamic disk. In addition, if the system needs to be rebooted before recovery is completed (for example, to replace a disk if hot-plug functionality is not available), the boot disk might require modifications to the BOOT.INI file, involving creation of an additional entry pointing to the other half of the mirror. This entry is selected following the reboot if the primary drive has not been recreated yet. This procedure is not required for hardware-level mirroring.

■ **Requirement for dynamic disks:** Software-based RAID requires use of dynamic disks (because they are managed by Windows Server 2003 Logical Disk Manager). This is not the case with hardware-based configurations.

■ **Support for fault-tolerant cluster shared disks:** Dynamic disks are not supported natively in Windows Server 2003 as clustered disk resources (although this is possible if VERITAS Logical Volume Manager is used). This means that disk fault tolerance in clustered configurations has to be accomplished through hardware-based RAID outside of the solutions offered by Windows Server 2003 Logical Disk Manager.

■ **Remote management:** High-end storage controllers support remote management through a command line or Web interface; however, lower-end ones require local access to the server. Software-based configurations are easily managed with a Disk Management MMC snap-in or DISKPART utility, both of which can be executed remotely.

■ **Dynamic reconfiguration:** Software-based fault-tolerant volumes do not support extending size of RAID 1 or RAID 5 disk arrays. While availability of such functionality is limited in hardware, there are RAID controllers that support it. It is, however, possible to extend partitions (on basic disks) and simple volumes (on dynamic disks) in Windows Server 2003 (including system volumes) with the DISKPART utility (but not the Disk Management console). The operating system is also capable of recognizing newly installed drives without a reboot (as long as hardware supports hot-pluggable disks). You should remember there are certain restrictions when extending basic partitions (NTFS formatted, unallocated space must be on the same drive and contiguous to the existing partition to be extended—that is, you cannot extend a basic partition by spanning it across disks. You also cannot extend the system or boot partition across disks on dynamic disks.).

Server Attached Storage Solutions

As we mentioned before, there are four basic categories of systems in regard to the storage access technology. The most traditional one, known as server attached storage, consists of a server (or servers, in more advanced, clustered scenarios) with either internal IDE/ATA or SCSI controllers and storage or host bus adapters connected directly to external devices.

We focus on SCSI-based solutions, despite the popularity of *parallel ATA* (also referred to as EIDE), because the latter reigns among desktops and workstations, rather than servers, which are of interest to us. This is due mostly to the inherent performance and distance restrictions of this technology. Even though *serial ATA* provides improvements in these areas, by increasing length and bandwidth of the interconnect, neither one allows for device sharing and both are severely limited in terms of the total number of devices supported on the bus.

The main component of the SCSI bus is a controller, which is a combination of firmware and circuitry implementing SCSI protocol, providing a means of communication between controller and SCSI storage devices, such as disks or tapes. Such a controller can be installed in a host system as the host adapter, or it can reside in an external storage subsystem. The other part of the SCSI channel is the I/O bus, which constitutes a path for transferring parallel-SCSI protocol commands and data. The channel is typically formed by connecting SCSI devices to each other in the daisy chain fashion and enclosed on both ends with terminators, preventing electrical signals from bouncing back. A diagram of a sample Server Attached Storage solution is shown in Figure 3.1.

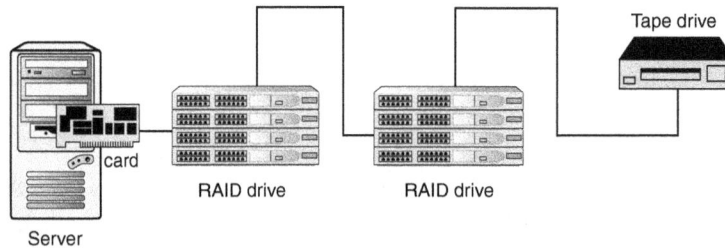

Figure 3.1   Server attached storage solution.

SCSI ID Assignments

Each device connected to an SCSI channel needs to have an assigned unique SCSI identifier, which also determines its priority. You should ensure that the SCSI ID 7, designating the highest priority device, is always assigned to the host bus adapter (that is, the SCSI controller installed in the host server). This facilitates proper bus arbitration (the method of determining which device has exclusive access to it because only one can be transmitting at any given time).

You might recall from our earlier discussion that the number of unique SCSI IDs is either 8 or 16, depending on whether you deal with narrow or wide SCSI (with at least one ID assigned to the SCSI controller). The number of addressable devices on a SCSI bus can be further extended using *Logical Unit Numbers* (LUNs), which represent individual disks within storage subsystems, connected to the main SCSI channel through an SCSI controller (which gets assigned one of the unique SCSI IDs). The number of available LUNs can vary from 8 to 254 per SCSI ID, depending on hardware devices and whether the Large LUN support is enabled, as explained in the Microsoft Knowledge Base article 310072 available at `http://support.microsoft.com/default.aspx?scid=kb;` `en-us;310072&sd=tech`.

Server attached storage solutions are inexpensive and simple to implement, but they suffer from a number of limitations. The I/O path contains numerous single points of failure (primarily, SCSI channel and SCSI controller), which cannot be easily eliminated. With the most current SCSI-3 specifications, the maximum data transfer rate is 320MB per second (provided all devices sharing the bus support it). Further, SCSI bus is prone to contention issues. Even though arbitration is used to keep simultaneous requests from SCSI devices in order, it is possible for those with higher priority to dominate communication. Reallocating disks to another server typically requires physical access, which complicates consolidation efforts and might lead to scenarios where some servers are underutilized while others are starving for additional space. Storage devices connected to separate servers cannot be managed collectively as a single unit. SCSI channel length limitations (between 12 and 25 meters, with declining signal quality, as the bus length and number of devices connected to it increase) impose restrictions on placement of hardware in data centers—storage units and servers have to reside in the same or adjacent racks. This also precludes suitability of SCSI-based configurations for disaster recovery solutions. Finally, meeting increasing storage space requirements could be problematic—adding a new disk might not be possible due to a lack of available SCSI IDs, server or rack space, empty PCI slots for SCSI host adapters on the server, or hitting the server's I/O throughput bottleneck.

Several modifications can be applied to mitigate at least some of these issues. For example, you can attach multiple SCSI host bus adapters to separate high-speed PCI buses in the host system to load balance I/O traffic and minimize contention issues. It is also possible to provide redundancy and fault tolerance by connecting two servers through their host bus adapters to a shared SCSI bus with storage devices attached to it. In Windows Server 2003, such a setup forms the basis of a cluster server. However, for this configuration to operate properly, you need to satisfy a number of other requirements outlined in Chapter 6 when we start working with clustering.

Network Attached Storage Solutions (NAS)

Network Attached Storage, similar to Server Attached Storage, provides file serving functionality using locally attached disks. What makes a NAS solution unique is the fact that the sole function of its operating system is to provide over-the-network access to the storage, which makes it very easy to configure and maintain. Most of the time, all that is required to make new storage available is to connect the device to the network, assign IP configuration parameters, set up volumes, and permission them properly. NAS devices come with server functionality already pre-installed, either as firmware or small-footprint software, optimized for file sharing. Therefore, in a slightly simplified interpretation, NAS can be viewed as a standalone storage device with some intelligence built into it, which is made available directly to clients over the network. Users can create a drive mapping to a share residing on the device, as if the share resided on a server-attached disk, and request files residing on it through client applications (typically over TCP/IP networks, although there are NAS solutions supporting UDP/IP and IPX/SPX protocols). The requests are received and processed following successful user authentication (Active Directory integration can be used for this purpose). Frequently, NAS storage devices also implement their own file system. A diagram of the Network Attached Storage solution is shown in the Figure 3.2.

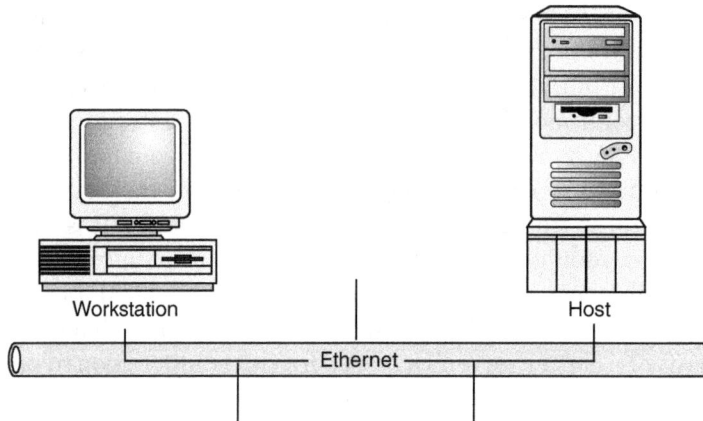

Figure 3.2   Network attached storage solution.

NAS devices, frequently referred to as storage appliances to reflect their simplicity and turnkey utility characteristics, can run either a feature-limited version of a standard operating system (such as a member of the Windows Server 2003 family—Windows Storage Server 2003), or a proprietary, device vendor-specific operating system (for example, Network Appliance's Data ONTAP). In both cases, underlying software is geared towards simplicity and file-serving efficiency. Deployment and configuration of such servers is extremely easy, the price is very competitive, the performance is excellent, and the functionality (as far as storage management and network file sharing are concerned) matches file servers based on other Windows Server 2003 editions.

Because a single NAS device functions as a unit, you no longer have to face issues relating to I/O bottlenecks or SCSI-bus length limitations (appliances can be installed in any secure area where sufficient network bandwidth is available). NAS devices also offer multiplatform support through their ability to communicate with clients using *Common Internet File System* (CIFS), *File Transfer Protocol* (FTP), *Hypertext Transfer Protocol* (HTTP), or *Network File System* (NFS) protocols, which cover a wide variety of operating systems (all versions of Windows and a range of UNIX and Linux flavors). CIFS, carrying *Server Message Block* (SMB) traffic, is the primary network file access protocol among Windows clients and includes such functionality as user-level security on the server (share-level security is also supported although rarely used), authentication (Challenge/Response or Kerberos starting with Windows 2000 Active Directory environment), as well as locking (ensuring that file access is properly controlled—for example, two users are not allowed to simultaneously make modifications to the same file). Network File System is used predominantly by UNIX systems and differs from CIFS in several areas—for example, it does not enforce locking and typically does not implement security on the server, but it relies on clients to ensure that requester's credentials are properly validated.

High-end NAS devices support a number of enterprise-class features, such as built-in synchronous or asynchronous replication, clustered failover, volume snapshots, integrated multi-level RAID, and superior scalability.

Note that NAS does not solve all problems associated with server attached storage solutions. All backup traffic still remains on the LAN, unless you attach a local backup device to each storage unit, which typically is not a realistic possibility. A more reasonable option involves installing an additional network adapter on each server and creating an isolated, dedicated backup network. This, however, requires a separate backup network infrastructure with cabling, interconnectivity devices, and management overhead.

Volume Snapshot Copy and NAS

Windows Server 2003 (including its NAS incarnation in the form of Windows Storage Server) offers significant improvement as far as backups are concerned, due to the presence of Volume Shadow Copy Service (introduced in Windows XP). This feature, also known as volume snapshots, has been available in third-party, hardware-based storage management products for some time, but its inclusion into the operating system makes it an interesting proposition from dependability, stability, and cost efficiency perspectives. The main concept behind this technology is the creation of "virtual" copies of a volume, which represent its data at arbitrarily chosen points of time. The copies do not contain all data from the underlying volume, but instead, they capture only changes applied to it since the most recent snapshot. The main benefits of this approach are savings in space and time necessary to allocate backup and the ability to back up open files. Microsoft's implementation of volume snapshot is based on the Volume Shadow Copy Service core operating system component and includes support for two native Windows Server 2003 features. The first one is the Previous Version, allowing users to recover older versions of a modified file (simply by selecting the Previous Version tab in the file's Properties dialog box within Windows Explorer); the second one is System Restore (identical to the one present in Windows XP). Both features are not dependent on types of volumes (they can reside on a local, clustered, or shared disk) or their file system (FAT32 and NTFS are supported).

Support for volume snapshots is included in Microsoft's most popular applications, such as SQL Server or Exchange Server, although third-party products are required to take advantage of these capabilities for the purpose of backups or more elaborate scenarios, such as cloning of live data for testing or disaster recovery purposes with minimal impact on the production environment.

Storage access traffic has similar characteristics. While this is not an issue when serving file shares directly to clients (because the same amount of traffic travels over the network, in the case of Server Attached Storage), the situation changes when NAS is used by server applications. In this case, if the bandwidth is shared with other applications and client traffic, congestion issues might cause significant problems; hence, the use of an isolated, high bandwidth, low latency network is strongly recommended.

In addition, you need to keep in mind a number of other considerations, which might not be relevant with NAS devices functioning purely as file servers, but are critical when using them for Exchange Server

2003 or SQL Server 2000 databases. Refer to Microsoft's Knowledge Base article 304261 (available at `http://support.microsoft.com/ ?kbid=304261`) for issues surrounding support for network SQL Server database files.

Storage Area Networks (SAN)

The primary difference between Storage Area Network (SAN) and two previously discussed technologies (Server Attached Storage and Network Attached Storage) is the method of connecting storage devices and servers. Instead of attaching storage devices directly to the server hosting the operating system, SAN topology separates them with a dedicated, Fibre-Channel–based network.

I Say "Fibre," You Say "Fiber"?

Do not be confused by the apparent misspelling of the word *Fibre*. This is intentional and is supposed to indicate that some of the cabling connecting storage and servers in SAN configurations might be made of copper. Keep in mind, however, that copper cable limits the supported maximum distance to about 100 feet and is susceptible to electromagnetic interference (compared with the distance of 10 kilometers with single-mode *fiber*-optic cabling with EMI resiliency). Fiber-optic cabling can be either single-mode (very thin with a 9-micron core), supporting longer distances, but at a higher price, or multi-mode (thicker with about a 50-micron core), which is less expensive but operates at shorter distances.

Fibre Channel network, unlike the SCSI-channel we discussed, carries electronic signals in the serial fashion (Fibre Channel protocol stack adapted serial implementation of SCSI-3 as its upper layer protocol). Serial communication is not subjected to limitations inherent to parallel technologies, which makes it capable of gigabit transfer rates over much longer distances (about 10 kilometers or even more, if specialized hardware is used). Another characteristic of Fibre Channel network, which makes it superior compared to SCSI channel, is its level of scalability. Depending on the topology and interconnectivity devices used, SAN practical limits range from about 50 (on hub-based loop networks where restrictions are imposed by arbitration, contention, and latency issues) to hundreds of devices (on switched fabric). Fibre-Channel disks are dual-ported (unlike standard, single-ported SCSI disks), which allows connections through a pair of redundant fibre links, increasing their fault tolerance.

Additionally, Fibre Channel offers improved arbitration compared to SCSI channel. For example, it is less common for a bus-wide SCSI RESET command to be required. Instead, much more efficient and less disruptive targeted LUN and SCSI ID resets are attempted first. You can read more about this at Microsoft's Web site: `http://support.microsoft.com/default.aspx?scid=kb;EN-US;301647`.

Addressable nodes on a Fibre Channel network are identifiable by the 64-bit (written typically in the format of eight pairs of hexadecimal characters) *World Wide Names* (WWN) , which are assigned to host bus adapters by their manufacturers (resembling, in this aspect, Media Access Control addresses burned into every network interface adapter card).

A Fibre Channel host bus adapter installed in each server connected to the SAN constitutes an entry point into the fabric. Its generic functionality is implemented in the Windows Server 2003 Storport device driver, which not only implements communication protocol necessary for communication with SAN devices, but it also provides a layer of virtualization, making SAN storage appear the same way as directly attached disks. Storport driver also includes support for bidirectional communication with miniport drivers and graceful recovery from error conditions. Hardware-specific miniport drivers can provide additional functionality and performance enhancements.

Similar to standard data networks, which are discussed in Chapter 4, Fibre Channel networks can be based on several different topologies. Among the most common ones are point-to-point, *Fibre Channel Arbitrated Loop* (FC-AL), and *Switched Fibre Channel Fabric* (SW-FC).

A point-to-point connection between a server with a Fibre Channel host bus adapter and a dedicated storage unit is the simplest and least expensive to implement and manage, but it does not offer the scalability or fault tolerance advantages of shared or switched configurations.

Loop topologies can use either hubs or loop-switches (which have Fibre Loop ports, allowing them to connect to loop-only devices). Interconnected servers and storage devices form a logical ring (physical star) known as a *Fibre Channel Arbitrated Loop* (FC-AL). Interconnecting devices, such as hubs or switches, are responsible for arbitration   and a number of other maintenance and management tasks, such as assigning addresses and keeping track of devices joining and leaving the network.

The FC-AL arbitration algorithm ensures lower-priority devices get their turn to transmit. Theoretically, the FC-AL supports up to 126 nodes, although due to contention and latency issues, 50 is considered the practical limit.

A diagram of a sample Fibre Channel Arbitrated Loop Storage Area Network (resembling a Token Ring LAN topology) is shown in Figure 3.3.

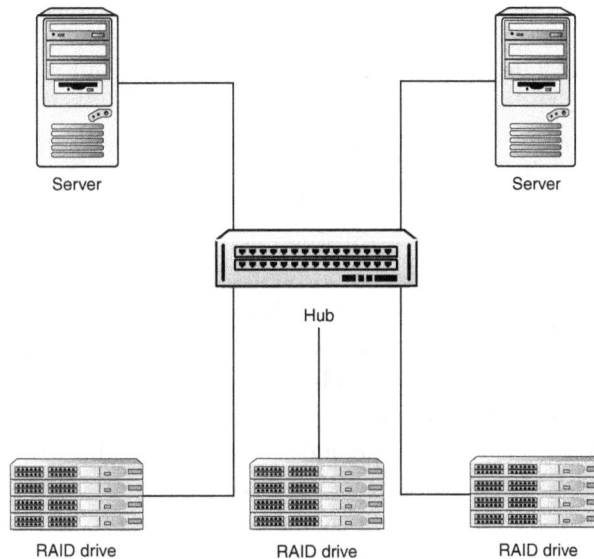

Figure 3.3   Fibre Channel arbitrated loop storage area network solution.

FC-AL configuration suffers from similar limitations as its hub-based shared LAN counterpart. Because the bandwidth is shared, only two devices can communicate at any given time. Larger numbers of devices increases the rate of contention, which makes arbitrated loops unsuitable for larger configurations (a typical hub has between 2 and 16 ports). While a Fibre Channel loop can be used in server clustering to provide access to a shared storage device, such configuration is limited to two nodes only. In addition, the process of loop initialization, which takes place during error recovery or bus resets triggered by a device joining or leaving the loop, negatively affect all nodes connected to the hub, causing time-outs or even potentially data loss.

Switched fabric resolves these issues. Fabric switches functioning as the interconnectivity devices, just like their LAN equivalents, allow simultaneous transmission between any pair of devices connected to them. Adding or removing a node or its recovery from an error does not trigger loop initialization and has no impact on the performance of remaining nodes.

This resiliency can be further enhanced by building a redundant switched fabric infrastructure. Hosts can be connected through redundant links and independently functioning switches to target devices. In this case, additional software running on host systems must be able to detect a failure of a link or switch behind it and automatically failover to another. The software also needs to properly handle the existence of two simultaneous paths to target storage devices and make sure it is presented to the operating system as one (this is the purpose of the Multipath I/O solutions we discuss later in this section). Another possibility involves creating a layer of federated, interconnected switches, which can detect communication problems and appropriately redirect server-to-storage communication. Switches can also form a scaleable hierarchy, resembling complex, multi-layered networks with redundant paths between each layer. In such a case, FC-AL hubs or point-to-point devices typically operate at the access layer (higher-end switches can auto-sense the device type and appropriately adjust their port parameters) with lower-end switches serving distribution tasks, and the high-end ones (fastest and with highest port density) residing at the core.

Switches handle the majority of management and operational tasks, such as keeping track of devices as they connect and disconnect, monitoring the integrity of transactions between them, and assigning unique addresses to each. The addressing scheme determines the theoretical maximum number of nodes supported on the Fibre Channel Switched Fabric. Because 3 bytes (or 24 bits) are used for this purpose, it is possible to create 2^{24} (or roughly 15 million) unique addresses; although, of course, the practical limits are in the range of hundreds.

A diagram of the Fibre Channel switched storage area network solution is shown in Figure 3.4.

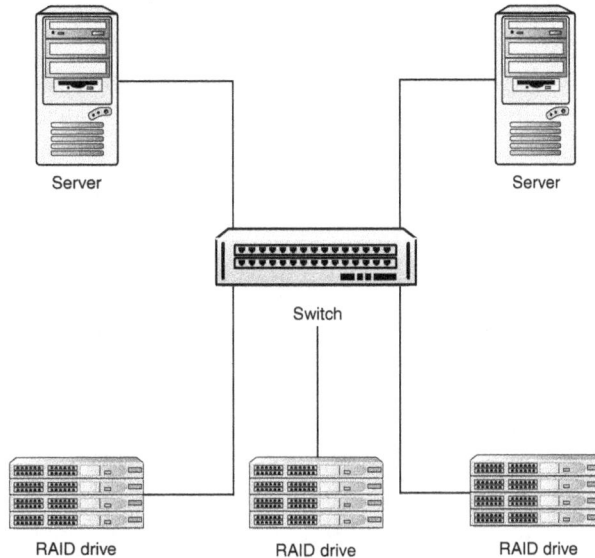

Figure 3.4   Fibre channel switched storage area network solution.

One of the problems that surfaces in a SAN environment where multiple servers and storage devices are interconnected is securing exclusive access to disk volumes. This is due to the fact that simultaneous writes from multiple servers to the same volume inevitably lead to data corruption. This issue requires extra attention in the Windows environment due to its tendency to spontaneously mount any new volume detected by the operating system (which is different from UNIX-based operating systems where mounts do not take place by default). It is possible to alter this behavior in Windows Server 2003 with the MOUNTVOL utility (by running it with the /N parameter) which restricts automatic mounting to only previously mounted volumes; however, it is important to consider more secure alternatives. Because the automatic mounting still remains the out-of-the box default, newly installed systems can easily wreak havoc in a SAN environment as soon as they get connected to the shared loop or switched fabric.

Two primary mechanisms provide the desired level of isolation—zoning and LUN masking (also called selective presentation). They are, in essence, mapping methods that ensure only designated server (or servers, in case of clustering) can communicate with specific storage devices. The zoning mechanism was developed specifically for switched

SANs, but it is conceptually equivalent to *Virtual LANs* (VLANs) in traditional switched networks. It creates dedicated paths spanning multiple devices connected to a switch (or a hierarchy of switches), which form separate zones. Traffic is allowed only between devices residing in the same zone (the same way traffic between network nodes belonging to the same VLAN can be isolated), although it is possible for a device to belong to multiple zones.

Zones can be implemented in firmware or software on one of the three main components of a switched SAN—switches, storage devices, or host bus adapters on servers. Depending on implementation, you can define zones using switch port designation or a World Wide Name assigned to the host bus adapter. With the scheme called *soft zoning*, the switch operates the name server, storing information about addresses all the devices are connected to it in port or World Wide Name format, and it operates the configurable access control list for each. *Hard zoning*, on the other hand, uses a routing table residing on the switch controlling the flow of traffic based on World Wide Names. We return to the discussion on zones in Chapter 4, "Highly Available Networks."

Unfortunately zone-based separation frequently is not granular enough. A storage controller with a single World Wide Name connected to an individual port on a Fibre Channel switch might contain tens of individual disks. To control access at the per-disk level, LUN (*Logical Unit Number*) masking is used (as explained before, LUNs designate individual devices within storage subsystems). LUN masking extends isolation of components connected to switch fabric beyond the switch port or host bus adapter level provided by zoning. This means that separate servers are able to view only their designated disks attached to the same controller and connected to the same port on the switched fabric, as long as they are associated with separate LUNs. LUN masking is typically handled by storage controllers and enforced by the host bus adapter drivers on host servers.

SAN architecture includes provisions for attaching legacy SCSI devices through SCSI-to-Fibre bridges and routers. A bridge contains a dual interface—one connecting to a Fibre Channel network and the other to a standard SCSI bus—and circuitry that translates Fibre Channel protocol into parallel SCSI signals. This way, multiple servers connected to a Fibre Channel network through a host bus adapter can take advantage of a common set of parallel SCSI devices. A router contains a single Fibre Channel interface and multiple parallel SCSI connections. Both bridges and routers are capable of restricting SAN traffic using access-control lists.

Two primary reasons for using SAN bridges and routers exist. The first one is allowing access to existing SCSI storage. The second one is implementation of LAN-free backup, in which data residing on SAN-attached storage is copied to SCSI-based tape libraries. This way, backup traffic does not impact the production network, and, at the same rate, a single backup unit can be used by multiple storage devices. Such a solution speeds up the backup process and limits hardware costs.

Server-free backup is a special case of the LAN-free backup. Its mechanism is based on the SCSI Extended Copy command and a component called *data mover agent*, implemented either in firmware on an FC-to-SCSI router device (connected, in turn, to SCSI tape libraries) or embedded directly into firmware on Fibre Channel tape libraries (connected directly to the switched fabric). Backup server performs only initial tasks, such as ensuring that media is mounted and reserved, connecting to a data mover agent on a router or FC-backup device, and sending an SCSI Extended Copy command to it. A data mover agent coordinates the rest of the process.

Other advantages of the SAN architecture exist. By creating a common communication path between storage devices, SAN-attached disks form a pool of redistributable resources, which can be easily reassigned from one host to another in response to changing storage needs. Modifications do not require physical access but can typically be accomplished with remote management utilities. Shared storage provides a strong foundation for building server clusters. Scalability and redundancy accomplished this way can be extended by creating duplicate Fibre Channel paths configured with failover and load balancing. You can also use SAN-attached disks to host boot and system disks for Windows Server 2003, as long as the conditions outlined in the Knowledge Base article Q305547 are satisfied. (This article is available at `http://support.microsoft.com/default.aspx?kbid=305547`.)

Unfortunately, when it comes to providing I/O path redundancy, additional precautions are required. Under normal conditions, having two separate communication channels to the same storage volume results in the operating system presenting it as two separate drives. To eliminate this problem, Windows Server 2003 includes native support for Multipath I/O (also available for Windows 2000 Server SP2 and later systems). Offered as a separate product (such as EMC PowerPath or HP SecurePath) by third-party Fibre Channel storage vendors for earlier versions of Windows, this software facilitates simultaneous operations of multiple host bus adapters connected to the same storage volumes through redundant I/O paths, yielding a single view of a target storage device. In addition, it supports such features as failover (automatic change from primary failed I/O path to a secondary one), failback (automatic change from a secondary I/O path back to the primary after it becomes available again), and load balancing (distribution of traffic among multiple available I/O paths leading to the same target storage volume).

Microsoft provides the core components for the Multipath I/O (bus, class, and filter driver); so, the host bus adapter's specific minidriver still needs to be developed by its manufacturer based on the development kit from Microsoft. This design ensures compatibility with other operating system components and features, such as clustering, power management, or Plug and Play.

The main drawbacks of Fibre Channel solutions are their high cost and incompatibilities with SAN components from different vendors. The slow adoption of SAN technology was exacerbated by its expensive dedicated fabric infrastructure, as well as the difficulty to design, implement, and manage its architecture. While prices of Switched Fibre Channel Fabric components are decreasing, other more cost-effective solutions, which also provide pooled, redundant, highly available storage, keep gaining popularity. We present one of them in the next section.

IP-Based Storage Solutions

IP-based storage is the latest of the technologies covered in this chapter. Its name indicates use of the TCP/IP network for transfer of storage data, which certainly does not sound like a new idea. After all, a typical communication session between a client and a file server involves network packets with payload containing portions of data files. While this is correct, it is the content of the payload that makes IP-based storage solutions unique. Instead of carrying files, network packets contain disk-level blocks and SCSI commands. Communication follows rules defined by IP Storage protocols, such as iSCSI (Internet SCSI encapsulating an SCSI command in TCP/IP packets for transmission over TCP/IP network), iFCP (*Internet Fibre Channel Protocol* providing connectivity between Fibre Channel devices separated by an IP network—a solution typically used to connect individual devices on two distinct, remote SANs), or FCIP (*Fibre Channel over IP* intended for communication between SANs through an IP-based tunnel—a solution frequently used for remote backups and restores, including maintaining disaster recovery sites).

The concept of providing block-level access to remote storage devices makes IP-based storage similar to Storage Area Networks, although in the case of the latter, request and response travel over a Fibre Channel rather than an IP network. So, in essence, you can think of the IP-based storage as a transition from SAN-based storage where the Fibre Channel network is replaced by an IP network. This transition makes sense because it eliminates the need for a separate, costly, and difficult-to-manage network infrastructure. IP networks are much more prevalent, as well as easier and cheaper to implement and maintain.

Redundancy offered by federated Fibre Channel switches can be emulated with duplicate paths through traditional network switches and routers, just as separation of devices through VLANs can serve as replacement for zoning (although there are more appropriate, iSCSI-specific methods that we discuss shortly). In addition, iSCSI is supported over copper Ethernet or fibre-optic cabling, just like Fibre Channel protocol, which ensures sufficient bandwidth. At the same time, IP-based storage solutions offer benefits similar to those provided by Storage Area Networks, such as shared access to highly available, easily manageable, and scalable storage.

It is superior in several areas—for example, it is better suited for disaster recovery scenarios because of its longer supported distances. It preserves investment in other storage technologies by allowing attachment of iSCSI devices into Storage Area Networks through interconnectivity devices, such as bridges, mutli-protocol switches, or storage routers. Such devices can also be used to bridge existing FC solutions, extending their reach beyond the 10km limit. IP Storage solutions combine multi-vendor components into a single storage network, eliminating interoperability issues typical for Fibre Channel technology. iSCSI also simplifies cluster configuration and management.

However, additional factors need to be considered to make IP-based storage solutions successful. The factors relate mostly to latency and contention issues (which were the primary reasons behind late adoption of this technology), imposing media, and distance limitations. We present these considerations in this section, while focusing on Windows Server 2003 implementation of iSCSI protocol because other IP-based storage protocols mentioned previously have not found their way into the Windows Server 2003 platform—although, they certainly may be used in combination with Windows Server 2003. For example, you can use iFCP gateways to connect a Windows Server 2003 with a Fibre Channel host bus adapter to a remote Fibre Channel storage device, separated by an IP network. Similarly, SANs connected through an IP tunnel established between two FCIP gateways over an IP network can have Windows servers attached to them. Nevertheless, in both of these cases, server platform is irrelevant and does not affect architectural design or implementation issues.

iSCSI is a standard (ratified by the Internet Engineering Task Force in February 2003) block-level transport protocol that allows sending and receiving serial SCSI-based communication (including SCSI commands, status messages, and block-level storage data) through Ethernet or Gigabit Ethernet-based TCP/IP traffic. This means that SCSI payload is included in iSCSI packets, which, in turn, are carried using standard TCP/IP communication. This way, iSCSI traffic inherits TCP/IP characteristics, such as routing and guaranteed delivery, which are essential for efficient and reliable transmission. However, because iSCSI communication can involve multiple TCP/IP sessions, implementation of sequencing and synchronization across these sessions is part of iSCSI protocol (instead of relying only on TCP capabilities). Similarly, iSCSI includes its own cyclic redundancy checks to ensure payload integrity.

iSCSI session typically involves four parties—*initiator* (typically a host server equipped with a standard network adapter or a host bus adapter with iSCSI over TCP/IP functionality), *target* (a storage unit with an equivalent adapter or an iSCSI bridge between IP network and Fibre Channel SAN), *interconnectivity device* (a standard Ethernet or iSCSI switches or routers), and a server running *Internet Storage Name Service* (iSNS) software. iSNS serves as a database (which can reside on any network host, including initiators and targets) where storage devices functioning as iSCSI targets register. (Fibre-Channel devices also have the ability to register through iFCP gateways, which were briefly described previously.) iSCSI hosts and targets are identified by unique *iSCSI qualified names* (iQN), which are functionally equivalent to World Wide Names assigned to Fibre Channel host bus adapters.

Microsoft iSCSI initiator software (downloadable from `http://www.microsoft.com/downloads/details.aspx?FamilyID=12cb3c1a-15d6-4585-b385-befd1319f825&DisplayLang=en`) is implemented as a miniport driver, which interfaces with either SCSIPort or Storport driver and runs on Windows 2000, XP, and Server 2003 platforms. The download also includes the Microsoft iSCSI driver, iSNS client, and management utilities (such as iSCSI Initiator Control Panel applet and command-line utility, iSCSICLI.EXE). Presence and status of targets is monitored through the iSCSI discovery DLL file, which communicates with iSCSI initiator and iSNS client through the Windows Management Instrumentation interface. iSNS server is downloadable from Microsoft (`http://www.microsoft.com/downloads/details.aspx?FamilyID=0dbc4af5-9410-4080-a545-f90b45650e20&DisplayLang=en`).

Microsoft iSCSI driver supports both basic types of hardware—standard Ethernet network adapters and specialized iSCSI host bus adapters. In the first case, processing is handled by the software running on the host server. The second, more expensive method offloads processing to hardware, minimizing CPU utilization of the initiator system.

iSCSI deployment is straightforward because, in essence, it only requires installation of iSCSI client software on the host server, connecting the host server and target iSCSI storage device to a (preferably dedicated) network, and assigning required parameters to both. iSCSI storage devices are typically managed with proprietary IP-based utilities, allowing you to create volumes and set authentication mechanism. Authentication can be handled with CHAP, which is used by the iSCSI initiator at the beginning of the session. Security is based on a username and password pair, known to both parties. Hashes of the password are computed independently and compared—a match between them indicates success.

You can point iSCSI targets and initiators directly at specific iSNS servers or configure them to use agent-based Service Location Protocol to locate them dynamically. Registration information is entered by iSNS clients running on iSCSI intiators and targets and is used subsequently to enumerate storage devices and initiate an iSCSI session. Alternatively, you can manually configure each initiator and target to allow their mutual communication. This method, due to administrative overhead, is appropriate only for small and relatively static implementations. iSNS has the capability to enforce access control through the feature called *discovery domains*, which is equivalent to SAN zoning. By defining multiple domains and assigning iSCSI devices to them, you can ensure a specific initiator is able to connect only to targets within the same discovery domain, down to the volume level. iSNS also provides *State Change Notification Service*, informing selected initiators and targets running iSNS client software of changes on the iSCSI network, such as the addition or removal of devices or discovery domain modifications.

The initiator must designate a specific logical unit within the target at the beginning of the session. The volumes visible to initiator (registered with iSNS server) are listed on the Available Targets tab of the Properties dialog box of the iSCSI Initiator Control Panel applet. To connect to them, you need to authenticate by clicking on the Log On button on the same page and specifying the username and password.

After the authentication completes successfully, initiator and its target negotiate communication parameters, such as security mechanism or buffer size. Discovered devices can be remembered throughout reboots of the initiator host, resulting in automatic mounts. This is configurable from the Persistent Targets tab of the iSCSI Initiator applet Properties dialog box.

As mentioned earlier in this section, SAN and iSCSI are conceptually very similar. The main difference between them is the type of network protocol carrying the SCSI payload. This, however, has important implications in terms of performance, which needs to be carefully considered. First of all, an IP network must satisfy increased bandwidth and latency requirements to be able to carry efficiently storage-related traffic. TCP/IP protocol has higher overhead than Fibre Channel because it was designed to operate in unreliable and slow environments. The same applies to the comparison between Ethernet switches or TCP/IP routers and Fibre Channel interconnectivity devices. To minimize this overhead, it is recommended you implement a dedicated iSCSI Gigabit Ethernet network and minimize network distance between iSCSI initiators and targets. Use of Jumbo Ethernet frames can additionally help maximize the percentage of effective payload.

You should also keep in mind potential issues with data integrity and security. Network errors are more likely to occur on a shared TCP/IP network infrastructure, especially when operating over lower bandwidth or long distance connections. Some of the error correction mechanisms are built into network protocol layers. The iSCSI-specific ones include acknowledgement of the process performed by the initiator (similar to the one performed on the TCP level), which maintains a buffer storing previously sent data. The initiator is also responsible for reestablishment of broken iSCSI sessions.

While IPSec can be used to protect the content of iSCSI packets, this increases processing load on their senders and recipients. This affects, in particular, iSCSI initiator host servers. To remedy this issue, the burden of processing network data can be offloaded from the main processors to circuitry on properly equipped network adapters.

Time-Out

We covered many different angles to the storage story. A sound strategy for storage is critical in the architecting of high availability, high-performance solutions. The first thing that comes to mind for an architect crafting a cluster for Exchange, SQL Server, or file and print is this question, "Which shared storage solution is going to be the best choice for the project at hand?"

Do you go for SCSI or FC, NAS or SAN? After you've decided on the storage solution, if you are looking for a highly available solution to meet a stringent SLA, then you need to consider that you'll need to get two of whatever storage solution you decide on.

Let's say you've decided to install an EMC SAN, a couple of terrabytes that costs six figures. Have you budgeted for two EMC SANs? Think about it. You have two servers in your cluster; each node has dual HBA adapters, dual NICs, redundant switches for the SAN fabric, and so on. If any node or device fails, you have a second one to failover two. But do you have a second SAN, a second SCSI enclosure, or a NAS storage unit? To be redundant from one end of the system to the other, you also need redundant storage, and two SANs can really do serious damage to the budget.

Not only do you need two SANs, but next comes the problem of replicating your data from the active SAN to the passive SAN. Now you have more expensive software to think about. And, how do your hosts failover to a standby SAN? They can't. You would need another cluster attached and waiting on the standby SAN, and there is no known way to failover a cluster to another cluster. Or is there? In Chapter 10, we'll introduce a solution that presents an elegant and very smart solution to the problem of redundancy in the shared storage tier, which actually brings with it some amazing collateral benefits.

CHAPTER 4

Highly Available Networks

Introduction

Without a backbone, most systems, both organic and mechanic, cannot exist. The backbone in the world of computers and software is the network. When designing highly available systems, whether they are load-balanced, failover, SANs, or simply redundant systems, a weak or flimsy backbone, an unstable or poorly designed network, presents the greatest risk to availability. If the hosts cannot communicate with each other, they are useless.

This chapter focuses on building a solid network and backbone before any high-performance, highly available architecture is put in place with respect to the actual systems themselves. We discuss backbone design for availability and scalability, network interface cards, hubs, switches, and routers, and then finish the chapter with a SAN topology primer. We also introduce the storage redundancy solutions like disk mirroring and replication.

Backbone Design for High Availability

When architecting a resilient network to support high availability or high-performance solutions, it is important to understand that your work usually begins with the backbone. This is, essentially, the core networking services, which begins with the provisioning of a root, a primary, or main switch, or router, that supports your primary network. Another term for this part of the network is the *core*, and some engineers call it the *head* or the *top*.

If your network is small or located in a single office supporting less than, say, 24 devices, your backbone really lives out of a single switch or *hub*—which is the device that lets all devices (hosts) communicate with each other.

You install additional routers and switches as soon as you have good reason to partition servers from clients on a single floor, or you need to connect two floors or buildings to each other. It doesn't take much equipment or much money these days to install a fast and highly sophisticated backbone, comprising of a core router, a switch for servers, a switch for client devices and printers, and a switch or more to connect floors, buildings, or workspaces to each other.

Regardless of whether you are installing one switch or if your backbone is comprised of numerous switches, the key is to architect and design a system of switches to form a *hierarchy*. A hierarchy lets you scale out and in easily and protects you against catastrophic failures.

In a hierarchy, the topmost router ports are devoted to interconnections between buildings (dedicated network services and segments) and router-to-switch or switch-to-switch connections. Of course, if you have a very small network, then the hierarchy is relatively shallow and narrow, for instance, one or two switches deep and wide. If you have a large network and are provisioning for one or more high-availability solutions, then your network contains many switches across the network and at several levels. This is demonstrated in Figure 4.1.

When architecting high-availability solutions, you should install redundant LAN *network interface cards* (NICs) on the servers with one NIC connecting to one port of the first redundant switch and another to the second redundant switch. You should never connect your servers directly to the root or core switch. They should be connected at the second- or third-level switches. By creating a hierarchy, you are guarding against communications failure by connecting your servers to the second or third tier's switch. This protects you from failures that may occur at the root of the hierarchy. And, if the network engineers ever need to rearchitect the root or upgrade equipment, the lower or base part of the hierarchy can still function.

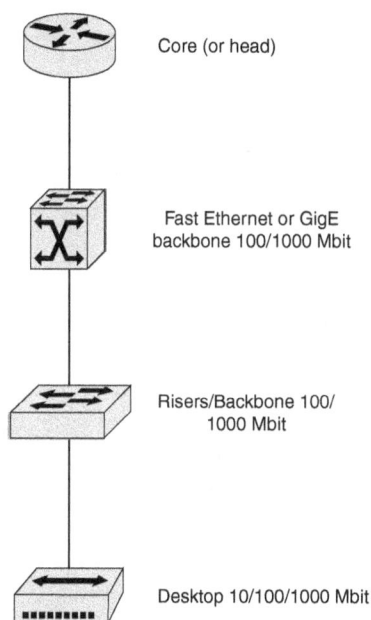

Figure 4.1   A scalable, hierarchical, highly available network.

Typically, your high-end, switch-cum-routers that connect backbones only have a few ports for switch-to-switch connections. The high-end Cisco 6500s series, the 7000 series, and so on are good examples of core equipment in large networks. Your 24- and 48-port switches, such as the series 2000, 3000, and 4000 switches, connect up to these core switches. If for any reason the backbone between the root or top-level switch goes, it will not take the extended backbone further down the hierarchy.

This design also lets you scale much easier; the ability to scale is one of the key components of a good network architecture.

NOTE: A discussion of what constitutes a good switch or router is beyond the scope of this book. Network equipment is being improved every day; so, it is best to consult your Cisco, Brocade, or Dell representatives, to mention a few, for this information.

Bandwidth Field Notes

Now that we have discussed the enterprise network, let's turn to what we never seem to get enough of on a network—bandwidth. Bandwidth is the second key issue when it comes to provisioning network for high availability. The advent of cost-effective high bandwidth technology has allowed us to start entertaining what was, for years, too expensive and too complex to entertain—clusters and load-balanced services that span geographical divides. It is now possible to split a cluster over data centers in a city, across a state, and even across a continent.

We briefly discuss what it takes to build geographic clusters and the options for distributing services over a large geographical area in Chapter 11, "Load Balancing," but most of us rarely are called upon to implement such systems. Instead, we are all architecting high-bandwidth networks within our local data centers and the backbones that service individual locations in the enterprise.

As we consolidate core network services, such as email, print, and file in corporate data centers, bandwidth becomes a critical focus of the solution, as much as the availability of the service. When consolidating, you offer more clients service on a smaller number of servers; so, you need to architect solutions that cannot fail. At the same time, having a highly available print server that cannot push print jobs over your network is pointless. So, before you go spending a lot of time and effort on your clusters to serve a bunch of remote sites, spend some time making sure you have the bandwidth faucet well greased.

Ethernet

First, a primer on the new gigabit technologies takes root. It's been more than 30 years since Ethernet became the de facto networking protocol, and it is very rare these days to find Token Ring, *Fiber Distributed Data Interface* (FDDI), and *Asynchronous Transfer Mode* (ATM), especially in server and client networks. Since Xerox introduced Ethernet in the 70s, we have seen it mature from standard Ethernet at 10 megabits per second (Mbps) to 100Mbps.

Most corporate backbones are still running at 100Mbps (Fast Ethernet) because of the cost and past slow vendor support for gigabit technology. However, gigabit is now much cheaper and easier to implement than ever before, with many standard NICS and switching supported and huge interest from vendors. Gigabit Ethernet and beyond is here.

Looking back at Fast Ethernet, you can see exactly where gigabit technology is going to go, and very soon it will completely replace Fast Ethernet as the simple, cost-effective backbone option. We like to think of Gigabit being bandwidth for the backbone, but Gigabit NIC prices are dropping so fast it will not be long before gigabit extends to the desktop and becomes the de facto standard for corporate networking. As of mid-2004, a Gigabit NIC can be purchased for less than a hundred US dollars.

How do we compare Gigabit Ethernet (or GigE) to its predecessors? Fast Ethernet is the foundation for Gigabit Ethernet. It sits atop of the Ethernet protocol but ramps up the transmission speed almost ten times to 1000Mbps, or 1 gigabit per second (1Gbps). The protocol is not so new either; it was standardized in mid-1998, but it took until late 2003 to drop enough in price to warrant fast adoption.

How does it work? To ramp up from 100Mbps, Fast Ethernet engineers made a number of physical interface changes to the interfaces of the day. Only from the data link layer upward does Gigabit Ethernet differ from Fast and standard Ethernet. Engineers focused on merging two Ethernet technologies: IEEE 802.3 Ethernet and ANSI X3T11 *Fibre Channel* (FC).

For networks that grow to more than a single floor in a building, or grow beyond 48 devices, GigE presents the ideal backbone. In high-availability environments, it has become essential to have GigE on the backbone. For example, print-server clusters under Windows Server 2003 have become highly efficient and can now host thousands of queues. Print spooler files are growing larger than ever. Thus, it goes without saying that while you might have seen sufficient throughput in the earlier years with Fast Ethernet coming out of Microsoft Cluster Server, today's needs and requirements are very different, especially when it comes to pushing print and spool files over the WAN.

Without spending too much time on the fine points of GigE, today's new copper interface cards present low-cost entries into the gigabit market. In architecting your backbone, you can place high-end gigabit switches that interconnect with fiber at the root of the architecture—connecting buildings, floors, and sites to each other. Lower down the backbone, your 24- and 48-port switches can be the cheaper copper GigE ports for direct connection to your servers.

Servers today from all vendors now come standard with 10/100/1000 GigE interfaces on the main board with copper interfaces, which still use RJ45 plugs and the standard CAT5 cable. This enables you to connect standard Ethernet cable to the interfaces, connecting the servers to the switches for server-to-server and server-to-client communications. This is demonstrated in Figure 4.2.

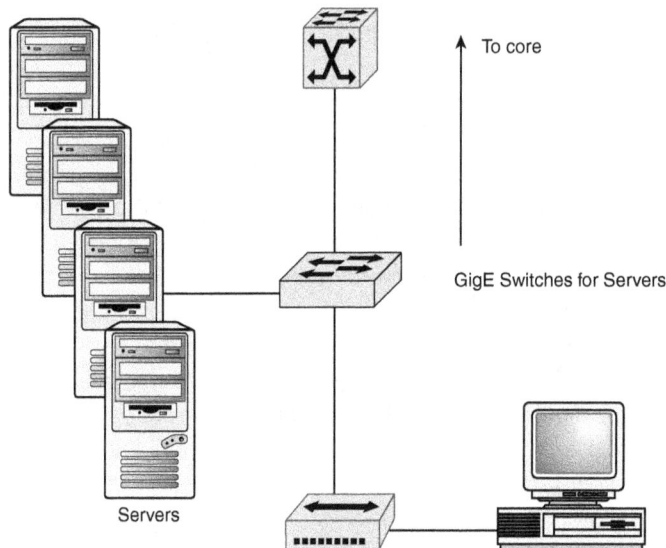

Figure 4.2   GigE on the corporate network.

Figure 4.2 shows your desktop-to-server-to-backbone architecture scaling from 10/100 at the desktop to 100Mbps up the riser to 1000 Mbps in the data center. Where do we go from here? Well, it's worthwhile to watch the advent of 10Gbit Ethernet, which is fast coming into focus on the horizon, sort of where 1Gbit was back in 1998. What this tells you is that it's not worth your time to consider architecting any longer for Fast Ethernet.

Can you have too much bandwidth? Yes, you can. The current technology in or at the server is slightly behind the curve of the advancement on the network. Internal components, computer busses, network interfaces, processors, memory, and the software cannot actually receive data thrown at it at the increasing speeds on the network.

Thus, thinking about doing anything faster than GigE at the present time may not make much sense. In fact, some systems now have technology built into it that becomes aware of data coming in too quickly by communicating with the switches and interfaces to delay transmission if the receiving host is having a tough time getting it all in.

No doubt, we will one day be plugging away at 10GB plus, but for now, sensibly architecting at 1Gbit is sufficient for the most demanding of high-availability requirements. Figure 4.1 also illustrates separating the network into three bandwidth levels: 10Mbit or 100Mbit at the desktops, 100Mbit at the risers, and 1000Mbit between the servers and connecting to the risers.

What to Look for in Network Interface Cards

Paramount in network architecture, and of prime importance when architecting a high-availability network, is making decisions about the NICs you are going to buy. Today, most servers come with at least two NICs on the main system board; so, you don't have many options but to go with what they give you. Of course, you can also choose to add additional PCI-based NICs installed at the factory (don't waste time buying them separately). Also, the high-density systems and blade servers don't have room to install NICs. Good news is all vendors put a lot of thought into the NIC and go with top-class products from the likes of Qualcom or Intel.

When it comes to larger hosts that require more than two NICs, for both LAN communications and NICs for cluster interconnects, it is up to you to decide what you need. Many engineers like to disable the onboard NICs for fear their demise requires you to replace the entire system board instead of just pulling the NICs. However, the reputation NICs have for failing has long since played out and, in any event, often the cause of NIC failure stems from handling NICs in unclean and statically charged environments.

When considering NIC, first consider the environment into which the servers are going. If you have the luxury of architecting a new backbone along with the high-availability network, you are able to decide on GigE from servers to the core and intermediate switches and install gigabit NICs from the outset.

You also need to decide on fiber versus CAT 5 (copper). CAT 5 NICs for the GigE network have come a long way, and the honor of pushing high bandwidth limits are no longer fiber's alone. Fiber is, however, more expensive in a number of areas. First, the cards themselves are expensive, although not that much more nowadays than copper GigE NICs; so, they won't break the budget of a HA data center. Second, fiber is delicate and requires a lot more care than CAT 5; pinch a CAT 5 cable and most of the time you can save the cable. A tiny pinch on fiber is likely going to "break glass" and render the cable useless. A fiber cable either works or it is broken.

NOTE: If a fiber device —NIC or adapter—stops working, do not—I repeat, do not—stare into the fiber optics to see if you see any light pulses. If the device does not have automatic shut off (*optical fiber control* [OFC]) you will damage your cornea permanently. FC emits laser beams. You will not burn a hole through your eye and out the back of your head, but you may have permanent eye damage that will only become noticeable later in life.

Fiber cables are much more expensive to replace than CAT 5. Thus, with cable, you have a much higher overhead when it comes to maintenance. Finally, provisioning every server with LAN-side fiber can be very expensive because the server must run fiber switches, and fiber switches result in you sharpening your budget pencils. Remember that it is not so much about NIC cost but about the topology. Rule of thumb: Fiber topology is more expensive and harder to maintain than CAT 5.

If you are going to use fiber for the backbone, put fiber at the switch-to-switch level. As indicated in Figure 4.3, collapse down to a copper GigE switch using a single fiber port on the CAT 5 switch, and then connect all the servers to the CAT 5 switch. Finally, building the SAN network, which we discuss later in this chapter, may require fiber provisioning; so, budget for fiber-based *Host Bus Adapters* (HBA NICs) and fiber switches for the SAN solution.

Also, remember that however you architect your network, provision for future bandwidth needs and scale-out. That copper switch you thought would do the trick for the backbone may have to be junked for a new fiber-based switch down the road. The network architects rule: Come up with a figure you think the network engineers (and purchasing) can live with, then add 20 percent for growth and another 20 percent if you need room for underestimation.

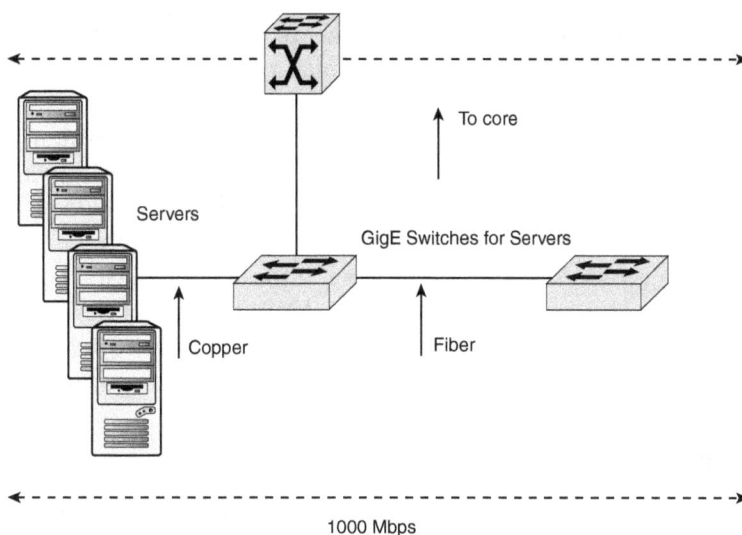

Figure 4.3   Fiber versus copper on the corporate network.

Hubs, Switches, and Routers

You may wonder how hubs are used in high-availability architecture. It is true that hubs are not intelligent like switches. Servers and devices talk to each other in hubs because the hub is a simple device in which all ports pass and receive information. You can think of the hub as a small communal swimming pool that everyone shares. While ten people in the pool may be okay, going above 30 or 40 starts to detract from the communal experience. Everyone starts bumping into each other and no one can carry on a private conversation. In essence, hubs can become very noisy, and noise on the network detracts from high-availability requirements.

There was a time when the cost of switches was such that hubs were attractive in small data centers or small offices. But nowadays you can buy a small switch the size of a small book and it costs the same and even less than a hub. Hubs are useful for small workgroups where network drops are hard to install. Everywhere else on the corporate network, switches should do the work.

Why do we even need to keep manufacturing hubs? In high availability architecture, hubs can play a very important role for hosting your cluster nodes. This is discussed in the next section.

Switches are another matter and came about as a result of many limitations encountered with hubs. Switches are able to forward packets directly to an individual *media access control* (MAC) address, direct to a port. The more expensive switches are also highly programmable, enabling you to partition the switch into routable virtual networks, otherwise known as virtual LANs or VLANS. They also offer security, monitoring, and so on. Let's now look closer at how switches, hubs, and routers are used in high-availability or load-balancing solutions.

Layer 2 Switches

The layer 2 switch, as discussed a few moments ago, is able to filter packets according to the MAC address that is interested in the packet. However, the layer 2 switch marries a port on its matrix with the MAC address that is able to talk to the server that's connected to it.

Servers communicate as usual, but the layer 2 switch forwards the packet directly to the machine for which the packet is intended. The switching matrix thus routes the packet directly from one port to another. The packet may be coming in from a port that leads to the backbone and down to the switch hosting the client machines, or it may be coming directly from another server connected to the switch.

Layer 2 technology can cause problems for both NBL and failover clusters because of the way clients connect to the virtual IP and MAC addresses used by these HA solutions. To understand the problem and how to provision for it, we must first discuss how the layer 2 switch works; however, we do not delve deeply into this subject.

On your network, when servers talk to each other and clients talk to the server by connecting to the layer 2 switch, the packets are not broadcast in a packet storm like they are in a hub. Instead, packets are switched directly to the machine for which the packet is intended, just like a telephone switch. Now the *address resolution table* (ARP) comes into play. If the switch does not have information about a particular MAC address in its ARP table, it broadcasts the address to all ports in the switch until a reply is obtained that claims to be the destination.

In NLB clustering arrangements, as you will later learn, all the servers in the cluster can claim the same IP and MAC address through the address virtualization process. Your switch may attempt to assign the virtual MAC address to a particular port on the switch. This causes the requests for the address to be targeted to only one node in the cluster instead of being load-balanced across all the cluster nodes, which defeats the purpose of the NLB cluster.

With fail-over clustering, a slightly different problem can occur. With all Microsoft fail-over clustering technology, the servers perform what is called a *gratuitous Address Resolution Protocol (ARP) request* when a failover occurs. The gratuitous ARP request is performed to update the network (computers, routers, and switches) with the MAC address that now owns the virtual server's IP address.

The problem is that your device may not forward the gratuitous ARP request to other devices. So, devices on the other side of the switch or router end up with the wrong information in their ARP tables and, thus, incorrect MAC address for the virtual server that has failed over. Most likely the situation corrects itself after a router or switch learns of the failure and updates its ARP table by performing a broadcast. By default, routers and switches are configured not to forward ARP traffic between subnets. This is done to prevent the occurrence of what is known as an *ARP storm*.

In a failover cluster, each computer node has a network adapter attached to the LAN, and each cluster node has its own IP address, network name (NetBIOS name), and MAC address. The virtual server also has a resolvable IP address and network name, but it uses the MAC address of the cluster node that is the current owner of the virtual server resources.

So, when failover takes place, the node receiving IP resources sends the gratuitous ARP request to update all devices with the new MAC address assigned to an existing IP address. If a switch or router does not pass the updated MAC-to-IP address mappings, network devices on other segments contain the old MAC address for the cluster node that is down and clients no longer are able to communicate with the virtual server. Essentially, the clients are waiting for the data train on the wrong platform.

For failover clusters, you should configure your switches and routers as follows: Have them forward the gratuitous ARP requests across all networks, so all devices receive the updated MAC-to-IP address mappings. This is done inside your switch or router; so you need to telnet to the router or log in to its private Web site, if it has one, to make the changes.

When configuring your systems for NLB clustering, you can configure the cluster to use *Unicast* or *Multicast* mode. Unicast is the default and, essentially, connects the IP address to a unicast MAC address. Unicast mode uses a MAC address mask, a substitute address, as its source MAC address when it sends the packets to the switch. This behavior prevents the switch from updating its ARP cache with the address and causes it to forward the packet to all ports in the switch, which is what you want.

Another lesson learned by seasoned NLB cluster architects is to connect all the NICs in the NLB "farm" to a hub instead, and then connect the hub to the layer 2 switch. The switch then records the virtual MAC address and associates it with the port connecting to the hub. The packets then arrive at the hub, which broadcasts it to all servers connected to the hub. However, if you use a hub, then you need to disable the MAC address masking behavior because now you *want* the ARP table to be updated with the MAC of the port that connects to the hub. To do this, you need to change a registry key of the Windows Server operating system. The key is found at the following location:

```
HKEY_LOCAL_MACHINE\SYSTEM\CurrentControlSet\Services\WLBS\
Parameters
```

You can find the following default information at this registry folder:

```
MaskSourceMAC
Data type = REG_DWORD
Range = 0 or 1
Default = 1
```

Change the value to **0** in Range. Setting the Range value to 1 masks the source MAC address in outbound packets, preventing switches from learning and forcing them to broadcast packets for unknown addresses to all ports. Setting this value to 0 disables masking of the MAC address.

You can also choose to disable port blocking (this enables unknown unicast and multicast packets to flood the specific ports). Known as Multicast mode, it makes use of a multicast MAC address for the virtual address and resolves it to a unicast IP address. This causes the switch to ignore recording which MAC address is associated with a single port. Instead, the switch now behaves like a hub and broadcasts the packets to all ports.

While the latter option is a simple quick fix, it is not a better option and detracts from the purpose of layer 2 switches. The switch does not associate the multicast MAC addresses to a port and, thus, sends frames to the MAC address on all the ports. IP Multicast pruning implementations cannot limit the port flooding and you may have to configure a virtual LAN as a solution. Multicast provides no advantage over unicast from the switches perspective. Performance decreases and will burden the layer 2 topology your networking team has spent time perfecting. Connecting the NLB hosts to a hub may be your best option.

Layer 3, Layer 4, and Beyond

The higher layer switches work in similar fashion to layer 2 switches, but the MAC address is not included in the switching equation. Instead, routing is based on IP addressing. This can be a problem for clustering because you now do not have the option of masking the MAC address as discussed earlier.

The best, and only, option in layer 3 and above switching environments is to connect your cluster nodes, NLB, and fail-over to a hub and connect the hub to a port on the layer 3 switch. If for some reason you must connect the nodes directly to a switch, then you have to provision for an intermediate layer 2 switch.

NOTE: The issues described are obviously pertinent to larger networks that have multiple switches and routers spanning the corporate network.

Routers and Routing in High Availability Architecture

Routers figure in all high-availability scenarios that cater to multiple subnets and network segments. Now that geographically dispersed clustering is becoming easier to achieve, routers actually sit between nodes of your clusters. In fact, lately it has become harder to discern the difference between switches and routers because many modern switches support router modules that are no bigger than a port on the chassis.

Some of the things you need to watch for in routed networks supporting high-availability architecture are that clients on the outer segments can connect back to a failover server or connect again upon failback. Again, the culprit that causes clients to not find the virtual servers is the ARP. The solution is to ensure routers are configured to bridge their ARP broadcasts across all the routers on the enterprise network.

Also, the use of address masking can cause problems at the router level. Routes typically do not record the ARP entry for the virtual server; so, you may need to add the entry to the router's table manually.

TIP: For better performance, configure the default gateway on your node's virtual interface only, and leave it out of the configuration dialog for the actual corporate network NICs in the machine.

Using Hubs for Failover Interconnects

Earlier we discussed the role of hubs in the high-availability architecture with respect to connectivity on the enterprise network. However, hubs can play an important role in the interconnect architecture for your failover clusters.

Later, in Chapter 8, "High-Performance File-Server Solutions," we talk about configuring failover clusters and, more specifically, configuring the interconnects. When a resource fails on a cluster node, the passive node takes over operations. It does this because it learns of the failure over a private network between the nodes in a cluster. How and why this works is discussed in Chapter 8, but for now, know that you need to set up a private network typically isolated from the main LAN or corporate network exclusively for node-to-node communications. When only two clusters are installed as part of a fail-over cluster in the same rack, the network is established using a crossover cable between the two nodes. A private IP subnet is used to enable all the nodes to talk to each other's IP address.

However, as soon as you add more nodes to the cluster, or add more clusters to the architecture, you have to install a small hub to cater to the interconnected private network. Using a hub also enables you to easily troubleshoot the interconnect traffic. You can join a client monitoring device or machine to the hub and capture the packets being sent and received on the interconnect network. The topology for hubs in the interconnect design is illustrated in Figure 4.4.

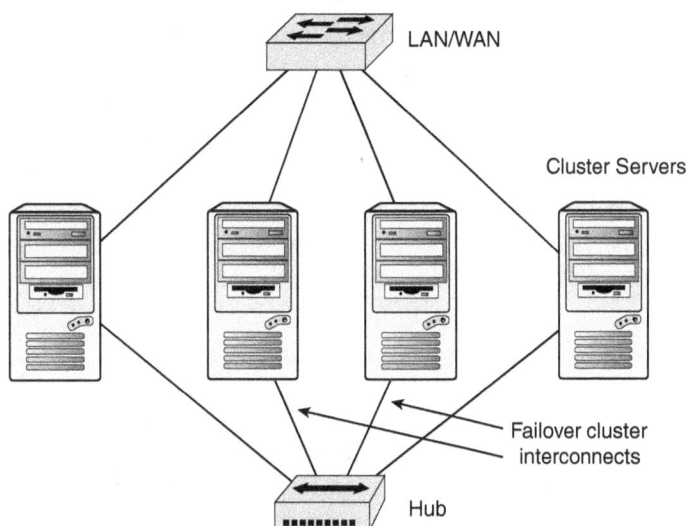

Figure 4.4 Using a hub for your interconnect network.

Almost all cluster interconnect topologies that have started as a single CAT 5 cable between two servers have ended up being removed in favor of a small hub. Remember one of the golden rules of architecting networks is to plan for the future, which is just around the next corner. So, place a cheap but reliable hub into the cluster rack from the get-go and save yourself the trouble of trying to add it later when the rack is full.

SAN Topology Primer

In Chapter 3, we touched on the subject of SAN networking and fabrics. Let's now look deeper into the subject from a SAN network architecting point of view. If you are new to SANs, then it is important to know the subject is vast, the technology is leading-edge, and often bleeding-edge. The entire subject cannot be covered adequately in one or two chapters. However, SANs are so key to high-availability solutions, we offer some insight and guidelines to get your taste buds working.

The difference between a SAN and the corporate network, from the server's point of view, is on the SAN, servers never talk to each other, they only communicate with the SAN. The only role the SAN network has is to provide the high-speed channel or data bus between the server and its hard disk drives. Sure, there is a lot of technology in between the SAN and the server, but the server only sees its LUNs and volumes as if they were local to the machine at the end of the standard SCSI cable. This is fundamentally what a SAN is—a network, instead of an 80-pin ribbon cable, that provides access to storage (see Chapter 3).

Servers interface to the SAN network with a NIC called a *host bus adapter* (HBA). While some SAN HBAs use copper media, fiber is more suitable, scalable, and functional. Fibre Channel (not fiber) SANs are still too expensive for small networks (see Chapter 3 on the subject of SCSI and ISCSI). However, if you are building a SAN that serves several clusters (and provides storage for hundreds and thousands of users), then you almost certainly should deploy Fibre Channel.

Our experience with Fibre Channel in a number of locations is that it is not a very difficult technology to deploy. However, because it is rarely deployed outside of the SAN implementation, most IT shops do not have in-house expertise on the subject. The lack of knowledge in deploying Fibre Channel for a SAN is one of the greatest contributors to the cost of your high-availability project.

Until you have expertise in-house, it is important to add an FC consultant to the project, even if just to get you up-to-speed. Alternatively, spend a few thousand dollars and get someone from the network team out to a SAN implementation course. Most of the SAN vendors, like private-label EMC or Hitachi SANS provide consultants. These come at great cost (typically no less that $10,000 for a two-day SAN project). They don't give you a lot of time, and they leave you with little transferred knowledge and a lot of PowerPoint slides.

Fibre Channel

To start you on the road to your SAN, let's talk a little about Fibre Channel. While FC is used in standard enterprise networking, it is ideal for SAN implementations for the following reasons:

- FC supports non-network protocols, such as SCSI-3 or video, and is thus ideal for data access.
- FC supports hot pluggable devices. This is critical for HA architectures.
- FC is a low-latency connection and connectionless service.

- FC offers superb *quality of service* (QoS) features. These include fractional bandwidth allocation and connections-specific bandwidth guarantee. This is useful, for example, in allocating bandwidth to high-performance backups to SAN-attached tape drive units when access to the file servers is at its lowest.
- FC offers a band rate of 1Gbps/2Gbps, with the ability to scale to 4Gbps.
- FC supports point-to-point, loop, switched, or hub topology.
- FC offers guaranteed delivery (both GigE or ATM do not offer this).
- FC offers data transfer with zero congested data loss.
- FC has a frame size that is variable to 2KB.
- FC supports both glass and copper media. Fibre Channel once only supported fiber optic cables, but, as discussed earlier, support for copper cable is now mature.

FC is actually a standard that defines a stack of protocols used for data transfer. Its upper-layer protocols include SCSI, IP, 802.2, IPI, and HIPPI. As data travels up or down the stack, it is mapped to the FC channel protocols for transfer. The layers are illustrated in Figure 4.5.

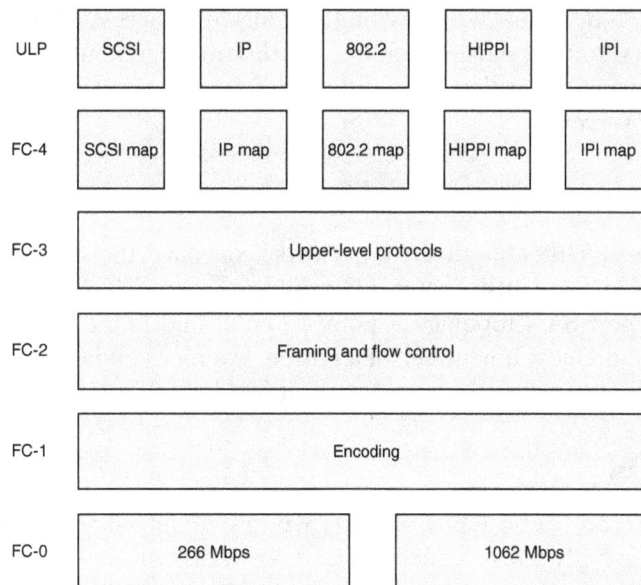

ULP	SCSI	IP	802.2	HIPPI	IPI
FC-4	SCSI map	IP map	802.2 map	HIPPI map	IPI map
FC-3	Upper-level protocols				
FC-2	Framing and flow control				
FC-1	Encoding				
FC-0	266 Mbps		1062 Mbps		

Figure 4.5 The Fibre Channel protocol stack.

When a server requests data from a disk, the SCSI-3 protocol essentially decides how the data is going to be retrieved. The data is then passed to the SCSI map of the FC protocol (see FC-4 in Figure 4.5). The data is then segmented into frames at FC-2, encoded at FC-1, and then onto FC-0 to begin its journey across the glass or copper media.

The data transfer is made possible by support for the SCSI-3 protocol at the adapter and server level. SCSI-3 defines what is known as serial SCSI. Instead of sending the data across parallel conductors in the SCSI ribbon cable, the data is sent in one transmission stream through the single line in the FC cable.

The HBA cards that you plug into your servers are the devices that take care of the aforementioned details for your servers. So, the server can talk the language they are already familiar with (SCSI) and not care how the data is sent and retrieved from the SAN and the disk array on the other end of the cable.

This magic over FC is replicated on the other side of the SAN fabric, the so-called weave of network technology that ties the SAN together (discussed in more detail in the next section). The disk arrays themselves can be thought of as servers, but their job is to handle the requests for data, fetch and store data from the arrays, and transfer them across to the servers on the other end of the fabric. SAN array processors use UNIX- or Linux-like operating systems (only accessible to the manufacturers) to do the data handling and disk management. The processor on the array controller is no different from the processor that resides in your server.

SAN Topology

When architecting a SAN network, you have the choice of three FC topologies: point-to-point, *FC arbitrated loop* (FC-AL), and fabric. The cheapest SAN topology is point-to-point and fabric is the most expensive, and most functional, of all three. We focus on fabric because it is by far the most desirable topology. But first let's discuss ports.

Ports

There are three types of ports we talk about when architecting SAN topology: N_Ports, which are ports on a disk or server system; F_Ports, which are ports on a SAN fabric switch; and L_Ports, which are ports that function in an arbitrated loop.

N_Ports only communicate with other N_Ports in point-to-point topology, or they talk to F_Ports on a SAN fabric. L_Ports alone do not exist. While they are built to function in arbitrated loops, they need to be combined with N_Ports or F_Ports to create FL_Ports. In other words, an FL_Port on a switch can connect to a node that can function in an arbitrated loop.

We also talk about E_Ports, which stands for *expansion* port. E_Ports connect switches to each other to scale the SAN fabric. Then there are G_Ports, which are *generic* ports on a switch that can function as FL_Ports or F_Ports depending on what they connect to.

Point-to-Point Topology

Point-to-point topology is comprised of two N_Ports that talk over a direct connection. This is illustrated in Figure 4.6, showing a single host server connected to an array over FC. FC-AL, pronounced "f-cal," actually came after fabric topology because, in the early days of SANs, fabric was prohibitively expensive for many small to medium implementations. FC-AL was thus offered as a cheaper alternative to fabric, but without the limitations apparent in a point to point-to-point topology.

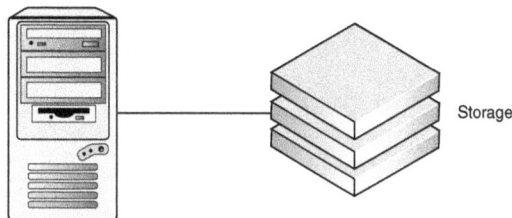

Figure 4.6   Point-to-point topology.

For obvious reasons, point-to-point topology is hardly suitable for larger high-availability solutions but is far better than SCSI arrays for clustering solutions.

FC-AL

The so-called "f-cal" loop is illustrated in Figure 4.7, where the topology is an actual loop. This topology requires the receiving and transmitting wires of the interconnecting cables be split. This was achieved with the invention of HBA adapters for FC-AL networks that actually split the fiber-optic cables. This topology is illustrated in Figure 4.7.

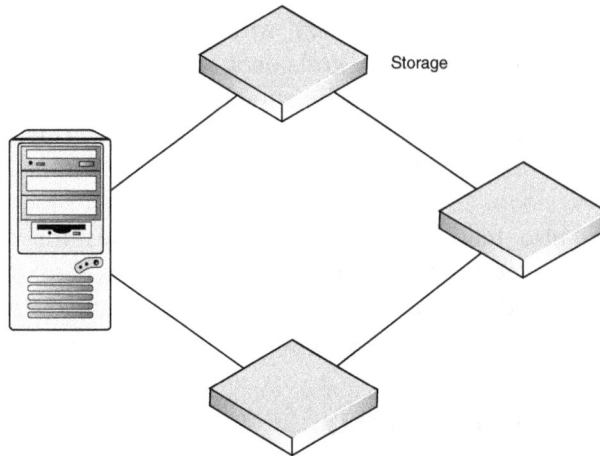

Figure 4.7 FC-AL topology.

It should be obvious from both Figures 4.6 and 4.7 that the limitations of FC-AL are distance and the number of supported devices. Another, more profound, limitation of the "loop" illustrated in Figure 4.7 is that the death of one HBA takes out the entire loop. This is unacceptable for any HA architecture. The advent of FC-AL switches allows you to overcome this limitation by forming a star topology. This is illustrated in Figure 4.8.

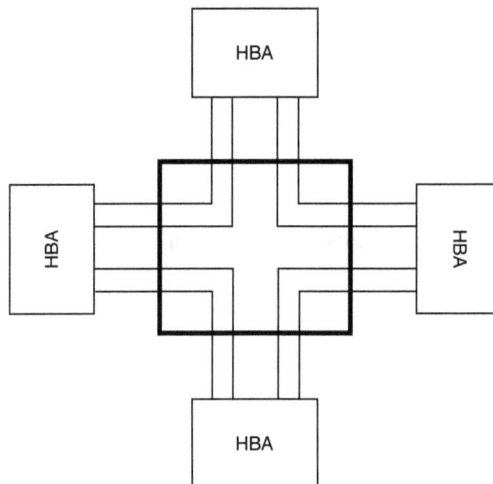

Figure 4.8 FC-AL hub.

In the star topology, you connect each NL-Port to an FC hub. The internals in the hub take care of the loop for you. Another factor of FC-AL over fabric is the arbitration factor (the "L" and the "A" in the acronym, as in *arbitrated loop*). Because FC-AL is a shared resource, nodes that wish to transmit have to arbitrate for that right.

Fabric

Fabric topology makes use of a special switch where each N_Port plugs into the F-Port on the switch. Each node is then assigned an address by the switch. To participate in the fabric, the node must log in to the fabric. Each address in a fabric is a 24-bit value; so, you can easily scale to 16 million devices on your SAN (not that the array itself would be able support that many).

The fabric topology thus allows the node that logs into the port to use the entire bandwidth of the port, which is similar to how the layer 2 and layer 3 switches work as discussed earlier. SAN fabric technology is fast making FC-AL technology obsolete, and fabric is quickly becoming the standard.

One of the advantages of fabric is the switch technology employed in the fabric is much more sophisticated and functional than a FC-AL hub. A fabric switch offers true switching and many other sophisticated features. One of the most appealing is the ability to run software that manages the switch for you. With switch software you create "zones" that enable certain servers to see only the volumes or devices you want them to see. For example, you can place a tape library in a zone and configure the switch to enable the servers to see only the tape library in that zone and not any of the other servers. The zoning, thus, allows the servers to see the tape drive and think they have exclusive use of it; that it is somehow locally attached to the server. More about this topic in the following section, "Zoning."

NOTE: As mentioned in Chapter 3, iSCSI can use standard IP switches for its shared storage topology, but fabric SAN switches are specially built for SAN topology, and they are more expensive. The three leading manufacturers of fabric switches are Brocade Communications Systems at No. 1, McData Corp at No. 2, and QLogic Corp. at No. 3.

The good news is fabric equipment is becoming cheaper by the day. The cost of the switches, from the likes of Brocade and McData, are dropping, as is the cost of the HBAs and the SAN arrays themselves.

Of course, if you want to start experimenting or have a small number of nodes to install on a high-availability SAN, FC-AL can be done much cheaper. Entry cost for FC-AL can be astonishingly low in comparison to fabric, especially for a lab setup. FC-AL hubs supporting up to nine devices can be found on the Internet for less than $200. The array controllers or processors are going to be the most expensive components, but you can still put up a small SAN on FC-AL for less than $5000. At the time of this writing, EMC's baby fabric SAN, the CSX200, is around $20,000 for a few nodes.

Now let's look at zoning in more detail.

Zoning

As mentioned in Chapter 3, zoning enables you to partition a SAN fabric in such a way that devices on the fabric are isolated from each other and only the servers zoned with certain devices get to use those devices. A very different scenario exists on legacy SCSI storage solutions, which allow all the servers on the SAN to see each other and all devices connected to the SAN. Unrestricted access has a number of implications for building in reliability, maintainability, and monitoring on your SAN.

Zoning throws off a lot of network engineers new to SAN topology; so, it's a good idea to liken it to technology with which network engineers are intimately familiar (and passionate about)—VLANs. Zoning is a lot like virtual LAN configuration. Network administrators partition a network using VLAN software in switches to group devices together to form collections of devices, protocols, ports, and addresses in the switch. A VLAN-capable switch can be easily segmented into, say, four VLANs, each VLAN routable to the other VLANs such that the switch appears to the network and the devices as four distinct networks.

VLANs can also span many switches, and a matrix of VLANs in an enterprise spanning multiple switches makes life easier for network engineers. A good example is how you can move a port from one VLAN to another without ever having to physically unplug a cable from any device. A port in one VLAN is not accessible from any other VLANs.

Zones are similar to VLANs in that zones can also span multiple fabric switches and control how traffic is distributed around the switches. The difference is that zoning is a way of partnering servers with devices on the SAN, such as LUNs and tape drive systems. This is illustrated in Figure 4.9.

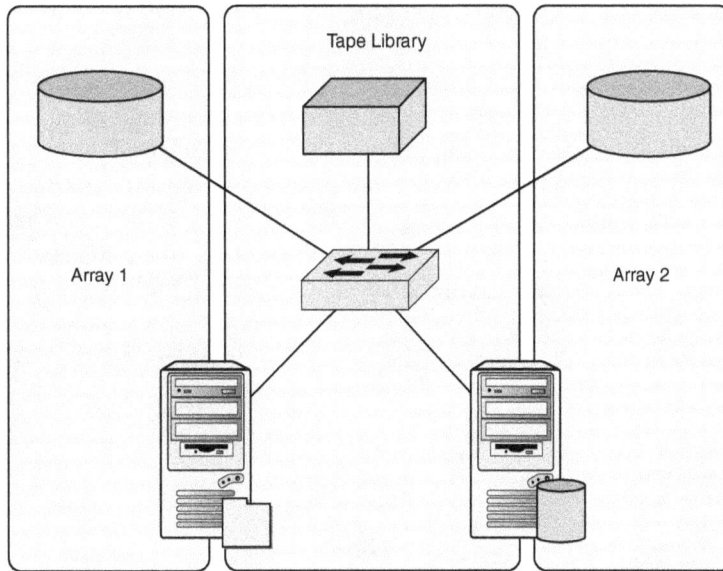

Figure 4.9   Zones associating servers with arrays.

Fortunately, zoning software has matured, but setting up the zones requires some assistance from the fabric expert, or you need to get yourself off to some intense training. Zoning is a knowledge you use time and time again, as long as you manage a SAN.

Architecting SAN Topology for High Availability

As a rule of thumb, when architecting and designing for the SAN network, the corporate network, the interconnect network, or the backbone, always determine the number of ports you need and then, as a rule, add 20 to 30 percent for expansion. Experience has shown that no matter how careful you study your network, there are some factors that always cause you to underestimate your requirements.

The larger your network, the more planning you need to do. Always start with your servers and high-availability needs. Determine the devices you are going to be installing; understand fully your backup device needs and your switching and zoning requirements. Leave port requirements for last.

One of the key reasons a SAN is so desirable in a high-availability environment is that you can design it to avoid a single point-of-failure in the path between the servers and the storage array. This is a problem in SCSI storage where hardware and network failure can trash the entire storage solution, and kill all access to the storage from the servers. Before you go architecting the SAN topology like a SCSI storage solution, consider an architecture that provides multiple paths between servers and devices.

Figure 4.10 illustrates the typical single point-of-failure SAN fabric.

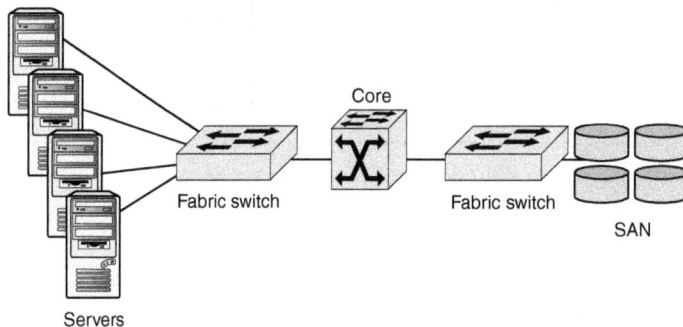

Figure 4.10   Single point-of-failure SAN fabric.

In Figure 4.10, servers only have one route to the storage array and the tape device. Thus, if you count the devices and ports between the servers and the arrays, it is not difficult to determine the number of points of failure that have a potential to bring down your cluster.

In Figure 4.11, we illustrate a multi-path topology for a highly available SAN fabric. You still have the same number of failure points, but as soon as a failure occurs in one path, you have yet another path to keep up the application.

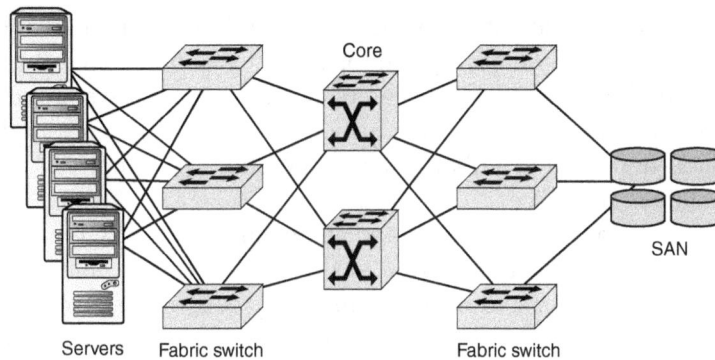

Figure 4.11   Multipath architecture for a high-availability SAN fabric.

Notice, however, that you still have only one SAN in the architecture. So, it is still possible to lose the system if the SAN itself, its processing unit, crashes. You do not lose the array if disks or switches go down because disks are configured in RAID arrays, and you typically install two or more switches in the SAN topology.

But a SAN is driven by a self-contained server, with a UNIX-like operating system, that is not crash proof. You cannot claim to have a SAN that is without a single point of failure unless you are replicating the data off the SAN to a backup mirror SAN somewhere. There are several technologies that can mirror or replicate volumes from one storage device to another to achieve a failover storage device. We will further explore the subject in Chapter 10, in architecting high availability storage for Microsoft Exchange 2003.

Time-Out

This chapter provided some food for thought on the networking subject. There is a lot to consider when it comes to crafting a sound network for a highly available solution. However, all too often network architecture is either ignored or undertaken without the consideration of the HA system needs.

When you receive a mandate to craft a system that must provide four or five nines availability, the first consideration is where to put your system. Very few businesses are fortunate enough to have a hardened

server room that has fire suppressions systems, unlimited and uninter-
ruptable power supply, generators, cooling systems, security, and more.
So, the first item on the design plan is to locate the systems off-site in a
data center or disaster recovery location. Depending on your design, the
data center can be either primary operations or standby in the event of
failure at the office.

In today's highly distributed and connected world, it makes sense to
locate the production system in the hardened data center where your
partners, clients, and users are primarily connected. Back at the office,
you can still use local domain controllers, file and print servers, email,
and database systems for local access, but you can mirror these systems
with the systems at the data center in the event the systems at the office
fail.

If the SLA mandates that employees should be able to continue
working, even in the event the primary employee workplace is taken
offline or shut down, then all employees and users should be able to
telecommute to the production systems in the data center and continue
working without leaving their homes.

Installing a system in a data center is going to place a lot of attention
on the network architecture. You need to consider how the main and
branch offices are going to connect with the data center. Are you going
to connect with a dedicated private network, or use a VPN over the
Internet? Are you going to route the traffic, or do you need to craft a flat
address space to meet your needs? What about firewalls, routers, and
network address translation? In Chapter 9, we investigate the architecture for such solutions using SQL Server applications in our design.

Preparing the Platform for a High-Performance Network

Introduction

Architecting for high availability Windows Server 2003 solutions requires vigorous planning and design. In this chapter, we cover what you need to do to prepare the platform (network operating system, Active Directory, and networking infrastructure) for your high-performance, fail-safe systems.

At first glance, this chapter may look like it belongs in a book on Windows networking and Active Directory. However, you cannot hope to be successful building a system of cluster servers, load-balanced clusters, redundant or high-performance server systems without first laying down a solid foundation. Every aspect of Windows infrastructure services, networking services, security, monitoring, and administration goes into the support of high-availability systems more than anything else.

DNS and your IP infrastructure must be spot on. Active Directory replication needs to be error-free, update services finely tuned, security bolted down airtight, and all aspects of your servers and supporting infrastructure must be highly monitored. This is what you need to put in place before you can build anything that your users can expect to be always available.

In this chapter, we look at the building of a new Active Directory network. If you already have an AD domain in place, then the pointers in this chapter can help you prepare or, alternatively, configure your infrastructure for adding HA/HPC systems. Of course, if you are not building an HA system and are just putting up a solid AD network, then this chapter is ideal for you as well. What we discuss here has you building and maintaining a highly available, high-performance Active Directory network, with or without cluster servers.

This chapter and the others to come are based on several case histories. One case study is on the HA network built for Broward County, Florida—a network supporting more than 7,000 employees of the county catering to the citizens of Broward. Other case histories include an HA data recovery center implementation for an online service, and yet a third is based on the implementation of a data center/disaster recovery site for an insurance company providing about $4 billion in coverage.

The Active Directory Architecture outlined in this chapter is a blueprint that details the Windows Server 2003/Active Directory architecture for a large organization with a number of subsidiaries, partners, and agencies. In fact, this network supports about 80 interrelated agencies. You can use it in your design, construction, and implementation phases for an end-to-end Windows Server 2003/Active Directory HA implementation project.

We also address the management and complexity issues involved in designing an Active Directory architecture for HA services (using Microsoft's Windows Server 2003 for the network operating system, Exchange 2003 Server for the messaging system, SQL Server 2000 for database systems, and Windows Storage Server 2003 and Windows Server 2003 for file and print services respectively—all running on Windows Server 2003 clusters). These vertical systems are further discussed in Part II, "Building High Availability Windows Server 2003 Solutions."

This chapter addresses security implications that arise and references the myriad design specifications for various services and solutions that arise from this implementation.

Architecting Primer

Before we get into the configuration, the following design principles should be kept in mind. The system design and architecture described here follows typical 4-D's methodology using the iterative procedures of (d)efinition, (d)esign, (d)evelop (labs, testing, and implementation plan), and (d)eployment (and sustaining).

Validation, which comes after deployment, assures requirements have been met and the systems operate according to the quality assurance (installation, operational, and performance qualifications) requirements of the stakeholders. Your validation can be either formal (required by law) or informal. Informal validation is up to you. If there is a lot of risk and revenue riding on the success of the implementation, then you should perform validation and quality assurance.

All systems you define for the HA project must be designed and tested in a lab and then migrated into production (cut-and-paste) or cloned (copy-and-paste) from the test plans on the production backbone in either the main or regional hubs or demilitarized zones (DMZ) you are providing. This can be difficult for HA systems architecture because it is rare you will have the budget to maintain expensive clusters and SAN systems in a lab environment; they usually end up in production after the lab phase. However, if you are installing new systems, you can easily wire the SAN and cluster equipment to a lab domain and go through your lab staging and proof of concept, only to later break down these systems and rebuild them in production.

The design provides fault-tolerant and redundant components. This is evidenced in the server hardware you obtain (such as power supplies, disk drives, NICs [Network Interface Controllers], and so on), the infrastructure services architecture (such as DDNS [Dynamic Domain Naming Service], and WINS and DHCP [Dynamic Host Configuration Protocol]).

While designing these systems is no simple matter, you should strive to keep your design as simple as possible while still meeting user requirements. Simple architectures and deployments are easier to explain, maintain, and debug in the long term.

Your design also should exploit available WAN bandwidth wherever possible, and you should consolidate as much as possible. The architecture in this chapter proposes a centralized design model over a distributed design model. Based on the case history, the architecture demonstrates consolidation to three almost identically configured data centers, which are also the domain hub sites (the high-level Active Directory services design is designed along the hub-and-spoke model).

Create a Design Plan

A *design plan* (DP) is a document that provides an overview of the design procedures for a new systems architecture. It is a treatise on how you intend to architect, design, test, evaluate, validate, and so on. In a nutshell, your DP is how you plan to build the system you are proposing.

Your DP for a Windows Server 2003 HA system should include the following elements:

- How you will use directory services using Active Directory. Include a design plan for administrative services, such as Group Policy, and administrative infrastructure (such as Microsoft Operations Manager outlined in Chapter 13," Looking for Trouble: Setting Up Performance Monitoring and Alerts").
- Active Directory preparation to accommodate high-availability applications and services that require directory services (such as Exchange, File, Print, and SQL Server).
- Network operating system (NOS) using Windows Server 2003 from Microsoft. These include DHCP, WINS, and DNS.
- Active Directory administration, group membership design, access to rights, and permissions (administrative privileges).

These elements are critical to get right because all Microsoft Server solutions (such as clustering, load balancing, SQL Server, and Exchange) depend on a sound Active Directory implementation.

Design Goals

The following design goals should be used to define the proposed Windows Server 2003/Active Directory architecture:

- **Achieve simplicity:** Your principle design goal should be to dramatically simplify the Windows NOS infrastructure. One of the design elements that greatly contributes to meeting this design goal is the installation of a sensible domain model. Large implementations typically follow the dual domain model (parent and child) in which all resources are maintained in the single domain beneath a root domain that does not contain user accounts. This root-child model provides the following benefit for medium to large implementations:

- A dramatic reduction in the authentication complexities due to the elimination of trusts, which carry heavy administrative burden
- Easier resource relocation (such as moving user accounts) because intradomain moves are far easier than interdomain moves
- Simplified creation and maintenance of GPOs (Group Policy Objects) because GPOs do not scale easily across domains
- Simplified creation and maintenance OU (Organizational Unit) structure because OU structure only needs to be implemented and maintained in one domain
- A simpler implementation and maintenance objective
- The capability to leverage new AD-integrated security technology, such as *Public Key Infrastructure* (PKI)
- The capability to delegate resource control and provide flexibility of administration
- **Achieve security:** Your design goals should not be achieved at the expense of security; thus, security architecture and design is implicitly embedded in the implementation of your architecture.
- **Site creation and server consolidation:** This is achieved by deploying an optimal number of Windows Server 2003 infrastructure servers in the various locations and exploiting the WAN and network to concentrate data, file, print, messaging, and line-of-business servers at the enterprise data centers (hubs).

After you have detailed your design goals, you can move onto specific components of your design, which is outlined in the next section.

Design Components

Our proposed Windows Server 2003 Active Directory infrastructure consists of many server-based services that provide the following services for high-availability application and service support:

- Windows Server 2003 domain controllers, which are the platform for "housing" Active Directory
- Authentication services
- Catalog services
- Active Directory integrated DDNS services

- DHCP services
- WINS services
- Microsoft Exchange Server 2003 on Windows Server 2003 Enterprise Server
- File Services on Windows Storage Server
- Print Services using standard Windows Server 2003 Enterprise Server
- SQL Server 2000 and SQL Server 2005 database services on Windows Server 2003 Enterprise Server

As you can see, the shopping list is rather extensive and requires strategic design decision-making.

Design Decisions

A design strategy to consider for this exercise is to develop the proposed solution incorporating "industry best practice" elements into each core component. Microsoft makes these readily available through a number of support services. The least expensive resource is a good book, like this one, covering field notes from actual implementations. The most expensive is hiring Microsoft Consulting Services. You can save a lot of consulting money by hiring a good architect, at least for the initial design phase.

In the case outlined in this chapter, the proposed solution was developed largely independently of any existing infrastructure. This is always the best option because upgrading existing systems can be a challenge to your mental health and physical endurance.

What or how you plan to migrate, upgrade, remove, or retire should be consistent with any HA design brief, which is to design and construct an "industrial-strength" AD network for the HA services we discussed earlier and which we implement in later chapters. You should at all costs avoid Windows 2000 Advanced Server as a platform of choice at this stage because compared to the Server 2003 platform, Windows 2000 is obsolete. Windows Server 2003 and services like Exchange 2003 and SQL Server 2005 represent a generational change in computing from anything else we have seen before. Any proposed solution must be designed with the foreseeable future in mind (at least five years); so, it makes sense to go with the latest systems as long as they provide a stable platform (which Server 2003 does in every way, shape, and form).

As you delve into this chapter further, you can see we are going to build a new Windows Server 2003 domain. A new domain name is used for the project. Here we design a complete network and engineer it such that users and computers are finally migrated to the new Windows Server 2003 domain.

This might not be what you are planning, but it indicates how best to restructure what you currently have to accommodate an HA system such as the one we are architecting in this chapter. The specifics for the domain we are creating are as follows:

- The proposed solution is to use the internal domain name (such as AD.MCITY.CTY) as the operational environment.
- The down-level (NetBIOS) domain name is AD.
- The proposed solution is to continue to use external domain names, such as MCITY.ORG for email and user principal names (such as jshapiro@mcity.org). This is accommodated in Active Directory.
- The Windows Server 2003 domain, AD.MCITY.CTY, is in native-mode and operates on the highest possible Active Directory schema level.

For the record, a native-mode Windows Server 2003 domain

- Is possible when only Windows Server 2003 DCs exist in the domain, and there is no interoperation with Windows 2000 or Windows NT 4.0 domain controllers.
- Offers additional functionality and security.

A native-mode Windows Server 2003 domain

- Is required when Windows NT v4.0 Domain Controllers still exist in the domain.
- Is used for migration/backward-compatibility work.
- Is not required if a domain migration, as opposed to a domain upgrade, occurs.

If at all possible, strive to build a native mode domain; it affords the best level of security Active Directory has to offer. Security is especially important for clustering because compromising the cluster itself can bring down all the servers in the cluster and, in effect, lead to a complete denial of service to your users.

NOTE: A domain migration has major implications for security, which should be addressed in a comprehensive security assessment.

Design Implications

The Active Directory and the *Security Accounts Manager* (SAM) represents the cradle of security in any Windows Server 2003 (or earlier) domain. An AD network, whether a single forest containing a single domain, or multiple domains, or an AD network of multiple forests, is only as secure as the administrative practices of the enterprise or organization.

The notion that highly sensitive resources can be secured only in their own domains or forests because of the administrative and security boundaries provided by them, is at best misguided and at worst a myth. Any value factored in from the utility of the administrative or security boundary is quickly eroded by the administrative burden in operating and managing multiple domains and forests.

Technically, a domain affords the ability of multiple entities of an enterprise, such as the subsidiaries of a company, to organize and administer its own security policy, its own group policy, its own distributed file system, and so on; but the domain boundary does not necessarily make it more secure. The reason is simple: The domains in a single forest trust each other through bi-directional, implicit, transitive trusts, and, thus, the domains are not separated by impenetrable security.

Only a separate forest fully secures two domains from each other because the trusts are not transitive, not bi-directional, and they have to be created explicitly, like the trusts between NT 4.0 domains and trusts between Windows Server 2003 and other NOSs, such as a UNIX realm. However, when forests are managed by the same team of people or resources need to be shared between them, the administrative boundaries tend to erode and are penetrated far easier and far quicker, and often without the knowledge of the organization, than the boundaries of a single resource domain. Doors are inevitably opened to ease the administrative burden.

All that is needed to bring down the domain or forest boundaries is the compromising of the key administrator accounts. It is clear for a single, large organization to entertain multiple domains, and multiple forests would result in a far more expensive and awkward architecture for its Active Directory implementation than a single forest and one operations (resource) domain for all its agencies.

The design and architecture described in this chapter is geared in every way, shape, and form around one operations domain that is subordinate to a forest root domain responsible for forest-maintenance operations. This enables all administrative burdens, resources, and tools to be exploited by a single domain's security and administrative team. The security of the domain is also ensured by installing a granular and hierarchical administrative design, described in this book, which is backed by the most sophisticated security mechanisms available to Active Directory and Windows Server 2003.

In this regard, it is critical to be aware that should you decide to forgo the single resource domain in favor of a multiple domain model, or possibly a multiple-forest model, this architecture described here will have to be significantly reworked to accommodate the new model, at a significantly greater cost in both the short and long terms. The architecture for hardware, software, tools, human resources, and WAN traffic will be significantly affected as a result.

Active Directory Services, Logical Architecture

We first began to write about Active Directory back in 1998, and later we described it as a universal distributed information storehouse into which all network objects, such as application configurations, services, computers, users, and processes can be accessed, in a consistent manner, over the full expanse of a network or internetwork. This is made possible by the logical structure of the directory, which we discuss in this section. If you are familiar with AD, you can forgo this section; however, we do address aspects of Active Directory in relation to the design and implementation of high-availability systems and services.

On the physical level, AD is two things: It is a database and a *database management system* (DBMS). The data it stores can be viewed hierarchically. The following list describes the directory services architecture underpinning AD:

- Active Directory supports and coexists with both DNS and LDAP; any kinks in its original design, since its release back in 1999, have been worked out. AD and LDAP are loosely modeled on the X.500 standard, especially with respect to its structural and organizational model. Active Directory supports open and interoperable standards, especially with regard to the widespread naming conventions in use today.

- Active Directory is seamlessly integrated into the Internet by virtue of Microsoft's total adoption and commitment to TCP/IP. All other protocols Microsoft supports are essentially provided for backward-compatibility with earlier versions of NT, other network operating systems, legacy transports, such as SNA and the DLC protocols, and NetBEUI clients. As you are probably aware, protocols like NetBEUI do not come built into the OS anymore. If you need these protocols, you have to install them from a CD.

- Active Directory provides a rich set of Visual Basic, C/C++, Java, .NET, and scripting language interfaces enabling it to be fully programmed against. (See the Active Directory namespace in the .NET Framework.)

- Active Directory is built on the Windows Server 2003 operating system, which is a direct upgrade of Windows 2000 (still at the core of Windows Server 2003), making it backwards-compatible with Windows 2000 and earlier versions of Windows NT, and forward-compatible with the next version of the Windows Server OS due in 2006. (Even though Windows Server 2003 is somewhat backwards-compatible with Windows NT, do not expect Microsoft to help you if you have an issue with integration. Windows NT 4.0 and earlier operating systems are obsolete and no longer supported by Microsoft.)

- Active Directory is a fully distributed architecture allowing administrators to write once and update everywhere from a single point of access, across any network. Of course, you do not see changes on the other domain controllers until replication has taken place. On a DC on the same network segment, the change is almost instant. It takes longer to appear on DCs on the other side of a router, especially across a WAN.

- Active Directory is highly scalable and self-replicating. It can be implemented on one machine, or the smallest network, and it can scale to support the largest enterprises in the world.

■ Active Directory's structural model is extensible, enabling its schema to evolve almost without limit. In this regard, Active Directory has to comply with the X.500 specification that extending the schema requires you to register the new class with a X.500 governing body. This compliance is achieved by registering an *Object Identifier* (OID) with the authorities. In the United States, the authority is the *American National Standards Institute* (ANSI).

AD has fully adopted the most popular namespace models in use today. It embraces the concept of an extendable namespace and marries this concept with operating systems, networks, and applications. Companies deploying AD are able to manage multiple namespaces that exist in their heterogeneous software and hardware.

More importantly, for any high-availability, high-performance system using Microsoft Windows Server 2003 components, AD is essential. However, as mentioned before, it is not enough to simply deploy AD for the sake of joining servers to it. AD should be specifically designed with cluster servers and high availability systems in mind. This means architecting and designing to ease administrative burden, increase security, maintain stability, and support rapid recoverability in the event of a disaster.

In virtually any situation where you have a cluster servicing many users, you will probably have a DC near the cluster nodes on the same LAN segment. You also need to make sure that should the nearest DC become unavailable, then the cluster needs to be referred to the next available DC in the site, or a remote site.

Forest Plan for Highly Available Systems

A Windows Server 2003 network is a networked collection of computers, running Windows Server 2003 and Windows XP that share a portion of the Active Directory namespace and distributed database and can be administered as a group.

A *domain* is a single security boundary of a Windows Server 2003 computer network. It is also an administrative boundary. A user with an account on the network can log on to and access his or her account from any computer in the domain or in a trusting domain. Administrators can centrally administer to the user and computer from any computer in the domain or in a trusting domain.

A *tree* is a set of one or more Windows Server 2003 domains with contiguous names (see Figure 5.1). That is, a Windows Server 2003 domain name adopts the parent Windows Server 2003 domain name as a postscript to its own name. So, for example, where the parent domain name is MCITY.CTY, a child/sub-domain name would be AD.MCITY.CTY. A *forest* is a collection of Windows Server 2003 domains. Forests serve two main purposes: to simplify user interaction with the directory and to simplify the management of multiple domains. Forests have the following key characteristics:

- **Single Schema:** The Active Directory schema defines the object classes and the attributes of object classes that can be created in the directory. Object classes define the types of objects that can be created in the directory. The schema exists as a naming context that is replicated to every DC in the forest. The Schema Administrators security group has full control over the schema.
- **Single Configuration Container:** The Active Directory configuration container is a naming context that is replicated to every DC in the forest. Directory-aware applications (such as Exchange 2003) store information in the configuration container that applies forest-wide. For example, Active Directory stores information about the physical network in the configuration container and uses it to guide the creation of replication connections between DCs. The Enterprise Administrators security group has full control over the configuration container.
- **Complete Trust:** Active Directory automatically creates transitive, two-way trust relationships between the domains in a forest. Users and groups from any domain can be recognized by any member computer in the forest and included in groups or *Access Control Lists* (ACLs). Complete trust makes managing multiple domains simpler in Windows Server 2003.

In previous versions of Windows NT, a popular model for deploying domains was the multiple Master Domain model. In that model, a domain containing primarily user accounts was called a Master User Domain, and a domain that contained primarily computer accounts and resources was called a Resource Domain.

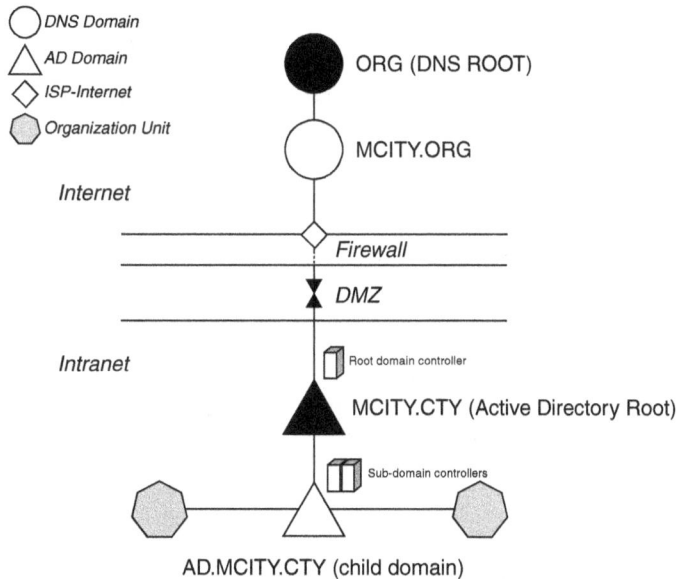

Figure 5.1 Dual domain model.

A common deployment consisted of a small number of Master User domains, each of which was trusted by a large number of Resource Domains. Adding a new domain to the deployment required several trusts to be created. With Windows Server 2003 Active Directory, when you add a domain to a forest, it is automatically configured with a two-way transitive trust. This eliminates the need to create additional trusts with domains in the same forest.

Single Global Catalog

The *Global Catalog* (GC) contains a copy of every object from every domain in the forest but only a select set of the attributes from each object. The GC enables fast, efficient searches that span the entire forest. The GC makes directory structures within a forest transparent to end users. Using the GC as a search scope makes finding objects in the directory simple. Logging on is made simpler through the GC and user principal names, and as such, a domain controller must be a GC for users to authenticate to the network.

In a very large organization, the appropriate AD architecture that provides a blueprint for the establishment of forests, trees, and domains is very important. The proposed solution is to implement a single Active Directory forest with two domains. This is illustrated in Figure 5.1. To sum up, the principal benefits of a single forest/dual domain are

- Simple design
- Simple replication topology
- A root domain that isolates the Schema Administrators and Enterprise Administrators security groups
- Child/Sub-domain
- Ease of administration and management
- Single security boundary
- Removes the need to duplicate policy definitions in GPOs (*Group Policy Objects*)
- A single forest/dual domain design provides a single security boundary. Administrative privileges within the child/sub-domain can be delegated to users or user groups over OUs (Organizational Units) as required.
- The ability to easily create child domains under the root should it ever become necessary to do so.

It goes without saying that the easier it is to administer and manage the domain and infrastructure services, the easier it is to administer to the high-availability systems and cluster servers.

Domain Namespace

Our architecture maintains firewalls between the Internet and its DMZ or perimeter networks and also between its DMZ and internal networks. For security reasons, the internal namespace was not made visible to the global community of the Internet. In such an environment, there are two common approaches you can consider when naming the internal DNS namespace:

- **Use the same name as the external namespace.** This can be accomplished either through split-brain DNS (different "views" of the same namespace) or by manual updates of two different DNS infrastructures. Two different infrastructures can be created when an ISP manages the external namespace and an internal group (your DNS administrator) manages the internal namespace. The potential for confusion and lost updates in such a situation is quite high. Strict segregation policies must be enforced to prevent name resolution "leakage" between DNS infrastructures.

■ **Delegate a sub-domain of the external namespace.** The internal domain can be dependent as a child name under the officially registered external domain. This is a popular point for placing a Windows Server 2003 root domain. The issue raised is one of domain naming because this option places the root (or first-in-forest) domain of the production forest further down the DNS naming hierarchy. This increases the length of the Windows Server 2003 domain name. Many enterprises prefer a shorter name for usability purposes. They don't want their users or application interfaces entering long names to identify them to the network. An example of this is jsmith@ad.co.mcity.fl.us, which illustrates the ungainly nature of a sub-domain concatenated with a long external name. A delegated sub-domain also adds complexity and administrative overhead in the management of DNS.

We adopted the following approach and recommend you do the same.

Separate discontinuous namespaces that preclude delegation or any connection between public DNS namespaces. The advantages of doing this are substantial:

■ The network security boundaries are clearly defined.
■ Anything in the first domain of the namespace is treated as an exclusive AD namespace for internal use, company confidential and restricted.
■ URL's (*Universal Resource Locators*) or hosts ending in *fl.us* or *.org* are presumed to be publicly accessible.
■ Proxy services are simpler to maintain when the internal and external spaces have separate names.
■ Access control lists are easier to write when public and private namespaces are split.
■ Network management in general, and network policy settings in particular, are simpler and easier to administer when it is clear whether a system is in the public or the private space.

External DNS Domain Name

We, thus, continue to utilize the external domains, such as mcity.org, for external communications. In the future, there may be additional externally visible domains. All hosts providing an externally accessible service must be named in one of the externally visible domains.

Domain Controllers (DCs)

Place your DCs according to the following rules:

- **User population:** DCs should be located where there is a high concentration of users logging on (this is a viable rule even when the link to a remote DC offers high bandwidth).
- **Cluster Services:** Place a DC in the site where you are placing cluster services.
- **Bandwidth:** Where bandwidth is low, a DC is used to speed up logon and authentication times.
- **Redundancy:** Consideration must be given to how functionality will be maintained in the event a DC fails. Consequently, multiple DCs should be available at key locations.
- **Applications:** Application reliance on DCs (such as Exchange 2003).

Fifty users are considered the break-even point for authentication traffic versus AD replication traffic. At a site with less than 50 users, Active Directory replication traffic generated by a local DC server actually creates more traffic on the WAN than authentication traffic generated by users being authenticated by a remote DC. The placement of DC servers has been modeled according to the best practices rules.

A local DC server is not required in a site when

- There are less than 50 users at the site and the WAN circuit to the hub/parent site (the site containing the closest DC) server has at least 64KB/sec of average available bandwidth. However, if this condition is true, then this circuit should be able to handle the authentication traffic. If this were not true, then we would consider increasing the bandwidth of the circuit by at least another 64KB/sec, and if that is not possible we would consider implementing measures that greatly reduce the authentication traffic needed to the site and frequency of group policy updates.

- The site can tolerate the expected duration and frequency of WAN circuit failures to the hub/parent site (that is, the site containing the closest DC) server. This could be ensured or provided by a backup/alternate WAN circuit. Generally speaking, if a WAN link to a site is not 100 percent available, then WAN logon and WAN access to resources is not viable for the site.

A local DC server is required in a site when

- More than 50 users work at the site, or a local Exchange server exists (likely if the site has more than 50 mailbox users and the link between the sites and a remote Exchange server is weak. Exchange servers require fast and reliable access to GC servers.)
- An application is heavily dependent on fast access to Active Directory, such as a database application that performs GC lookups, and so on.

This information should be taken as a guideline and not as gospel. Always test your assumptions. Each site or location differs in how much load is placed on the network, the domain controllers, and the servers. Before you decide to add or exclude a domain controller from a site, perform sufficient analysis and testing with the infrastructure provided to determine if you really need a domain controller or if you are safe excluding it. Often going out to the site, monitoring the people working, analyzing the network traffic, and experiencing actual network performance is the best way to determine your needs.

Multi-Master Operations (Global Catalogs)

Global Catalogs or GCs contain a partial replica of the Active Directory and, consequently, act as an extremely efficient Active Directory search engine. A GC has to be a DC and incurs additional overhead as a result of searches and the need for additional replication.

When placing GCs, take into consideration what you would for any DC. A GC is required in each site that has been determined to require a DC, especially when that site contains an Exchange 2003 server. The GC acts as a search engine for the Active Directory and improves the performance of the Exchange 2003 Server.

Single Master Operations (FSMO Roles)

Windows Server 2003 DCs host the Active Directory and provide directory services to participating clients and servers. Windows Server 2003 DCs can be configured to hold FSMO (*Flexible Single Master Operations*) roles. The servers that hold these roles are known as the *operations masters*.

Windows NT v4.0 DCs supported a single-master replication model. All updates occur on the PDC (*Primary Domain Controller*) and are periodically replicated to BDCs (*Backup Domain Controllers*). Windows 2000 and Windows Server 2003 DCs, instead, support multi-master updates for the replication of objects (such as user and computer accounts) in the Active Directory. In a multi-master model, objects and their properties can originate on any DC in the domain.

However, certain domain and enterprise-wide operations are not well-suited to multi-master replication. The advantage of single-master operations is to prevent the introduction of conflicts while an operations master is offline, rather than introducing potential conflicts and having to resolve them later. Having a single-master operation means, however, that the FSMO role owner must be available when dependent activities in the domain or enterprise take place, or to make directory changes associated with that role.

Active Directory defines five FSMO roles as follows:

- **Forest Roles:** The Schema Master and the Domain Naming Master
- **Domain Roles:** The RID (*Relative Identifier*) Master, the PDC, and the IF (*Infrastructure*) Master

A forest with one domain has five roles. Every additional domain in the forest adds the three domain-wide roles described in the previous bullet on domain roles.

When the first Windows Server 2003 DC in a forest is created, all five roles are assigned to it. When the first Windows Server 2003 DC is created in a new domain in an existing forest, all three domain roles are assigned to it. In a mixed-mode domain (containing both Windows NT v4.0 and Windows Server 2003 DCs), only Windows Server 2003 DCs can hold FSMO roles. A DC for any domain within a forest can hold a per-forest role for that forest; but only a DC for a specific domain can hold a per-domain role for that domain.

Schema Master

The *Schema Master* is the DC responsible for performing updates to the directory schema. The *directory schema* is a definition of the classes and attributes within a directory. This DC is the only one that can process updates to the directory schema. After the directory schema is updated, it is replicated from the Schema Master to all other DCs in the directory.

A product that applies updates to the directory schema (such as Exchange 2003, NetIQ, *Microsoft Directory Synchronization Services* [MSDSS] and the GroupWise Connector) must have access to the Schema Master when it is installed. Access is obtained by logging onto the network as a user that is a member of the Schema Admins domain local security group. There is only one Schema Master per directory.

Domain Naming Master

The *Domain Naming Master* is the DC responsible for making changes to the forest-wide domain name space of the directory. This DC is the only one that can add or remove a domain from the directory. It can also add or remove cross-references to domains in external directories. There is only one Domain Naming Master per directory.

RID (Relative Identifier) Master

The *RID Master* is the DC responsible for processing RID (*Relative Identifier*) pool requests from all DCs within a given domain. It is also responsible for removing an object from its domain and putting it in another domain during an object move.

When a DC creates a security principal object (such as a user or user group), it attaches a unique SID (*Security Identifier*) to the object. This SID consists of a domain SID (the same for all SIDs created in a domain) and a RID that is unique for each security principal SID created in a domain.

Each Windows Server 2003 DC in a domain is allocated a pool of RIDs it is allowed to assign to the security principals it creates. When a DC's allocated RID-pool falls below a certain threshold, that DC issues a request for additional RIDs to the domain's RID Master. The RID Master responds to the request by retrieving RIDs from the domain's unallocated RID-pool and assigns them to the pool of the requesting DC. There is only one RID Master per domain in a directory.

Primary Domain Controller Emulator

In a Windows Server 2003 domain, the PDC Emulator role holder retains the following functions:

- Password changes performed by other DCs in the domain are replicated preferentially to the PDC Emulator.
- Authentication failures that occur at a given DC in a domain because of an incorrect password are forwarded to the PDC Emulator before a bad password failure message is reported to the user.
- Account lockout is processed on the PDC Emulator.

The PDC Emulator role becomes unnecessary as down-level workstations, member servers, and DCs are all upgraded to Windows Server 2003, in which case the following information applies:

- Windows Server 2003/Windows XP clients (workstations and member servers) and down-level clients that have installed the distributed services client package do not perform directory writes (such as password changes) preferentially at the DC that has advertised itself as the PDC; they use any DC for the domain.
- After BDCs (*Backup Domain Controllers*) in down-level domains are upgraded to Windows Server 2003, the PDC Emulator receives no down-level replica requests.

Windows Server 2003 clients (XP workstations and member servers) and down-level clients that have installed the distributed services client package use AD to locate network resources. They do not require the Windows NT Browser service. There is only one PDC Emulator per domain in a directory.

Infrastructure Master

When an object in one domain is referenced by another object in another domain, it represents the reference by a number of means (the GUID, the SID, and the DN of the object being referenced). The Infrastructure Master is the DC responsible for updating an object's SID and DN in a cross-domain object reference.

There is only one Infrastructure Master per domain in a directory. A DC that is not a GC server must hold the Infrastructure Master role. If this role is hosted on a GC server, cross-domain object references in that domain are not updated. The Schema Master, Domain Naming Master, PDC Emulator, RID Master, Infrastructure Master, and GC role holders are as listed in Table 5.1 and presented visually in Figure 5.2.

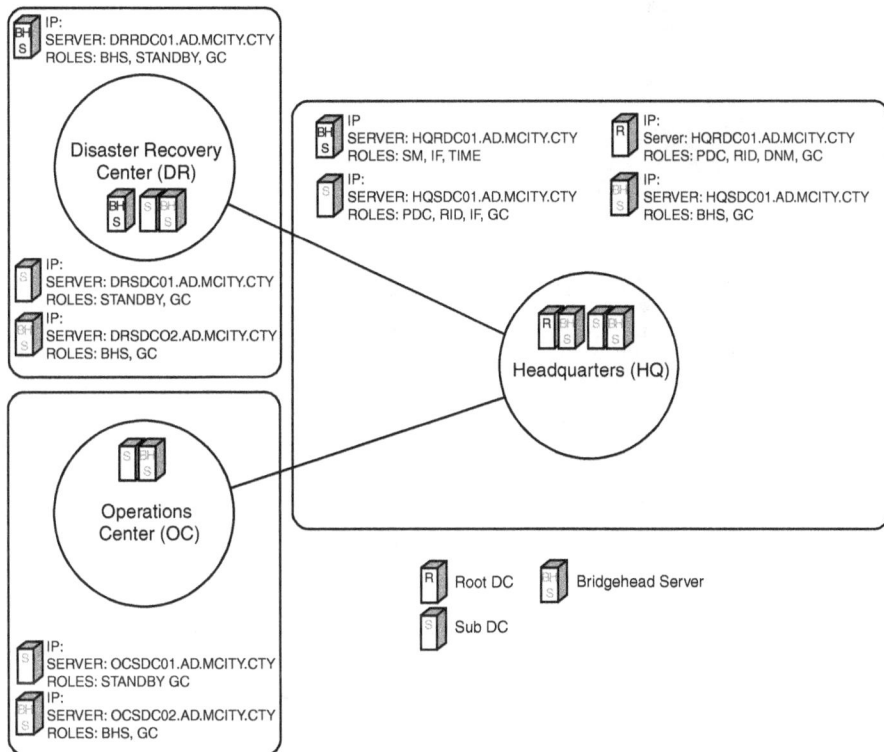

Figure 5.2 AD FSMO roles.

Table 5.1 List of FSMO Roles

Server#	Name	Hub	Schema Master	Domain Naming Master	PDC Emulator	RID Master	IF Master	Standby	GC
Flexible Single Master Operations									
Regional Hub Sites Root (mcity.cty)									
1	HQRDC01	HQ	X				X		
2	HQRDC02	HQ		X	X	X			X
3	DRRDC01	DR						X	X
Sub-domain (ad.mcity.cty)									
4	HQSDC01	HQ			X	X	X		X
5	HQSDC02	HQ						X(PDC)	X°
6	DRSDC01	DR							X
7	DRSDC02	DR							X°
8	OCSDC01	OC						X	X
9	OCSDC02	OC							X°

Miscellaneous Roles for Domain Controllers

Two miscellaneous roles indirectly related to Active Directory services need to be defined for domain controllers. They are the *Preferred Group Policy Administration Domain Controller* and the *Time Service Server*.

Preferred Group Policy Administration Domain Controller (GPDC)

Group Policy should always be updated on the same DC, no matter how many DCs exist in the domain. This DC should always be in the first hub site of the domain. This policy serves to avoid replication collisions when administering GP and forces centralization of GPO development and assignment. The DC should also be the only DC on which GPTs (*Group Policy Templates*) are administered (see the section "Group Policy" later in this chapter).

Time Service

All computers running a Windows Server 2003 OS, XP, or Server 2003 must synchronize to a common time source in the forest. The time source is typically the DC keeping the PDC Emulator role, which maintains the Time Service. The overview and architecture of the Time Service is beyond the scope of this book.

Organizational Units

This section discusses *Organizational Units* (OUs), which are logical containers that belong to AD domains. OUs are connected to the domain in which they are created—their parent—and cannot be moved between domains.

OUs are containers into which similar resources (objects) are grouped. OUs can contain computers, users, printers, various network objects, such as shares, and other OUs (which are nested). In this regard, they make a domain easier to manage by gathering a large collection of objects into smaller collections. AD OUs are very similar to *Novell Directory Services* (NDS) OUs and are useful in partitioning domains along various organizational partitions, such as administrative, departmental, or geographic boundaries.

While most AD implementations provide OUs along administrative boundaries, many larger directories partition the domain along departmental lines or business groups, which are usually also their administrative boundaries. This is illustrated in Figure 5.3.

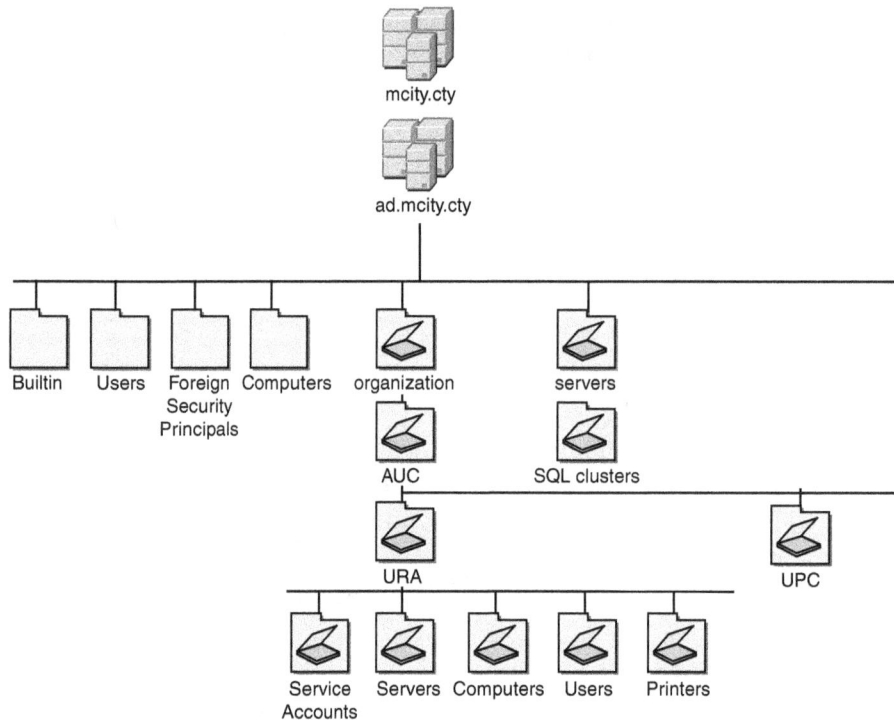

Figure 5.3   OU architecture.

OUs are easier to move around the domain, and they easily can be modified, renamed, and deleted. While domains remain larger administrative boundaries, OUs are better suited to delegating administration and the assignment of administrative roles within an organization.

OUs are also the smallest container to which group policy can be applied (see the discussion on group policy in the next section). OUs are thus essential for the finer application of Group Policy. When a *group policy object* (GPO) is created, it normally links to the OU in which it is created, thus influencing only the objects contained in the OU. However, a group of users or computers can be the target of group policy regardless of the OU in which it is created. OUs make it easier to apply group policy to a collection of objects. It should be clear, however, that OUs do not provide the mechanisms for generating and applying policy. Unlike NDS OUs, AD OUs do not apply rights and permissions.

OUs are not visible to end users nor can users use the containers in any meaningful way; thus, how you partition the domain into OUs need only be for administrative needs and group policy application. While it may be prudent to partition along regional or geographic lines, it always makes more sense to further partition to administrative levels (usually along departmental or agency boundaries). When creating an OU hierarchy, three primary considerations are

- How group policy can be easily applied and managed with the hierarchy
- How administrative privileges can be easily delegated and managed
- How objects in an OU can be effectively managed as a group

The third consideration, which is important for large implementations, allows you to consider how best to use Active Directory to reflect organizational structure and to aid management. It is important to compartmentalize Active Directory in such a way that it can be easily navigated by third-party applications and administrators alike. In this regard, the OUs can be laid out in a way that reflects a hierarchical, flat, matrix, team, or project-oriented structure. Some companies have partitioned AD to more closely mirror their organizational chart. This is not always practical, but it may be the best starting point for large companies with many autonomous divisions.

Most importantly, for HA systems, you need to place your load-balanced systems, clusters, and mission-critical applications in their own OUs so you can apply specialized group policy to them. Cluster servers require certain rights on the domain and on the actual server operating systems, and the best way to manage these rights and permissions is through group policy objects. Chapter 6, "Building the Foundations for a Highly Available Architecture," shows exactly what group policy settings are going to be required in these GPOs. While AD provides a very efficient inheritance mechanism for propagating group policy to the deeper levels of an OU hierarchy, nesting to too many levels begins to impact the performance of AD in the application of GP. It is also harder to manage a domain that has a deeply nested or overly complex OU structure. Again, the idea is to keep it simple.

The OUs in the architecture described here were partitioned to four tiers. There is a root Tier-1 for broad administration and application of common GP settings. This Tier-1 level is used for administration of resources that reside in the *enterprise datacenters* (EDC) of the organization (the major hubs' sites and regional data centers supporting AD) and its DMZs. Administrative authority and application of GP at this level is the widest in the domain.

There is a second-level tier (Tier-2), which represents the root of the organizational tree. This second level is used for partitioning agencies and major divisions into their respective OUs. The Tier-2 boundary provides delegation of administration and application of GP specific to an agency or major division.

There is a third-level (Tier-3), which represents a departmental container for departments and groups (functional) within the organizational or division OUs, and their collections of resources.

And finally, there is a resource level (Tier-4) for the collections of users, computers, and printers used by each group.

Group policy and administrative control of resources is available to the agencies and divisions from their root organizational OU down. This tiered design is illustrated in Figure 5.4.

An OU is created to support an agency or division, which takes ownership (administration and GP) of that OU. This design emulates multiple domains for autonomy; however, mandatory domain policy (which is minimal) still applies to all resources in all OUs.

Each agency or division can create additional OUs under its root OU to collect departments, groups, and resources (such as Users, Computers, Groups and Printers), and to delegate required administrative privileges. The latter OUs provide a facility for the most focused or targeted delegation of administrative privilege and GP at the OU level. This design is reflected in Figure 5.4.

While it is possible to place all users or computers in a single OU, or a few large OUs, this is not considered because it distracts from the ability to administer, monitor, and affectively manage GP and to delegate effectively. The county is comprised of more than 100 agencies and thousands of groups, offices, divisions, and collections of workers and their computers. The OU design presented here thus caters to the widely distributed organizational structure of Broward County. For example, grouping collections of users and computers intelligently allows administrators to target workstations and groups for activities such as application of patches, hot fixes, and virus inoculation. The granularity of the OUs also facilitates new technologies, such as SMS 2003 for software distribution and patch management. The resources are grouped into at least four OUs as shown in Figures 5.3 and 5.4.

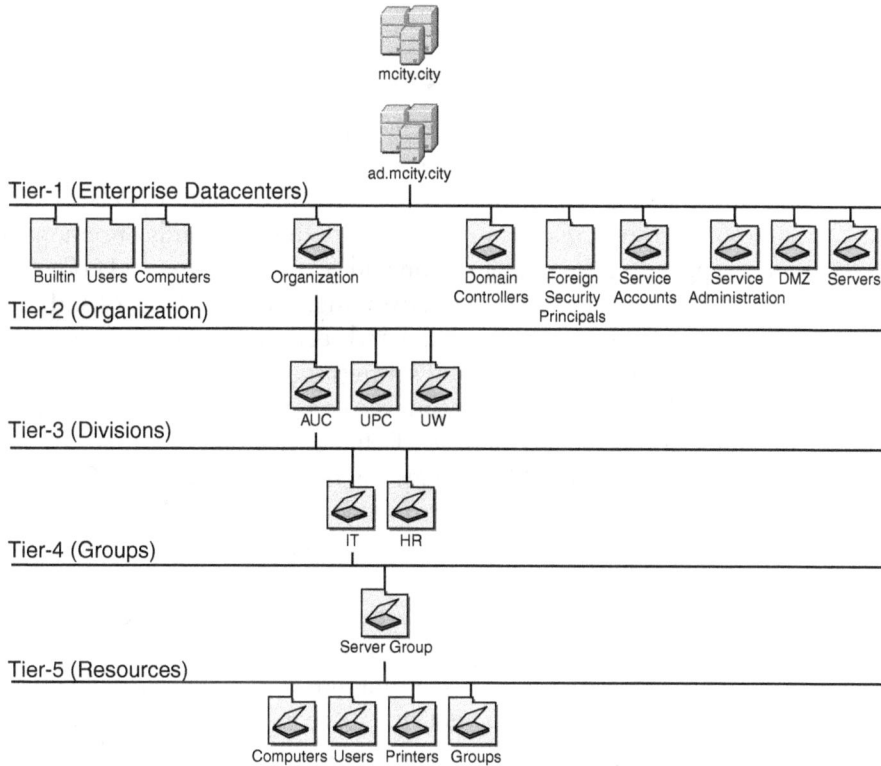

Figure 5.4 Group Policy architecture.

So where would we put our clusters and NLB servers, our Exchange systems, SQL Server, and so on? These go at the top-most level of the domain, the first tier. At this level, the administrative partition allows only the most senior engineers to actually administer and access the cluster servers.

For more information on GP, see the next section. Agencies administer to their own OUs and are free to move resources around these OUs as they deem fit. However, to facilitate domain-wide activities, such as patch management and antivirus management, it is crucial to maintain the structure illustrated in Figure 5.3.

This chapter provides the guidelines for naming conventions, namespace design, and rules to follow for the creation and population of resource OUs.

Group Policy Backgrounder

This next section discusses Group Policy: what it is, how it gets used, and the architecture for this blueprint.

Group policy (GP) is one of the most important aspects of Active Directory. Group Policy is used to specify the thousands of options that can be applied to the configuration and control of users and computers. Group Policy governs security, networking, software delivery and usage, remote installation services, folder redirection, Internet Explorer (IE) maintenance, and registry-based settings (controlled through the use of administrative templates). It is thus the core technology in Active Directory that can control and manage IT change in an organization.

Hundreds of major GP settings can be manipulated in a *Group Policy Object*, and all these settings contain many variables resulting in a myriad of configurations that can be applied to various collections of objects.

GP affects everything and everyone in an Active Directory domain, from the ability to log on to the domain through logon scripts and settings and password policy to such minute options as specifying that a particular group of users cannot open Access 97 databases into Access 2003, or that one group of users spell checks using a UK English dictionary while another group uses the US English dictionary.

Only Windows 2000, Windows Server 2003, and Windows XP operating systems can use GP. These systems contain client-side functionality that acquires GP from domain controllers as soon as a computer logs into the network. This means poor group policy management or the inadvertent deletion or corruption of a GPO can easily adversely affect a client or collection of clients. Through GP, even the ability to execute an application can be prevented, regardless of whether or not the application is installed on the user's desktop.

With the power of GP comes complexity. It is the single-most complex function in AD management and should be allocated to the care of a small team of skilled administrators who have the knowledge and experience to create GPOs, allocate them or link them accordingly, place them under change control, and create new administrative templates as needed.

GP provides a directory-based desktop configuration for all users in a domain. The entire computing experience of the individual user can be very tightly controlled to manage change and reduce the cost of administering in a Windows domain. Many settings in GP templates are only known to the most experienced administrators. And some features of GP, such as the ability to create custom administrative templates and scripts, are only accessible to highly experienced administrators who have more than a modicum of software development expertise.

GP settings are selected and targeted to users and computers in Group Policy Objects. These objects are created by selecting settings from GP templates and then including them in a GPO. The settings are then applied to the user or computer through reading and applying the GPO to a group at the lowest level and through membership or association to an OU, domain, or site at a much higher level. Thus, GP can be easily applied to users where they are located in Active Directory and not where they are physically located. The GP administrator also has the ability to determine the priority of GP application and what settings must be inherited or possibly blocked at the lower tiers in the OU hierarchy.

The broader the policy—such as password settings—the higher the level at which the GP is placed. For example, password settings must be consistent across a domain, and thus password policy only can be enabled and applied in the Default Domain Policy. By placing an enterprise-wide or organization-wide policy in the Default Domain Policy, you ensure every user and computer in the organization follows the same policy.

The various levels at which GP is automatically applied is as follows:

- **Site-level GPO:** A site-level GPO affects all the users and computers that are members of a site. It does not affect other users and computers that are not explicitly linked to the GPO.
- **Domain-level GPO:** A domain-level GPO affects all the users and computers that are members of a particular domain. It does not affect other users and computers that are housed in other domains in the same forest.

- **OU-level GPO:** An OU-level GPO affects all the users and computers that are members of an OU. It does not affect other users and computers that are not explicitly linked to the GPO.

The three levels discussed here are often referred to as the *Site-Domain-OU* hierarchy for GP or SDOU. As mentioned in this overview, GP can be further applied to security groups by enabling the group, in the *access control list* (ACL) of the GPO, to read and apply the settings from any GPO anywhere in Active Directory. However, group enabling for the application of GP should not be the norm because it is difficult to manage GP at such a low level.

GP policy at the lowest level of the SDOU hierarchy always wins over a policy from a higher level OU or the domain and site OUs. In other words, the last GPO applied has the final application. So, if an administrator restricts access to a certain console at a parent OU and another administrator allows access to the console at a child or nest OU level, the access to the console is not restricted.

This behavior can naturally be overridden but only if an administrator allows the higher-level policy to be blocked at the lower levels. This does not apply to certain security policies found in the Default Domain Policy because such policy settings are not available for OUs.

GP settings are also cumulative. In other words, all the settings from all the GPOs that apply to an object are combined to provide the so-called effective policy. For example, if the last GPO to apply to an object contains a setting that has been configured, and if no earlier GPO configures that setting, then the setting is added to the effective policy.

There is another type of GPO that does not live in Active Directory. It is the local policy that lives on each computer running a Windows 2000, Windows Server 2003, or Windows XP operating system. Local policy is applied to an individual machine whenever AD Group Policy is not accessible, and some settings are applied in any event.

The essential configuration defined in the domain-level GPOs are controlled in the following sections:

- Password Policy
- Account Lockout Policy
- Kerberos Policy (see Chapter 7, "High-Performance Print-Server Solutions." These policies are set in the Default Domain Policy)
- Audit Policy

- Event Logs
- User Rights Assignments
- Security Options
- System Services
- IP Security Policies
- Group Policy
- Display
- Start Menu and Task Bar

Every domain contains a Default Domain Policy, and this GPO is modified in both the root domain and the child domain. A Default Domain Policy is always linked (active) for a domain; albeit, initially, it contains default settings, which provide a relaxed implementation of security policy.

The broadest security policy that needs to be defined for a domain is configured in the Default Domain Policy. It is a single GPO intended to extend certain mandatory security settings to all users and computers in the domain, no matter where they reside in Active Directory. The policies in the Default Domain Policy cannot be overridden by GPOs that are applied at some point after its application.

Account policies affect local and domain connected computers. When applied to a local computer, the account policies apply to the local account database that is stored on the computer. When applied to domain controllers, the account policy affects domain accounts for all users logging onto the domain from Windows Server 2003 or XP computers.

Domain-wide account policies are defined in the Default Domain Policy. All DCs pull the domain-wide account policy from the Default Domain Policy regardless of where that DC is placed in the OU hierarchy of the domain. For this reason, it is imperative a paper copy of the GPO, listing the settings, is maintained in the event the GPO becomes corrupt. The use of third-party GPO management tools, such as FAZAM2000, NetIQ's Group Policy Administrator (a licensed version of the former that is packed with advanced features), and the *Group Policy Management Console* (GPMC), obviates this need because these tools store the settings of GPOs offline, and they can be easily restored or rolled back in the event the GP becomes corrupt and the default policy must be re-created.

While there may be different local account policies for member computers in different OUs, there cannot be different account policies for domain accounts. The Default Domain GPO, thus, enforces the requirement for all domain accounts.

Computers that are not DCs also receive the Default Domain Policy. This can, however, be blocked at the lower level by blocking the domain policy from applying. Ensuring the "No Override" option on the GPO is enabled can prevent the circumvention. As long as a member server is joined or authenticated to the domain, its local policy is overridden by domain policy. Thus, you cannot specify a local security account policy and succeed at applying it unless the server, or workstation, is removed from the domain or no longer pulls down AD Group Policy.

Under Local Policies in the Default Domain Policy, the recommended practice is to define the minimal audit policy for the domain. User Rights Assignment and Security Options are also defined under Local Policies but these will be configured on Default Domain Controllers Policy and GPOs at the root OU levels for the various server groups, such as file servers and print servers. A Default Domain Controllers Policy is always linked for a domain; albeit, initially, it contains default settings, which are insufficient for secure implementation of security policy. The polices in these so-called "default" GPOs are discussed later in this chapter.

Password Policy

The password policy proposed here meets Microsoft's recommendation for password complexity and management. Password complexity was once enforced using a custom-built password filter or the default filter provided with the Windows NT 4.0 SP2 password filter (passfilt.dll). The password filter is a *dynamically linked library* (DLL) that is accessed when password complexity is defined in Group Policy. Today, however, the complexity checking algorithms are built into the system, and you do not need to access the passfilt.dll in any way.

The password policies include the following options:

- **Maximum password age:** This specifies the number of days a password can be used before the user is asked to change it. Changing passwords regularly is one way to prevent passwords from being compromised. Typically, the default varies from 30 to 42 days.

- **Enforce password history:** This setting specifies the number of unique, new passwords that must be associated with a user account before an old password can be reused. When used in conjunction with Minimum Password Age, this setting prevents reuse of the same password over and over. This setting is a value greater than 10 to prevent reuse of the same password, which is a security risk.

- **Minimum password age:** This setting specifies the number of days a password must be used before the user can change it. The default value is zero, but Microsoft recommends that this be reset to a few days. When used in conjunction with similarly short settings in Enforce Password History, this restriction prevents repeated reuse of the same password.

- **Minimum password length:** The minimum number of characters a user's password can contain. The default value is zero. Seven characters is a recommended and widely used minimum.

- **Passwords must meet complexity requirements:** A password must have the following characteristics:
  - Does not contain your name or user name
  - Contains at least six characters
  - Contains characters from each of the following two groups:
    - Uppercase and lowercase letters (A, a, B, b, C, c, and so on)
    - Numerals
  - Symbols (characters that are not defined as letters or numerals, such as !, @, #, and so on)

Table 5.2 lists the password policy and the GPO in which it is configured.

Table 5.2   Password Policy

Setting	Policy	Default Value	Required Policy	Unit	GPO
Windows Settings\ Security Settings\ Account Policies	Enforce password history	1	15	Passwords remembered	Default Domain

continues

Table 5.2   Password Policy (continued)

Setting	Policy	Default Value	Required Policy	Unit	GPO
	Maximum password age	42	45	Days	"
	Minimum password age	0	4	Days	"
	Minimum password length	0	8	Characters	"
	Passwords must meet complexity requirements	Disabled	Enabled		"
	Store password using reversible encryption for all users in the domain	Disabled	Disabled		"

Account lockout is a facility that automatically disables accounts, thereby locking out the user or computer, when a number of lockout criteria are presented to the security sub-system. Using this facility enables the administrator to block attempts to break passwords and detect attempts to hack into the network using random password generators. The facility provides three criteria that must be met to trigger the lockout of the account. A locked-out account cannot be reused until an authorized administrator or help desk administrator resets it.

- **Account lockout threshold:** This setting specifies the number of failed logon attempts the security system allows to go unnoticed until the lockout is activated. The threshold can be set from 1 to 999 failed attempts. You can also specify that the account is never locked out using the value of 0 in the threshold field. Failed attempts at CTRL+ALT+DEL or failed attempts to cancel a password-protected screen saver do not count towards the threshold. Failed attempts to logon remotely, however, do count toward the lockout threshold. To apply this setting, navigate to the following GP configuration: Computer Configuration\Windows Settings\Security Settings\Account Policies\Account Lockout Policy.

- **Account lockout duration:** This setting specifies the number of minutes (1 to 99999) that can elapse before an account is unlocked automatically. To require an administrator to be the only means to unlock the account, set the duration to zero. By default, this policy is not defined because it only has meaning when an Account lockout threshold is specified.
- **Reset account lockout counter after:** This setting lets you determine how many minutes (1 to 99999) must elapse before the failed logon counter for an account resets to 0.

By default, these settings are disabled in the Default Domain Group Policy object and in the local security policy of workstations and servers. Table 5.3 outlines the policy chosen for this architecture.

Table 5.3 Account Lockout Policy

Setting	Policy	Default Value	Required Policy	Unit	GPO
Windows Settings\ Security Settings\ Account Policies	Account lockout duration	Not Defined	0	Minutes	Default Domain
	Account lockout threshold	0	5^1	Invalid logon attempts	"
	Reset account lockout counter after	Not Defined	4320^2	Minutes	"

continues

[1] This setting specifies the number of times in the duration logon attempts can be made before an account is locked out.

[2] The higher the value for the reset option, the longer it will take for a locked account to automatically unlock.

Table 5.3 Account Lockout Policy (continued)

Setting	Policy	Default Value	Required Policy	Unit	GPO
Windows Settings\ Local Policies\ Security Options	Interactive Logon: Prompt user to change password before expiration	Not Defined	Enabled	10 days	"

Audit policy for both the root and child domain is defined as follows:

- **Audit account logon events:** Whenever a user logs on to a domain, the logon is processed at a DC. If auditing of Account Logon events is defined for the domain, the logon activity associated with the logon event is recorded in the event log of the DC that processes the logon attempt. The event is processed with the security subsystem processes and validates the user's credentials. Account logon events are only processed at DCs and are only recorded in the DC event logs.

  These can be viewed under the Security tab of the server's event viewer. If credentials are presented to the local SAM, which means the user is not authenticating to the domain but rather to the local machine, the event is recorded in the local server's security event log.

  The consolidation of event logs for the domain enables the security administrators to track and analyze all Account Logon events for the domain. A report should be created for the account logon events, which would filter out all other event logs and provide the security administrators with a clean audit trail for all logon authentications for the domain. A well-designed report can quickly highlight disconcerting logon patterns in the domain.

- **Audit account management:** The Account Management auditing is used when users and groups (security principals) are created, changed, or deleted in the domain. This audit tells the security administrator when a security principal was created and who created the object.

- **Audit directory service access:** All Active Directory objects have a *system access control list* (SACL) associated with it, and thus object the security administrators can extensively audit access. AD user and group accounts are audited using Account Management facilities; however, you can also audit the modification of other objects in the directory naming contexts, such as the Configuration and Naming contexts. This is achieved by auditing for object access, which is done by defining the SACL for the specific objects to be audited. Audit information is generated when users and groups listed on the SACL of the AD object attempt to access the object.

- **Audit logon events:** Logon events record when a user logs on or off a computer, which is not the same thing as account logon events. Logons can be generated at any time after a user logs on with an account. In other words, the logon events are generated after a user authenticates to the domain, whereas account logon events usually only occur once.

  When a user logs onto a remote server, say, using the Terminal Services client, the logon event is generated in the remote server's security log. These logon events are created when the user's logon session and access tokens are created and destroyed.

  Logon events are useful to the security administrators to track attempts to logon interactively to servers. They can be used to investigate potential security violation launched against servers from specific locations. Success audits generate an audit entry when a logon attempt succeeds and failure audits generate an audit entry when the logon attempt fails.

- **Audit object access:** Auditing for all objects throughout a Windows Server 2003 domain can be achieved using the SACL of the objects. Each object's SACL contains a list of security principals (usually groups) that specify actions to audit. Just about every object created in a Windows Server 2003 domain has its own SACL, and it can be audited for access control. Important objects to audit include files, folders, drives, printers, and even registry keys.

The SACL contains *Access Control Entries* (ACEs). Each ACE contains three items of information critical to the object auditing process:

- The security principal to be audited (a user or group object).
- The specific access type to be audited. This is known as the *access mask*.
- A flag that indicates whether to audit for failed access, successful access, or both.

For events to appear in the security log, Auditing for Object Access first must be enabled in Active Directory. Then the SACL for each object must be defined.

- **Audit policy change:** Auditing for policy enables the security administrator to monitor attempts to change policy. Not only can you audit to track and monitor attempts to change policy that governs user rights and other policies, but also attempts to alter audit policy itself.

- **Audit privilege use:** Administrators at various levels in a Window 2000 domain exercise certain rights they are given to administer a domain. Such privileges include backup of files and folders, restoring files and folders, changing the system time, shutting down the system, and so on. Auditing the use of privileges for success and failure generates an event for each time a user attempts to exercise a user right.

  Enabling the Privilege Use audit does not automatically audit use of every user right. By default, the following rights are excluded:

  - Bypass traverse checking
  - Create a token object
  - Replace process level token
  - Generate security audits
  - Backup files and directories
  - Restore files and directories

- **Audit process tracking:** Processes running on Windows Server 2003 computers can be audited to provide detailed information showing attempts to create processes and end processes. Security administrators can use this facility to audit a process' attempt to generate a handle to an object or even to obtain indirect access to an object. It is very useful in the hacker prevention arsenal.

- **Audit system events:** System events are generated every time a user or process alters an aspect of the computer environment. The security administrator can thus audit for events, such as attempting to fiddle with system time (often a target in a hacking scenario) or shutting down a computer.

This facility also lets you audit attempts to clear the security log. This is important because users or hackers planning to infiltrate the network almost always attempt to cover their tracks by purging the security logs and, thereby, hiding changes they make, or attempt to make, to the environment. It is important to constantly pipe event log information to SQL Server or a similar repository (the archiving process); so, in the event a hacker succeeds to purge the event log, the event leading up to the purge, or events close to the actual purge event, are logged.

The minimum audit policy defined for Broward County's domains are listed in Table 5.4.

Table 5.4   Audit Policy

Setting	Policy	Default Value	Required Policy	Unit	GPO
Windows Settings\ Local Policies\ Audit Policy	Audit account logon events	Not Defined	Success and Failure		Default Domain
	Audit account management	"	Success and Failure		"
	Audit directory service access	"	Success and Failure		"
	Audit logon events	"	Success and Failure		"
	Audit object access	"	Failure		"
	Audit policy change	"	Success and Failure		"
	Audit privilege use	"	Failure		"
	Audit process tracking	"	Failure		"
	Audit system events	"	Success and Failure		"

It should be noted that audit policy for Application, Security, and System applies on all computers in the domain, including workstations. However, password policy for the servers, especially the clusters, is specialized for these applications. You would not, for example, cause your cluster service accounts to require new passwords every 45 days, nor would you enforce a policy that causes the account to lock out the cluster service at certain times. This would simply cause your clusters to stop working.

Base policy for auditing on desktops should be enabled with custom settings defined for desktop events. These then take precedence for the desktop over the domain-level settings. Only events that apply to the local workstation are recorded, which provides a useful record of activity on a workstation and the necessary data required for troubleshooting. Remote access tools, like the SMS client, can read these logs and determine the cause of application or system failure or security breaches. A wide range of events flowing to the report and alert systems helps you maintain a proactive, watchful eye on your systems.

Event Log

Table 5.5 lists the required event log settings. These are typically set in the Default Domain Policy. These settings are sufficient for the HA systems as well.

Table 5.5   Event Log Settings

Setting	Policy	Default Value	Required Policy	Unit	GPO
Windows Settings\ Event Log	Maximum application log size	Not Defined	65,536	KB	Default Domain
	Maximum security log size	"	184,320	KB	"
	Maximum system log size	"	65,536	KB	"
	Restrict guest access to application log	"	Enabled		"

Setting	Policy	Default Value	Required Policy	Unit	GPO
	Restrict guest access to security log	"	Enabled		"
	Restrict guest access to system log	"	Enabled		"
	Retain application log	"			"
	Retain security log	"			"
	Retain system log	"			"
	Retention method for application log	"	Override events as needed		"
	Retention method for security log	"	Override events as needed		"
	Retention method for system log	"	Override events as needed		"
	Shut down the computer when the security audit log is full	"	Disabled		"

Group Policy Objects for Cluster Servers

Most cluster installations fail because the cluster service account does not get the proper rights it needs on each of the cluster nodes. First, the cluster service account must be in the local administrators group. You can create a domain cluster service account as long as you create a separate account for each cluster. You can name the account something like filvs01.cl.adm (where "adm" is short for administrator) or filvs01.cl.ad (where "ad" is the Active Directory domain the account is in) and make it a member of the local administrator's group on the node. The reason for creating separate accounts for each cluster is to lessen the risk of an account compromise so it only affects the cluster nodes it is assigned to, and not all the cluster nodes.

If your cluster is failing (and you'll notice this because resources will fail), then it is possible that group policy has come down on top of your local policy. To ensure that the right policy gets the clusters, you can create a GPO for cluster services and link it to the OU in which you place your cluster server objects. The following list provides the group policy settings for this cluster server GPO. Verify that the Cluster Service account has explicitly been given the following rights:

- Log on as a service
- Act as part of the operating system
- Back up files and directories
- Adjust memory quotas for a process
- Increase scheduling priority
- Restore files and directories

Active Directory Physical Architecture

The physical architecture of Active Directory consists of its replication architecture, which takes into account subnets, replication between domain controllers within sites, replication between domain controllers in different sites, LAN and WAN speeds, server placement, and server configuration.

Subnets

As mentioned in Chapter 4, "Highly Available Networks," subnets are a critical component of AD architecture and topology, and every subnet that contains computers that logon to the Windows Server 2003 NOS must be defined to AD. This section provides an overview and the architecture for the subnets used in a widely distributed AD site and replication topology. Having accurate and up-to-date information is critical for the architecting and design phase and eventual implementation and deployment (both pilot and final roll-out).

Of course, our systems would not be considered highly available if the sites, subnets, and network architecture were designed in such a way that could risk clients losing connections with the domain controllers and DNS servers. Without access to these resources, there is no way a client can find the file and print servers, Exchange, SQL, or any other system. So, a highly available network, supporting always-available DNS, DHCP, and WINS servers, is critical; otherwise, you would have cluster servers that no one would ever access.

All computers on the TCP/IP subnet requiring access to back-end systems need to be assigned to a site according to the subnet on which they are placed. Subnet information is used to group computers in a way that identifies their location on the network and their proximity to AD domain controllers (locality). When computers log onto an AD network, they first look for a DC on the same subnet (site) for which they are configured. Subnets are also used to formulate site topology (discussed in the "Sites" section) for replication purposes to determine the best routes between domain controllers.

Site information is also cached to mobile devices and notebook computers that log on to the AD network. This means mobile users can easily logon in any office or facility on the network and receive an IP configuration that enables AD to accommodate the user even if she is not in her home site or subnet.

A large number of subnets are identified to AD, which may or may not translate into AD sites that have domain controllers. No correlation should be assumed between IP subnets, sites, and organizational units. Sites may be composed of numerous subnets, and OUs may span numerous sites. The number of AD sites chosen depends on a variety of factors, of which a subnet is one.

The concept of a site was introduced in Windows 2000. It did not exist in Windows NT. Sites provide AD with knowledge of the physical network upon which it is functioning. Sites and domains are independent concepts. A site can belong to multiple domains and a domain can span many sites. Sites are retained as objects in AD, stored in the *Configuration Naming Context* (CNC). The architecture and implementation of site topology is discussed in this section.

Sites in AD typically define locality (for service requests of domain controllers) and replication topology. Sites are defined to AD as locations containing domain controllers that are well connected in terms of speed and cost. A site is created and named after the location that contains a large number of users, has a powerful LAN, and provides the key route through which remote locations and centers connect to a core data center.

If there are multiple domain controllers in a site (such as a hub site or a regional site with hundreds of users), they replicate with each other through a built-in configurable notification system. Domain controllers in remote sites replicate using a user-configurable replication scheme, which can be scheduled to meet the needs of the WAN topology and the available bandwidth.

For the purposes of this architecture, the following convention for referring to sites and locations is used:

- **Hub Site:** One of three main data centers that contain the root domain controllers, FSMO role servers, bridgehead servers, and disaster recovery architecture. The hub sites comprise the county's three redundant data centers. You may have more or fewer hub sites, depending on the size of your network. Some implementations have dozens of hub sites.
- **Regional Site:** An autonomous location that contains at least one domain controller holding the role of Global Catalog server for LAN speed logon (typically for more than 50 users). A regional site is connected to the hub site through a WAN link.
- **Center:** A remote location that does not contain a domain controller and is logically part of a larger regional or hub site. The subnets of centers that logon over the WAN to the hub site are thus included in the collection of subnets that make up a hub or a regional site.

Only sites with domain controllers are defined to AD. In other words, site objects are created in AD to provide a means for clients to authenticate to domain controllers in their sites. The domain controllers in the hub sites are load balanced, and any one domain controller is able to pick up the load should another domain controller fail or be scheduled for maintenance. Regional sites have at least one domain controller, and a hub site domain controller is available to service the regional site in the event of DC failure.

Replication between domain controllers within sites (intersite) takes place as needed. Replication between domain controllers in different sites (intrasite) takes place on a schedule. The intrasite schedule defined in this architecture is such that it does not burden the network on the one hand, while exposing AD to potential information update latency problems on the other hand.

Replication to regional sites can occur once a day, every six hours, or every two hours depending on requirements. Replication between the domain controllers in the hubs can occur more frequently (for example, every 15 minutes) to keep the hubs as concurrent as possible. This is possible because of the high-bandwidth links that exist between the hub sites. In this regard, a bandwidth of at least 512Kbit between the hubs is sufficient (and recommended to be reserved (using QoS algorithms) for inter-hub replication, and replication between the hubs should be allowed to occur as frequently as possible.

As mentioned earlier, a site is defined around a collection of networks connected by fast, reliable backbones. In other words, a LAN (which runs at 10-100Mbits) is considered a fast network and accommodating of a site. A WAN link between LANS should have a net 512Kbs available to consolidate them into the same site. Naturally, available bandwidth even higher than 512Kbs is preferred to consolidate the locations into sites. See Chapter 3, "Storage for Highly Available Systems," on the subject.

LAN speeds alone do not necessarily require the location to have a local DC. Most centers have local 10-100Mbit LANs and 1.5Mbit connections to their nearest regional or hub sites. And as discussed in Chapter 3, bandwidth is becoming more available as we progress into the world of fiber.

To qualify as a regional site that needs a domain controller, the logon and authentication traffic generated by the site over the WAN must be more than the traffic generated by AD replication on the same WAN link. Logon and authentication traffic begins to surpass replication traffic at about 50 users.

Intersite replication is very fast and very efficient because data is compressed. Depending on the application and user requirements, analysis may show the intersection or break-even to be at less than or more than 50 users. Server consolidation objectives may prefer that the links to the regional site be upgraded rather than place a DC in the site. In any event, Windows XP logon times (when Group Policy is applied) and lingering hourglasses are good indications that a GC should be located at the site.

AD uses site information to determine how best to use available network resources. This makes the following types of operations more efficient:

- **Service Requests** (in other words, authentication): The local net logon is built into Windows clients. The client makes a call to the logon API that queries AD, through DNS, for the GC situated closest to the client (determined by IP subnet information). The client is directed to logon to a GC in the same site as the client, or the closest site that contains a DC. Selecting a DC that is nearest to the client that placed the request makes handling the request more efficient. DC location is cached at the client so repeated calls to the API are avoided. Mobile computers that connect at multiple sites request a DC when the cached information is no longer valid.

- **Replication:** Sites streamline replication of directory information. Directory schema and configuration information is distributed throughout the forest and domain data is distributed among all DCs in the domain. By strategically reducing replication, the strain on the network can be similarly reduced. Active Directory replicates directory information within a site more frequently than among sites. This way, the best-connected DCs, those most likely to need particular directory information, receive replications first. The DCs in other sites receive all changes to the directory, but less frequently, reducing network bandwidth consumption.

  - A site is defined for each physical site that contains a domain controller. In other words, hub sites and regional sites initially represent candidates for sites.
  - A site is defined according to its subnet and the IP subnets of other regional sites or centers.
  - If there is no need to replicate DC data to and from a site, it is considered a center.
  - Users in centers are authenticated by the DC in their site across the WAN.
  - Site names are typically formed by combining a site's acronym of its canonical name with other data. Site links usually include the acronym of the notification site and the partner site with which it replicates. However, sites currently slated to replicate with the MR hub, as indicated, may replicate with another hub in a later phase in the life of the network. (Prepare a site naming convention for this.)
  - Users in regional sites are only able to log on to domain controllers in their hub sites should their local domain controllers be unavailable. They cannot log on to domain controllers in other hub sites or in other regional sites. This is prevented in DNS by configuring Net Logon appropriately on the DNS servers at regional sites. Users in centers directly connected to regional sites use the domain controllers in the regional sites instead of one of the central hub sites. In this regard, the regional site that services a center can be thought of as a mini-hub.

The hub and spoke model that was designed for this architecture consisted of three rings—with Ring 1 being the highest bandwidth ring where all sites positioned on Ring 1 connect to the same backbone and where information is routed around the ring simultaneously to reduce replication latency.

Ring 2 sites (spoke sites) get connected to their hub's sites on lower bandwidth connections but do not connect to other spoke-sites. As Ring 2 sites attach directly to the backbone, they become Ring 1 sites. The subnets of centers without domain controllers use the domain controllers in Ring 2 sites as their logon servers, and the domain controllers in the hub sites are available as backups.

This hub and spoke topology and ring design is illustrated in Figure 5.5.

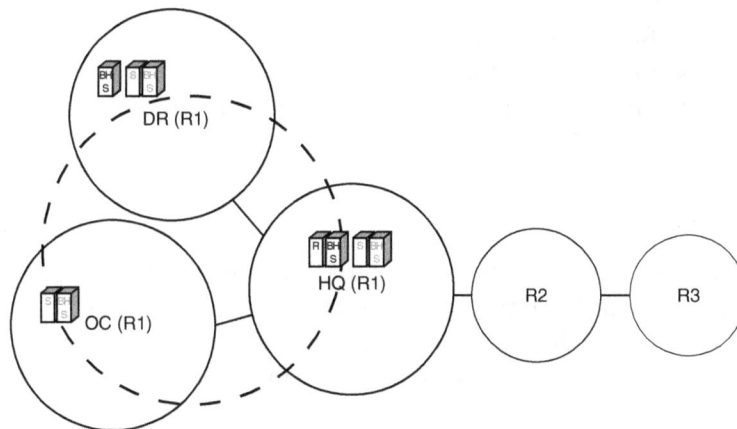

Figure 5.5 Site architecture.

Site Links

Site links are objects that represent configurations of physical connections between sites. They are used to model the amount of available bandwidth between sites. A site link is typically slow (less than 10Mbits/sec) and a potentially unreliable network that connects two, or more, sites.

In general, site links should be configured to map WAN connections, connecting only two sites. A very fast link that is operating near its full capacity that has a low-effective bandwidth can also be considered a site link.

The WAN speed at Ring 1 is higher than what AD considers for an intersite connection (T3 bandwidth is usually the upper limit); however, reliability of the WAN, geographical distribution of the user base, and redundancy warrant configuring the county's three data centers as corresponding hub sites. In this regard, intersite change notification on intersite transports is enabled to take advantage of the high bandwidth available at Ring 1 (100Mb). This is further explained in the following section.

Site links have four parameters:

- Cost
- Replication schedule
- Replication interval
- Transports (the transports used for replication)

Cost

The cost value of a site link is an arbitrary number that helps the replication system determine when to use the link compared to other links. Cost values determine the paths that replication takes through the network. To obtain cost factors, the following formula is typically used:

$$\text{Cost} = 1024 / \text{Log(available bandwidth in KB)}$$

Table 5.6 provides the site link chart that is used in the site/replication topology covered herein. As you can see, Ring 1 links have the lowest cost values.

Site links assist the *Knowledge Consistency Checker* (KCC), and AD integrated replication topology generating mechanism, to identify the appropriate Active Directory replication topology; thus, it is important that any manually created connections are relevant to the underlying network topology.

Table 5.6 Site Link Chart

Available Bandwidth	Cost*
9.6	1042
19.2	798
38.8	644
56	586
64	567
128	486
256	425
512	378
1024	340
2048	309
4096	283
8192	261
16384	242
32768	227
65536	212
131072	200

---

* You can use a simple descending or ascending cost table (such as 100, 200, 300); however, scientifically calculated costs derived from a cost formula lessen the chance of assigning incorrect cost factors to various links.

The KCC is the application that automatically creates replication connections between AD servers within sites and between sites. For example, if Site A is network-connected to Site B, which in turn is network-connected to Site C, then the logical site link topology should be the same. It does not make sense to create a site link topology of "SiteA-SiteLink" connected to Site C and "SiteC-SiteLink" connected to Site B.

Site links are critical to the KCC to identify the appropriate AD replication topology and, thus, must be configured correctly. A clear naming standard can assist you. The importance of this grows as the number of WAN links grows.

Replication Schedule and Notification

Intrasite replication topology is automatically configured by the KCC. Whenever changes are made at a DC, a timer begins a countdown from five minutes before peer domain controllers in the site are notified of the changes. As soon as notification goes out, the notified domain controllers immediately begin to pull changes from the source DC. The default topology created by the KCC is accepted for intrasite replication and should not be changed.

Intersite replication is configurable to allow engineers to fine-tune the replication topology between sites and to take into consideration factors like available bandwidth, peak times on the WAN, and routes.

A site link has an associated schedule that indicates at what times of the day the link is available to carry replication traffic (in other words, it can be thought of as a replication window). Hubs' sites at Ring 1 have all the bandwidth they need for frequent replication. The interval is, thus, every 15 minutes. Replication to Ring 2 sites is every hour (see Table 5.7).

Usually you cannot configure notification on intrasite links and there is no means to set notification on any intrasite MMC screen. However, on the links connecting the hubs (on Ring 1) notification is enabled at the registry level to make the intersite replication sitting on a very high-bandwidth backbone work more like intrasite replication. This keeps the three hub sites continuously up-to-date and enables them to work like a single site over the WAN.

Table 5.8 provides the schedule and notification data to be used for the implementation of the replication topology (see Chapter 6, "Building the Foundations for a Highly Available Architecture").

Table 5.7   Schedule and Notification Data

Link Schedule/Notification Data		
	Intersite	
Ring	**Schedule**	**Notification**
Ring 1	Every 15 minutes	Yes
Ring 2	60 minutes	No
Ring 3	Once a day at midnight	No
Intrasite		
N/A	Automatic	Every five minutes

Urgent changes, such as account lockouts and password updates, are replicated immediately. This can be done on the links in the Active Directory Sites and Services console or in the Replication Monitor application (both utilities are available on AD administration workstations).

Transports

While intrasite replication is achieved through standard Windows Server 2003 *remote procedure calls* (RPC), different transports are used to achieve replication between DCs in different sites. This intersite replication can be achieved using the following two transports:

- DS-RPC (Directory Services RPC [over IP])
- ISM-SMTP (Intersite Messaging-Simple Mail Transport Protocol)

Intrasite replication is always RPC-based. The replication is also synchronous and cannot be scheduled. Intersite replication can use either RPC- or SMTP-based transports. The replication data is always compressed regardless of the transport if the data is larger than 50KB. In other words, AD expects intersite replication between sites to be over low-bandwidth links.

Compression algorithms run on the bridgehead servers, which is why good disks and good processors are important on these servers. Data is compressed down to between 10 and 15 percent of the original size of the packet. Intersite replication is fully schedulable as mentioned earlier. Table 5.8 shows intrasite replication features versus intersite replication features.

Table 5.8   Instrasite Replication Versus Intersite Replication

Feature	Intrasite	Intersite
Transport	RPC	RPC or SMTP
Topology	Ring	Spanning Tree
Replication Schedule	N/A	Replication Window
Replication model	Notify and Pull	Optional Notify, Pull
Compression	None	On all packets >= 50KB
Secure channel	No	Yes (requires a CA)

The available bandwidth on the entire WAN is such that SMTP replication would not be recommended. RPC over IP is the preferred transport protocol to be used in all cases.

The RPC links between the DCs cannot be configured to directly use certificates like secure SMTP. SMTP requires that an enterprise *certificate authority* (CA) be made available to secure the replication traffic. This is not possible with the RPC channels, and IPSec is installed to domain controllers NICs to secure the intersite replication traffic. IPSec also requires a CA.

Connection Objects

Connection objects are the communication channels used by site links to affect the replication. Connection objects are also stored in AD, and they contain attributes that provide information about replication partners, the sites they belong to, and the transport (RPC/IP versus SMTP) that the connections use to transfer the data.

During the creation of the forest topology, the KCC creates two connection objects between two root DCs: one is used to replicate the configuration naming context and the schema naming contexts, and the other is used to replicate the domain naming context. When a third DC is promoted and becomes a child domain controller, no domain-naming context needs to be replicated between the root and the child DCs because the domain-naming context is only replicated within a domain.

The connection objects are created by the KCC, which uses a built-in process that automatically creates and then optimizes the replication topology by automatic generation of the connection objects.

Connection objects can also be created manually, and replication can be manually forced over them; however, this is usually required only in very large domains where the KCC needs to be manually overridden. Manually overriding the KCC occurs due to a built-in limitation it has on very large implementations (it does not scale well when the number of sites exceeds 100).

Manual creation of connection objects should be reserved in only exceptional circumstances because the KCC does not own or know about them. They have to be manually managed by the administrator who created them, and they are not affected by any automatic replication schedules.

Site Link Bridge

A *site link bridge* creates transitivity between a set of site links. If a site link over a slow WAN connects one site to another HQ (*headquarters*) to DR (*disaster recovery*) (HQ-DR), and a slow link connects HQ to OC (*Operations Center*) (HQ-OC), then a site link bridge called DR-OC connects Government Center to One University. The bridge essentially enables the domain controllers in one hub to create replication connections with the domain controllers in another hub. In other words, the site link bridge creates a link between two sites that do not explicitly have a site link between them.

It is not necessary to explicitly create site link bridges between the three hub sites because the network is powerful enough to allow the KCC to automatically develop replication topology between the DCs in the three hub sites. This is known as *site link transitiveness*.

Site Layout and Topology

The domain controllers configured as bridgehead servers affect replication between sites. When bridgehead servers accumulate changes for replication, they wait on remote sites to begin pulling the data during the replication window. As mentioned earlier, the bridgehead servers in the hubs' sites are configured to notify replication partners in the replication window, which is opened every 15 minutes.

The configuration change to allow intersite notification of changes needs to be made at the registry on each bridgehead server. The procedure is outlined in the Active Directory Implementation Plan.

To ensure that the correctly configured servers are assigned the role of *bridgehead server* (BHS), a preferred list of bridgehead servers is installed to AD. This section defines the architecture for the core infrastructure servers in each hub site. Each of the three hub sites are built out as central redundant Active Directory, Windows Server 2003, Windows 2000 Server and Advanced Server, and Exchange 2003 data centers. In addition to the AD infrastructure servers, the data centers also accommodate centralized file servers, email servers (MS Exchange 2003), print servers, and service-level and O&M servers (*Operations and Maintenance*) used for monitoring, disaster recovery, and backup/restore.

AD Integrated DDNS (Dynamic DNS)

DNS is used to translate a host name to an IP address. Dynamic DNS (for integration with Active Directory) is characterized by the following:

- Active Directory integrated zones
- Secure dynamic updates
- Active Directory-integrated zones can only be hosted on a DC server for that domain; other servers (member servers and/or DC servers) can only hold secondary read-only copies

Domain controllers use DNS to locate other domain controllers that are hosting Active Directory. DNS is the lifeblood of an Active Directory domain, so to speak; thus, every domain controller is configured as an AD integrated DNS controller to help ensure that a DNS server is always available, that DNS is always backed up, and that DNS is secure and up-to-date. AD integrated DNS stores the DNS records in AD, and the information is replicated and kept up-to-date with all domain controllers in the forest.

Using Active Directory-integrated DNS zones simplifies the configuration required because you do not need to create the zone files on each DNS server, which is a security risk, and a potential hazard for adhering to the SLA.

As mentioned, AD-integrated zones are stored in the directory and are replicated to each domain controller along with other Active Directory data. When you start a domain controller that also runs DNS, the DNS Server service detects the zones in the directory and uses them. You can, however, create secondary zones for AD in root, parent, or non-AD integrated domains so domains on the AD namespace can resolve resources in each domain if necessary. The best practice, however, for resolving resources in other domains on the same AD tree is through delegation. To resolve resources in other forests or out on the Internet, best practice requires the use of forwarders.

See Chapter 6 for how to do this. Secondary zones in other domains are read-only. They are updated through zone-transfers from the primary DNS servers. Legacy or non-AD integrated DNS servers, even Windows Server 2003 non-domain DNS servers, are not included in the AD-integrated DNS architecture because a new, separate namespace has been chosen to support AD.

The root DNS server of the domain should use any non-domain DNS servers inside the private network for external resolution. This enables clients to always resolve external hosts by resolving up the DNS chain to a server authorized to return an external name address resolution. For example, if a local client browses to www.foxnews.com, the non-AD domain DNS server returns the resolution to the client through the services of AD-integrated DNS architecture.

DNS Architecture

As mentioned earlier in this chapter, the DNS namespace for Active Directory is not part of the external Internet namespace maintained by the organization and its ISP. A separate DNS namespace exists and is maintained on the domain controllers of both the root and child AD domains. The first DNS server residing on the first root server is not a root server. Any non-AD host and service queries that it cannot resolve as the authority for the domain are seconded to external DNS servers. See Figure 5.6 for a look at DNS topology.

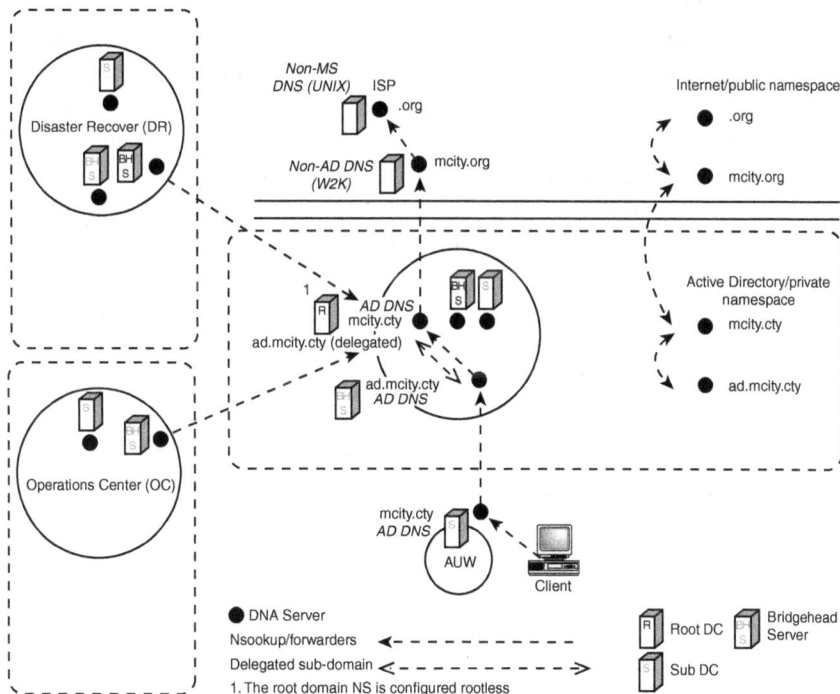

Figure 5.6   DNS topology.

The DDNS architecture is characterized by the following:

- A DDNS service is installed on all domain controllers for all sites in the forest (Active Directory integrated zones can only be hosted on a DC server for that domain).
- All clients and servers have both a primary and alternate DDNS server configured, except in the case of the root domain controllers.
- The primary and alternate DDNS servers are always located within the same regional hub as the client or server and never across the major WAN links to a remote hub site or region. (Even with high-bandwidth availability across links between hub sites and regions, it is prudent to keep DNS lookup traffic local to a region and its hub site.)

Hub Sites

- HQ: Primary and alternate DDNS servers are local. Servers forward to the DMZ DNS for external (Internet) resolution.
- DQ: Primary and alternate DDNS servers are local. Servers forward to the DMZ DNS for external (Internet) resolution
- OC: Primary and alternate DDNS servers are local. Servers forward to the DMZ DNS for external (Internet) resolution
- Regional Sites: The primary DDNS server is local and the alternate server is at the hub site.
- Centers: The primary DDNS server is at the regional site higher up on the spoke or at the hub site and the alternate DDNS server is at the hub site.
- DDNS is integrated with Active Directory so no zone transfers need be carried out. There is no notion of a primary and secondary zone with AD-integrated DDNS.
- The DNS for the child domain is delegated to a sub-domain controller in the child domain. The root DNS, therefore, delegates the hosting of the child DNS to the first bridgehead domain controller.

Resolution of external names (names on the public Internet) are forwarded to a name server that is not part of the AD-integrated namespace.

Administration of DNS Servers

Connection to and administration of DNS servers is restricted to members of the domain local groups listed in Table 5.9.

Table 5.9   DNS Administration Data

Group	Access
DNS Users	Read only
DNS Admins	Full (modify)
Domain Admins	Full
Administrators	Full

Only users belonging to the DNS Admins, Domain Admins, or Administrators domain local groups can modify DDNS information and configuration and manage the DDNS services.

DDNS Configuration

The DDNS servers are listed in Table 5.10; the TCP/IP addresses are added at the time of implementation.

Table 5.10   DDNS (Dynamic Domain Naming Service) Servers in Hubs

	Host IP	Primary	Alternate	Site
Note: IP address configuration subject to change.				
HQ				
HQRDC01	10.10.20.21	10.10.20.24	.22, .25	HQ
HQRDC02	10.10.20.28	10.10.20.30	.29, .31	HQ

continues

Table 5.10   DDNS (Dynamic Domain Naming Service) Servers in Hubs (continued)

HQ				
HQSDC01	10.10.20.34	10.10.20.38	.35, .39	HQ
HQSDC02	10.10.20. 41	10.10.20.44	.42, .45	HQ
DR				
DRRDC01	10.20.20.21	10.20.20.24	.22, .25	DR
DRSDC01	10.20.20.28	10.20.20.30	.29, .31	DR
DRSDC02	10.20.20.34	10.20.20.38	.35, .39	DR
OC				
OCSDC01	10.30.20.21	10.30.20.24	.22, .25	OC
OCSDC02	10.30.20.28	10.30.20.30	.29, .31	OC

WINS

WINS is used to translate a computer name (NetBIOS name) to an IP address. WINS is an infrastructure service used extensively by Windows 9.x and NT v4.0 to locate servers and resources. It is also useful as a resolution service for technology and applications that make use of NetBIOS names, such as the names of virtual servers on Microsoft Cluster Services implementations, and for DFS. However, even virtual server names can and should be resolved on DDNS. This architecture provides a WINS implementation at the hubs sites. A replication partner can be installed on the regional site's domain controller if WINS is needed at a regional site.

The WINS architecture is characterized by the following:

- The organization is migrating all WINS-dependent computers to Windows Server 2003 and Windows XP ahead of the migration to the Windows Server 2003 NOS and Active Directory; thus, the WINS services are not overburdened. It is sufficient to place WINS servers in the hub sites.
- There are three WINS servers servicing the domains.
- Only servers in the child/sub domain are WINS servers.

■ All clients and servers have both a primary and secondary WINS server.

■ The primary WINS server is always located within the same hub region as the client or server and never across the main WAN links to a remote hub site.

■ The secondary WINS server is always located across the main WAN links to a remote hub site.

Hub Sites

■ HQ: The primary WINS server is local and the secondary WINS server is remote (DR).

■ DR: The primary WINS server is local and the secondary WINS server is remote (HQ).

■ OC: The primary WINS server is local and the secondary WINS server is remote (HQ).

■ Regional Sites: They use the same WINS configuration as the closest remote hub site.

The following best practice for WINS servers should be noted:

■ Do not place WINS servers on any DC serving a large site of down-level clients (such as Windows 95), especially a DC in a hub site. If a WINS server must be placed onto a DC (for example, to consolidate servers) or into a regional site, then it can be installed on a domain controller that services a small regional site (less than 50 down-level users) or a small number of Windows 95 clients. WINS is a process- and disk-intensive service and can impact NTDS performance in large environments heavily dependent on WINS.

■ The primary WINS server value given to a primary WINS server must be the address of the primary WINS server itself.

■ WINS servers must not be provided with values for secondary WINS servers.

■ To minimize WAN link usage, inter-region pull replication is less frequent (240 minutes) than intra-site pull replication (30 minutes or 120 minutes).

- Inter-region push replication (replication initiated after an arbitrary number of updates) may be effectively disabled (that is, by setting a 9,999 count).
- Inter-region replication is controlled to occur at specified intervals only (pull replication).
- To minimize intra-region convergence time, intra-region replication between well-connected sites is more frequent (pull replication 30 minutes and push replication 20 count) than intra-region replication between not so well-connected sites (pull replication 120 minutes and push replication 40 count).
- To minimize both intra-region convergence time and intra-region WAN link usage, intra-region replication between not so well-connected sites is less frequent (pull replication 120 minutes and push replication 40 count) than intra-region replication between well-connected sites (pull replication 30 minutes and push replication 20 count).
- Relatively infrequent intra-region replication occurs between the WINS server in the hub sites.

Administration of WINS Servers

Connection to and administration of DHCP servers is restricted to members of custom domain local groups.

DHCP (Dynamic Host Configuration Protocol)

DHCP (*Dynamic Host Configuration Protocol*) is used to provide DHCP clients with IP configuration details. IP configuration details include IP address, subnet mask, default gateway, primary and secondary DNS servers, primary and secondary WINS servers, domain name and NetBIOS node type, and so forth. DHCP configuration provides the primary and alternate DNS server configuration for all dynamically addressed computers. If a dynamically addressed client cannot access DNS information, it cannot participate on an Active Directory network.

DHCP Architecture

DHCP is extended to clients across many of the networks through the services of BOOTP relay agents and router-based IP helper services. Depending on the configuration of the IP helper devices, this service can detract from an Active Directory migration if Windows Server 2003 DHCP Server configuration and router-based IP helper configuration is not coordinated.

The DHCP architecture for this architecture is thus characterized by the following best practices:

- DHCP servers should be placed in the primary subnet of a site where there is a domain controller. This provides redundancy (using super-scope/split-scope configurations) and load balancing and keeps DHCP local to the subnets requiring the services.
- As far as possible, BOOTP should be kept to a minimum on an AD/DHCP/DDNS integrated network.
- A distribute network of DHCP servers on a large routed WAN is much preferred over one or more large DHCP servers sitting on the backbone of the WAN in a few locations.
- The DHCP server service can be easily accommodated on the site's DC. It is accommodated on both GC and BHS servers in all hubs' sites.
- All Windows Server 2003 DHCP servers on the network must be Active Directory authenticated. Non-AD–authenticated servers must either be retired or authenticated to AD.
- Only DC servers in the child/sub-domain are DHCP servers (DHCP services are not required for the root domain).
- The DHCP scopes are split across DHCP servers dependent upon whether the DHCP server is local or remote to the site.
- The DHCP scopes for the main hub sites and large regional sites are split across two servers for redundancy. The split is 50/50 between two domain controllers in each site.
- Each hub's DHCP server also contains scopes to service regional sites in the event the regional DHCP servers cannot (failure or overflow). These scopes are split 50/50 with the regional (local) site leasing 100 percent of the addresses needed and the hub site (remote) leasing out the remaining 50 percent of the scope when needed.

DHCP Parameters

DHCP parameters can be configured according to server options or scope options. In other words, where configuration is identical across all scopes hosted on the server, the configuration should be a server option. Server options automatically apply to all scopes unless they are overridden by scope options. Scope options only apply to the scope in which they are defined.

The DCHP server follows the following protocol:

- A server option is used when all scope options are the same.
- A scope option is used when an option on one or more scopes is different for the other scopes.

Scope Details

Each DHCP scope must be configured with information peculiar to the subnet it is servicing. Document how each DHCP server needs to be implemented. See Chapter 6 for the steps required to configure and activate DHCP Servers when installing domain controllers.

Naming Conventions

Before implementing systems, as described in the next chapter, it is very important for you to develop a solid naming convention document, or add such a section to your Active Directory architecture document. The document should contain both naming conventions and labeling for logical and physical components. There are many reasons for this document. The obvious one is to maintain consistency of labeling as your implement your systems; but such a document has become more important because of how Microsoft Operations Manager (MOM) works. Without a consistent, well thought-out naming convention, it will be difficult to track alerts to various devices and locate information provided in these reports.

The following list of the most important components must consistently be named and labeled:

- **Server Names:** It is important to group your servers according to the roles they serve or the functions they provide in your organization before naming them. This is in keeping with role organization best practices suggested by Microsoft, introduced in Windows 2000, and adhered to more acutely in Windows Server 2003. Before you name a server, first establish what role it will play or what it does and then provide an acronym for that role. Major roles are roles that a single server or a cluster of servers is dedicated to. A sub-domain controller is considered a major role, as is a root domain controller. However, AD integrated DNS and DC-hosted DHCP are not considered major roles because they need to survive on the same server as a domain controller. WINS, on the other hand, is considered a major role if it is placed on a dedicated server. For example, if a WINS server is supporting a large number of NetBIOS clients or replicates with several partners, it should be on its own server. Stand-alone DHCP and DNS servers can be classified major role servers. A suggested naming convention for servers could be <Site or Location Name><Server Role><Server Number in series>. For example, the second sub-domain controller in the HQ hub site is thus HQSDC02 and the server name for the file server in the DR site is DRFIL01.
- **Virtual Server (Cluster) Names:** These names need to be unique on the network and need to be resolved for both access and management. Simply use the server naming convention described above and add VS to the name to signify virtual server. Such as DRFILVS01 or DREVS01 which is the first Exchange Virtual Server (EVS) in the DR site.
- **Server Drive Volume Labels:** Server drive volume labels must be consistent across all servers. Drive volume labels will show up in reports, software, alerts, and events and thus need to be report-, code-, and monitor-friendly. The naming convention for drive volume labels should reflect the major function of the drive. Volume labels should be in title case (initial capped) and two words should be separated with an underscore. Labels for volumes on drives owned by clusters should be uppercase. The quorum resource or drive should be labeled after the server node

using it. For example, the quorum resource for the second SQL Server cluster is labeled MRSQL02Q. Disk Q would also work in a small company with one or two clusters.

- **Server Drive Letters:** You should always reserve drive letters A through O for drive mappings and shares. Drive letter P onwards can be used for disk resources on your clusters. We talked about the Q drive for the Quorum resource.

- **Cluster Resource Labels:** Due to their critical application, cluster resources are constantly monitored and assessed for performance. Service level and data center operations will dictate that cluster resources be frequently reported on by services such as MOM. Cluster resource failure, for example, is by MOM, which means it is possible to pull a report—for example, on the number of times a network or disk resource failed during a given time. It is thus important that cluster resource names be consistent across the community of clusters installed at the various hub sites and locations in your enterprise. See Part II for examples of cluster resource naming.

- **Network Interface Card (NIC) Labels:** NICs labels should be consistent across all servers in the enterprise. When naming NICs differentiate between on-board components, public NICs, private or heartbeat NICs and so on. An example is "Primary – onboard – Public" or "Secondary – heartbeat."

- **Sites:** The naming convention for AD sites should be simple. Consider a short acronym or abbreviation named after the primary location for the site, such as HQ for Headquarters or DR for Disaster Recovery.

- **Sites Links:** The naming convention for site links should be the sending site name acronym described in the Sites section followed by a hyphen followed by the receiving site acronym. For example, HQ-DR.

- **Group Policy Objects (GPOs):** The naming convention for GPOs is best implemented using the camel-case notation proposed by the .NET Framework. This allows uniformity while enjoying the freedom to provide a descriptive name. A good example is defaultWorkstationsPolicy or accessSaveRestrictions. You can also initial cap the first part of the name—for example, SoftwareRestrictions. The more complex and cryptic Hungarian notation for naming objects—such as GPO_Access_Restricitions and adding numbers and dates in the GPO—is not recommended.

- **Service Accounts:** A service account is the user account used by a service to obtain access and authentication to NOS resources. Service accounts need to gain authentication at various levels both interactively and programmatically. A network administrator or server administrator usually enters service accounts in the Service Control Manager.
- **Organizational Units (OUs):** Two or three characters in uppercase works the best. Examples are Finance and Administrations (FA), Underwriters (UW), and Information Technology (IT). Some companies prefer longer names that are more descriptive, and this works for small- to medium-size entities. Examples are Accounting, Agents, Sales, and Marketing.

Time-Out

This chapter covered the Active Directory and network infrastructure sevices we need to have in place before we can implement high availability services. In Chapter 6, we take the architecture discussed in this chapter and implement the systems and services that comprise the high-availability platforms.

Building the Foundations for a Highly Available Architecture

Introduction

A lot of theory has been covered in the previous chapters. Now it's time to start implementing. This chapter and the ones to follow take what we have discussed up to now and roll it into an implementation plan for a data center that tens of thousands of users will rely upon.

First, we introduce clustering as it is accomplished on the Windows Server 2003 platform. We also discuss cluster concepts, models, and architecture. Then we implement the Active Directory architecture and network architecture as discussed in Chapter 5, "Preparing the Platform for a High-Performance Network," and lay the foundations for a highly available and reliable Web, database, and email server architecture, a network that will eventually comprise NLB IIS servers, NLB application servers, SQL Server clusters, Exchange clusters, and file and print clusters.

You can look at this chapter as the foundation implementation plan. It is what you need to follow if tasked with constructing and deploying a highly available solution. In the practical part, this chapter first outlines the process of building the forest and forest root domain, on either your lab or production network. It also covers the process of providing a resource for OS installations, tools, utilities, and patches. Then we prepare the cluster virtual server to begin hosting resources.

In this chapter, you implement Active Directory. At first glance, it seems that you are doing nothing more than setting up the usual AD network. But as you install the various cluster servers and services, you see that what is laid down in this chapter provides the solid foundation for the future systems. Then we deal with the actual process of clustering the servers, setting up cluster resources, and getting ready to activate the fail-over resources in Part II, "Building High Availability Windows Server 2003 Solutions." This is something you cannot do unless AD is well implemented beforehand.

Windows Clustering 101

There was a time in the not-too-distant past when the thought of clustering Windows servers sent a chill down the spines of network engineers and caused them to go take out long-term care insurance. Those days are gone with the clustering services that are now built into the Windows Server 2003 operating system. Only Windows Server 2003, Enterprise Edition and Windows Server 2003, Datacenter Edition can create clusters. Windows Storage Server 2003 is a version of Enterprise Edition for clustering file share resources.

There are two parts to clustering a high-availability service or application, such as Exchange 2003 or SQL Server 2000 or SQL Server 2005. The first part entails setting up the base cluster service and getting a virtual server going. The second part entails creating the resources that failover on that virtual server. Most of the second part of clustering is dealt with in Part II of this book.

By the time you are ready to cluster Exchange or SQL Server, you will be able to failover the virtual server resources from one node to the other and keep services, like drives and network interface cards, under the control of the cluster.

The Cluster Model

With Windows Server 2003, you have three models from which to choose; they are built into the operating system and are, thus, supported by Microsoft. The third option may require third-party software. Table 6.1 discusses the models in order of increasing complexity.

The most common cluster model (and inherited from Windows 2000 and Windows NT) is the single quorum cluster model in which multiple nodes of a cluster share a single quorum resource. In this model, all nodes communicate with each other across a local interconnect, and all nodes share a common disk array (in a SAN or a SCSI enclosure).

Windows Server 2003 also introduces the concept of a single node cluster, which is a cluster that is comprised of a single node or server. For obvious reasons, a single node cluster runs host cluster resources, but the cluster resources cannot fail-over to anything.

Then there is the geographic cluster or so-called "geo-cluster" in which the nodes that comprise the cluster are separated over a geographic divide. A wide area network usually separates the nodes and the geo-cluster nodes can be in different buildings or even across the country. They don't share storage or a quorum.

The central repository of data in a cluster is the so-called quorum resource. You can think of the quorum as the brain center of the cluster. The idea of a cluster is to provide system or server redundancy. In other words, when a server in the cluster fails, the cluster service is able to transfer operations to a healthy node. This is called failover. The quorum resource data is persistent and the quorum must survive node failure in the cluster or the resources cannot fail to the healthy node and start up.

This is why in a traditional, single quorum resource cluster, the quorum cannot be mounted into any single device on the node of the cluster unless the cluster can gain exclusive access to the device (and unless it can be moved or transferred upon node failure, which is technically possible even on a local disk resource as we will soon see). There are two exceptions to this rule: the single node cluster and the so-called geo-cluster, a concept in clustering now possible with Windows Server 2003.

Each of the cluster models discussed employs a different quorum resource type. Table 6.1 discusses the models.

Table 6.1   Cluster Model Options

Cluster Model	Application	Location of Cluster Configuration Data
Single Node	Ideal for labs, testing, development, and hosting applications on a virtual server	The quorum resource maintains the cluster configuration data either on a cluster storage device (an external drive array) or as a local drive on the node. Setup requires selection of the Local Quorum resource type.
Single Quorum	Typical local Active-Passive and Active-Active clusters	The quorum resource maintains the cluster configuration data on the single cluster storage device to which all nodes in the cluster are connected. Setup of this model ratifies the Physical Disk resource type (or other storage class resource type). The cluster installation will fail if this resource time does not test true as a viable quorum (we demostrate this later in the chapter).
Majority Node Set	Geographically dispersed server clusters	Geographic clusters are separated over wide area networks; therefore, each node maintains its own copy of the cluster configuration data. The quorum resource ensures the cluster configuration data is kept consistent across the nodes.

Single Node

Of particular interest is the Single Node cluster model in which the quorum resource can be maintained on a storage device on the local node. The idea behind the single node model is novel. With previous versions of the operating system, it was impossible to establish a virtual server, what users attach to, on a cluster comprising only one node. The single node cluster enables this. The Single Node cluster model is illustrated in Figure 6.1.

NOTE: This chapter covers the creation of a single quorum cluster. However, we do touch on the subject of geo-clusters in Chapter 10, "High Availability, High-Performance Exchange."

You can use the single node cluster for lab testing of applications that have been engineered for clustering. You can also use it to test access to storage devices, quorum resources, and so on. The lab or development work is, thus, used to migrate the cluster-aware application into production as a standard single quorum cluster. It is also possible to simply cluster the single node with other nodes at a later time. The resource groups are in place and all you need to do is configure fail-over policies for the groups.

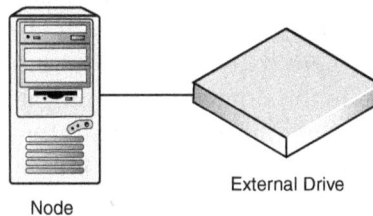

Node   External Drive

Figure 6.1   Single Node cluster model.

A single node cluster can also be used to simply provide a virtual server that users connect to. The virtual server service and name, thus, survives hardware failure. Both administrators and clients can see the virtual servers on the network and they do not have to browse a list of actual servers to find file shares.

What happens when the server hosting the single node cluster and the virtual server fail? The Cluster service automatically restarts the various application and dependent resources when the node is repaired. You can also use this service to automatically restart applications that would not otherwise be able to restart themselves.

For example, you can use this model to locate all the file and print resources in your organization on a single computer, establishing separate groups for each department. When clients from one department need to connect to the appropriate file or print share, they can find the share as easily as they would find an actual computer.

You can move the virtual server to a new node and end users never know the physical server behind the virtual server name has been changed. The real NetBIOS name of the server is never used. The downside of this idea is downtime. Moving the virtual server name to a new server requires downtime. Therefore, this is not suitable for a high-availability solution.

Single Quorum Cluster

This cluster model prescribes the quorum resource maintains all cluster configuration data on a single cluster storage device that all nodes have the potential to control. As mentioned earlier, this is the cluster model available in previous versions of Windows. The Single Quorum cluster model is illustrated in Figure 6.2.

Microsoft discounts the perception that the cluster storage device can be a single point of failure and promotes the idea that a *Storage Area Network* (SAN) where there are often multiple, redundant paths from the cluster nodes to the storage device mitigates in favor of this solution. While not discounting this model, if you study how a SAN is built, you discover there is some truth that a SAN is a single point of failure.

You can indeed have multple paths to the storage device (the "heart" of the SAN) as discussed in Chapters 3, "Storage for Highly Available Systems," and 4, "Highly Available Networks." However, the SAN controller is really nothing more than a server with an operating system that is dedicated to hosting the drive arrays in its enclosures. Unless you have redundant controllers, your SAN will fail if a component in the SAN controller fails. SAN memory can fail, its operating system can hang, the processors can be fried, and so on. Thus, to really eliminate every single point of failure in this model, you really need to have two SANs on the back end. This idea really opens a can of worms. After all, most IT shops do not budget for two SANs for every cluster. The SANs of today have many redundant components within their single footprint (usually a very large footprint) in the data center. To deploy two-mirrored SANs on a cluster is not only a very expensive proposition, but it is technically very difficult to install and manage.

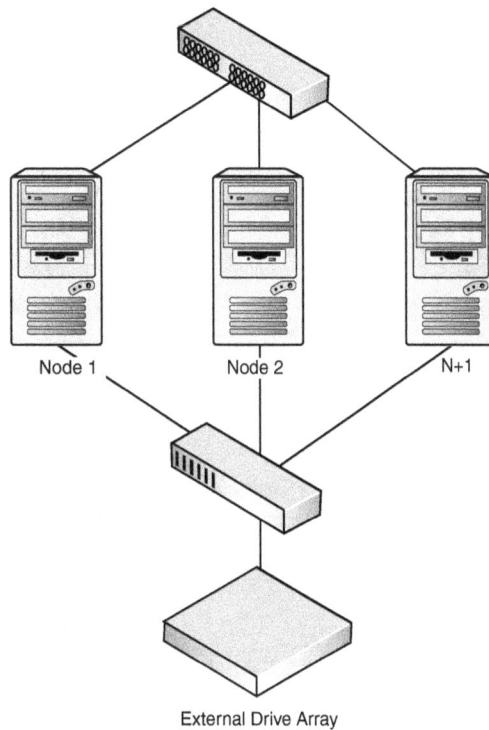

Figure 6.2   Single Quorum cluster model.

Majority Node Set

As mentioned, geo-cluster nodes can reside on opposite sides of the planet because each node maintains its own copy of the cluster configuration data. The quorum resource in the geo-cluster is called the Majority Node Set resource. Its job is to ensure the cluster configuration data is kept consistent across the different nodes; it is essentially a mirroring mechanism. The Majority Node Set cluster model is illustrated in Figure 6.3.

The quorum data is transmitted unencrypted over *Server Message Block* (SMB) file shares from one node to the other. Naturally, the cluster nodes cannot be connected to a common cluster disk array, which is the main idea behind this model.

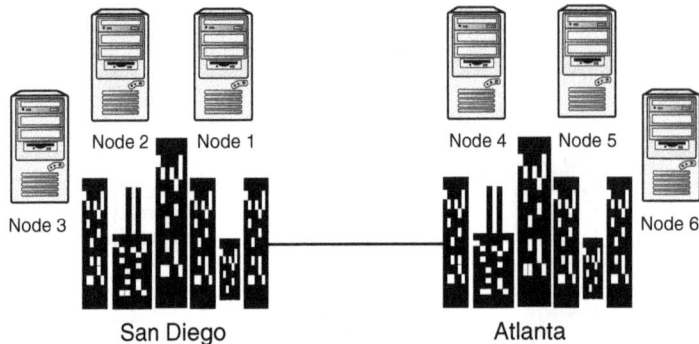

Figure 6.3   Majority Node Set cluster model.

You can use a majority node set cluster in special situations, and it will likely require special third-party software and hardware offered by your *Original Equipment Manufacturer* (OEM), *Independent Software Vendor* (ISV), or *Independent Hardware Vendor* (IHV).

Let's look at an example. Let's say we create an 8-node geo-cluster. We could, for example, locate four nodes in one data center, say in Atlanta, and the other 4 nodes in another data center in Phoenix. This can be achieved, and you can still present a single point of access to your clients. At any time a node in the geo-cluster can be taken offline, either intentionally or as a result of failure, and the cluster still remains available.

You can create these clusters without cluster disks. In other words, you can host applications that can failover, but the data the application needs are replicated or mirrored to the quorum data repositories on the other nodes on the cluster. For example, we can use this model with SQL Server to keep a database state up-to-date with log shipping. In Chapter 10, we investigate the particular solutions offered by NSI Software: Double-Take and GeoCluster.

The majority node set is enticing, but there are disadvantages. For starters, if more than half the nodes fail at any one time, then the entire cluster itself fails. When this happens, we say the cluster has lost quorum. This fail-over limitation is in contrast to the Single Quorum cluster model discussed ealier which will not fail until the last node in the cluster fails.

The Quorum Resource

Every cluster requires a resource which is designated as the quorum resource. The idea of the quorum is to provide a place to store configuration data for the cluster. Thus, when a cluster node fails, the quorum lives to service the new active node (or nodes) in the cluster. The quorum essentially maintains the configuration data the cluster needs to recover.

This data in the quorum is saved in the form of recovery logs. These logs store the changes that have been saved in the cluster database. Each node in the cluster depends on the data in the cluster database for configuration and state.

A cluster cannot exist without the cluster database. For example, a cluster is created when each node that joins the cluster updates its private copy of the cluster database. When you add a node to the existing cluster, the Cluster service retrieves data from the other active nodes and uses it to expand the cluster. When you create the first node in a cluster, the creation process updates the cluster database with details about the new node. This is discussed in more detail in the section "Clustering" later in this chapter.

The quorum resource is also used by the cluster service to ensure the cluster is composed of an active collection of communicating nodes. If the nodes in the cluster can communicate normally with each other (across the cluster interconnect), then you have a cluster. Like all service databases on the Windows platform, the cluster database and the quorum resource logs can become corrupt. There are procedures to fix these resources and we cover this a little later in this chapter.

When you attempt to create a cluster, the first node in the cluster needs to gain control of the quorum resource. If it cannot see the resource (this quorum), then the cluster installation fails. We show you this later. In addition, a new node is allowed to join a cluster or remain in the cluster only if it can communicate with the node that controls the quorum resource.

Let's now look at how the quorum resource is used in a two-node cluster, which is the type of cluster we will in the coming chapters.

When the first node in the cluster fails, the second node continues to write changes to the cluster database that it has taken control of. When the first node recovers and a fail-back is initiated, then ownership on the cluster database and quorum resource is returned in the fail-back mechanism.

But what if the second node fails before the first is recovered? In such a case, the first node must first update its copy of the cluster database with the changes made by the second node before it failed. It does this using the quorum resource recovery logs.

If the event the interconnect between the nodes fails, then each node automatically assumes the other node has failed. Typically, both nodes then attempt to continue operating as the cluster, and what you now have is a state called *split brain sydrome*. Imagine both servers succeeded in operating the cluster, you would then have two separate clusters claiming the same virtual server name and competing for the same disk resources. This is not a good condition for a system to find itself in.

The operating system prevents this scenario with quorum resource ownership. The node that succeeds in gaining control of the quorum resource wins and continues to present the cluster. In other words, whoever controls the "brain" wins. The other node submits, the fail-over completes, and the resources on the failed node are deactivated.

What constitutes a valid quorum resource? The quorum can be any resource that meets the following attributes:

- It can be accessed by a single node that must be able to gain physical control of it and defend the control.
- It must reside on physical storage that can be accessed by any node in the cluster.
- It must be established on the NTFS file system.

It is possible to create custom resource types as long as developers meet the arbitration and storage requirements specified in the API exposed by the Microsoft Software Development Kit. Let's now look at some deployment scenarios.

Deployment Scenarios

Let's discuss some example deployment schemes, namely the *n*-node fail-over scheme, the fail-over ring scheme, and the hot-standby server scheme.

In the *n*-node fail-over scheme you deploy applications that are setup to be moved to a passive node when the primary node on a 2-node cluster fails. In this configuration, you limit the possible owners for each resource group. You will see how we do this in Part II of this book.

Let's consider the so-called N+I hot-standby server scheme. Here you reduce the overhead of the 2-node failover by adding a "spare" node (one for each cluster pair) to the cluster. This provides a so-called "hot-standby" server that is part and parcel of the cluster and equally capable of running the applications from each node pair in the event of a failure of both of the other nodes. Both of these solutions are called active/passive clusters—*n*-node and *n*-node+1 (or N+1).

As you create the N+1 mode cluster, you will discover it is a simple matter to configure as the spare node. How you use a combination of the preferred owners lists and the possible owners list depends on your application. You typically set the preferred node to the node that the application runs on by default; and you set the possible owners for a given resource group to the preferred node and the spare node.

Then there is the concept of a *Failover Ring*. Here you set up each node in the cluster to run an application instance. Let's assume we have an instance of SQL Server on each node of the cluster. In the event of a failure, the SQL Server on the failed node is moved to the next node in sequence. Actually, an instance of SQL Server is installed on every server. Fail-over simply activates the SQL Server instance, and it takes control of the databases stored on the SAN or SCSI array. We call this the Active-Active cluster.

You can also allow the server cluster to choose the failover node at random. You can do this with large clusters and you'll just not define a preferred owners list for the resource groups. In other words, each resource group that has an empty preferred owners list is failed over to any node in random fashion in the event that the node currently hosting that group fails.

We will leave the clustering subject now and return to the creation of the infrastructure to support our clusters.

Forest Creation Process

Assuming we are starting from scratch, a so-called green fields site, we must first create a forest into which your systems will be integrated. This is called the forest creation process. This is the process that starts with the provisioning of an installation server through the creation of the forest.

Installation of Support Server

The first server installed in your network, you may be surprised to know, is not a domain controller. It is not even a new server. It should be a non-service server installed with either Windows 2000 or Windows Server 2003 in its own workgroup. This server is placed on the lab or future production subnet, initially as a workgroup server, and exposes a number of shares used for accessing operating systems, tools, software, utilities, and patches. The idea is to provide a secure, closed network that does not have access to the outside network that might likely contaminate your implementation. The support server is used for patches, access to tools, resource kits, and so on.

It is critical at this stage that none of your new servers "touch" the Internet or are exposed to the outside. It is very easy to "catch" a virus and not notice it until the entire forest is created and all your servers start croaking.

This server is eventually joined to the network as a temporary *Windows Update Server* (WUS). The server may also function as a temporary DHCP server. To configure the support server, do as follows:

1. Log on to support server as Administrator while this server is still in the lab.
2. Create a folder named C:\ADSTUFF and share as ADSTUFF (actually any name will do).
3. Create a folder named C:\ADSTUFF\Adminpak\.
4. Create a folder named C:\ADSTUFF\Support\.
5. Create a folder named C:\ADSTUFF\Exchange Tools\.
6. Create a folder named C:\ADSTUFF\SQL Server Tools\.
7. Create a folder named C:\ADSTUFF\QA documents\.
8. Crate a folder named C:\ADSTUFF\Scripts\.
9. Create a folder named C:\ADSTUFF\RKTools\.
10. Copy needed tools, MSI files, scripts, data, packages, and so on to these folders.
11. Install anti-virus services and make sure the support server has the latest anti-virus DAT files and is performing the correct scans of its file system.
12. Install Software Update Services Software Update Services on the support server.

13. If needed, create distribution folders for operating system images. You can call the shares STDINST for the Windows Server 2003 Standard Edition or ENTINST for the Windows Server 2003 Enterprise Edition operating system.
14. If needed, create the distribution folders named C:\WEBINST and share as WEBINST for the Windows Server 2003 Web Edition operating system.
15. If needed, create the distribution folders named C:\XPINST and share as XPINST for the XP workstation images.
16. Create distribution shares (for example, C:\..\I386) and copy installation sub-folders and files to the distribution shares (see Table 6.2). This process can be done automatically using the Setup manager utility (setupmgr.exe) on the operating system CD's Support, Tools folder. Setupmgr is found in the deploy.cab file.
17. Configure Software Update Services on the installation.
18. Validate this server (including last scan for anti-virus).

Table 6.2 Example Configuration of Support Server

Item	Description
Server Name	SHQPSERVER
Server IP address	10.10.20.6
W2K3 STD install share	STDINST
W2K3 ENT install share	ENTINST
AD/W2K3 Tools	\..\ADSTUFF
Server Administrator account	Administrator (local machine)
Password	(see your specs)

With the support server in place on your isolated network, you can begin working on the creation of the forest and the domains, accessing your server for support materials as if it were your own mini Microsoft.com Web site.

Installation

Upon installation of the support server to the isolated network, proceed to the installation procedures.

1. Rack and stack your servers in the production racks or on the data center floor with access to the isolated network.
2. Power up the support/installation server.
3. Log on to the installation server as Administrator on the isolated subnet.
4. Reset the Administrator password.
5. Change the IP configuration to statically assigned addressing.
6. Assign the IP address of 10.10.20.23 (on a /22 subnet where the 10.10.20.0 space is reserved for the data center servers).
7. Assign the same IP address as the gateway and DNS.
8. Install DHCP and configure the new scope for the subnet (see Table 6.3).

At this point, the installation and provisioning of the support server is complete.

Table 6.3 Example Configuration of DHCP on the Support Server

Scope	Split	Excluded Range	Default Gateway	CIDR	WINS	DDNS
10.10.20.0 to 10.10.20.254	NA	10.10.20.1 to 10.10.20.20	NA	/22	10.10.20.23	10.10.20.23

After the DHCP server has been installed on the support server, reserve IP addresses for the root domain controllers. This ensures the root DCs obtain the correct IP addresses as soon as their IP configuration is changed from static addressing to DHCP-assigned.

One note to consider before we move on: The subnet we have used here will provide sufficient addresses to meet the needs of a high availabilty network. Don't short change yourself with IP addresses. You should be good to go with a subnet that provides more than a thousand

IP addresses. High availability systems use a lot of IP addresses. A typical two-node cluster should be allocated a block of about 24 addresses for future expansion.

Installation of Root Domain

This section covers the promotion of the root domain controllers. By promoting root domain controllers, we are, in fact, creating the forest in which all future high-availability systems will be installed (see Chapter 5 for the discussion of the dual domain [root-and-child] model). The prerequisite to this process is installation of the operating system (Windows Server 2003, Standard Edition) to the domain controller computers on a RAID-1 array. See Chapter 4 for instructions on the configuration of RAID-1 on this server. The servers should be configured for second and third RAID-5 arrays as required.

It is critical this process completes and proceeds as described herein. Deviation from the process or shortcuts may render the root domain useless and it will have to be rebuilt. The updating of the domain controller servers with the required software updates and security patches can take place after promotion, QA, and validation. (See Chapter 5 for the overall architecture this implementation supports.)

Process

Name the Root Domain DCs. Upon completion of the server installations, the root domain controllers will be given miscellaneous names, and they will be a member of the workgroup setup on the support server. Change the names of the root domain controllers to the names provided in your Active Directory Architecture (discussed in Chapter 5). For the corporate hub, the server names we use here are HQRDC01 and HQRDC02 (for later implementation).

It is important to remember to rename the servers to their DC names prior to running DC promo. The names cannot be changed after promotion of these servers to domain controllers, and they have to be destroyed if the names are incorrect. Do not change the workgroup when changing the names.

Configure TCP/IP on HQRDC01. Log on as Administrator to the server designated to become the root DC (HQRDC01). Open the

TCP/IP properties of the network interface card (NIC), and enter the parameters listed in Table 6.4.

Table 6.4   TCP/IP Configuration on HQRDC01 Support Server

Resources (RDC01)	Configuration
IP	10.10.20.21
Subnet Mask	255.255.252.0
Default Gateway	10.10.20.1
Preferred DNS	10.10.20.21
Alternate	<null>

Configure TCP/IP on HQRDC02. Log on as Administrator to the server designated to become the root DC (RDC02). Open the TCP/IP properties of the NIC, and enter the parameters listed in Table 6.5.

Table 6.5   TCP/IP Configuration on UVRDC02 Support Server

Resources (HQRDC02)	Configuration
IP	10.10.20.24
Subnet Mask	255.255.252.0
Default Gateway	10.10.20.1
Preferred DNS	10.10.20.24
Alternate	<null>

To install DNS, do as follows:

1. Log on as Administrator to the server designated to become the root DC (HQRDC01) and install DNS on this server. This is achieved by opening Control Panel, Add or Remove Programs, and Add/Remove Windows Components. This launches the Windows Components Wizard.

2. Select Networking Services in the wizard and click the Details button. In the Networking Services dialog box, check the option to install Domain Name System (DNS).

3. Complete the procedures and, when prompted by the installation procedure for the Windows Server operating system CD, provide a CD or browse to the I386 folder under the STDINST share (the source for OS installation files) on the installation or support server.

4. Complete the process to install DNS on the server. Repeat the process for all hub root domain controllers.

Now you can create the Forest Root Zone on HQRDC01. To create the forest root zone, perform the following steps (note: this process is not repeated on HQRDC02 or any other root server destined to become a DC):

1. Start DNS and right-click on the HQRDC01 icon.

2. Select New Zone. The New Zone Wizard launches. Click Next.

3. Select the option to create a Primary zone and click Next.

4. Select Forward Lookup zone and click Next.

5. Enter the domain name (such as MCITY.CTY) as the name of the zone and click Next.

6. Keep the default DNS file name (it should be MCITY.CTY. dns) for the zone file name and click Next.

7. If prompted for Dynamic Update configuration, choose the option to allow Dynamic Updates. Click Next.

8. Complete the process by selecting Finish.

Create the Reverse Lookup Zone on HQRDC01. To create the reverse lookup zone for the forest, perform the following steps:

1. Open the DNS console and expand the HQRDC01 server icon.

2. Select Reverse Lookup Zones and click on New Zone. The New Zone Wizard launches.

3. Select options for a Primary non-integrated zone and click Next.

4. Enter the IP address range for the zone; this is the 10.10.20.X network.

5. Click Next and select the options to enable dynamic update.

6. Complete the process by selecting Finish.

Create the Forest Root Domain Controller on HQRDC01. To create the forest root domain, perform the following steps:

1. Click Start, Run, and type **DCPROMO** on HQRDC01.
2. Choose the options for creating a root domain controller in a new forest.
3. Choose the root domain name as the full DNS name for the new domain (MCITY.CTY).
4. Accept the default NetBIOS name for the domain.
5. Choose the default path for the SYSVOL folder on the RAID-5 array. However, the drive letter should point to the RAID-5 array on (D, E, or F) and not C:\ (for example E:\Windows\...). Choose the path options provided for the NTDS Active Directory database and its log files, changing only the drive letters to point to the RAID 5.
6. Accept permissions compatible with Windows 2000 and Windows Server 2003.
7. Enter the Directory Services Restore Mode Administrator password (this should be a complex password, choose something like 4NTDS@mcity), ignoring the quotes. (Remember the server's local Administrator password becomes the password required to log on to the DC after promotion.)

Review the settings, and click Finish to begin the process. Restart the server when prompted.

Enable Active Directory Integration of the Forest Root Zone and the Reverse Lookup Zone. To enable AD integration for the root zone, do as follows:

1. Open the DNS console and expand the root server HQRDC01 icon.
2. Expand the Forward Lookup Zones folder and select the MCITY.CTY zone. Right-click this zone and select Properties.
3. The Properties dialog box for MCITY opens. On the General tab, select the Change button on the Type option. The Change Zone Type dialog box launches.
4. Select the option to change the zone to Active Directory Integrated and click OK.

Perform the same procedure on the Reverse Lookup Zone folder. Verify HQRDC01 Name Registration. To verify name registration, perform the following actions:

1. Open the DNS console and expand the root server HQRDC01 icon.
2. Expand the Forward Lookup Zones folder and select the MCITY.CTY zone.
3. Verify whether _msdcs, _sites, _tcp, and _udp sub-domains are registered under MCITY.CTY.
4. If these sub-domains are not registered, then start a command prompt and type **NET STOP NETLOGON**. Wait for the service to stop and then type **NET START NETLOGON**.
5. Repeat steps 1 through 3 to verify the registration.
6. Verify the Reverse Lookup Zone has replicated.

Verify DNS name resolution on HQRDC02. Before HQRDC02 can be promoted as a root DC, DNS first must be verified. This can be achieved as follows:

1. Log on to HQRDC02 as the Administrator.
2. Open the command prompt and type **NSLOOKUP MCITY. CTY** and press Enter. You should see the following result:
   C:\>nslookup MCITY.CTY
   Server: HQRDC01.MCITY.CTY
   Address: 10.10.20.21
   Name: MCITY.CTY
   Address: 10.10.20.21

If you do not see this, check to see whether the IP settings on HQRDC02 are correct. It should have HQRDC01 (10.10.20.21) as its preferred DNS server. Do not proceed with DCPROMO of HQRDC02 until DNS is working properly.

Perform DCPROMO on the server HQRDC02. To create the second domain controller, perform the following steps:

1. Click Start, Run, and type **DCPROMO** on HQRDC02.
2. Choose the options for creating an additional domain controller for an existing domain and click Next.

3. You are prompted for access to the root domain. Choose the Administrator account because this account has Enterprise Administrator credentials. See the previous steps for account and password information.
4. Choose the default path for the SYSVOL folder on the RAID-5 array. However, the drive letter should point to the RAID-5 array on (D, E, or F) and not C:\. Choose the path options provided for the NTDS Active Directory database and its log files, changing only the drive letters to point to the RAID 5 volume as previously mentioned (see Chapter 4).
5. Enter the Directory Services Restore Mode Administrator password for this server (this should be a complex password; choose 4NTDS@MCITY). DCs can and should have the same Directory Services Restore Mode Administrator password to simplify administration.

Review the settings and then click Finish to begin the process. Restart the server when prompted. Verify HQRDC02 Name Registration. To verify name registration, perform the following actions:

1. Open the DNS console and expand the root server HQRDC02 icon.
2. Expand the Forward Lookup Zones folder and select the MCITY.CTY zone.
3. Verify whether _msdcs, _sites, _tcp, and _udp sub-domains are registered under MCITY.CTY.
4. If the sub-domains are not registered, then start a command prompt and type **NET STOP NETLOGON**. Wait for the service to stop and then type **NET START NETLOGON**.
5. Repeat steps 1 through 3 to verify the registration.

Verify the Reverse Lookup Zone has replicated. Update the Preferred DNS Parameters on HQRDC01. Log on to HQRDC01 and open the TCP/IP properties for the NIC. Change the preferred DNS server from 10.10.20.21 to 10.10.20.24.

Create *Automated System Recovery* (ASR) media for the domain controllers. The creation of the root domain and promotion of the first domain controllers is now complete. System recovery using ASR media now must be performed on the domain controllers. After the ASR disks have been created, you can start the QA discussed in the next section.

Quality Assurance

QA and validation must be performed before continuing further. QA can be achieved by following these steps:

1. Join a clean Windows XP SP1, SP2, or higher workstation to the root domain. Remember to follow the naming convention for the workstation according to Active Directory Architecture.

2. Install the WSO3 support tools on the workstation. The tools can be accessed from the ADSTUFF\SHQPORT\TOOLS share on the installation server. Install the tools to the default path on the C: drive.

3. Install the ADMINPAK on the workstation. This installs management tools, such as DSA.MSC, to the workstation. The tools can be accessed from the ADSTUFF\ADMINPAK share on the installation server. Install the tools to the default path on the C: drive.

4. Install the Resource Kit tools to the workstation. This installs tools, such as DNSDIAG, DCDIAG, and DSQUERY to the workstation. The tools can be accessed from the ADSTUFF\RESKIT share on the installation server. Install the tools to the default path on the C: drive.

5. Open a command console and run DCDIAG /s:<domain controller name> /a /f<logfile> /ferr<errlogfile>. Perform the DCDIAG against both HQRDC01 and HQRDC02. The data generated by DCDIAG is piped to the default log file location on the workstation.

6. Perform DCDIAG several times a day during the installation.

7. Open the replication monitor and check that replication is occurring without errors between the domain controllers.

Finally, you can run DSQUERY against the domain controllers to see that all FSMO roles are intact (the roles are moved later on in the implementation). Much of this manual diagnostics and QA can be left to Microsoft Operations Manager (MOM) to handle. Without MOM, QA can become something of an endurance during the life of a long project to stand-up a high availability infrastructure.

Forest Preparation, DNS, and Exchange

This section covers the preparation of the forest for the addition of Exchange 2003 and the creation of a child domain. Before the child domain can be created, the schema is extended in the forest root to cater to the addition of domains and the installation of Exchange 2003 into the forest. All activities in the root domain on the domain controllers are done using the root domain's Administrator account. In addition, we prepare the first site and associate it with the new subnet and perform some housekeeping. The process of preparing the forest is outlined as follows.

Move Domain Operations Master Roles. HQRDC01 is a GC server and also holds schema and domain naming operations. It is important to move the domain operations roles to HQRDC02.

1. Start Active Directory User and Computers on HQRDC01.
2. Right-click the root node and select Connect to Domain Controller. Choose HQRDC02 and click OK. You are now on RDC02.
3. Right-click the MCITY.CTY domain and select Operations Masters.
4. The RID Master Role appears first. Select Change to move it to HQRDC02. You are able to select the target computer from a list if necessary.
5. Click Yes to confirm the transfer.

Repeat these steps for the PDC Emulator and Infrastructure Master roles.

Configure DNS Forwarders. We cannot leave the DNS Servers in the root domain as root servers because they assume they have root authority and users are unable to resolve addresses in the external namespaces the county owns and on the Internet. To add DNS forwarding, we first have to delete the root DNS zone (if it exists) and add DNS forwarder addresses. This is done as follows:

1. Right-click the "." folder under the Forward Lookup Zones and select Delete.
2. Right-click the DNS Server name HQRDC01 and select Refresh.

3. Right-click the server name again and select Properties. Click the Forwarders tab and check the Enable Forwarders check box.

4. Enter the IP addresses of the external, private DNS server (primary and alternate) for MCITY.CTY (most likely these are your external domain's ISP) and click Add. (The addresses of these servers are usually obtained from the Datacom or Network Group in your enterprise.)

When all addresses are entered, click OK to close the dialog box.

Perform ASR backups of the root domains controllers.

Verify Credentials of the root domain's Administrator Account. Before continuing with schema changes, it is worthwhile to confirm the credentials of the Administrator because, at this stage, no other account has the rights needed to perform forest operations:

1. Open Active Directory User and Computers (DSA.MSC) and expand the Users folder.

2. Double-click the Enterprise Admins group and verify whether the Administrator account is present. Add the account if it is not.

3. Perform the same verification on the Schema Admins group. If Administrator is not present, then add the account. Close down the DSA.

4. Prepare the forest for Exchange 2003. This process requires the Exchange 2003 Installation CD.

5. Insert the CD into the drive. If the Exchange installation process boots, then close it down.

6. Open the command prompt on HQRDC01 and enter the following command: **<CDDRIVE>:\setup.exe /ForestPrep**. During ForestPrep, you are prompted for the account for the Full Exchange Administrator. Use only the MCITY\Administrator account (which can be removed later).

7. When the ForestPrep completes, remove the Exchange CD and check for any errors in the event logs. Report any errors related to ForestPrep for review and copy the ForestPrep progress log files to the Service Admin workstation. (It is important that the DC on which you perform this can "see" the DC that has the Schema Master role, otherwise ForestPrep will fail.)

8. Allow root domain controllers enough time to replicate the changes made before moving onto the next step. Never rush into the next step, and if possible give your new domain at least 12

hours before continuing. You can check to see whether the schema additions have replicated by confirming the presence of the exchange object in ADSI Edit. Connect ADSI Edit to both domain controllers. They should both show the exchange objects in the Configuration container.

9. Review DCDIAG results during the replication cycle as previously described.

Change the Default-First-Site-Name. This step takes place after all forest changes have replicated and DCDIAG results are normal. To do this, do the following:

1. Start Active Directory Sites and Services.
2. Expand Sites.
3. Right-click Default-First-Site-Name and select Rename. Enter HQ (corporate headquarters).
4. Do not close down the console.
5. Add the Subnet Associated with the Site. In this step, we add the subnet and mask associated with HQ.
6. With the console still open, right-click the Subnets folder and select New Subnet.
7. Enter the Network ID (10.10.20.0) for the subnet associated with HQ (you need to select HQ in the sites list).
8. Click OK and close the console.
9. Perform QA.
10. Create new ASR media.

You are now ready to move on to a child domain.

Installation of Bridgehead Servers and the Child Domain

This section outlines the steps required to build the bridgehead servers for the main hub site (HQ) and promote the domain controllers into the child domain AD.MCITY.CTY. The process is outlined in the next section. You typically do not need to specifically set up bridgehead servers on small domains (with less than 100 domain controllers).

The first procedure to perform on the bridgehead or sub-domain controllers is the configuration of DNS, particularly forwarding. The process is similar to the configuration of DNS in the root domain.

1. **Name the Child Domain DCs:** Upon completion of the server installations, the child domain controllers are given miscellaneous names, and they are a member of the workgroup created when you installed the support server. Change the names of the child domain controllers to the names provided in your Active Directory Architecture. For the HQ hub, the server names are HQSDC01 and HQSDC02. It is important to remember to rename the servers to their DC names prior to running DC promo. The names cannot be changed after promotion of these servers to domain controllers, and they have to be destroyed if the names are incorrect. Do not change the workgroup when changing the names.
2. **Configure TCP/IP on HQSDC01:** Log on to the server designated to be promoted first (HQSDC01) as Administrator. Open the TCP/IP properties of the NIC and enter the parameters listed in Table 6.6.

Table 6.6 TCP/IP Configuration of SDC01 Domain Controller

Resources (SDC01)	Configuration
IP	10.10.20.27
Subnet Mask	255.255.252.0
Default Gateway	10.10.20.1
Preferred DNS	10.10.20.27
Alternate	10.10.20.30

3. **Configure TCP/IP on HQSDC02:** Log on to the server designated to become the second DC to be promoted (HQSDC01) as Administrator. Open the TCP/IP properties of the NIC and enter the parameters listed in Table 6.7.

Table 6.7   TCP/IP Configuration of SDC02 Domain Controller

Resources (SDC01)	Configuration
IP	10.10.20.30
Subnet Mask	255.255.252.0
Default Gateway	10.10.20.1
Preferred DNS	10.10.20.30
Alternate	10.10.20.27

4. **Install DNS:** Log on as Administrator to the server designated to be promoted first (HQSDC01), and install DNS on this server. This is achieved by opening Control Panel, Add or Remove Programs, and Add/Remove Windows Components; this launches the Windows Components Wizard. Select Networking Services in the wizard and click the Details button. In the Networking Services Dialog box, check the option to install DNS. Complete the procedures and, when prompted by the installation procedure for the Windows Server operating system CD, provide a CD or browse to the I386 folder under the STDINST share on the installation server.

5. **Complete the install:** Finish the process of installing DNS on the server. Repeat the process for all hub child domain controllers (prior to promotion).

Configure Forwarding. Log on as Administrator to the server designated to be promoted first domain controller (HQSDC01), and open the DNS console to configure forwarding:

1. Right-click the server name and select Properties.
2. Select the Forwarders tab.
3. Check the option Enable Forwarders.
4. Enter the IP addresses for the forest root servers, HQRDC01, HQRDC02, and DRRDC01 (the root domain controller at the DR site).
5. Check the option Do Not Use Recursion.
6. Click Apply and close the DNS console.

7. Verify forwarding by performing a NSLOOKUP on AD.MCITY. CTY. The lookup should fail because the zone for the AD domain is not yet created. However, you should see whether the query correctly forwarded to one of the root DCs. If you get a timeout on the request, then forwarding is not set up correctly. Check the forwarder settings and, if you are still getting a time-out, go down to the network layer and make sure the child DCs can ping the root DCs.

Repeat these steps on all child domain controllers.

Delegate the AD DNS domain to HQSDC01. To delegate the child domain, you need to open the DNS console on the root DC HQRDC01. This can be achieved by opening the DNS console on the service admin workstation that has an account in the root domain:

1. Select the MCITY.CTY domain and right-click. Select New Delegation. The New Delegation Wizard launches. Click Next.
2. In the Delegated domain field, enter the name of the domain to be delegated, namely AS (the FQDN is, thus, AD.MCITY.CTY). Click Next.
3. On the Name Servers page, click Add. This lets you enter the name of the DNS server that hosts the sub-domain. Enter the FQDN of the server in the server FQDN field and attempt to resolve the IP address of the server. If you cannot resolve the name (which is likely to be the case at this point), then enter the known IP address for the HQSDC01 server. Click OK and then click Next.
4. Click Finish to create the delegation.

Create the DNS zone on HQSDC01. To create the primary DNS zone for AD, perform the following steps (this process is *not* repeated on HQSDC02 or any other server destined to become a DC in the HQ hub):

1. Start DNS and right-click the HQSDC01 icon.
2. Select New Zone. The New Zone Wizard launches. Click Next.
3. Select the option to create a standard Primary zone and click Next.
4. Select Forward Lookup zone and click Next.
5. Enter **AD.MCITY.CTY** as the name of the zone and click Next.

6. Keep the default DNS file name (it should be AD.MCITY.CTY.dns) for the zone file name, and click Next.

7. If prompted for Dynamic Update configuration, choose the option to allow dynamic updates. Click Next.

8. Complete the process by selecting Finish.

Create the Child Domain Controller and Domain on HQSDC01. To create the child domain, perform the following steps:

1. Click Start, Run, and type **DCPROMO** on HQSDC01.

2. Choose the options for creating a domain controller for a new domain; that is, select the domain controller for a new domain option. Click Next.

3. Select the option Create a New Child Domain in an Existing Domain Tree, and then click Next.

4. Enter the Enterprise Administrator credentials (MCITY\ Administrator), and in the Domain box, enter **AD.MCITY.CTY**.

5. Provide MCITY.CTY as the parent domain.

6. Enter AD as the child domain and click Next.

7. Click Next to accept the default NetBIOS name AD.

8. Choose the default path for the SYSVOL folder on the RAID-5 array. However, the drive letter should point to the RAID-5 array on (D, E, or F) and not C:\ (for example, E:\Windows\...). Choose the path options provided for the NTDS Active Directory database and its log files, changing only the drive letters to point to the RAID 5 volume as previously mentioned (see Chapter 4).

9. Click OK if you receive a message indicating the DNS server for the domain was not found. This occurs if there is no A record for the domain yet.

10. Accept permissions compatible with Windows 2000 and Windows Server 2003.

11. Enter the Directory Services Restore Mode Administrator password (this should be a complex password, so choose something like 4NTDS@ MCITY). Remember the server's local Administrator password becomes the password required to log on to the DC after promotion.

Review the settings and click Finish to begin the process. Restart the server when prompted. Enable Active Directory Integration of the AD Zone. To enable Active Directory integration for the zone, do as follows:

1. Open the DNS console and expand the root server HQSDC01 icon.
2. Expand the Forward Lookup Zones folder and select the HQ. MCITY.CTY zone. Right-click this zone and select Properties.
3. The Properties dialog box for AD opens. On the General tab, select the Change button on the Type option. The Change Zone Type dialog box launches.
4. Select the option to change the zone to Active Directory Integrated and click OK.

Verify HQSDC01 Name Registration. To verify name registration, perform the following actions:

1. Open the DNS console and expand the root server HQSDC01 icon.
2. Expand the Forward Lookup Zones folder and select the AD.MCITY.CTY zone.
3. Verify whether _msdcs, _sites, _tcp, and _udp sub-domains are registered under AD.MCITY.CTY.
4. If these sub-domains are not registered, then start a command prompt and type **NET STOP NETLOGON**. Wait for the service to stop and then type **NET START NETLOGON**.
5. Repeat steps 1 through 3 to verify the registration.

Verify DNS name resolution on HQRDC02. Before HQSDC02 can be promoted as an additional child DC, DNS first must be verified. This can be achieved as follows:

1. Log on to HQSDC02 as the Administrator.
2. Open the command prompt and type **NSLOOKUP AD.MCITY.CTY** and press Enter. You should see a resolution to AD.MCITY.CTY from 10.10.20.27.

If you are not able to resolve the domain, check to see whether the IP settings on HQSDC02 are correct. It should have 10.10.20.30 as its preferred DNS server address and 10.10.20.27 as the alternate. Do not proceed with the DCPROMO of HQSDC02 until DNS is working properly. DCPROMO the HQSDC02 server. To create the second domain controller, perform the following steps:

1. Click Start, Run, and type **DCPROMO** on HQSDC02.
2. Choose the options for creating an additional domain controller for an existing domain and click Next.
3. You are prompted for access to the child domain. Choose the Administrator account for AD. The Administrator password is the same as the server password before the DC was promoted.
4. Choose the default path for the SYSVOL folder on the RAID-5 array. However, the drive letter should point to the RAID-5 array on (D, E, or F) and not C:\. Choose the path options provided for the NTDS Active Directory database and its log files, changing only the drive letters to point to the RAID 5 volume as previously mentioned (see Chapter 4).
5. Enter the Directory Services Restore Mode Administrator password for this server (this should be a complex password; choose 4NTDS@MCITY). DCs can and should have the same Directory Services Restore Mode Administrator password to simplify administration.

Review the settings and then click Finish to begin the process. Restart the server when prompted. Verify HQSDC02 Name Registration. To verify name registration, perform the following actions:

1. Open the DNS console and expand the root server HQSDC02 icon.
2. Expand the Forward Lookup Zones folder and select the AD.MCITY.CTY zone.
3. Verify whether _msdcs, _sites, _tcp, and _udp sub-domains are registered under MCITY.CTY.
4. If these sub-domains are not registered, then start a command prompt and type **NET STOP NETLOGON**. Wait for the service to stop, and then type **NET START NETLOGON**.
5. Repeat steps 1 through 3 to verify the registration.

Move the Domain Operations Master Roles. HQSDC01 is a GC server and becomes the preferred bridgehead server (Active Directory does this automatically in Windows Server 2003). To lessen the load on this server, the RID operations master needs to be moved to HQSDC02. We also should move the IF and PDC roles to HQSDC02.

1. Start Active Directory User and Computers on HQSDC01.
2. Right-click the root node and select Connect to Domain Controller. Choose HQSDC02 and click OK. You are now on HQRSC02.
3. Right-click the AD.MCITY.CTY domain and select Operations Masters.
4. The RID Master Role appears first. Select Change to move it to HQSDC02. You are able to select the target computer from a list if necessary.
5. Click Yes to confirm the transfer.

Repeat these steps for the PDC Emulator and IF roles. Create ASR media for the Domain Controllers. The creation of the child domain and its controllers is now complete. System recovery using ASR media now must be performed on the domain controllers.

Quality Assurance and validation must be performed before continuing further. QA can be achieved by following these steps:

1. Open a command console and run DCDIAG /s:<domain controller name> /a /f<logfile> /ferr<errlogfile>. Perform the DCDIAG against both HQSDC01 and HQSDC02. The data generated by DCDIAG is piped to the default log file location on the workstation.
2. Perform DCDIAG several times a day and run DCDIAG at the enterprise level.
3. Open the replication monitor REPLMON, and check to see whether replication is occurring without errors between the domain controllers. You also can use REPADMIN to check the update vectors and force replication between the replication partners.
4. Finally, you can run DSQUERY against the domain controllers to see that all FSMO roles are intact.

Also, load the replication monitor and ensure infrastructure changes between the domains are replicating. (See Chapter 13 on using MOM for alerts and monitoring.) The Windows Server 2003 replication service (FRS) Management Pack can get this going for your in no time flat.

Installing DHCP and WINS Services

This section covers installing the DHCP and WINS services on the sub-domain controllers. These services are essential to support the client network so they do not have any problem accessing the client network. In this process, we first install the services for both DHCP and WINS, and then we configure them to provide the required services. For the time being, we only configure the DHCP servers to service the 10.10.20.0 subnet and import the scopes from the legacy DHCP servers (should we need to) after the implementation is released to production.

The process of installing the DHCP and WINS service is as follows:

1. While keeping the standby DHCP server going, provide a static IP address for HQSDC01 and HQSDC02. These addresses can be the ones that were originally assigned these servers during the creation of the sub-domain. Notice that we are not going to install DHCP on the root domain controllers. Ensure that these addresses cannot be obtained by other clients on the network. This is achieved by reserving a range of IP addresses for static assignment.

2. Install the DHCP and WINS service from the Windows Components facility on both HQSDC01 and HQSDC02. The files required for the installation can be obtained from the \STDINST\i386 directory on the installation server we discussed at the beginning of this chapter.

3. Upon completion of the installation of the DHCP servers, authorize both servers in Active Directory. This can be done in the root domain using the DHCP console. Log on to the root domain as the Administrator. This operation requires Enterprise Administrator credentials, which the root Administrator has.

4. On HQSDC01 only, create a scope called "Server Subnet" with the parameters listed in Table 6.8. Upon creation of the scope, ensure the scope is deactivated (the default upon creation is deactivated). To deactivate the scope, right-click the scope name and select Deactivate.

Table 6.8 DHCP Server Settings

Parameter	Value
Scope Name	Server subnet (for example, 10.10.20.0)
Scope	10.10.20.1 to 10.10.22.254
Exclusion	10.10.20.1 to 10.10.20.41
003 Router	10.10.20.1
015 DNS Server	10.10.20.27, 10.10.20.30
044 WINS/NBNS Servers	10.10.20.27, 10.10.20.30
015 DNS Domain Name	AD.MCITY.CTY
046 WINS/NBT Node Type	0x08

As soon as the scope has been configured according to the values in Table 6.8, you can deactivate and stop the DHCP service on the installation server. After this service is offline, you can activate the scope on HQSDC01. First, however, you should create the superscope as outlined here:

1. To create the superscope, select the server icon (HQSDC01) and right-click.
2. Select New Superscope and click Next.
3. Provide a name for the superscope. You can name it something like HQ on HQSDC01. Click Next (do not add the word "Superscope" to the name because Windows adds it anyway).
4. Add the HQ scopes this server is hosting to the superscope.
5. Click Next and then Finish to create the superscope.

At this point, there are no other scopes to configure on the server. There is also no WINS server configuration required at this time. However, after setting up the DHCP servers, DHCP server HQSDC02 must be configured to offer the legacy scopes that might be migrated from any legacy DHCP servers on a preexisting network. To migrate the scopes (from a Windows 2000 or Server 2003 machine), you need to export the

DHCP settings from the legacy server that is being replaced by HQSDC02. This can be achieved as follows:

1. Run DhcpExim.exe (this tool is available on the CD that accompanies the Windows Server 2003 Deployment Kit; it can also be downloaded from Microsoft) against the DHCP server from which you are exporting.
2. In the DhcpExim dialog box that loads, select the option Export Configuration of the Local Service to a File.
3. In the DHCPEXIM Export to a File dialog box, enter the file name and location to save the file, then click OK.
4. In the DhcpExim Export dialog box, select all the scopes on the list to migrate; ensure you select to migrate all the settings on the server. Do not select the Disable the Selected Scopes on the Local Machine Before Export option because the scopes are needed to continue service for a few weeks after the export.
5. Click OK and wait for the message "The operation was completed successfully."
6. Copy the exported file to media that can be installed onto the installation server on the isolated 10.10.20.0 network. You cannot download the setting through any network connection between the old DHCP server and the new one.
7. To import the settings into HQSDC02 where the second DHCP server is running, open the command console and enter the command **netsh DHCP server import <path to export file> all**.

Confirm the import of the scopes into the HQSDC02 and then place them under the superscope called Legacy for HQ site, creating the superscope as demonstrated earlier. For WINS, ensure the WINS services are installed on both child domain controllers; however, only activate the WINS server on the DC that is not holding the PDC role. Ensure the superscope is deactivated until needed.

Patching and Updating Domain Controllers

Before continuing to configure any further services in the root domain, the root domain controllers should be patched and updated from the makeshift Windows Update Server (WUS). By installing WUS (or its predecessor *Software Update Services [SUS]*)on the isolated network, all servers in the isolated network can pull down updates and patches to bring them to the latest patch level and to ensure that critical software updates, especially security updates, are applied.

The process of ensuring all root domain servers are regularly updated while being staged on the isolated network is as follows:

1. Create a new group policy object at the domain level (root and child domains).
2. Call the policy SoftwareUpdatePolicy.

This GPO is created so the policy can persist after security templates and group policy are imported into the default domain policy later in the installation process.

After the policy is configured, all Windows 2003 Server, Windows 2000 Server SP3 and later, and all Windows XP clients are serviced by the SUS server.

WUS is beyond the scope of this book, but it is critical in the maintenance of a high availabilty network. Microsoft publishes excellent white papers on update services. They can be accessed on the Microsoft Web site (simply search for SUS or WUS).

Exchange Domain Preparation

This section covers the preparation of the child domain for the addition of Exchange 2003. This process entails running the /DomainPrep switch using Exchange setup.exe, similarly to what was performed during the /ForestPrep process. The domain preparation creates the groups and permissions in Active Directory necessary for Exchange operation. Domain prep also creates several folders and performs a variety of tasks needed to install Exchange 2003 into the domain. Obviously you cannot install an Exchange cluster like we will do in Chapter 10 until this process is complete.

Prepare the domain for Exchange 2003. This process requires the Exchange 2003 Installation CD as is described as follows:

1. Log in as Administrator to the *primary domain controller* (PDC) emulator in the child- or sub-domain. Domain Admin credentials are needed for this process. The account does not need

Enterprise Administrator or Schema Administrator credentials; therefore, in this process, AD\Administrator will do.

2. Insert the CD and, if the Exchange installation process boots, then close it down.

3. Open to the command prompt on the PDC DC and enter the following command: **<CDDRIVE>:\setup\i386\setup.exe /DomainPrep**.

4. When the DomainPrep completes, remove the Exchange CD and check for any errors in the event logs. Report any errors related to the process for review and copy the DomainPrep progress log files to the Service Admin workstation. Reboot the DC if required.

5. Allow root domain controllers to replicate the changes made before moving onto the next step.

Review DCDIAG results during the replication cycle in Step 4. (See also Chapter 13 on deploying Microsoft Operations Manager for monitoring Exchange.)

Creation of Initial Service and Administration Resources

This section covers the creation of the initial service and administration accounts and services. These accounts and resources are created before security and group policy are applied to the domain and forest. The resources are needed to flesh out the core servers and services of the Windows Server 2003 network and Active Directory.

The process of installing these services is outlined in Figure 6.4.

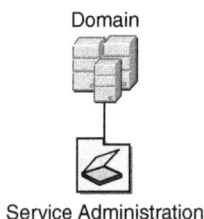

Figure 6.4   Creating Service and Administration Resources.

To create the necessary services, do as follows:

1. Create a Tier 1 OU called Service Administration.
2. Create three child OUs under Service Administration called Users, Computers, and Groups.
3. Select the Users OU, right-click and select New and then select User.
4. In the New Object – User dialog box, enter the first and last name of the user (for example, Mickey Mouse).
5. In the Full Name edit field, follow the guidelines in your Active Directory Architecture for service and administration accounts (make sure the logon account name is the same as the Full Name field).
6. Enter the password provided and then follow the password reset guidelines for the service accounts.
7. Select Finish and create the account.

After the account is created, open the account and provide it the appropriate group membership. Create more of the same account using the Copy account facility (this retains group membership for all accounts). Perform this on the Tier 1 OU called Service Accounts.

Next, create a root OU at the same level as Service Administration, and call it Servers. Under this OU, create three sub-OUs for cluster servers and call them Exchange, SQL Server, and File and Print. The OU namespace is demonstrated in Figure 6.5. The reason for this namespace is such that you can create GPOs for the Exchange, SQL Server, and File and Print Servers, respectively.

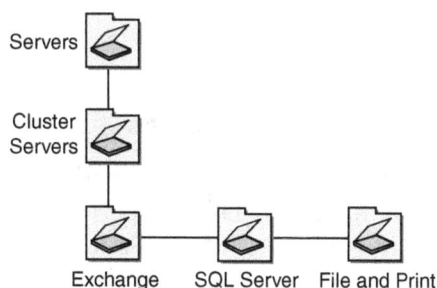

Figure 6.5   Creating OUs for cluster servers.

Next, we install the line of business servers that are configured and clustered for high availability.

Clustering

A number of steps must be completed before a cluster with multiple nodes is complete. Figure 6.6 provides a flow-chart of the steps to peform.

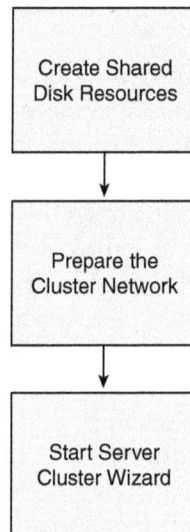

```
┌───────────────────┐
│   Create Shared   │
│   Disk Resources  │
└───────────────────┘
          │
          ▼
┌───────────────────┐
│   Prepare the     │
│  Cluster Network  │
└───────────────────┘
          │
          ▼
┌───────────────────┐
│   Start Server    │
│  Cluster Wizard   │
└───────────────────┘
```

Figure 6.6   Cluster creation flow-chart.

Create Shared Disk Resources

The first step in creating the cluster is the configuration of the disk drives. Obviously, the cluster creation fails if it does not find or recognize drives. If you are going to cluster on a SAN or a SCSI-shared storage array, then you first need to install your *host bus adapters* (HBAs) in the servers and configure them. This step might entail installing special drivers for the cards, management software, and any patches that may be necessary to get them working in Windows Server 2003.

After the adapters are installed and the interface management software sees the controllers working, you'll connect them to the SCSI array or to the switches of the SAN fabric. By now, your disk arrays are installed and ready to go.

This looks like a small step from the flow-chart in Figure 6.6, but it's not. It can take a lot of time and effort to set up the SAN devices, and the effort can vary greatly between different SANs SCSI arrays or disk replication solutions, such as the one provided by NSI-Software (see Chapters 9 and 10). The installation and configuration of the SAN, fabric, zoning, and so on, is very complex and beyond the scope of this book.

Make sure your servers see the external or replicated drives. If everything is configured properly, your Windows servers see the drives as if they are installed on the same server. You are able to manage the new drives the system sees from the SAN management software and various server utilities, including the Computer Management utility. This is demonstrated in Figure 6.7.

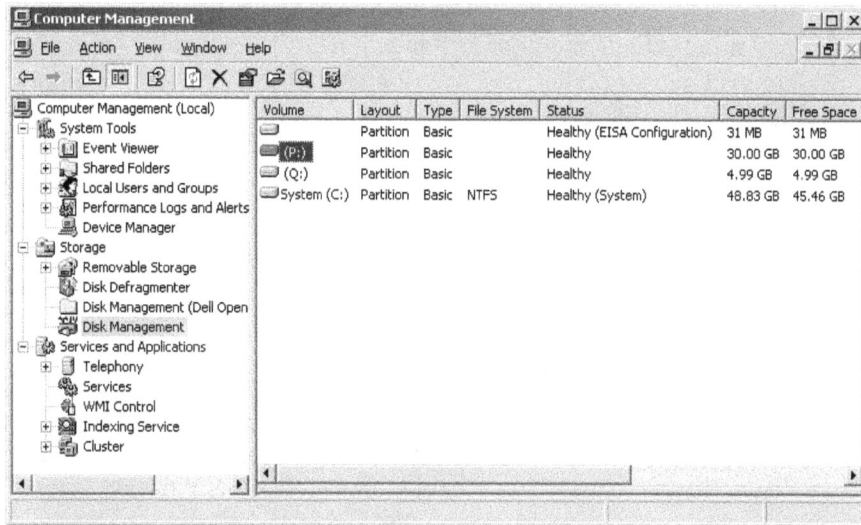

Figure 6.7 Computer Management recognizing the shared disk drives.

In Figure 6.7, notice the presence of the P and Q drives. In this case, we have configured the P drive for the application and the Q drive is the drive that holds the quorum resource. The "Quorum" drive is essential for the cluster and accommodates the so-called Quorum resource.

Prepare the Cluster Network

The next step is to prepare the cluster network or interconnect between the nodes in the cluster. If you are installing a 2-node (active-passive) cluster, it is possible to install an interconnect network between the nodes using a single network cable attached NIC to NIC. The network link needs to be crossed over, but you may not need a cross-over cable because most modern servers employ NICs that recognize the need to cross over the datapaths.

Your interconnect IP configuration must be different to the LAN NICs. In other words, you should set up a private subnet between the servers (unless you are setting up geo-clusters and don't have enough cable to stretch your cluster from NY to LA). For example, if your LAN is on a subnet configured as 10.10.20.0, then put the interconnect on a 192.168.0.0 subnet. The IP on a one-node is, thus, 192.168.0.1, and the NIC on the other node is 192.168.0.2. Leave the gateway addresses on both NICs vacant. As long as the .1 can ping .2, your interconnect is ready.

If you are going to install an N+1 node or any configuration comprising of more than two nodes, then you need to use a hub for your interconnect network. This issue was discussed in Chapter 4. Remember, you don't need a switch.

One last word: Make sure your interconnect NIC's IP addresses do not end up in the DNS configuration as belonging to your virtual server (the cluster name) because that can result in problems for clients connecting to the name resource. In other words, they can look up the resource IP address, but they are unable to connect to it.

Start Server Cluster Wizard

You can install a cluster interactively using the GUI of the Server Cluster Wizard, or from the command line with command-line parameters passed to the "cluster" executable (cluster/create). We recommend that until you know enough about what makes the cluster service tick, you should work with the wizard. The remainder of this chapter discusses installing a cluster using the wizard.

At this point in the cluster configuration and installation, shut down all potential cluster nodes except the first node. It is important you install the first node without the possibility that other nodes might interfere with the installation process. The cluster is created on the first node because it is allowed to gain exclusive use of the shared resources. It installs a cluster only if it discovers that it is the first node in the cluster. After the cluster has been created, the next node is added to the cluster, and the procedure is different.

Also, when you power on and start the operating system, make sure it is only the first node that has access to the cluster disk. If another server can see and access the disks, the data on them can be easily destroyed and would have to be reformatted. To prevent the corruption of the cluster disks, you should shut down all but the cluster node you are going to make the first node in the cluster. You can use other techniques (such as, *Logical Unit Number* or LUN masking, selective presentation, or zoning) to protect the cluster disks before creating the cluster, but we have learned that it's safer to simply power down all the other nodes until you have a cluster. After the Cluster service is running properly on one node, the other nodes can be powered up and then added to the cluster as needed.

When you create a cluster, the physical disk resources are automatically created for cluster disks that use drive letters. As mentioned earlier, follow a sound naming convention for all your resources and keep the names consistent. This is critical to do as you will see in the final chapter in this book when we configure and use Microsft Operations Manager. The alerts and logs are not much help if you can't identify the devices and the servers they are on in your MOM data.

To get started, open Cluster Administrator from Adminstrative Tools. Select File, Open Connection, and then select Create New Cluster from the Action list in the dialog box that appears. This is demonstrated in Figure 6.8. Click OK to launch the Server Cluster Wizard.

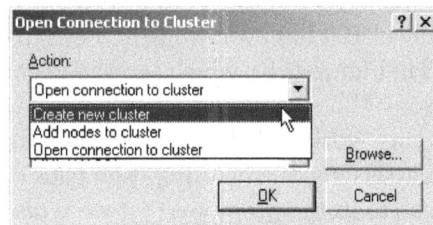

Figure 6.8   The Create New Cluster option in Cluster Administrator.

The first request the wizard makes is for the domain name of the cluster and the cluster name. For the deployment shown in this chapter, we make sure that we have the correct domain name and that the name you use for the virtual server is the cluster name. This is demonstrated in Figure 6.9. You can set up additional network names for the actual application resoureces (such as SQL Server) as we show in Part II of this book.

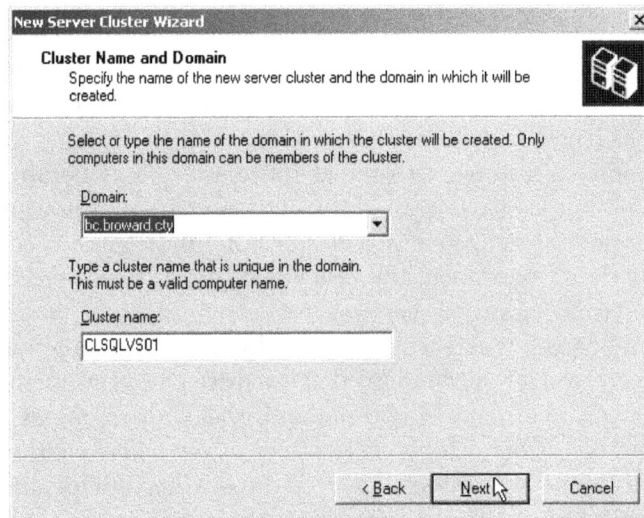

Figure 6.9   Cluster domain and cluster name.

Enter the domain name and cluster name and then click Next. The Select Computer Name dialog box appears. Enter the name of the node you are installing (typically the server on which you started the Cluster Administrator), and then click Next. The wizard now analyzes the configuration to check if it has everything it needs to create a cluster. This is demonstrated in Figure 6.10, which shows the cluster has failed due to a variety of reasons. When you see a lot of red and yellow in the dialog box, it's a sign you have work to do before you can move forward.

If the analaysis fails, you can simply go back or cancel out of the wizard and proceed to fix the problems that were discovered in the configuration analysis stage. The wizard then can be restarted at any time. Figure 6.11 shows that now the configuration analysis has succeeded. You are looking for check marks in all areas and a solid green line on the progress bar. When you have a clean analayis, click Next to continue installing the cluster.

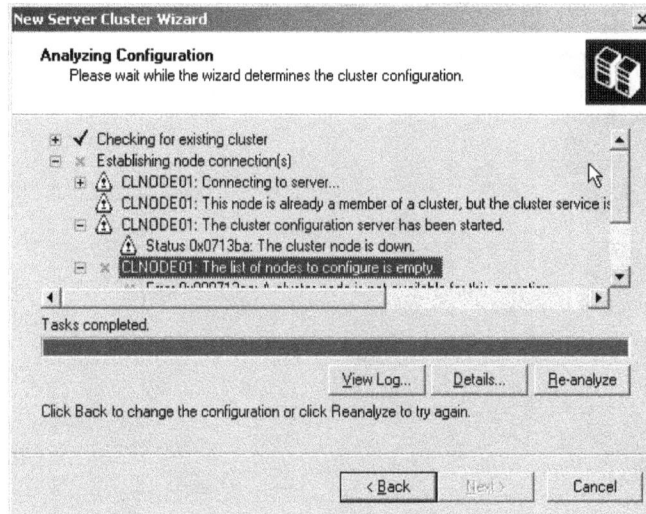

Figure 6.10 Cluster configuration analysis has failed.

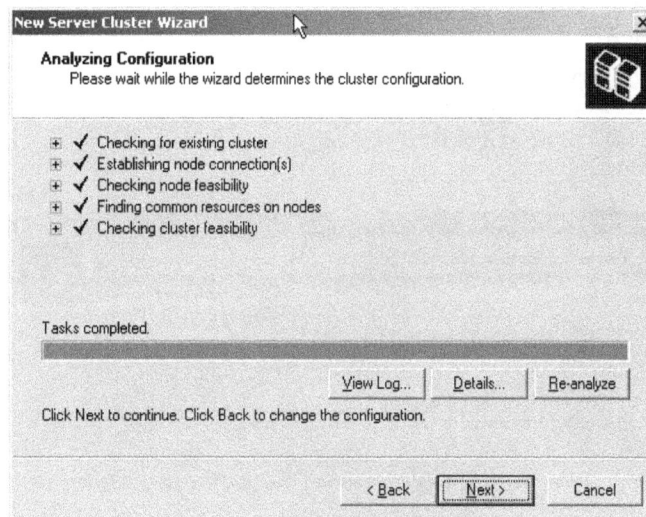

Figure 6.11 Cluster configuration analysis has succeeded.

The next dialog box prompts you for an IP address that Cluster Administrator can connect to. This is shown in Figure 6.12. Enter the IP address and click Next.

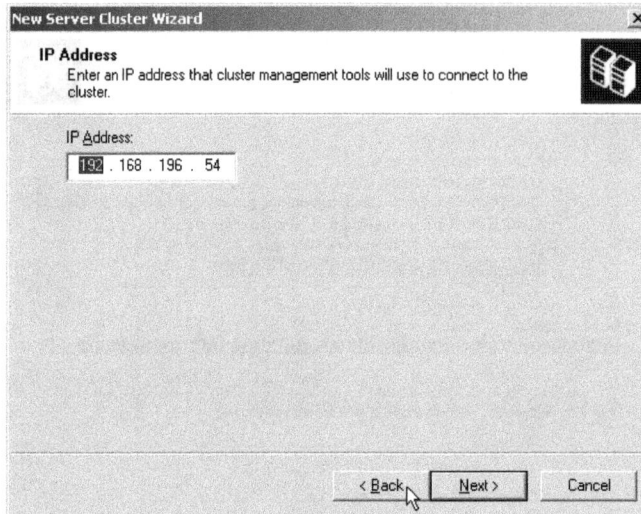

Figure 6.12   Cluster configuration IP address requirement.

The Cluster Service Account dialog box now appears. This is shown in Figure 6.12. You need to enter an account name, its password, and domain before continuing. Create an account specially for the cluster services account (create a separate account for each cluster). See Figure 6.13 for creating a cluster service account.

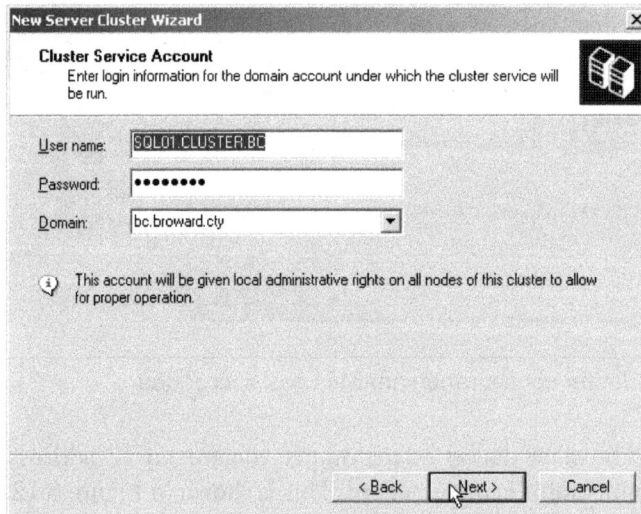

Figure 6.13   Cluster service account configuration requirement.

In the example shown, it is clear from the account name that the cluster service account is intended for the first SQL Server cluster. Under no circumstance make the account a member of Domain Admins. Making the cluster service account a member of Domain Admins was a common practice with earlier version of Windows. With Windows Server 2003, the account only needs to have administrative rights on each knot of the cluster. Upon entering the account data, click Next. The proposed cluster configuration is presented in the next dialog box. You can confirm the configuration and then go back to make a change if needed. If everything checks out, then click Next to begin the installation. Upon successful creation of the cluster, the dialog box shown in Figure 6.14 appears. When you again have a solid green line in the progress bar, you have yourself a cluster. The next dialog box gives you an opportunity to examine the cluster installation log.

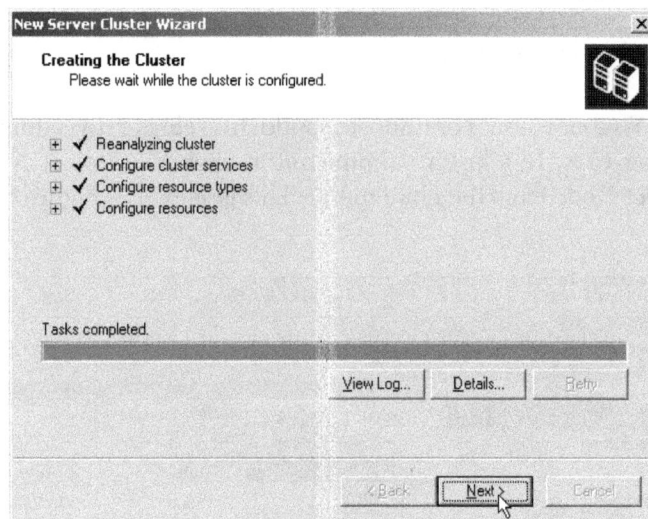

Figure 6.14　The cluster has been successfully created.

Now you can close Cluster Administrator and then reopen it to attach to the local node where you now have a single node cluster running. You attach Cluster Administrator to the name of the cluster or you can use the . (dot) notation, which is the symbol for local. If the Administrator attaches to the node successfully, the cluster can be accessed and your configuration can continue. This is demonstrated in Figure 6.15.

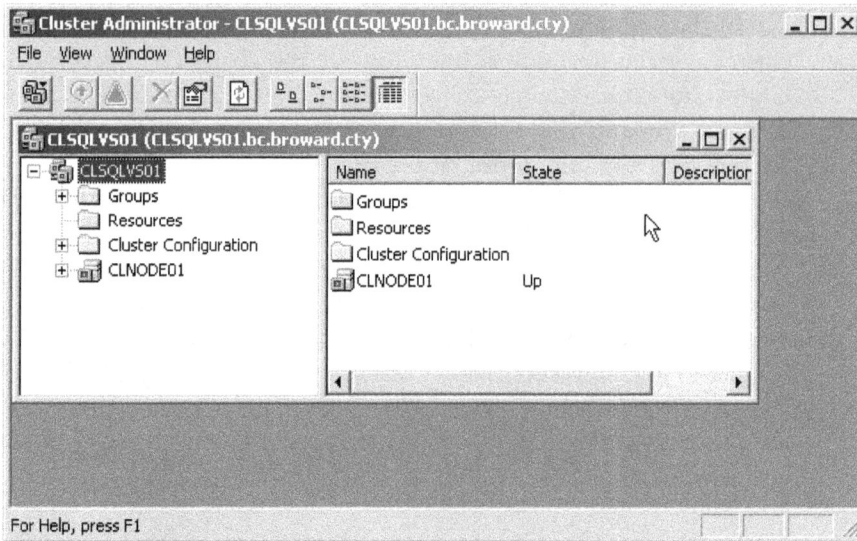

Figure 6.15   Attaching to the cluster.

You can now continue to build the cluster by adding additional nodes to it. In Cluster Administrator, click File, select New, and then select Node from the child menu. This is shown in Figure 6.16.

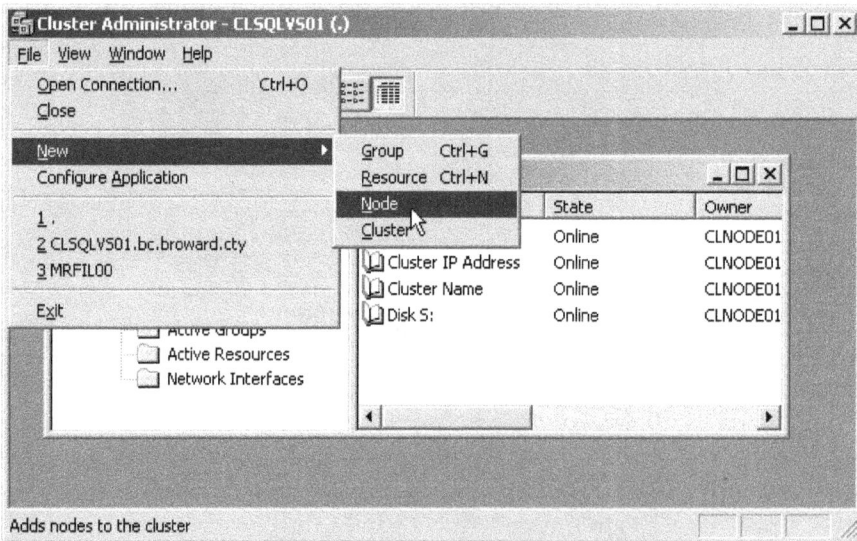

Figure 6.16   Adding nodes to the cluster.

Upon selecting New, the Add Nodes Wizard appears and prompts you to enter the name of the server that will be added as a new node to the cluster. This dialog box is shown in Figure 6.17.

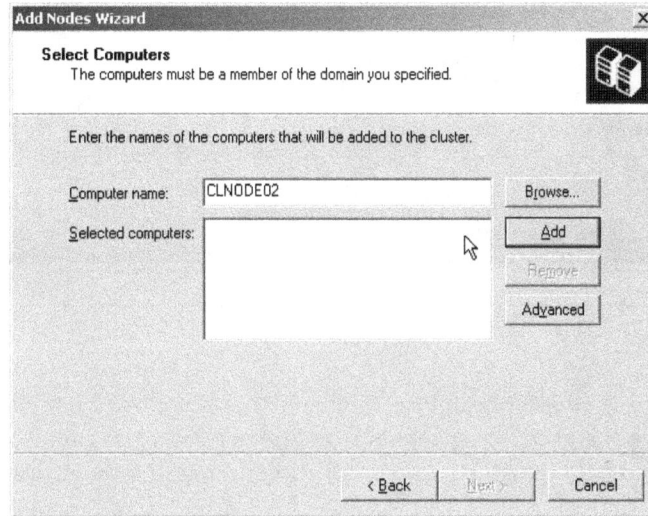

Figure 6.17   The Add Nodes Wizard.

Add the computer details and click Next. From now until the end, the process is the same as before for the first node. You are asked again for cluster service account information, and you have to provide the same service account used for the first node in the cluster. The Add Nodes Wizard again performs Configuration Analysis. When you see a green progress bar, you have a two-node cluster and you are ready to begin configuring resources for the cluster.

Cluster Administrator can tell you whether the cluster is operating properly. Open a command prompt and enter the command **cluster.resource**. This action lists the status for the available resources of the cluster. (You can issue this command even before you have added the second node to the cluster.) This is illustrated in Figure 6.18.

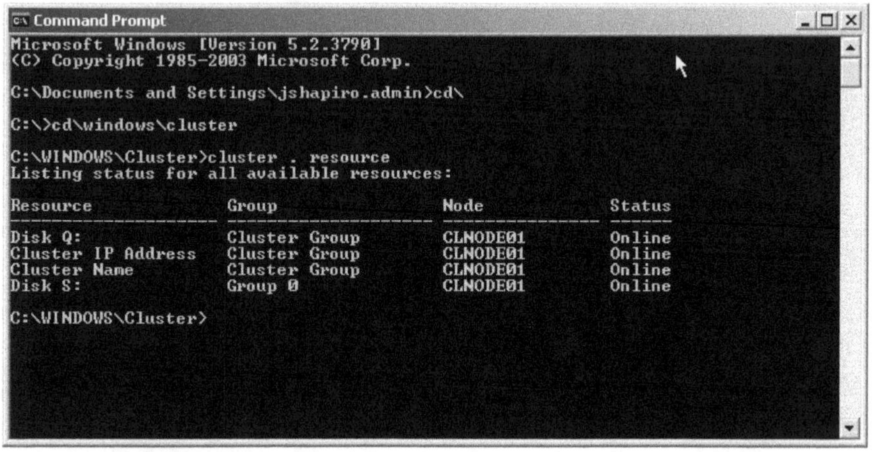

Figure 6.18   Checking cluster resource status.

It is also important to check whether the cluster has been registered in DNS and can be accessed from the network. You can do this by simply pinging the cluster name from the command line as demonstrated in Figure 6.19.

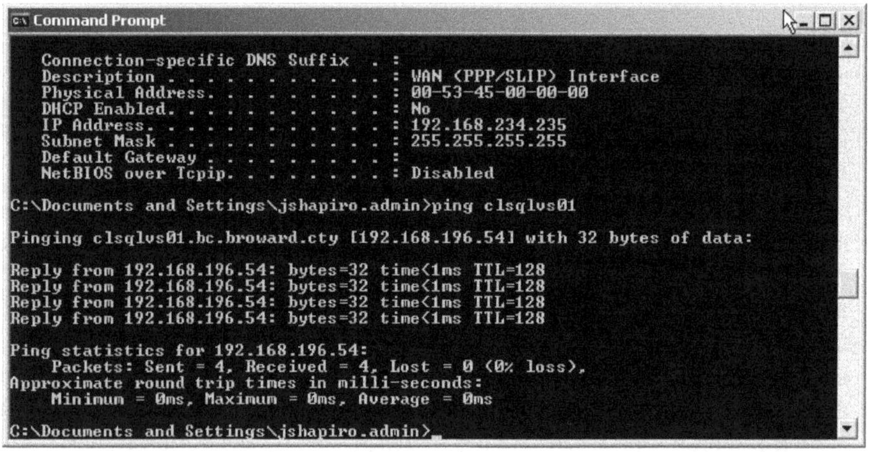

Figure 6.19   Ping the virtual server or cluster name on the network.

During the cluster creation process (using the Quorum button on the Proposed Cluster Configuration page), you are able to select a quorum resource type (that is, a Local Quorum resource, Physical Disk, or other storage class device resource, or Majority Node Set resource).

Troubleshooting

If things go bad and the cluster fails, you can simply back out of the clustering process, fix the errors, and restart the process. Usually the clustering process simply starts again with no issues. It is possible to corrupt the cluster database or contaminate it with invalid data. You may have to back out a node from the cluster, and it may not be possible to do this cleanly.

If you need to evict a node from the cluster, you can do this from the Cluster Administrator. Figure 6.20 shows the process of evicting a node that has for some reason become inoperable.

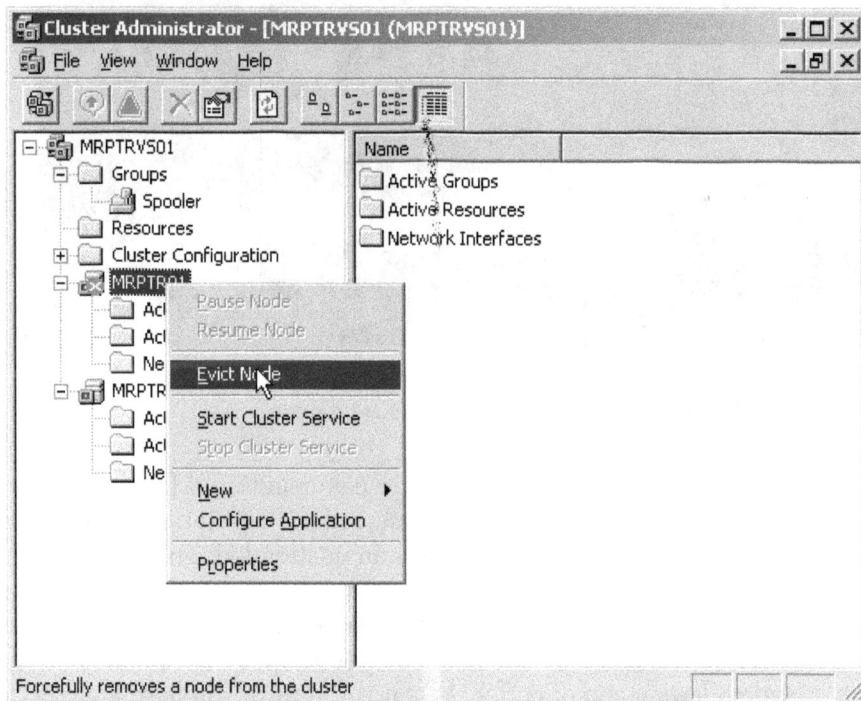

Figure 6.20   Evicting a node from the cluster.

Now, if the database is corrupt, it might not be possible to evict the node, and you may have to destroy the cluster and start all over again. When you shut down a cluster, you do not remove the cluster database (it's like the WINS or DHCP database; it's always there). It remains on the disk and it *can* remain in corrupt state. You are unable to re-create a cluster until the database is clean again. If you have cause to blow away the cluster and start all over again with a clean database, then perform the following steps.

Open up the command window on each node and change the directory to the Cluster folder in the system root (such as C:\Windows\ Cluster). Then run the **/forcecleanup** command. The exact command you use is very important and not easily remembered. See Figure 6.21, which demonstrates this.

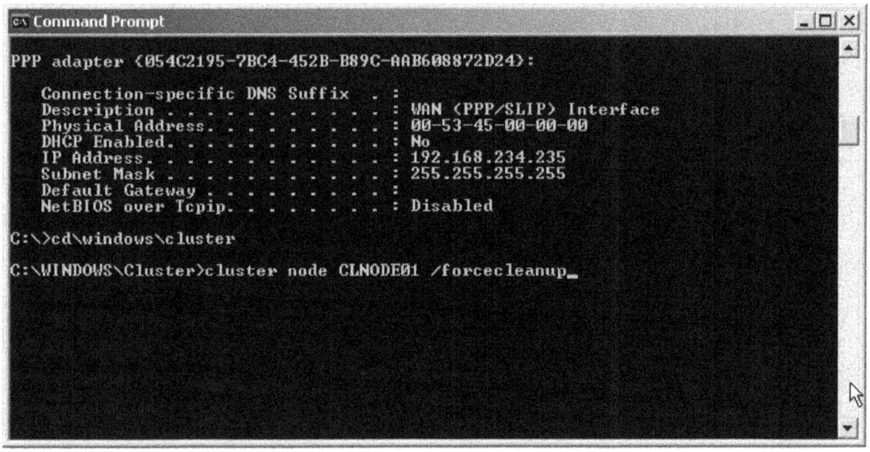

```
Command Prompt                                                        _ □ ×

PPP adapter (054C2195-7BC4-452B-B89C-AAB608872D24):

        Connection-specific DNS Suffix  . :
        Description . . . . . . . . . . . : WAN (PPP/SLIP) Interface
        Physical Address. . . . . . . . . : 00-53-45-00-00-00
        DHCP Enabled. . . . . . . . . . . : No
        IP Address. . . . . . . . . . . . : 192.168.234.235
        Subnet Mask . . . . . . . . . . . : 255.255.255.255
        Default Gateway . . . . . . . . . :
        NetBIOS over Tcpip. . . . . . . . : Disabled

C:\>cd\windows\cluster

C:\WINDOWS\Cluster>cluster node CLNODE01 /forcecleanup_
```

Figure 6.21   Cleaning up the cluster database on a node.

Now you have seen the Cluster command used for more than one reason. It is obviously clear you can call the Cluster executable from a script and configure a cluster after an unattended setup. As soon as the operating system is online, you can run a script to invoke the cluster **/create** command and supply it the the necessary configuration parameters at command line. Imagine that you drop a CD into a blank server and go have a cup of coffee. When you return, you have a cluster running and serving tens of thousands of users.

Time-Out

So, what was accomplished in this chapter? We did a few things. We set up a network around a single support server used for updates, patches, tools, installation bits, and DHCP services. We then set up the root domain controllers to create the forest and extended the forest to accommodate Exchange 2003. We performed quality assurance and set the scene to implement the child domain. Remember all high availability systems are installed into the child domain as are Exchange 2003 servers. After the network was established, we installed the cluster nodes and established the clusters. Let's now move onto the next chapter, which begins with configuring the applications that run on these clusters.

Building High Availability Windows Server 2003 Solutions

CHAPTER 7

High-Performance Print-Server Solutions

Introduction

Much has changed in recent years in how we do business. We have technology to thank for playing such a large part in that change. One business operation that has not changed much is printing. The demand for printing is as high as ever, with many companies still spewing out tons of paper and ink into the environment every day. Take a small insurance agency. Such a business can easily chew up three reams of paper in a day, even when business is in a slump.

Printers themselves have not changed much. Many mid-1990s' laser printers are still chomping away. While computers themselves have changed dramatically over the years, printers have not. Sure, the dot-matrix is practically extinct (expect in pawn shops), but the LaserJet IIIs, 4ls, 5Sis, and so on still keeping rolling. Bottom line: If a shop that depends on print output every day cannot print, it is essentially out of business.

This chapter guides you through the steps to implement a highly available print-server cluster. If you have set up a print-server cluster on the Windows 2000 or Windows NT platform, then you know how tedious a process it can be. With Windows Server 2003, Microsoft reworked the bits that install print-server clusters and greatly simplified the process. You now only need to install the printer drivers once on a single node, and the cluster service automatically replicates the drivers to the other print-server nodes in the cluster.

Other big improvements over earlier versions of the cluster service include support for 64-bit print server clusters, up to eight cluster nodes, majority node set quorums, and terminal server operations on print-server cluster nodes.

Some of our clients have many agencies and departments that would not function without printers and print-servers. It was thus deemed essential that 80 percent of all printing be supported on highly available print-server clusters on the Windows Server 2003 platform. For the architecture described in Chapters 5, "Preparing the Platform for a High-Performance Network," and 6, "Building the Foundations for a Highly Available Architecture," the print-server clusters for 60 percent of the users were deployed in three hub sites, catering to the bulk of the print demand. This chapter focuses on the first of the key *five 9's* systems to describe the process for setting up the print cluster resources and their configuration.

Design Specifications

A single print-server cluster can host print queues for hundreds, if not thousands, of queues. Print spooler files, however, still grow rather large, and you need to carefully consider your bandwidth needs when it comes to pushing files over the WAN.

As long as the demand at the remote site is not very heavy, your print server cluster can easily cater to the remote users on links with bandwidth as low as 64K. Naturally, if your WAN links are high-bandwidth, such as the links that connect the various buildings on a university campus, or a corporate complex like the Microsoft campus, then a single two-node cluster will do the job.

It is very easy to calculate the demands printing will place on the WAN links. Simply calculate the average number of jobs printing at the site and factor that into the available bandwidth at the busiest time of the day. If print files are large (like your average PDF print-out) and more than, say, six people are printing at any given time, then a T1 link that offers you around 720K at any given time will not provide good performance. Nevertheless, Windows Server 2003's print server bits have been engineered to improve the experience of serving WAN users; so, it is worth your while to consider keeping a site's print server at the hub to save on hardware and provide the desired high availability.

In the design described in this chapter, 2-node print-server clusters are placed in each hub location. The printers are naturally close to their users, but in this design, each hub site caters to several thousand users connected to the high-bandwidth backbone. In other words, the wire between the print-server cluster and the printer is on a LAN-speed network (10/100/1000MBits).

Users connect to the printer shares on the cluster the same way they connect to printer shares on a non-clustered node. Instead of connecting to the UNC of the node name, the user simply prints to the UNC name of the virtual server and any one of the printer share names given to the printers somewhere on the network. Naturally, your users can connect to the IP address of the virtual server, followed by the printer share, but such a practice is not recommended because virtual server IP addresses may change in the future.

Each print server cluster is configured for any one of the printers on the network. Remember, printers that "hang" off your print-server clusters must be network printers (connected to the network using a reception device such as an HP JetDirect). A printer connected directly to the server's LPT port is inaccessible from the virtual server, and there is no way you can failover the LPT port itself.

Also be aware that if a node fails in the middle of a print job (say, at page 10 coming out of the printer), the job itself does not fail over to the other node. In other words, the active node does not pick up from page 11. Instead, the active node merely restarts the job and the user has to discard any duplicate printouts.

Moving the spooler resource or manually taking it offline does not lose jobs in process. The cluster service waits until all jobs in process are finished.

Setting up the printers on the cluster is not more difficult than setting up the printer on a single-node print server. After your cluster has been installed and is up and running, you can begin the job of installing the printers to it. This process is described in the section "Installation" later in this chapter.

Before installing the print-server cluster, gather up the information needed to complete a design blueprint as described here.

Name your print-server clusters and virtual servers according to standards outlined in your Active Directory architecture documentation. Table 7.1 provides an example of names used for print-server clusters.

Table 7.1 Print-Server Cluster Configuration

HQ Hub Server Name	Site	IP Address
HQPRNVS01 (virtual server)	MI	10.10.20.16
HQPRN01 (node)	MI	10.10.20.14
HQPRN02 (node)	MI	10.10.20.12
DR Hub Server Name	**Site**	**IP Address**
DRPRNVS01 (virtual server)	AT	10.10.30.16
DRPRN01 (node)	AT	10.10.30.14
DRLPRN02 (node)	AT	10.10.30.12
OC Hub Server Name	**Site**	**IP Address**
OCPRNVS01 (virtual server)	CH	10.10.40.16
OCPRN01 (node)	CH	10.10.40.14
OCPRN02 (node)	CH	10.10.40.12

Next, prepare a table for each print-server cluster. The table should contain the print-server cluster service configuration. Table 7.2 provides an example of the information you need handy as you begin to configure the cluster service.

Table 7.2 Cluster Service Configuration

Parameters	Value
Domain for clusters	mcity.inc
NetBIOS name of the cluster (its virtual server name)	hqprnvs01
Shared disk for cluster data (quorum)	Q:
Shared disk for print spooler resource	S: or P:
Node Names	See Table 7.1
Node IP addresses	See Table 7.1

Parameters	Value
Cluster Service account name	hqprnvs01.cl.sa
Cluster Service account password	●●●●●●●●●●●●
Account membership	See Chapters 5 and 6 for account memberships.
Group Policy	See Chapter 11 for group policy settings that affect clusters.

Table 7.3 contains the cluster group configuration parameters. For more information and details concerning these parameters, see Chapter 6.

Table 7.3 Cluster Group Configuration

Parameters	Value
Group Name	Print Spooler Group, or it can be "DRPRNVS01"
Description	Print Spooler Group
Preferred owners	DRPRN01, DRPRN02
Failover threshold	10 (default)
Failover period	6 (hours)
Failback policy	Prevent Failback (default)

Table 7.4 contains the cluster print spooler resource configuration parameters. For more information and details concerning these parameters, see Chapter 6.

Table 7.4 Print Spooler Resource Configuration

Parameters	Value
Resource Type	Print Spooler
Resource Name	Spooler Resource (this name is for administrative purposes)

continues

Table 7.4   Print Spooler Resource Configuration (continued)

Parameters	Value
Description	Spooler on DRPRNVS01 (remember MOM needs to report this name)
Preferred owners	DRPRN01, DRPRN02
Dependencies	Disk P: (Disk), DRPRNVS01 (Network Name)
Restart (Advanced tab on resource)	Yes, default settings for Threshold and Period
"Looks Alive" poll interval	Keep default settings
"Is Alive" poll interval	Keep default settings

With the configuration data in hand, you are now ready to begin building the print-server cluster.

Installation

To install the print-server cluster, first get your base cluster servers up and running as described in Chapter 6. Make sure that Microsoft Operations Manager (MOM) bits are installed on the server and you are getting your initial monitoring from the servers.

Print-Server Preparation

Performance of the print-server cluster can be greatly improved if you disable or remove any unnecessary services on the cluster. The print servers do not require IIS/FTP components, media streaming, or any special network infrastructure services (such as WINS or DHCP). Configure the server for remote administration. You can also install the Telnet daemon in a secure environment. The Telnet command line is useful for gaining quick command-line access to the print-server console.

Remember your spooler resources on the cluster must be configured for shared storage; so, you provision your "S" or "P" disk as you do for SQL Server data files or the File Server cluster folder hierarchy. Spool files, however, are not permanent fixtures on your hard disks; so, the "S" drive on the print-server cluster does not need to be very big. This conserves SAN or shared storage hardware. Also, as mentioned in Chapter 3, "Storage for Highly Available Systems," spooler files prefer to live on RAID-1 arrays; so there is no need to carve the spooler drive out of a RAID-5 array.

Install Spooler Resources

Your cluster becomes a highly available print server after you install the Print Spooler resource on the cluster. You can create many Print Spooler resources on the cluster; however, as you have seen with the other cluster resources, you cannot have more than one spooler resource per cluster group.

Printer drivers and printer ports are installed on the virtual server, the same vitual server that contains the spooler that supports the printers. As you install drivers to the virtual server, the cluster service replicates the drivers to each node in the cluster only when the cluster fails over to the other nodes. After all the drives are installed and the active node is printing, fail-over to the passive node to replicate all the driver bits.

To configure the cluster to fail-over print servers, you need to perform the following steps:

1. Select a cluster group and in it create a Print Spooler resource. (See Chapter 6 for instructions on how to create cluster resources.)
2. Make the Print Spooler resource dependent on the Network Name and Physical Disk resource.
3. Bring the resource online. Fail-over the group to the other node and back again to validate the test operation. If the resource fails back with no issues, you are ready to install the printers to the virtual server.
4. Open the virtual server. You can do this by clicking Start, Run, and then targeting the UNC of the virtual server. For example, type **\\YourVirtualServer** in the open: field.
5. Open Printers and Faxes and then right-click on Server Properties.
6. Click the Drivers tab to install the printer drivers.

7. Reopen the virtual server from Start, Run (if you need to), and then click the Ports tab on the virtual server. Add a port for your printer.
8. Open the Remote Printer folder on the virtual server and, using the Add Printer Wizard, create the print queue.
9. Now share the printer so your users can access it. You need to share the printer (and publish it in Active Directory) on the virtual server itself.

That's all there is to setting up a print-server resource on your cluster. As long as your printers are supported on the Windows server platform, you really don't have anything more complex to do.

The LPR and Standard TCP/IP Port that ship with Windows Server 2003 are supported for clustering; however, not all ports are supported on a cluster server. Check with the printer's documentation to see if the printer can use the standard ports that ship with Windows Server 2003.

You may also need to install custom ports shipped by the *Independent Hardware Vendor* (IHV). If the IHV port is compatible with the cluster service, you have to install the port monitor on each node of the cluster.

Time-Out

Clustering print services is one of the easiest projects you can commission in your quest to meet a stringent SLA and provide high availabilty for your users. You must remember, however, that when a print server fails, for whatever reason, print jobs in the process of printing are lost. Fail-over always has latency, and a large print spooled file cannot be rolled back to print on the newly active print server. This means your users may have to reissue jobs lost during failure.

In Chapter 8, "High-Performance File-Server Solutions," we deal with file servers, the second of our critical five-9's systems.

High-Performance File-Server Solution

Introduction

The file servers war is over and Microsoft has won. With the advent of the *distributed files system* (DFS), Windows Storage Server, disk qoutas, encryption, and so on, Microsoft has surged ahead of the field in functionality, distribution, and performance. With clustering and the DFS, Microsoft's file server solution is far and away the leading industrial strength file server solution you can buy today.

Over the years the Windows file server system has accumulated many interesting and useful features. Much has been written about them; so, we do not delve into the subject of the file server and what makes it tick. This chapter does cover not only clustering and data replication, but architecting the domain DFS for high availability solutions.

Scale-Out Versus Scale-Up with File Servers

You have two roads to travel when deciding how to provide constant and powerful service to your users. By scaling-out, you split your user and group shares across several files servers. The logic here is that the loss of one file server only affects the group of users that are "homed" to that server. Having less users on a file server also helps in the response and performance area.

There is also the question of locality. Certainly the closer a file server is to its users (in other words, on the same LAN segment), the better their file sharing experience. Users do not have to pull and push files over the WAN.

The downside of multiple file servers is just that—multiple file servers. The more servers you have, the higher the administration cost or burden. Broward County, Florida, for example, while still running a NetWare network, had more than 100 NetWare file servers sprinkled all over the county.

Another negative of multiple file servers is how you cater to roaming users and what happens to users who lose a server. If the solution only offers scale-out and not high-availability, then when a server goes down, the users are out of luck.

So, if your solution is to scale-out or place a number of file servers in various locations, you need to decide what to do in the event of a server failure. Figure 8.1 illustrates the choices. Starting at the top, you have a single server and only a small number of users. If the server fails or becomes unresponsive, then your only option is to rebuild the server and restore the data from the last backup.

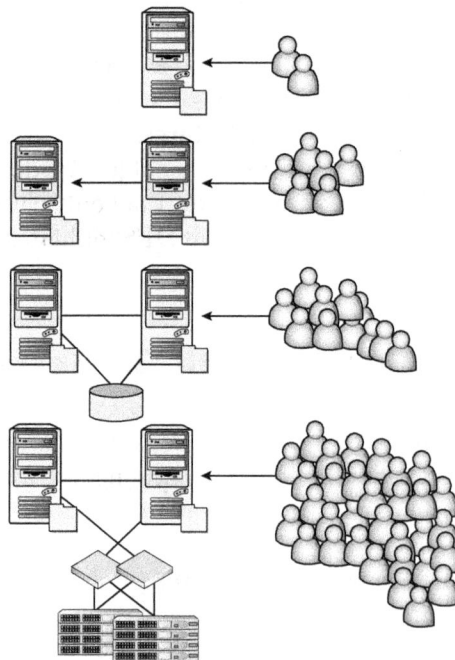

Figure 8.1 Options in the event of a server failure.

If the business cannot stand the first option, then you need to either beef up the machine (such as a RAID 5 array) or install a second standby server and replicate to it using replicating and mirroring software. See the section "High Availability Using Replication and Domain DFS" later in this chapter.

FRS Foilings

Windows Server 2003 is a marvelous operating system but the version of FRS that lies at the heart of the DFS is not as solid as we would like it to have been. It does not take much to break it. The glass jaw is unfortunately at the core of the service. It needs to be completely overhauled for the next version of the operating system. It is still not stable enough that you can use it to mirror and replicate data. In all fairness, Microsoft does not promote it as a mission-critical replication-mirroring service; and if you are looking for instant reliable replication of data (at the transaction or byte level), then you need a service specifically crafted for that purpose. Duplication and mirroring of data is covered extensively in Chapter 10, "High Availability, High-Performance Exchange."

The larger sites may require a solution like clustering for failover, with redundacy on the storage side in the form of a SAN. As we discussed in Chapters 3, "Storage for Highly Available Systems," and 4, "Highly Available Networks," SANS and shared storage arrays do crash; they can also be a single point of failure. Last on the list in Figure 8.1 is replicating data to secondary storage systems. The cheaper option is to replicate server-to-server (you can replicate over a WAN) or replicate SAN-to-SAN. Replicating SAN storage obviously requires a second SAN or a second storage location. If you don't have users attaching to the second SAN or storage device, then you obviously need to justify the cost.

Scaling up a file server means adding more memory, processing power, and storage. Performance monitoring, as discussed in Chapter 9, "High Availability, High-Performance SQL Server Solutions," points out the time you need to scale-up a particular server, be it stand-alone or a node in an active-active cluster.

Now, let's look at designing the file server solution.

Design

A small company, say 60+ users, may have a critical dependency on the file server. High availability may be a requirement if the cost of downtime is substantial. As mentioned earlier, hardware redundancy and fail-over clustering may or may not be affordable, and it all depends on the needs of the business and the users. As mentioned in Chapters 3, 4, and 7, "High-Performance Print-Server Solutions," you can cluster along traditional lines using *direct attached storage* (DAS), *storage area network* (SAN), or by providing availability using replication products like Double-Take or DFS.

The main case study in this chapter architects a storage solution for thousands of users in many agencies from dozens of locations, which means it is very difficult to estimate the exact availability needs of all the agencies. In such a situation, it becomes necessary to provide for continous availability and high performance for everyone. Thus, SAN, DFS, replication, and fail-over clustering are all part of the architecture, design, and final implementation. We decided to install major file-serving hubs in our Active Directory hub sites described in Chapter 5, "Preparing the Platform for a High-Performance Network," as well as smaller file server solutions in locations that needed a significant network upgrade.

Also included in the equation, and a considerable factor at that, is bandwidth. With a large number of users on WAN links, it's critical you have sufficient bandwidth to provide a useful user experience. If your bandwith is so low users see hour-glass icons when they open or save files, then providing them with consolidated file server access and storage from a handful of data centers is not a good idea. You might as well place file servers in remote locations and maintain good backups on site, or replicate data over the WAN.

If you can provide your remote users with sufficient bandwidth, then you will find it makes both economic and technical sense to implement a SAN and traditional file server clusters for availability. In this architecture, most of the users (thousands) were on LAN speed connections, in the same building as the SAN, or over high-bandwidth network links. We thus implemented part of the SAN for file servers, using clustered Active-Passive Windows Storage Server boxes for the file servers.

Users connect to the file server shares on the cluster in the same way they connect to file servers shares on non-clustered servers. Instead of connecting to the UNC of the node name, the user simply maps to the UNC name of the virtual server and any required share. In addition, with DFS in the mix, users do not need the name of the servers at all. In other words, they could be connecting to shares on any of a dozen high availability nodes without even having to know the name of the server hosting the share. Even better, with a domain DFS, they only need to know the domain name and the name of the share. To the end-users, the share looks very close at hand and accessible. In reality, the shares are actually on SAN storage behind both the domain DFS and the clustered storage servers.

If the number of users on your file server is small or the file server is also an application server or hosts a number of services for the company, possibly even Exchange or IIS, then you will likely make your file server out of Windows Server 2003 Standard, or Enterprise Edition, if you are going to cluster. If, however, you need to dedicate the file server to file services, period, then the best choice for server is Windows Storage Server 2003.

What is the Windows Storage Server? Windows Storage Server is a version of the Windows Server operating system dedicated to file server work. In other words, Microsoft has stripped a lot of overhead out of the OS to allow it to do one task well—file serving and storage access. This does not mean the OS is dumbed down; you can still cluster the server and add various services and applications to it. However, you just don't use it as a Web server, a mail server, or a database server. It is used for what it does best—serving up files.

The companies that ship Storage Server solutions, like Dell, HP, and IBM, do so using the so-called *Software Appliance Kit* (SAK) that Microsoft provides to OEM companies. The SAK is not new; Microsoft shipped OEMs the SAK for Windows 2000 storage solutions. These systems were, and still are, known as *network appliances* or NAS (*network attached storage*) servers.

Windows-based NAS solutions are built with so-called Microsoft-qualified server hardware, which are optimized for serving networked storage, typically a SAN. The advent of Windows Storage Server 2003 represented a major boost in storage performance and functionality from the previous NAS-appliance offerings from Microsoft, or other companies.

While a number of NAS solutions are available from various vendors, the Windows Storage Server 2003-based NAS solutions deliver critical functionality in several key areas, including virtualization, heterogeneous device management, security, and a highly-integrated operating environment.

The most significant advantage of the Windows-based NAS is that it is part of the Windows Server operating systems and, thus, works seamlessly with other integral parts of the Windows operating environment. You also get best integration with the Windows Active Directory services, which helps further improve the operational efficiency. This is key for security and virus protection. Its solid integration and manageability with the likes of Group Policy reduces complexity and helps keep costs down.

You can also leverage existing Windows skills to support your Storage Server infrastructure. Finally, one of the best reasons to install Windows Storage Server 2003 is it supports a variety of server hardware from multiple vendors that have worked for years on the Windows platform. This deployment flexibility enables Storage Server solutions to satisfy a wide range of performance requirements for the right price. As an industry-standard operating environment, Windows is widely supported. In fact, the Windows-based NAS gateway stands out as the most broadly supported NAS-gateway solution in the market.

The following sections are comprised of the steps towards the implementation of our highly available file server solutions, based on Windows Storage Server 2003.

Develop Lab Systems

Before implementing your system into production, you should test the design in your lab to ensure it follows the architecture completely. You need to test all configuration changes, updates to architecture, and proof of concept before you can begin installation of production systems, disaster recover, and availability trials.

Most important in the lab environment is to test replication over simulated WAN links. If you have a big IT department, you can have the datacom team install some old routers in the lab and simulate various bandwidths. If you need to simulate slow links, you can use modem-to-modem equipment and set up two old Windows 2000 servers as routers (or more modern servers running trials of Windows Server 2003 and ISA Server 2004). Unfortunately, you will not get a good representation of your actual WAN traffic. The WAN simulators are so expensive you might as well spend the money on field trials and the production WAN.

In addition, you need to test clustering, DFS concepts, disaster recovery, disk quotas, and so on in your lab.

Configure Hardware

This step requires configuration of the NAS equipment—such as Dell PowerVaults—on the network, configuration of network services, and required protocols. You don't need to install an operating system on a NAS appliance because these servers come with the Storage Server software preinstalled. OEMs and Microsoft do not typically make the OS available to you.

Configuration of the file servers is done on the NAS appliances; however, file services such as DFS and any coexistence equipment (such as gateways and staging servers) need to be developed and ratified in the lab. See Chapter 4 for information on NAS/SAN storage design.

Configure 2-Node Cluster Services

The NAS files servers are typically configured as 2-node (Active-Passive) clusters using standard Microsoft Cluster Server Configuration for file servers. See Chapter 6, "Building the Foundations for a Highly Available Architecture," for further information.

Deploy Standard File System Configuration

The standard file system configuration is comprised of UNC share names and server-based folder hierarchy. See the section on share resources later in this chapter.

Define and Implement Backup/Restore Procedures

Test backup and restore of data on the NAS attached to the SAN or NAS storage system. We do not discuss backup and disaster recovery in this book, but it is essential you spend enough time in the lab to test disaster recovery and backup/restore procedures. Unless you simulate disasters, failures, and loss of data on the file servers and storage devices, you will not have the benefit of hindsight when the real disaster happens.

Disaster recovery procedures are defined for the file servers in the event of cluster failure, network failure, SAN failure, and so on.

Create a File Server Security Plan

This part defines how security is ensured on the file server. It dictates to your administrators how to administer to shares, permissions, and general administration of the servers. As part of the security plan, you will create DFS Admins and FileServer Admins Group. Make sure you include a file server security plan in your project.

Configure Root of a Domain DFS

This step requires configuration of the domain DFS on the file servers, which is done on the NAS appliances (as opposed to DFS roots being installed on domain controls and standalone file servers).

Set Up File Server Administration Tools

This part provides for the configuration of the file server administration tools. Each vendor's Storage Server solution provides its own file server administration tools. These tools typically include browser-based utilities for managing the file server. Some solutions also include content management software.

Define and Implement File Server Antivirus Strategy

This is an important step, and you need to be sure the antivirus software itself does not cause problems in some of your file shares.

General Configuration

The following items also need to be extensively tested in your lab. You can read all you want about the various features of the Windows file server, but on Windows Storage Server 2003, with clustering, replication, and so on, they may not behave as you would expect or have experienced with standalone servers.

This short list should be extensively covered in your lab:

- **Define and configure namespace and upper-tier share-points.**
- **Test quotas:** Quotas are defined in Windows Server 2003 and through the NAS appliance management software.
- **Create Test Security Groups for NTFS Object Access:** Domain and global security groups need to be installed and tested against the file shares.
- **Configure Coexistence or Migration Topology:** Technology, such as the NetIQ migration tools and Netware File Service, may need to be installed on the file servers or interact with your clusters.
- **Configure and test encryption.**
- **Configure and test compression.**
- **Configure and test group policy.**
- **Configure replication topology:** The *File Replication Service* (FRS) is critical in a DFS for the replication of data required on all file servers or replication partners.
- **Configure monitoring with *Microsoft Operations Manager* (MOM):** MOM is the key technology used for monitoring the file systems. See Chapter 13, "Looking for Trouble: Setting Up Performance Monitoring and Alerts," for MOM specifications.
- **Clustering Windows Storage Server 2003.**

With these steps complete and with the core cluster services running, as described in Chapter 6, you can begin configuring the file share resources on which the cluster relies. First, let's look again at configuration.

Each of your file servers should be part of a distributed files server hierarchy. The file servers should mirror some of each other's functionality, such as file replication services; however, each file server plays various roles to support their users and to provide services to the hub site in which they reside. The various roles the servers play and the services they provide are discussed in the following sections.

Configuration for File Server Clusters

In the following section we describe the configuration for the three 2-node file server clusters, one in each datacenter or hub site (the sites are called HQ, DR, and OC). The configuration of each of the three clusters is described in Tables 8.1 to 8.4.

Table 8.1   File-Server Cluster Configuration

HO Hub Server Name	Site	IP Address
HQFILVS01 (virtual server)	HQ	10.10.20.16
HQFIL01 (node)	HQ	10.10.20.14
HQFIL02 (node)	HQ	10.10.20.12
DR Hub **Server Name**	**Site**	**IP Address**
DRFILVS01 (virtual server)	DR	10.10.30.16
DRFIL01 (node)	DR	10.10.30.14
DRFIL02 (node)	DR	10.10.30.12
OC Hub **Server Name**	**Site**	**IP Address**
OCFILVS01 (virtual server)	OC	10.10.40.16
OCFIL01 (node)	OC	10.10.40.14
OCFIL02 (node)	OC	10.10.40.12

Prepare a table for each file-server cluster. The table should contain the file-server cluster service configuration. Table 8.2 provides an example of the information you need handy as you begin to configure the cluster service.

Table 8.2   Cluster Service Configuration

Parameters	Value
Domain for clusters	mcity.inc
NetBIOS name of the cluster (its virtual server name)	hqfilvs01
Shared disk letter for cluster data (quorum)	Disk Q:
Shared disk letter for file share resource data	Disk S:
Node names	See Table 8.1
Node IP addresses	See Table 8.1
Cluster Service account name	hqfilvs01.cl.sa
Cluster Service account password	✱✱✱✱✱✱✱✱✱✱✱✱✱
Account membership	See Chapter 6 for account memberships.

Table 8.3 contains the cluster group configuration parameters. For more information and details concerning these parameters, see Chapter 6.

Table 8.3   Cluster Group Configuration

Parameters	Value
Group Name	File Share Group or it can be "DRFILVS01"
Description	File Share Group
Preferred owners	DRFIL01, DRFIL02
Failover threshold	10 (default)
Failover period	6 (hours)
Failback policy	Prevent Failback (default)

Table 8.4 contains the cluster resource configuration parameters.

Table 8.4 Cluster Resource Configuration

Parameters	Value
Resource Type	File Share Resource
Resource Name	File Share Resource on DRFILVS01 (this name is for administrative purposes)
Description	File Shares for Users on DRFILVS01 (remember MOM needs to report this name)
Preferred owners	DRFIL01, DRFIL02
Dependencies	Disk S: (Disk), DRFILVS01 (Network Name)
Restart (Advanced tab on resource)	Yes, default settings for Threshold and Period
"Looks Alive" poll interval	Keep default settings
"Is Alive" poll interval	Keep default settings

With the configuration data in hand, you are now ready to begin building the file-server resourced on your Windows Storage Server cluster.

Installation

To install the file server resource, first get your base cluster-service up and running as described in Chapter 6. Make sure the Microsoft Operations Manager bits are installed on the server and you are getting your initial performance monitoring from the servers.

The central service behind the file server cluster is the share resource type. In other words, the high availability component of the file server cluster is a share point that can failover to an active node when the current node fails. The file share resource can be used as either a standard file share or a share for publishing or hiding subdirectories. These are described in the next section.

Standard File Share

The standard file share resource is used to provide a basic file share, using a single share name. It functions in the same fashion as a share on a standalone file server.

Share or Hide Subdirectories

This share resource is used to publish several network names. You can publish for each root file folder and all of the subordinate folders. Using this resource makes it easy to create a large number of file shares on the server. A good example of the application for this resource is your user folder's namespace. With this share, you can also hide the subdirectory shares so users do not see the shares when they browse the network.

Installing the File Share Resource

As with the print spooler cluster configuration described in Chapter 7, you need to be a member of the Administrators group on the local computer. As a member of Domain Admins, you have this ablity. You also need to verify that the Cluster service account has Full Control rights to the folder for which you are configuring a resource and for the NTFS file system. To do this, follow these steps:

1. Open Cluster Administrator from Control Panel, double-click the Administrative Tools, and then double-click Cluster Administrator.
2. In Cluster Administrator, create a Physical Disk resource for the drive on which the folder is located, a Network Name resource, and an IP Address resource. Place these resources in the same resource group. You should set up the File Share resource such that it is dependent on the Physical Disk resource as well as the Network Name resource.
3. Create a File Share resource in the same resource group as the aforementioned resources. You can now click Advanced to change the File Share resource type from Normal to DFS root or Share subdirectories. If the file share is configured as a DFS root, it must be dependent on a Network Name resource (see the following sidebar on clusters, "Domain DFS").
4. From the details pane in Cluster Administrator, click the File Share resource you created, then from the File menu, click Properties. On the Parameters tab in Path, type the path to the folder whose subfolders you want to share.
5. You can now bring the file share resource online.

You are now set to build your folder namespace. Always use the Cluster Administration tools rather than Windows Explorer to manage the file shares. If you make the mistake of using Explorer, the shares will be lost when you failover to any other nodes in the cluster. In fact, after you have configured an extensive file server cluster, you should test the availability of the cluster-aware file shares by failing over and making a passive node active. If any file shares have been created on the cluster with Windows Explorer, they will not show up on a newly active node.

Domain DFS

You noticed when configuring the file share resource that you can set up the file share to host a DFS root. However, you can only fail-over a standalone DFS root, you cannot fail-over a domain DFS root. To configure a file server cluster to support domain DFS systems, simply create the virtual file server as you would for the standard file share resource and then configure your domain DFS link paths to the virtual server that represents the cluster (as opposed to the UNC name). The domain DFS root can also be homed to the nodes of the clusters making them always available.

High Availability Using Replication and Domain DFS

Let's now look at a solution that lands in the middle of the options shown in Figure 8.1: the replicated disk scenario. There are a number of replication options. However, for a high availability file server "cluster," the following scorecard must be applied:

- The replication technology must be fast and robust or failover cannot happen. In other words, as soon as a file is changed it is replicated to the partner node.
- The replication technology must be optimized for network bandwidth. The best technology does not replicate the entire file; it replicates just the bytes that represent the changes in the file.
- The replication technology must automatically failover, if desired (in other words, if the source file server fails, the target allows users to continue working with their files). Failover implies serveral requirements, and we'll look at those shortly.
- The replication technology must work with Microsoft Windows Server 2003 native file server features, such as DFS and ShadowCopy.

There are several products that can do the work just described. The two most popular products are EMC²'s Legato Co-StandbyServer AAdvanced and NSI Software's Double-Take. In terms of cost (less than $2000 per node), power and robustness, and ease of use and speed, we are partial to Double-Take.

We have mentioned Double-Take previously in this book, but what is it exactly? Double-Take installs on the nodes of a replicated disk cluster set and includes many-to-one, one-to-many, chained, and same server configurations across any IP-based LAN or WAN. The many-to-one capability also enables one target machine to support multiple source machines.

Double-Take also provides a transmission control option for real-time or restricted transmission based on bandwidth usage. This preserves bandwidth for other applications or scheduled events. In other words, you are able to specify criteria for Double-Take transmission when real-time transmission is not practical. This is a great feature for scheduling replication at certain times (for example, for backup or disaster recovery operations). And you can use this to restrict data flow to private links or a public network.

Double-Take also allows "loosely coupled" communications, which means that Double-Take can operate asynchronously and enable source machines to continue processing events when the network link is congested or unavailable. Double-Take simply tests the link and resumes transmission when the network or bandwidth comes back. And it is ideal for disaster recovery and backup/restore.

Its ability to replicate changes even in open files means that you can replicate data from a number of servers to a central target that has a tape-drive unit attached. Now you only need one tape backup system in one location, which cuts cost of ownership of hardware, software, and adminisration. There are a number of configurations you can consider:

- **One-to-One, Active/Standby:** One target machine acts as the standby and cannot have any production activity. The target is dedicated to support one source machine. You can use this configuration for offsite disaster recovery, failover, and critical data backup. Source server applications can include the likes of Exchange, SQL Server, and Web servers. While this configuration is the easiest to implement, support, and maintain, it requires the highest hardware cost because you need a target machine for every source machine.

- **One-to-One, Active/Active:** You can use this configuration for both failover and critical data backup. This configuration also provides better return-on-investment because you do not need to dedicate a target machine for each source, and thus both machines can be used for production. This configuration is, however, more complex than the Active/Standby configuration because during replication each machine continues with its own production work. You must also be careful not to include the destination folders in the replication set of the other server, or you'll end up with a replication loop. You also have to be sure that if one machine fails over to the other, the active machine is able to handle the workload of both machines.

- **Many-to-One:** With this configuration, your multiple source machines are protected with one dedicated target machine. This configuration is most often used to provide centralized tape backup. As mentioned earlier, this configuration spreads the cost of one target machine and many source machines, and consolidates backup to one server, which drastically reduces the cost of administration. Your target must have enough disk space and RAM to support replication from all of the source systems. You can also use failover in this scenario.

- **One-to-Many:** Here one source machine partners with multiple target machines. This configuration provides offsite disaster recovery, redundant backups, and data distribution. You can use this configuration to replicate data to a local target machine and separately replicate a subset of the mission-critical data to an offsite disaster recovery machine. An important consideration for this sceraio is that the updates are transmitted multiple times across the network; and if one of the target machines is on a WAN, the source machine becomes burdened with WAN communications.

- **Chained:** This configuration can be used for integrating local high availability with offsite disaster recovery. This configuration can be used to move the processing burden of WAN communications from the source machine to an intermediate target/source machine. One downside of this setup is that the intermediate machine could become a single point of failure for offsite data protection.

- **Single Node:** The last and most simple configuration allows you to replicate folders on the same node. Thus, source and target are folders on the disks of the same machine. You can use this to relocate data within existing machines so that open files can be backed up. This configuration can also be used to mirror drive arrays on the same computer. For example, you can replicate the data from one RAID 5 array that is attached to the server to another RAID 5 array that is attached to the same server.
- **Cluster-to-Cluster and Cluster-to-DR:** Here Double-Take is used with its sister product, GeoCluster, to replicate cluster storage to standby clusters, passive servers positioned at remote locations, and to target Double-Take server for offsite backups. GeoCluster is discussed in depth in Chapter 10.

Let's now look at an Active/Active "cluster" using Double-Take. While this solution does not use the Microsoft Cluster Service, we consider it a cluster because the servers can failover to each other. Even if one of the servers stands by as a passive node, the failover service simply transfers network names and IP addresses to the healthy node and users connect to identical data on the new server.

Setting up the replication of data between the nodes is so easy it's not worth showing here. The wizard lets you select the source folders or volumes (the target folders or volumes) and then lets you create and name a replication set.

Failover is just as easy to set up. Figure 8.2 shows selection of the source server to monitor for failover in the Connection Manager dialog box.

The Failover tab on the Connection Manager dialog box lets you select the source address to monitor as well as the criteria (for example, thresholds). You simply need to tell Double-Take what it should consider to be signs of failure at the source. This is shown in Figure 8.3.

Now, it's easy to set up the failover pairs or triplets when all the servers are on the same subnet. It's a little more difficult to have a server failover its IP address to a server on another subnet (and network address translation [NAT] would make it impossible). In this case, you might need to set up a geographic or stretch cluster, as described in Chapter 10, "High Availability, High-Performance Exchange," and use Microsoft Cluster Service to failover the resources.

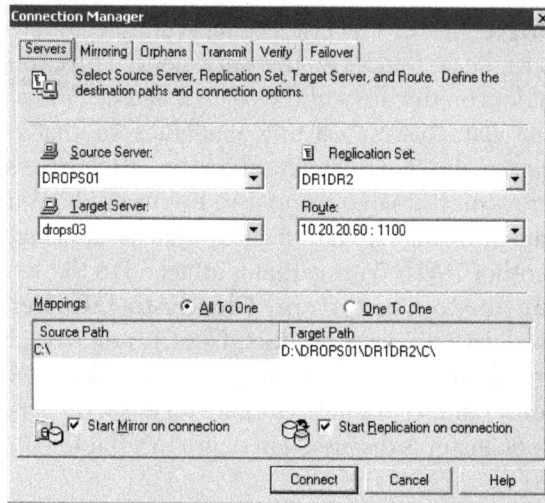

Figure 8.2   Selecting Target and Source servers for failover configuration.

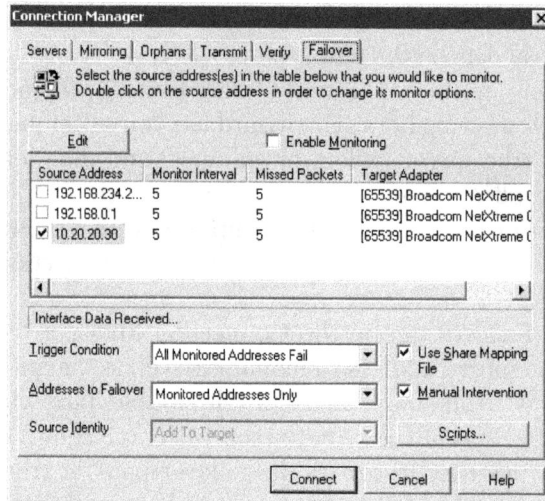

Figure 8.3   Seting up Failover parameters and configuration.

But our customer required us to set up a geographically-separated cluster in which one server replicates data from headquarters (HQ) to a disaster recovery datacenter (DR). The cluster as Active/Active would allow telecommuters to use a portion of the DR file server namespace (home and data folders) while most office users are attached to the HQ file server. The DR server thus replicates data back to the HQ server where daily backups are monitored by the onsite administrator, while the HQ server replicates part of its folder namespace to the DR server for offsite disaster recovery (to be accessed in the event the HQ server becomes inoperable). Instead of using the failover, in this instance we set up DFS on both servers, allowing users to simply connect to DFS links regardless of which server was available.

Time-Out

In the previous two chapters, we configured cluster services for file and print. As you have seen, it is not a difficult exercise to create the services (starting with the base cluster service as demonstrated in Chapter 6). In the next few chapters, the cluster services become a little more complicated to configure with advanced SQL Server 2000 and Exchange Server 2003 services.

CHAPTER 9

High Availability, High-Performance SQL Server Solutions

Introduction

I t's all about data. And for Microsoft's data technolgy, it's all about SQL Server. No matter what the IT shop is supporting—home-grown client applications, CRM, Web applications, enterprise, and line-of-business— SQL Server 2000 and SQL Server 2005 are the only Microsoft database technologies engineered to provide a highly available data tier.

Before we explore the data tier further, it should be noted that this chapter has been based mostly on SQL Server 2000. While SQL Server 2005 can obviously support clustering, the product had not been issued as beta at the time this chapter was written. Although we have been working extensively on the recent beta and alpha versions, this book is based on supported technology that has been released to manufacturing (RTM).

Future versions of this book, should they be required, no doubt will reference SQL Server 2005. Because SQL Server 2005 is at least a year away from RTM, we focus on SQL Server 2000. However, it does not matter whether you cluster or scale-out SQL Server 2000 or 2005, the underlying high availability technology, Microsoft Clustering, is the same—supported on Windows Server 2003, Enterprise Edition.

Of course, some small differences between the two versions exist, such as improvements in log shipping and distributed transactions. It is worthwhile mentioning that SQL Server 2005 includes database mirroring, the first time it has been introduced by Microsoft. You probably have noticed we talk about mirroring a lot in this book and have a lot to say about NSI Software's Double-Take and GeoCluster software, anticipating that mirroring technology most certainly will mature.

Scale-Out Versus Scale-Up with Microsoft SQL Server

Many database administrators typically think of adding resources to their existing database servers when the going gets tough. They tend to think "scale-up" before "scale-out." When server response time starts to degrade because of increased workload or higher database capacities, the most common initial reaction to a performance problem is to add bigger, faster, and more expensive hardware.

At present, hardware vendors are doubling the performance of their devices every 18 to 24 months; so this may seem viable, but you eventually reach a point of diminishing return. Many problems are associated with constant hardware upgrades. First, hardware *does* have its limitations. Given hardware performance doubles every two years, and assuming you have the money to upgrade your hardware every two years, what do you do when you max out your new system after only 12 months? Do you just suffer with poor performance for the next year? That is probably not an option, especially after that expensive upgrade.

Even though hardware vendors are making eight-processor systems for the Intel platform, with gobs of RAM, fiber-meshed, SAN-connected computers still have the problem of scalability. Sooner or later you have to wait for your hardware vendor to release the next version of super hardware to catch up with your desired performance counters. It gets more complicated. When a system reaches a certain point, further scaling-up becomes cost-prohibitive and is not worthwhile. Even beyond the hardware and compatibility issues, you'll probably encounter problems with software accessing your system when you're trying to scale-up past a certain point.

Take the /3GB /PAE switch in boot.ini with Windows 2000 Server, for example. If you are not familiar with this issue, it was a problem with systems not correctly using and identifying memory at 4GB and above. Some software systems, such as database engines, have internal algorithms handling transactions, locking, and multi-user or three-tier database issues. These software structures do have limited efficiency. These limits can hamper the ability to continue to scale upward. It's a Bell curve—sooner or later, at the top of that curve you'll need very expensive hardware upgrades to get even the smallest levels of increased performance.

Scaling out still means more hardware. The idea is more hardware, not bigger hardware. Scaling out can provide an effective answer to the problems of the scale-up scenario for database servers. Here, the design is not *shared-everything* architecture, it is *shared-nothing* architecture. Essentially, shared-nothing architecture means each computer system in the cluster operates independently. Each system in the cluster maintains separate resources (CPU, memory, and disk storage that other systems cannot directly access).

To address capacity issues by scaling out, you add more hardware to the pool—not bigger hardware to a single entity. Scaling out can address the cost factor associated with scaling up because adding several smaller systems is typically less expensive than upgrading a single large mainframe-class system and costs less in emotional pain than a total "forklift" upgrade to a new platform.

When you scale-out, the size and speed of a single system doesn't limit total capacity. Shared-nothing architecture also jukes the software bottleneck by providing architecture that supports multiple, multi-user concurrency mechanisms. Because the workload is divided among the multiple servers, total software capacity and throughput increases.

Even though scaling out provides solutions to the built-in limitations of scale-up architecture, this method has inherent problems as well. First, the ceiling is only so high. Scaling out requires additional administrative overhead, subject matter expertise, and of course money. The pitfalls can be potentially as great as the performance gains it offers. Even so, scaling out might be a viable solution to database implementations that have reached the hardware limits of scaling up.

Design

Let's look at a database server hosting multiple databases for multiple clients that depend on many applications. The server was upgraded this year to the newest high-performance model. You have had almost 100 percent uptime. You haven't had to reboot your server in months, and now your monster is ready for some scheduled downtime. This is a good thing because you are either a lazy database administrator (DBA), or your business cannot afford the maintenance window. If you have not rebooted in months, it means there are a few service packs and security hotfixes waiting for your attention.

With all the preparations out of the way, you set out on the quest of updating and rebooting the server, most likely more than once. After almost an hour of updates and reboots, it has finally come time to reboot for the last time and go live. But there is a problem. One of the hard disks on the mirror containing the OS has failed. After rebuilding the disk and rebooting, you find the problem unresolved. So you go and get a spare disk.

When the server was upgraded, so were the hard disks. You don't have anything compatible on-hand (and the spares you had have now been stolen by the Exchange administrator). Gold support is a four-hour wait for new hard drives. Should we restore from a backup to a different server and point applications to the new data source? What about migrating all the configurations in the system databases? Do we steal the hard disks back from the Exchange administrator (a mean Belgian who wrestles alligators in his spare time)? This is the ultimate nightmare scenario, and you would be surprised how often it plays out in data centers across the globe.

Now, if the SQL Server is part of a cluster, your back is covered (actually your boss' back is covered). If the machine that failed is part of a cluster, then it has a twin that understands its role—it understands how to service clients, and it has been engineered with high availability in mind.

Clustering SQL Server provides the capability to recover from resource failure immediately and provides seamless connectivity to your clients and client applications. The resources that can put your data tier in the dark upon failure can be physical, such as hardware, or logical, such as a service failure. When resource failure is identified, the failed resource and any resources that are dependent on the failed resource are moved from the failed node.

Clustering is not limited to one failover server. In Windows Server 2003, clustering supports up to eight nodes. Clustering configurations can be as simple as a two-node solution, such as one active server and one standby partner waiting for a resource to fail, to as complex as eight servers running individual applications. If there is a resource failure on any node, the remaining partners are able to claim ownership of resources and essentially *pick up* the work of the failed node.

To have a cluster effectively act as one entity, the nodes need to be able to talk to each other. With Microsoft clustering technology, this communication is achieved in two ways. The first is through the data written to the Quorum disk. The second is through the *heartbeat* (see Chapter 6, "Building the Foundations for a Highly Available Architecture").

The Quorum disk is a shared disk resource. While the Windows Server operating system does not allow multiple machines to *own* the same disk resource, the Quorum disk resource operates on a shared disk subsystem. It is a dedicated resource to which all machines can have access. A record of current activities and resource ownership is constantly written to and read from the Quorum disk by each node in the cluster.

The individual servers also must talk directly to each other to ensure operability. This task is accomplished through the heartbeat network interface. The heartbeat depends on a network interface card (NIC) on each participating cluster node configured to communicate with only the other member nodes. If Node-1 owns resources and fails, Node-2 needs to know immediately. As soon as an available node does not receive a reply from a current owner, ownership of the resources owned by the failing node are transferred to an available node. The algorithms that ensure the cluster *gossip* is reliable are beyond the scope of this book. Suffice it to say, the deadly malaise of clusters called *split brain syndrome*, in which nodes misinterpret failure, has been eliminated.

The importance of clustering for any mission-critical database system is paramount. But let's go behind the scenes for an example. SQL Server 2000 and SQL Server 2005 are enterprise-class database server systems. They can withstand a barrage of business rules and are wonderful in their flexibility. The SQL Server platform has also proven itself in speed and reliability over the years. Behind the scenes of our clustered SQL Servers, we find a database engine managing thousands of transactions per second, scheduled jobs, and continuous evaluation of business logic in its stored procedures, triggers, and functions.

While your SQL Server is chugging away, a klutzy new intern emerges from behind the server rack with the coffee in his mug missing. Next thing you hear, the SQL Server power supply unit is exploding. The active transactions being written to the database log files were too abundant to all fit in the memory cache on the SCSI controller card that houses your hard disks. Some transactions are lost. The worst enemies of a DBA have come to visit: coffee in the data center (punishable by death), data corruption, and unpredictable consequences (such as loss of employment). After the smoke has cleared, you realize you have orphaned transactions that cannot be recovered.

With a clustered set of servers, only the intern would be out of luck. Clustered servers either save data to a shared disk or replicate the data through a replicated disk. See Chapter 6, which describes the base cluster service and the configuration of nodes. It shows the most common design, a generic shared bus with two servers attached to it and a few disks chopped up in varying RAID configurations. While Node-1 goes up in smoke, the transactions being written to the log file are generally stored in memory on the disk array controller. These transactions are then written to disk as necessary.

The cache memory space of the array is exponential compared to a traditional SCSI controller. Your transactions have made it to the shared disk (in specialized replicated disk scenarios, the transaction is replicated as soon as it completes). Now Node-2 realizes Node-1 is no longer available (it does not care the server took a "coffee break"). It takes ownership of the resources Node-1 owned before failure, reads the Quorum disk for information about current activity, initializes all necessary resources, and starts where Node-1 left off. This includes reading the SQL Server transaction log. As with any DBMS, if a transaction was not completed, it is rolled back; if it resided in the log completely, it is rolled forward. While you might not recover every single transaction, the number of orphaned transactions is greatly reduced. Worst case, the Web server reports an error and the user resubmits the transaction.

Failover for SQL Server

Failover is the heart and soul of clustering. When any given resource fails, no matter what the reason, no matter what the resource, the participating nodes must respond. Abstract solutions call for abstract thinking. Clustered nodes communicate through the Quorum disk and heartbeat NICs. While the Microsoft Clustering Service (MSCS) monitors these resources, SQL Server runs its own processes in the background.

When an SQL Server resource becomes unavailable, MSCS transfers ownership to another participating node, and that node initializes the resource. MSCS monitors all resources necessary for one or more SQL Server instances. The bottom line is this: When resources necessary for SQL Server to service requests properly become unavailable, the ownership of this and all other dependent resources is given to another participating node, and that node initializes and manages the resource and its dependents. Dependent resources also are transferred.

Common configurations for clustered SQL Servers include disk resources, heartbeat network connections (also known and referred to as *private* networks), public network connections (for client network access and geographically dispersed cluster nodes), SQL Server services, SQL Server Agent services, MSDTC (Microsoft Distributed Transaction Coordinator) service resources, and the SQL Server virtual network name (what the clients connect to). Sound like a lot? Almost all are interconnected to form a unified system.

SQL Server Cluster Design Specs

Planning is vital for the success of your SQL Server cluster (and all clusters for that matter). A clear understanding of the needs of your databases and the applications they support is paramount. This chapter provides the necessary information for you to design a solution that best fits your scenario. Let's discuss the particulars and some different configurations.

Documenting the Dependencies

We mentioned this in earlier chapters, but let's review it here for SQL Server clusters. First, start with the physical disk as the first resource on which SQL Server depends. Without physical disks, you cannot read any data and begin service. So, when SQL Server fails over, you need to make sure the first resource claimed by the new node is the disk. Next, you can fail-over the public network, then the network name, and so on.

It helps to sketch or chart the resources and the sequence of the failovers, so you can see which things depends on what. Failing over the SQL Server virtual server before the network does not make much sense.

Understanding SQL Server Active/Passive Configurations

In *active/passive* configurations, you typically provide two nodes. One node is the workhorse. It processes all workload while the other waits; it's *active.* The *passive* node is really a hot standby partner. In the event of resource failure, the passive node gains ownership of all dependent resources and becomes the *active* node.

The active/passive configuration must guarantee there is minimal or zero performance degradation due to added workload. This configuration ensures applications have the insurance of a dedicated resource in case of failure. Given this also doubles the associated hardware cost, it is not always the most feasible option.

With active/passive SQL Server cluster configurations, usually only a single instance of SQL Server is running. This instance has all the resources it needs—SQL Server services, physical disk resources, SQL Server network name, and SQL Server instance IP address.

Active/Active Configurations and Multiple Instances

In *active/active* SQL Server cluster configurations, each participating node in the cluster has requests to serve. The term *active/active* can be potentially misleading; so let's clarify it. When MSCS resources are not shared between nodes, the ownership of resources is cut-and-dry. Either you own the resource or you don't. If you own the resource, you must serve the requests for that resource and any dependent resources. If you fail to do this, ownership is transferred to another node that can fulfill the request.

Active/active may appear as if multiple servers are sharing the load of responding to client requests from multiple sources. This is not the case for failover clusters. This is, however, what load-balanced clusters do, and for that you need to turn to Chapters 11, "Load Balancing," and 12, "Internet Information Server."

With regard to SQL Server, *active/active* actually means *multiple instance.* Each SQL Server installation can support up to 16 instances of SQL Server.

When clustering SQL Server as multiple instances, each node of the cluster owns all resources and dependent resources required for an individual instance of SQL Server to function properly. In turn, the other nodes own all resources and dependent resources needed for a separate individual instance of SQL Server to function properly. It is important to understand they do not share a database, and transactions are localized to the instance databases. An individual node can own other instances of SQL Server. It is better to refer to a multiple instance rather than active/active (this is also true for Exchange clustering). This configuration addresses the cost factor by utilizing all hardware all the time. Instead of the passive node wasting its life away (a costly server doing nothing), it should be put to work.

But you need to be careful. In a production environment with a multiple instance of SQL Server clusters, when failure occurs, one of the participating nodes gains ownership of the resources the failed node owned. This simply means performance suffers because the surviving node now takes over the load of the failed server while still contending with its own load. The amount of degradation associated with this depends on the amount of requests the failing node serves. If the cost of an active/passive configuration is too much to bear, and you choose to use a multiple instance configuration, you will take a hit in performance in the event of resource failover. However, poor performance is a better alternative than downtime. As long as the nodes in the clusters have enough resources to take over the failed node, you can maintain service level until the failed node is fixed. Naturally, you would not succeed if the failover was made to a server already running ragged.

In light of this, new factors need to be considered when choosing to go with an active/active cluster. Database design, database interaction, federated database, and replication are all considerations that help facilitate a high availability solution utilizing MSCS and SQL Server clustering.

Real-world scenarios are very often not cut-and-dry. For example, you have an SQL Server database that your business has decided is vital and needs to be highly available. This database and even other databases related to the function and health of your application need to be clustered. As we have found, databases in these types of scenarios most often play multiple roles.

Two primary schools of thought exist for the DBMS. The first is that the database is just *dumb storage*, and you can create robust devices for creating and managing business logic. The second school of thought is that most of the databases that require an elevated level of availability are not just *storage*; these databases are often the engines that power the Windows and Web applications of a business. They are the primary repositories used for reporting from Web sites serving both internal and external customers, and they are used for end-of-month and fiscal reporting. They are the lifeblood of the business.

With databases that are not just for storage, why not leverage the investment of a cluster for increased performance as well? Why not create an automated restore that restores our production databases from clustered Node-1 to a different instance of SQL running on Node-2, and point the reporting engines to the named instance currently running on Node-2, where we just restored the database?

All reporting traffic and queries no longer affect the production system. Have you ever had a developer drop or truncate a table necessary for clients for production? If you haven't, then you cannot call yourself a DBA. If you have a database used for reporting, why not leverage it? Use DTS to create a copy of the data from your hot standby database, and focus on recovering the data from the standby reporting server that may have been lost in between by recovering the transaction log. Why not have a fully functional, hot standby database to which you can point your primary applications if the primary database becomes corrupt, unusable, deleted, or hacked? These are all cases for having a clustered, multiple instance SQL Server solution.

N+1 Configurations

N+1 configurations are the best of both worlds for clustering technology. In N+1 configurations, N refers to number of nodes, while +1 refers to an additional node running on standby. This means in a failure scenario, the +1 virtual server takes ownership of the failed resource and any other dependent resources. This also means you can receive more resource productivity out of your hardware and still have a hot standby node to be a dedicated resource in the event of resource failure.

In an N+1 configuration of four nodes, three of the nodes are serving requests actively and the fourth is serving the hot standby partner to which any node can fail. Using an N+1 configuration is more cost-effective than a traditional active/passive configuration because it is not a one-to-one, active-to-passive ratio. You can support multiple instances of SQL Server, and, in the event of a single node failure, performance is not adversely affected. An N+1 configuration also addresses cost. Because N+1 configurations have a standby node, it is more expensive, but it doesn't have the one-to-one, active-to-passive ratio; so it is not waiting for the failure ratio that active/passive configurations have. This makes it more cost-effective than active/passive configurations. This also means you must have at least three *active* nodes for a true N+1 configuration.

Let's talk about resources again. In active/passive configurations, there are as many instances of SQL Server as you want, but the same server owns them all. One node of the cluster owns all resources all the time. When resource failure occurs, all resources are transferred to the other node. In active/active configurations, there are at least as many installed SQL Server instances as there are servers participating in the cluster. Because of this, all the clustered nodes are actively working and using their available resources. So, what are those resources?

For the *default* instance, you need:

- Clustered Host server
- SQL Server Network Name (this is the Virtual SQL Server name)
- SQL Server Network IP address
- Physical disk resources for the data and log files (a best practice is to have these on separate disks to maximize performance)
- MSSQLServer Service
- SQL Server Agent Service
- SQL Full Text Search Service

For any *named* instance, you need:

- Clustered Host server
- SQL Server Network Name (this is an instance name of SQL Server, such as "virtualservername\instance name")
- SQL Server Network IP address
- Physical disk resources for the data and log files (a best practice is to have these on separate disks to maximize performance)
- MSSQLServer Service
- SQL Server Agent Service
- SQL Full Text Search Service

With multiple instance configurations, each instance of SQL Server acts independently of the other. Each instance needs its own distinct set of resources. These instances only interact if and when the same node owns multiple instances of SQL Server. Your primary consideration should be performance planning. Multiple instances require their own resources, and that takes careful planning and coordination. This involves all dependent resources, which are discussed in the following sections.

Physical Disks

Physical disks have grown in capacity and are more resilient with the SAN and disk arrays that are available these days, but they come with a high price. Conventional disk storage arrays are cheaper, but many are not expandable and have only small amounts of memory cache. Because shared storage is a prerequisite for clustering, you must have some form of shared storage—SCSI arrays, SAN arrays, or replicated disk arrays.

As previously stated, each instance of SQL Server needs its own disk resource dedicated to only the function of that instance of SQL Server. Don't just give SQL Server a *chod*, or *chunk-of-disk-space*. SQL Server databases are comprised of data and log files. The data files store the data that exists in an SQL Server database. All the tables, indexes, and logic are stored there. The SQL Server log file is where the transactions are written.

When data is inserted or updated into the database, it first is written to the transaction log. These sequential logs are then committed to the data file by a process called a *checkpoint*. During a checkpoint, the database engine writes (also known as *flushes*) all committed transactions (dirty pages) to the data file on disk. The transaction log is written sequentially; so it knows to keep track of long-running transactions that may not complete between checkpoints.

SQL Server also reads from this transaction log when select statements are executed against the database tables and views. If we update a record at 12 p.m., and you select that same record at 12:01 p.m., and there has been no checkpoint issued, how is the correct record returned to you? The transaction log file is read, and those dirty pages are referenced to show the updated record set. Do you remember your RAID levels? Here are the most common levels and how they relate to SQL Server.

RAID 0, Striped Disk Array without Fault Tolerance: RAID 0 has no associated overhead trying to be redundant and is not truly RAID as RAID stands for *Redundant Array of Independent Disks* and should not be used because it is *not* fault-tolerant.

RAID 1, Mirrored Disks: This configuration takes two disks to configure and has a possible one write or two reads throughput per mirrored pair. 100 percent redundancy of data means no rebuild is necessary in case of a disk failure, just a copy to the replacement disk. RAID 1 is redundant. Both disks are duplicates of each other. This is especially meaningful with RDBMS technology. The database files hold the storage data. The transaction log file holds each and every transaction that will be or has been executed against the database it is referencing. These transactions must be secured against loss and corruption.

RAID 1 also has some drawbacks, like the highest disk overhead of all RAID types (100 percent)—which means it has to do work twice and is, therefore, inefficient. Typically, the RAID function is done by system software—loading the CPU/Server and possibly degrading throughput at high activity levels. Configuring RAID 1 disk sets at the hardware level is strongly recommended.

RAID 5, Independent Data disks with distributed or rotating parity blocks: This configuration has the highest read data transaction rate; a medium write data transaction rate; a low ratio of parity disks to data disks, which means it has high efficiency; and it has a good aggregate transfer rate. Disadvantages include disk failure, which has a medium impact on throughput performance, it is more difficult to rebuild in the event of a disk failure (as compared to RAID level 1), and individual block data transfer rates are the same as a single disk (with no additional throughput). With RAID 5 arrays, you can lose a single disk of the array and not lose any data. RAID 5 stores parity information but not redundant data (however, parity information can be used to reconstruct data). RAID 5 arrays require at least three individual hard disks. The best throughput is accomplished when there are at least five disks constituting the RAID 5 set.

RAID 10, Very High Reliability combined with High Performance: RAID 10 is implemented as a striped array whose segments are RAID 1 arrays. Effectively, these are striped mirrored sets, and that may not sound redundant, but RAID 10 has the same fault tolerance as RAID 1. RAID 10 has the same overhead for fault tolerance as mirroring alone and is an excellent solution for sites that otherwise would have gone with RAID 1 but need some additional performance boost. The mirroring provides the fault tolerance, and the disk striping aids in this performance boost. Disadvantages of this solution are that it is very expensive and has high overhead. Also, all drives must move in parallel to properly track lowering the overall sustained performance. RAID 10 is limited in its scalability and has a very high inherent cost when upgrades are deemed necessary. This is sometimes referred to as a mirrored RAID 5 set.

Many other RAID implementations exist, and each scenario has its own requirements to consider. As a best practice, baseline SQL Server transaction logs should be kept at least in a RAID 1 or RAID 10 disk set.

In most disaster scenarios, this prevents data loss and does not degrade performance until a disk recovery is necessary. SQL Server data files should be kept at least in a RAID 5 or RAID 10 disk set. In most disaster scenarios, this prevents data loss. RAID 5 also has the best-read capability, which is an important factor when dealing with the data file. The two key points to remember for successfully managing an SQL Server are uptime and speed. If the database is not available, there is a serious problem. If clients can connect, but using the applications that carry on regular activities is difficult, then we are not offering a high availability, high-performance solution.

Planning for disk utilization comes in more flavors than just deciding on which RAID implementations to place your data and log files. Depending on the number of disks and their individual capacity, there are considerations. SQL Server uses a temporary *scratch pad* to hold temp tables and other temporary database objects and processes.

This scratch pad is *TempDB*. The information in TempDB is released when it is no longer needed, such as when the transaction in question has completed or the temporary database object is no longer needed. Because this data does not require any redundancy, why place it on a partition that has a redundant RAID implementation on it? In large implementations, it may be a good idea to move TempDB to a partition of disk that doesn't have any redundancy.

This requires a more complex disk array configuration, but it may also save you a few gigabytes of disk space, which will go a long way to ease potential performance bottlenecks in the future. In large database implementations, it is often common and a best practice to create multiple file groups to house different internal components of SQL Server databases. The most common of these objects are indexes. Creating multiple filegroups—one to hold tables and another for indexes—can greatly increase performance for all aspects of database operations. Breaking existing databases into multiple filegroups may not have been an option prior to deciding to cluster your SQL Server installation, but now that you have decided to cluster your SQL Server and you have shared storage, it may be an ideal time to separate key portions of your database structure for performance tuning and longer term database planning.

Any type of additional database services, such as OLAP and Microsoft Reporting services, need special attention. It is a best practice to create OLAP cubes in their own RAID set. This is because OLAP is especially disk-intensive. When OLAP services create cubes, they compile data into multidimensional structures and pre-compute all possible computations of the given data sets. This is usually aggregate data.

If cost and administration overhead is an issue in the beginning, estimate the size of the databases, the number of connections you expect, and the application or business. Follow the guidelines in Chapter 13, "Looking for Trouble: Setting Up Performance Monitoring and Alerts," to monitor disks for performance. You can always start with a simple RAID 5 configuration and place all your databases on a single partition. Then as the number of transactions begin to climb—and you are approaching the performance threshold, and as a budget becomes available—you can always opt for a SAN, more local disks (for the replicated disk option), or a bigger SCSI array.

A nice feature of the replicated disk option is that you can maintain the service level on one single node while you drop a SAN into the scenario and drop each server onto the SAN one server at a time. You also can increase disk resources on each node because all you need to do is evict a node from the cluster, rebuild it, bring it back online, replicate the disk resource again, move ownership to the new node, and then rebuild the second node. All this time the application is available.

As an example, when we tested NSI Software's GeoCluster solution, we were able to drop nodes in and out of the cluster as we tried various disk configurations while keeping SQL Server available all the time.

Memory

Memory on each node of the cluster is another item to be addressed. SQL Server is an application that uses as much memory as it is allowed. The more transactions SQL Server can hold in memory, the faster the server feels to the end user. When planning for failover capacity, the amount of resources for all failed instances must be taken into consideration. Memory management can be explicitly configured through SQL Server using the Memory tab on the properties of the database server instance or by running the *sp_configure* stored procedure.

Memory management can be left to SQL Server to dynamically manage (see Figure 9.1). A fixed-value of memory dedicated to SQL Server also can be configured. If you are running SQL Server in an active/active cluster, you may want to manually configure how much memory each instance of SQL Server can use, so should a failover occur, both instances of SQL Server have the ability to grab the amount of RAM they need to run efficiently.

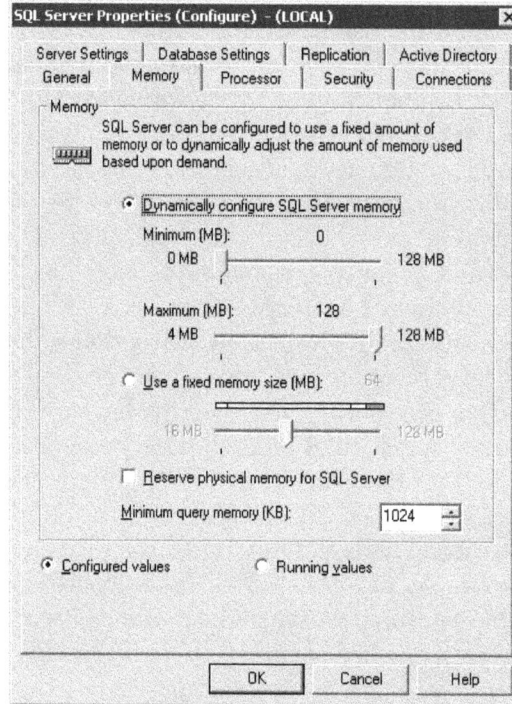

Figure 9.1   Configuring memory usage on an instance of SQL Server.

A minimum amount of memory also can be configured for queries. These values and configuration options, whether statically or dynamically configured, should be the same on each node of the cluster. In the event of failover, if the settings are different, there could be a significant degradation in performance.

Local Disks

The local hard disks of a clustered server house the individual operating system and program files. These disks need to be redundant. What good would a cluster be if a single point-of-failure was built into the foundation of the cluster? A mirrored disk set is usually the configuration option for most clusters.

A mirrored disk set provides redundancy, good speed, and little or no performance degradation in the event a disk needs to be rebuilt after failure. Local disks should be as fast as possible, and adequate amounts of virtual memory for the operating system should be allotted. Any data that is to be used by any node in the cluster set does not belong on the local disks of the server, unless the local disks are part of a replicated disk resource.

The local disks are going to house the program files and clustering files for the participating node. With Windows Server 2003, temp files are stored in the profile of each individual user who logs on to each server. In an effort to streamline the cleanup of this, you can change the system environmental variable that points to the profile for temporary file space and consolidate this into a single directory that generally resides in a root folder location. This is illustrated in Figure 9.2. Note the destination folder needs to be created ahead of time.

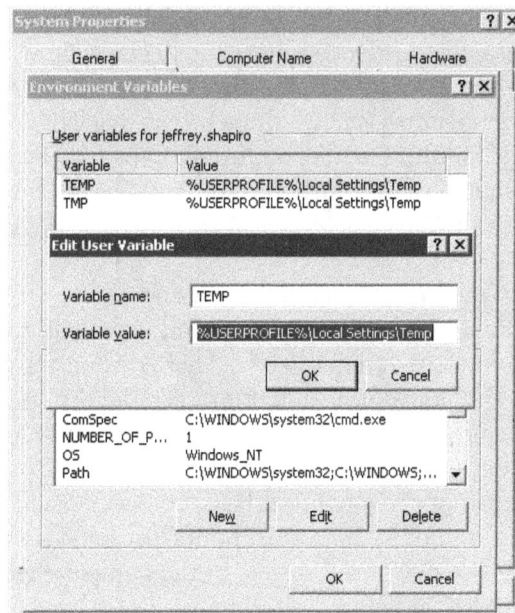

Figure 9.2   Changing the location of server temp files.

Standby Services—Advantages and Disadvantages

Definite advantages and disadvantages exist when it comes to clustering standby services. Some are obvious while others are not. Some of the items that we review can be an advantage or a disadvantage depending on the perspective (IT staff versus Accounting) from which you are viewing these items.

High availability is the single most important factor when weighing advantages and disadvantages of clustering to an administrator. While most DBAs think performance is at the top of the list, performance problems cannot be easily addressed without considering a cluster. Using standby services—that is, services and resources that are not actively being used and are waiting for failure to occur—is most often a decision based on the availability of funding. High availability goals for your business can be achieved through a clustering solution that does not have standby services.

Multiple instance or active/active clustering is the predominant form for a solution like this. The performance of your applications, from the database perspective, is where the decision on whether or not to use standby services is made. If standby services are not used and a multiple instance architecture is used, there are no available unused resources in the event of failure. The failed burden of the load is dispersed across the rest of the nodes of the cluster. In our instance, all resources for multiple installations of SQL Server are now owned and managed by a single server.

What if the load is too much for a single server to bear? The application may time out, report errors to end users, fail to serve requests, or even crash the server completely. That is when my worst two enemies show up—data corruption and unpredictable results. Is your application still truly highly available? In the event of a disaster, can one server truly hold the entire load? The costs for hardware, software licensing, and a paid administrator is not cheap. Have you ever calculated the cost of one hour of downtime? 12 hours? 24 hours? In some scenarios, more than a few minutes of downtime results in the company facing a real loss and the challenge of finding a new administrator.

Advantages of standby services are abundant, most notably the ability to be redundant and the resiliency to recover from resource failure. In the event a single node fails, there is no performance degradation because a twin of the failed system is available to serve requests at a moment's notice. Another advantage to standby services is the capability to continually provide services and stay up-to-date with Windows and security updates.

This is a challenging feat in environments where managing multiple instances threaten the uptime of a server. With standby services, each node of a cluster can own the resource pools as the opposite nodes are brought up-to-date and rebooted if necessary, thus resulting in a greater amount of total uptime for connected clients and processes.

Clustering SQL Server

Preparation for SQL Server 2000 clustered installation starts with the basics. The operating system of the individual nodes comes first. Are the security patches up-to-date? Are the most up-to-date service packs applied? See Chapters 5, "Preparing the Platform for a High-Performance Network" and 6, "Building the Foundations for a Highly Available Architecture," which review architecture and platform implementation. Does the server pass the MBSA penetration tests? (See the "Troubleshooting, Maintenance, and Best Practices" section.) Is anti-virus installed and configured properly? It is very important to lay a strong foundation from within the operating system before the installation CD is even inserted (if you can't install anti-virus software before the operating system).

Also, make sure the minimum system requirements are met. It may sounds silly, but it is definitely worth the time it takes to verify the requirements and that you meet them. Download the latest service packs, hotfixes, and security patches from the Microsoft SQL Server Web site (www.microsoft.com/sql) ahead of time. Better yet, check to see whether the Active Directory administrators have Software Update Services (SUS) up and running and whether they are online. Make sure you have all the most recent updates available on the local hard disk.

Next, you should have all the necessary clustered installation resources information ready ahead of time. Here is a basic list of what you need before you begin:

- Appropriate cluster hardware that has been certified by Microsoft.
- Windows Server 2003, Enterprise Edition, with its latest updates installed properly as a cluster (clustering is not possible on the Standard Edition).

- Windows Server 2003 Cluster Services must have been properly installed and configured. Refer to Chapter 6 if you have never clustered your servers.
- The Windows Server 2003 Cluster Service needs to have been thoroughly tested to ensure it is working correctly and the cluster service account has been properly created. This means ensuring the domain [user] account you are using for the SQL Server services has been added to the local administrators groups of all participating servers and is *not* a member of Domain Admins.
- Ensure you (the installer) are a local administrator on all participating nodes of the cluster.
- Have a copy of the SQL Server installation CDs.
- Pick a name you can assign to the SQL Server cluster. This is the virtual name clients use to access SQL Server. This name must consist only of letters or numbers, no special characters. You can default to the name of the cluster, but that is not always a practical solution.
- Have an IP address you can assign to the SQL Server cluster. This IP address is assigned to the virtual server that clients use to connect to SQL Server.

To install SQL Server onto the cluster, do the following:

1. Click Setup on the SQL Server CD. When the Welcome dialog box loads, select Next.
2. Enter the name of the virtual server. This is the name of the server your clients connect to. It is also the name used in the connection strings and tools, like Enterprise Manager. This is illustrated in Figure 9.3. Click Next.
3. Enter your user information if it is not automatically selected, and click Next.
4. You are presented with a request to acknowledge the licensing agreement. Select Yes and continue with the installation.
5. You now need to insert the IP address used by the virtual SQL Server. Under Network to Use, select your public network connection. This is the network connection that is connected to the LAN for client access (not the heartbeat). This is illustrated in Figure 9.4.

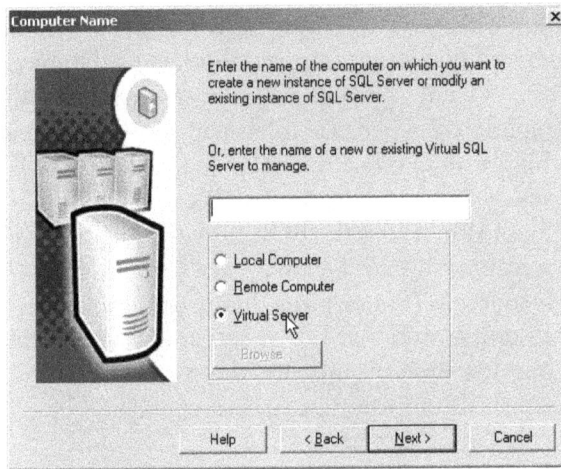

Figure 9.3 Setting the virtual server name.

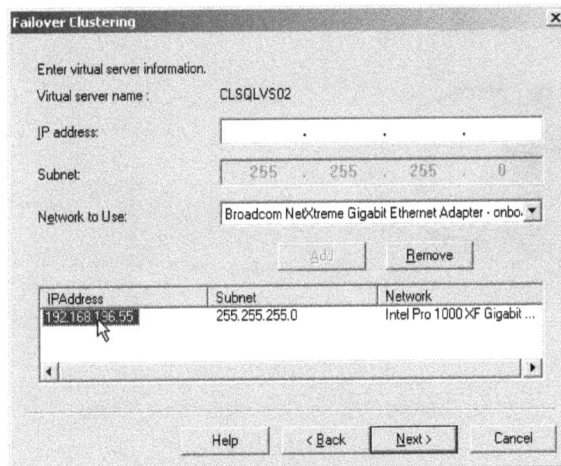

Figure 9.4 Setting the IP address for the virtual server.

6. It is possible to add additional virtual IP addresses for multiple instance clustering, but that is not necessary to configure the default installation nor is it necessary with active/passive, single instance installations of SQL Server on a cluster. Click Next to continue.

7. You must now tell SQL Server setup which logical disk of your shared disk array to place the logical database files. Make sure you do not select the Quorum drive (just thought we would mention this because it has happened). This task is illustrated in Figure 9.5. What this step really does is tell the SQL Server setup wizard where to install the SQL Server system database files. Also, it tells the SQL Server setup wizard the disk resource selected should become part of the SQL Server clustering resources. This ensures that if resource failure occurs, the disk resource used by SQL Server for system databases fails over as one resource group with the rest of the dependent resources. Select the appropriate drive and click Next.

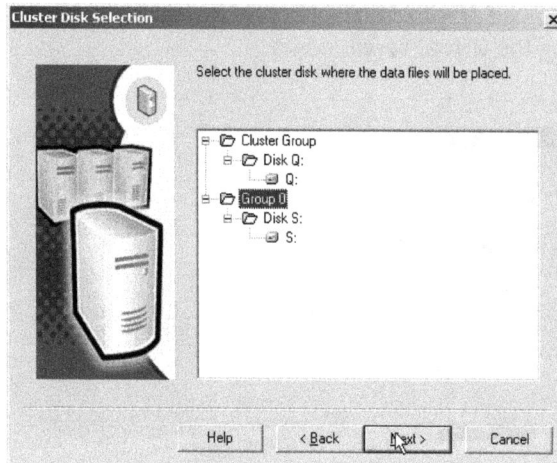

Figure 9.5   Specifying the disk for the logical database files.

8. At this point, you need to define which of the available nodes of the Windows cluster set should be available for SQL Server failover in the event of resource failure. This depends greatly on your business scenario and the type of Windows cluster configuration you have decided on. This decision can be as simple as the two available nodes, both configured as available cluster nodes, or it can be as complex as deciding that individual nodes should be excluded from this cluster because their role will be as a

member of a different clustered SQL Server installation at a later time. Figure 9.6 illustrates this. When you are finished, click Next.

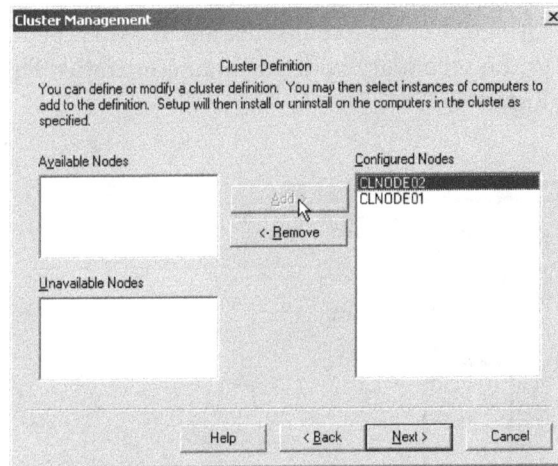

Figure 9.6   Specifying available nodes.

NOTE: Remember the N+1 clustered SQL Server 2000 configuration? With multiple instances of SQL Server 2000, you have the ability to dictate the participation of particular nodes of a cluster in different installations of SQL Server 2000. This is left to administrator discretion. You are given a four-node Windows 2003 Server cluster set. If you wanted to create an N+1 configuration, you could install three separate instances of SQL Server 2000, leaving a single node idle and waiting for resource failure to occur. During the installation of SQL Server 2000, on a clustered server set, you can choose to exclude particular nodes from assuming resource ownership from that installation of SQL Server 2000, and that is configurable here.

9. At this point, you must prove you have the appropriate rights to install SQL Server instances on this clustered set of servers. This form requires explanation because it is more than what it appears to be. The current wizard installs SQL Server on the local drive of both nodes of the cluster, along with the shared

disk arrays logical drive you selected in one of the previous steps. One of these nodes, the *primary node*, is the server where the wizard is currently running. The other node is called the *secondary node*. To install SQL Server on the secondary node from the primary node, a remote SQL Server 2000 installation is performed. For remote installation to work, the wizard must log in to the secondary node as an administrator. This is illustrated in Figure 9.7.

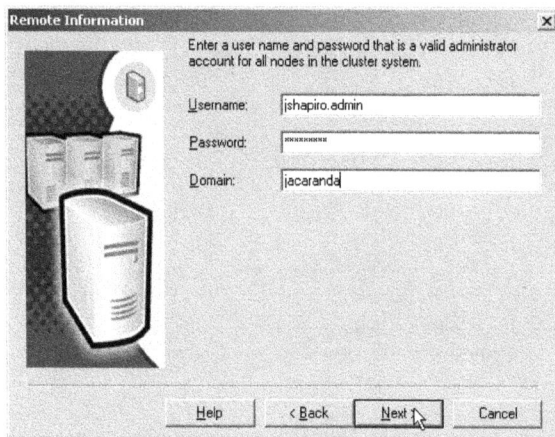

Figure 9.7 Remote installation to the other nodes.

This dialog box tells the SQL Server setup wizard the name of the instance of SQL Server you are currently installing. The figures represent a default instance of SQL Server on the cluster; this is a *default* installation. A named instance is only required if you intend to run more than one instance of SQL Server on the cluster, creating a multiple instance installation leading to active/active clustering and N+1 configurations.

10. At this point, you have arrived at what looks like the setup screen for SQL Server 2000, shown in Figure 9.8. The *Destination Folder* locations should be of interest to you. These should not have to be changed. If the destination folder for your SQL Server data files is not the logical drive on your shared storage disk array, that you specified earlier during setup, there is a

problem. The SQL Server 2000 *Program Files* need to be installed on the local disk of each node, not on the logical drive on the shared array. Verify this is correct for your setup, and click Next.

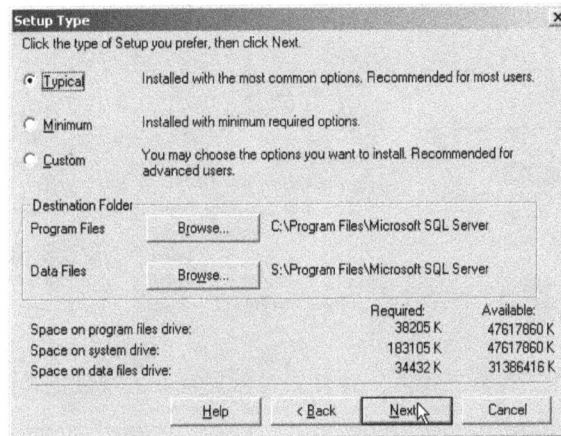

Figure 9.8 Destination folders.

11. At this point, the installation proceeds much like it does on standard installs. Select which components you want to install. The default options are usually sufficient.

To finalize the installation, enter the SQL Server 2000 service account information; this is necessary for any SQL Server 2000 installation. Choose the appropriate authentication mode for your situation, the appropriate SQL Collation, the appropriate network libraries (usually TCP/IP) licensing mode, and you are done.

The SQL Server 2000 installation can finally commence. The messages displayed change, giving you a watered-down explanation of what is going on behind the scenes. This process takes a fair amount of time to complete. Although you are not prompted to do so, after the install is complete, it is highly recommended you reboot all nodes of the cluster.

First, reboot the primary node (the node on which you have just run the SQL Server installation wizard). Make sure it comes up successfully, as shown in Figure 9.9. Then reboot the secondary node(s) and be sure they come up successfully. After you have a successful installation of SQL Server 2000 on the cluster, it is time to install the most recent SQL

Server 2000 Service Pack. Even if you did not reboot the nodes of the cluster, you are prompted to reboot them before you can install the service pack.

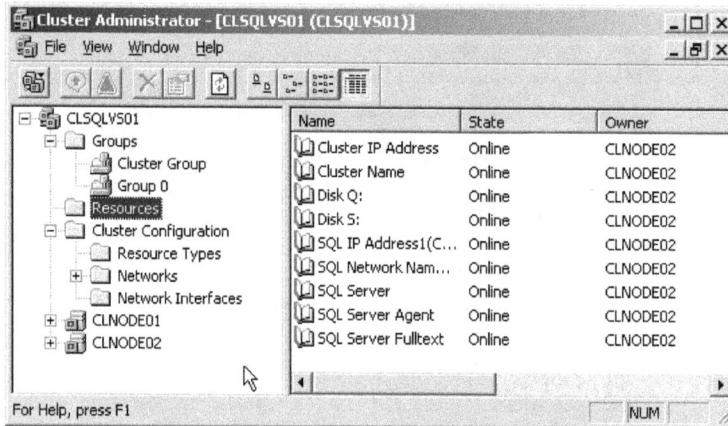

Figure 9.9 A successful SQL Server cluster installation.

Some additional items can be extremely helpful when running this installation. This includes copying the installation media to the local hard drive and running it from there instead of the CD-ROM drive. Having the most updated service packs, hot fixes, and security patches copied to the local disk drive for installation is also helpful.

High Availability, High-Performance Notes

With the SQL Server cluster up and running, you are ready to attach databases from the development servers. Let's review some architectural issues concerning high availability, high-performance SQL Server.

Storage Notes

Where to store your data depends on the kind of data it is. SQL Server 2000 data storage is not of the same ilk as your operating system. SQL Server Data Structure breaks down into the following:

Pages and extents are structures that house SQL Server data. The actual data in your table is stored in pages. BLOB (binary large object) data is excluded. If a column contains BLOB data, then a 16-byte pointer record is used to reference the BLOB page. A page is the smallest unit of data storage in Microsoft SQL Server. A page contains the data from the actual rows of the table. A row can only reside in one page. Each page can contain 8KB of information, due to this structure; the maximum size of a row is 8KB. A grouping of eight adjacent pages is called an *extent*. A *heap* is a collection of data pages.

Heaps and the Index Allocation Map (IAM) are structures to help identify where data is stored and located. Heaps have one row in sysindexes. The column sysindexes.FirstIAM points to the first IAM page in the chain of IAM pages that manage the space allocated to the heap. Microsoft SQL Server 2000 uses IAM pages to navigate through the heap. The data pages and the rows within them are not in any specific order and are not linked together. The only logical connection between data pages is that they are recorded in IAM pages.

All SQL Server indexes are B-Trees. There is a single "root" page at the top of the tree, branching out into N number of pages at each intermediate level until it reaches the bottom, or leaf level, of the index. The index tree is navigated by following pointers from the upper-level pages down through the lower-level pages to the leaf level. In addition, each index level is a separate page chain. The number of levels is dependent on the index key width, the type of index, and the number of rows or pages in the table. The number of levels is important in relation to index performance.

Two primary types of indexes exist: *clustered* and *nonclustered*. A *nonclustered index* is very similar to an index in a book. The data is stored in one place on the disk, and the index is in another place on the disk, with pointer records to the storage location of the actual data. The items in the index are stored in the order of the index key values, but the information in the table is stored in a different order. If no clustered index exists on the table, the rows are not guaranteed to be in any particular order.

Similar to the way you use an index in a book, Microsoft SQL Server 2000 searches for a data value by searching the nonclustered index to find the physical location of the data value in the table; it then retrieves the data directly from that location. This makes nonclustered indexes the optimal choice when searching for values to match identically because the index contains entries describing the exact location of the queried data values in the table.

A *clustered index* writes data in the physical order of data in a table. A clustered index is very similar to a telephone directory, which arranges data by last name. Because the clustered index writes data in the physical storage order of the data in the table, a table can contain only one clustered index. However, an index can be created that compiles multiple columns (a composite index). A clustered index is most efficient on columns that are queried based on a range of values. Clustered indexes are also efficient for finding a specific row when the indexed value is unique. A primary key constraint creates clustered indexes automatically if no clustered index already exists on the table. Because of these factors, it is a best practice to make physical disk housing SQL Server data and log file a dedicated resource for SQL Server operations whenever possible.

Failover Resources

Resource failover usually means there is a problem, and the clustered servers are doing their best to ensure client requests are served. Resource failover can be done manually as well. Failing over resources is a proper way of testing your failover scenarios. Before the SQL Server installations are created, you should have a very high comfort level with resource failover. This requires a lot of testing.

Pulling out network cables, disconnecting attached storage cables, unplugging power cables, and so forth are possible scenarios for these clustered servers to failover. Create these disaster scenarios ahead of time and evaluate how the cluster reacts. After SQL Server 2000 is installed, it is time to failover resources again. Try to create potential disaster scenarios for your servers to produce failover scenarios.

Compare what happens during failover to what your expectations were. Cluster resources can be an abundance of different resources. Cluster resources can be a physical disk, a Windows service, a network name, and more. Resources are assembled into resource groups. Resource groups are generally grouped by dependency. Dependency is configurable, and dependency can be configured wrong, too! Dependency for SQL Server 2000 can be broken down into the following lines.

The SQL Server Agent resource depends on the SQL Server resource, and the SQL Server Full Text resource depends on the SQL

Server resource. The SQL Server resource depends on the SQL network name resource and the physical disk resources that hold its data. The SQL network name resource depends on the SQL IP address resource. The SQL IP address resource and the physical disk resources do not depend on any resources. The only time the dependency of these resources should be altered is when you add physical disk resources to the SQL Server resource so that SQL Server can use additional drives for additional file groups, disks for transaction logs, or other disk resources. Improper altering of dependencies can lead to a dependency loop where no resources can be brought online.

Enterprise Manager

SQL Server 2000 Enterprise Manager is a graphical tool for the management of database operations. When using Enterprise Manager to connect to a clustered installation of SQL Server, you must connect to the SQL Server virtual server name for default instances or connect to the Virtual SQL Server name\instance name for named instances. Attempting to connect to the local host for SQL Server access becomes a frustrating process.

Other tools are present on a clustered server that may be familiar to you if you have used SQL Server in any depth before. The SQL Server 2000 Services Manager is a prime example. Attempting to stop clustered SQL Server services using Services Manager does not produce the desired results. Clustered resources need to be managed through the Cluster Administrator console. SQL Server Query Analyzer is a tried and true command or code-based tool to administer SQL Server 2000.

When using Query Analyzer, you must again connect to the SQL Server Virtual server name for default instances or connect to the Virtual SQL Server name\instance name for named instances. Enterprise Manager is a versatile GUI tool and does not auto-refresh. This has been known to pose a problem of *seeing* changes in real-time. Most of the applets in Enterprise Manager can be manually refreshed to identify and verify changes. Whenever you want to verify changes to database objects using Enterprise Manager, we would suggest manually refreshing the object that was changed. Enterprise Manager fools you if you let it.

Transactions and Logs

Transaction logs are a vital and often overlooked component of SQL Server 2000 database architecture. They are often overlooked because these logs are not scrupulously checked and altered or actively maintained like other database objects contained within a database. A transaction log is a sequential record of all changes made to the database. The actual data stored in the database is stored in a separate file.

The transaction log contains enough data to roll back all changes made to the data file as part of any individual transaction. The log records the start of a transaction, all the changes contained in the transaction including changes made to associated database objects, and then the final commit or rollback of the changes contained in the transaction. Each database has at least one physical transaction log and one data file that is a dedicated resource for only the database for which it was created. SQL Server keeps this log as a buffer of all the changes to data for speed and performance reasons.

SQL Server writes items to the transaction log immediately, but it does not write changes to the data file until a checkpoint is issued. A checkpoint is written to the transaction log to indicate that a particular transaction has been completely written from the buffer to the data file. This process is also known as flushing dirty pages to disk. When the SQL Server service is restarted, it identifies the most recent checkpoint in the transaction log and rolls forward all transactions that were recorded from that point forward because it is not guaranteed to have been written to the data file until a checkpoint is entered in the transaction log. Pages prior to the checkpoint being entered are not committed to disk and are therefore still dirty.

This prevents the loss of transactions that were in the buffer but not yet written to the data file. Transaction logs usually become a problem because they are often forgotten about until an issue occurs. The log continues to grow as operations are performed within the database if *autogrow* is set to *automatic*, and the disk still has space to allocate. While the log continues to grow, the available disk space decreases. Unless action is taken to prevent this, the transaction log inevitably grows to the full capacity of the disk.

This scenario leads to a problem. When the physical disk runs out of space to allocate to a growing file, the database stops functioning. Regularly scheduled backups of the transaction log help prevent it from consuming all the disk space and are the most efficient way of dealing with this problem. The backup process truncates old log records that are committed and, therefore, no longer needed for recovery.

The truncation process marks committed records as inactive; so they can be overwritten, which helps prevent the transaction log from growing too large. If frequent backups are not made or scheduled, then the database needs to be configured with the *simple recovery model* option. The simple recovery model forces the transaction log to be truncated automatically each time a checkpoint is processed. Using a simple recovery model severely limits your capabilities to recover from disaster.

Using a simple recovery model only enables you to recover a database to the last full backup of the database. The truncation process that occurs as a result of a backup or the issue of a checkpoint marks committed log records as inactive, which can be overwritten, but it does not reduce the actual size of the transaction log.

The logs continue to own all the space allocated, even if it is not used. Transaction logs play a vital role in the function of a database. Because of the nature of their role, they can have a direct impact on overall system performance.

Certain configurations can be made that optimize the performance of transaction logs. This is where a dedicated disk resource with an appropriate redundant disk configuration is necessary. Configuration options for transaction logs themselves also exist. These options encompass how the log file grows, when necessary. The log file can be configured to grow at a percentage of the total size of the log file or at a predetermined, set physical size. Regardless of which option you have chosen, the growth of the file should be sufficient enough to prevent the log from needing to continually expand. If the growth setting is set too low, the log may need to continually expand. This is unnecessary overhead and consumes system resources. This scenario has a negative effect on system performance.

Configuration and Planning

Multiple options are available for providing high availability solutions involving SQL Server 2000 clustering. Effective planning for a solution that fits your scenario starts long before an SQL Server solution is prepared. Many decisions need to be made ahead of considerations for SQL Server 2000 clustering. Here is a short list:

- Hardware. How many servers are members of this cluster?
- What type of shared storage disk array is used to house the cluster and database resources?
- How do the members of the cluster communicate with each other? Do they communicate through their own private network, or is all traffic passed on the public network? How do you provide redundancy and eliminate a single point-of-failure for these communications?
- What hardware is used to connect the members of the cluster to the shared storage array?
- Does your proposed hardware solution meet the requirements for SQL Server 2000? Is this hardware on the Microsoft HCL? (This can be found at `http://www.microsoft.com/whdc/hcl/default.mspx`.)
- Software. How many servers are members of the cluster for operating system licensing and SQL Server 2000 licensing? Does Windows Server 2003 standard satisfy your clustering goals?
- How many instances of SQL Server do you plan on implementing?
- How do you license SQL Server 2000? By CAL or by processor?
- Capacity. How large is the data set you are currently using?
- What is the growth rate percentage of your current data set over the last 3 months? 6 months? 12 months?
- What is the anticipated growth rate for the next 6 months? 12 months? 24 months?
- Solution. Is the proposed solution scalable enough to meet your anticipated requirements?

These questions are just some of the questions that need to be answered to ensure proper planning and help facilitate a lasting solution. Your individual scenario and goals will mold your other questions to develop a long-term solution.

The Role of Replication

SQL Server 2000 replication is a powerful tool that can provide another layer of redundancy and resiliency from resource failure. Multiple forms of replication exist in SQL Server 2000. Some are not formally called replication, but replicated data is the backbone of their function. SQL Server replication allows you, as the database administrator, to distribute data to multiple servers throughout an organization. You may wish to implement replication in your organization for a number of reasons, such as

- **Load balancing:** Replication allows you to distribute your data to a number of servers and then distribute load placed on these individual servers. These servers can be part of a clustered server environment to further promote redundancy and load balancing.
- **Offline processing:** You can manipulate and alter data from your database on a server that is not always connected to the network. This can provide a hot standby or an up-to-date and valid testing environment containing real-time data.
- **Redundancy:** Replication allows you to build a failover database server that is ready to pick up the processing load at a moment's notice.

Regardless of which replication scenario you choose, there are two main components:

- Publishers have data to offer to other servers. Any chosen replication scheme can have one or more publishers.
- Subscribers are SQL Server 2000 database servers that receive updates from the Publisher when data is altered or at scheduled intervals.

Any server can act as both a publisher and subscriber. In large-scale redundant database environments that entail multiple database structures, it is common to see a single clustered set of servers exchanging data with another clustered set of servers and vice versa. This provides a redundant environment for both sets of clusters. Microsoft SQL Server supports three types of database replication—*snapshot replication*, *transactional replication*, and *merger replication*.

Snapshot replication behaves much like the name sounds. The server that offers data for transfer, the publisher, takes a snapshot of the entire database to be replicated and offers it to the subscribers. This is a very resource-intensive process. It is also very time-consuming. The larger the dataset, the more resource-intensive it is, and the duration of the replication is longer. Because of this, snapshot replication is generally not used as a regularly scheduled event. Most administrators don't use snapshot replication on a recurring basis for databases that change frequently. Two scenarios exist where snapshot replication is commonly used. First, it is used for databases where the data is very static. Second, it is used to set a starting point for databases that use merge or transactional replication to establish a common data set from which to get started.

Transactional replication is much less resource-intensive and is a flexible solution for databases that are altered regularly. Transactional replication uses an agent to monitor and track changes made to database objects. The agent can present the changes to the subscriber immediately or at scheduled intervals. Using transactional replication is much less resource-intensive and is much faster than snapshot replication due to the relatively smaller amount of data that is being replicated.

Merge replication allows the publisher and subscriber to independently make changes to their databases. Both entities can work without an active network connection. When they are reconnected, merge replication uses an agent to check for changes on both sets of data and alters each database to reflect the changes. If there are any changes that conflict each other, the merge replication agent uses a conflict resolution algorithm to determine which changes to implement. Merge replication is a common solution for users and processes that cannot be constantly connected to a publisher, such as laptop mobile device users. This is also a potential solution for SQL Servers that are separated by expensive WAN links. In this scenario, SQL Servers have to compete with end users and other processes for network bandwidth. Using merge replication during off hours can promote savings on network bandwidth.

Another type of replication that uses a different name is *log shipping*. SQL Server 2000 log shipping is a process that involves replicating data from one SQL Server database to another using transaction log file backups from one server and restoring them to another. This process uses a simple architecture of backing up transaction logs, copying those logs across the network, and restoring them on a log shipping partner server.

This is a scheduled process. At virtually any interval, the transaction logs can be backed up and restored. With SQL Server 2000 log shipping, you can have a hot standby server on which the data is only as old as the amount of time you specify. This amount of time is calculated by adding the amount of time of the interval of the backups, the amount of time to copy the logs, and the amount of time to restore the transaction logs. Just like transactional replication, using a log shipping scenario is much less resource-intensive and is much faster than snapshot replication due to the relatively small amount of data that is being replicated.

Each one of these replication techniques serves a purpose and may be best suited to facilitate additional redundancy for your particular, individual database scenario. These techniques can be *mix-matched* across a single database or multiple servers to create a redundancy strategy that best suits your business. They can be instituted in various ways to be as flexible or as rigid as your business dictates.

Disaster Recovery

More than likely you are aware of the need for a comprehensive disaster recovery plan. This plan produces questions that form the starting point for the development of a plan tailored to the unique needs of your organization.

The first step in developing a solid disaster recovery plan is to develop an idea of what constitutes an acceptable loss for your organization. In the event of a disaster, there *will* be a loss. First, examine the results of losing data stored in your database(s). Would you be able to recover from the loss of an hour's worth of data?

The type of business mechanism you are administering shapes the actions you take. If you're managing an infrastructure employee database, you could deal with a disaster by instructing your personnel to reenter data entered during the period of the disaster. If you're running the database supporting a financial institution or a Web-based application receiving financial transactions, the loss of an hour's data could bring an instant wave of disgruntled clients and regulators along with significant monetary losses for your business.

Backups of the database and use of transaction logging provide protection against these types of losses. Second, consider the loss of access to the database itself. How would your business be affected if access to the database was lost for an extended period of time? After you've determined the level of acceptable loss for your organization, develop a strategy to minimize the impact of a catastrophic event on your database. Your first step is to develop a comprehensive backup strategy.

HA for Analysis Services (OLAP)

Online Analytical Processing (OLAP) enables users to access information from multidimensional data warehouses, almost instantly, to view information in any way they like and to cleanly specify and carry out sophisticated calculations. Although many commercial OLAP tools and products are now available, OLAP is still a difficult and complex technology to master.

SQL Server 2000 Analysis Services provides fast access to data warehouse data by creating multidimensional cubes from information in the data warehouse fact and dimension tables. OLAP is a way to extend traditional reporting. This feature *piggybacks* SQL Server technology and enhances the power of the database engine by enabling more in-depth analysis of the compiled data.

Let's say you run a typical report each month for monthly sales. Then the management team decides they want a more granular report that also shows weekly sales. Somehow we get the feeling you know what is coming next. The weekly report isn't enough; now management wants a report that compiles a data set for each day as well. With OLAP, this functionality is a breeze.

This data set can be called from a single cube. When management decides they require more details of the sales report, do you go and create new reports for each subset of information and the intervals in which they want to see them? Not with OLAP. OLAP compiles the data set to your specifications. Take our management team's approach. With a single OLAP cube, you can give them a sales report that shows sales by month, week, day, even to the minute, and there is so much more power to be unleashed. Why not find out how many widgets by month, week, and day? How about how many widgets by month, week, day, who sold them, which location they were sold from, and then aggregate the entire data set depending on which timeframe you are looking for? The sky is the limit.

Actually, hardware is what limits you. The cube creation process is very disk-intensive. To minimize the load placed at the client end, OLAP cubes are precompiled with the entire dataset and all possible computations that the data set can derive. This data is *wrapped* into a cube.

OLAP cubes can be viewed through a pivot table. Pivot tables can be manipulated through Excel. The tools are native. With pivot tables, that data set to which the pivot table is connected can be manipulated into a view that is most helpful for the user. No more copying and pasting between Excel spreadsheets. No more rekeying data between reports. Simply drag-and-drop a dimension on your pivot table, and the report shows a different perspective. Analysis Services is an extremely powerful tool used to quickly create a process to view and coordinate statistical data. Therefore, OLAP is an advanced topic and requires understanding.

Clustering Analysis Services

Here are instructions on how to set up SQL Server Analysis Services 2000 as a clustered service. Even though Analysis Services is not a cluster-aware application, you can install and configure Analysis Services as a generic service on a cluster, thus making it a cluster-aware instance of the application. You should not need to go through the steps outlined here for SQL Server 2005 because support for clustering Analysis Services is now fully supported.

When Analysis Services is configured in the manner outlined in the following numbered list, you can operate it in a clustered environment, which provides a high availability solution for Analysis Services. Here is an overview of the steps for configuring Analysis Services:

1. Install Analysis Services on Node-1.
2. Set the Analysis Server service to manual startup on Node-1.
3. Create a "domain OLAP Administrators" group.
4. Add the "domain OLAP administrators" to the Node-1 OLAP Administrators group.
5. Move the Analysis Services Query Log database.
6. Remove sharing from the MsOLAPRepository$ share on Node-1.
7. Force a failover.
8. Install Analysis Services on Node-2.
9. Set the Analysis Server service to manual startup on Node-2.

10. Add "domain OLAP Administrators" to the Node-2 OLAP Administrators group.
11. Remove sharing from the MsOLAPRepository$ share on Node-2.
12. Move the Analysis Services repository.
13. Create a cluster share in the Analysis Log folder.
14. Modify the registry keys for the Analysis server on Node-2.
15. Configure the Analysis Services service as a generic service.

You must have a clustered set of servers. Also, the cluster resource group where you configure Analysis Services always runs the same node as the default cluster group, which contains the cluster IP address and cluster network name.

This outline refers to the node that currently has control of the cluster server virtual name, IP address, and shared disk where you want to store your Analysis Services data files as Node-1. You can configure the computer running SQL Server that stores the repository and the query log off the cluster. This configuration is the easiest to configure for Analysis Services because you only have to make connection string changes to point to the computer running SQL Server.

You can configure the computer running SQL Server that stores the repository and the query log on the cluster. This configuration implies that this computer also is clustered in an active/passive configuration. This configuration requires more steps for Analysis Services to be clustered. At this point in time, we configure Analysis Services to act as a clustered application.

All management functions should be made through cluster administrator or through the Analysis Services snap-in referencing the Virtual Server name. This is no longer a local resource. The possibility exists that resources may be visible to the individual node. All access to the Analysis Services resources needs to be made through the Cluster Administrator or Analysis Administrators consoles connecting to the Virtual Server name.

Install Analysis Services on ClusterNode1:

1. Run the Setup program located in the MSOLAP\Install folder on the SQL Server 2000 CD, or click SQL Server 2000 Components. Install Analysis Services on the Autorun menu that appears when you insert the SQL Server CD.

2. In the Welcome dialog box, click Next.
3. In the Software License Agreement dialog box, click Yes to accept the agreement.
4. In the Select Components dialog box, make sure you select all the components, and then accept the default location for the Destination Folder. Click Next.
5. The Data Folder Location dialog box is a shared disk location of the cluster that stores your Analysis Services data files. A best practice for performance dictates that this is a location separate from the location of your SQL Server database data and log files. A dedicated disk resource is recommended. Click Yes, and then click Next.
6. In the Select Program Folder dialog box, click Next to accept the default location. This is for the program files.
7. When the setup completes, click Finish to exit the setup program.

Set the Analysis Server service to manual startup on ClusterNode1. Now open the Services management console. Locate the MSSQLServerOLAPService service in the list, and then double-click the MSSQL-ServerOLAPService service name to open the Properties dialog box.

1. On the General tab, change the Startup Type to Manual.
2. If the Service Status is Started, click Stop.
3. Click OK to close the Properties dialog box.
4. Close the Services management console.

Create Domain OLAP Administrators Group

Analysis Services requires the OLAP Administrators group have access permissions to the shared directory where the Analysis Services repository resides on your shared storage location disk. Because the shared directory must be available regardless of which node in the cluster is active, you will create this shared directory as a cluster share in a later step in the configuration process. The cluster share requires domain-level accounts. You must create the OLAP Administrators group as a domain-level group and manage OLAP Administrator group member-ship through the domain-level OLAP Administrators group.

1. Log on with an account that has Domain Administrator privileges.
2. Use either Active Directory Users and Computers or User Manager for Domains, and create a new domain-level group named OLAP Administrators.
3. Add all the users who should be Administrators for Analysis Services to the OLAP Administrators group.
4. Close the Active Directory Users and Computers or User Manager for Domains.

To add domain OLAP Administrators to the ClusterNode1 OLAP Administrators group:

1. On ClusterNode1, right-click My Computer, and then click Manage.
2. Expand the Local Users and Groups node located under System Tools.
3. Click the Groups folder.
4. Right-click the OLAP Administrators group located in the right-hand window, and then click Properties.
5. In the OLAP Administrators Properties dialog box, click Add.
6. In the Select Users or Groups dialog box, make sure you select the domain in which you created the OLAP Administrators group.
7. Locate the OLAP Administrators group in the list, and then double-click the name to add the OLAP Administrators group.
8. Click OK to close the Select Users or Groups dialog box.
9. Click OK to close the OLAP Administrators Properties dialog box.

Microsoft Analysis Services stores statistical sampling of the queries sent to the server in a Query Log database in MS Access named Msmdqlog.mdb. The Optimization Wizard uses the Msmdqlog.mdb database to tune cube performance. Analysis Services uses a shared folder to allow access to the Msmdqlog.mdb database from remote

OLAP management stations that run Analysis Manager. This shared folder should be separate from the data folder; however, it should be on the same shared disk resource in the cluster, thus making it available regardless of which node has ownership.

To move the Analysis Services Query Log database, perform the following steps:

1. Open Windows Explorer.
2. Select the same shared disk you chose for the data folder in the preceding "Install Analysis Services on ClusterNode1" section.
3. Create a new folder named AnalysisLog.
4. Navigate to the C:\Program Files\Microsoft Analysis Services\ Bin folder.
5. Copy the Msmdqlog.mdb file from this directory to the Analysis-Log folder you created on the shared disk of the cluster.

To remove sharing from the MsOLAPRepository$ share on Cluster-Node1

1. Navigate to the C:\Program Files\Microsoft Analysis Services\ Bin folder.
2. Right-click the Bin folder, and then click Sharing.
3. Click to select the Do Not Share This Folder option button.
4. Click OK to close the Bin Properties dialog box.
5. Close Windows Explorer.

To force a failover

1. Start the Cluster Administrator console.
2. Open a connection to the cluster.
3. Right-click the cluster group that contains the IP address and cluster name, and then click Move Group.
4. Right-click the cluster group that contains the physical disk in which you stored your OLAP data files and AnalysisLog directory, and then click Move Group.
5. Close the Cluster Administrator.

To install Analysis Services on ClusterNode2

1. Run the Setup program located in the MSOLAP\Install folder of the SQL Server 2000 CD, or click SQL Server 2000 Components...Install Analysis Services on the Autorun menu that appears when you insert the SQL Server CD.
2. In the Welcome dialog box, click Next.
3. In the Software License Agreement dialog box, click Yes to signify your acceptance of the agreement.
4. In the Select Components dialog box, make sure you select all the components, and then accept the default location for the destination folder. Click Next.
5. In the Data Folder Location dialog box, select the same folder on the shared disk resource of the cluster that you selected when you installed Analysis Services on ClusterNode1 of the cluster. Click Next.
6. In the Select Program Folder dialog box, click Next to accept the default location.
7. When the setup completes, click Finish to exit the setup program.

To set the Analysis Server service to manual startup on ClusterNode2

1. Open the Services management console. Locate the MSSQLServerOLAPService service in the list, and then double-click the MSSQLServerOLAPService service to open the Properties dialog box.
2. On the General tab, change the Startup Type to Manual.
3. If the Service Status shows Started, click Stop.
4. Click OK to close the Properties dialog box.
5. Close the Services management console.

To add domain OLAP administrators to the ClusterNode2 OLAP Administrators group

1. On ClusterNode2, right-click My Computer, and then click Manage.
2. Expand the Local Users and Groups node located under System Tools.

3. Click the Groups folder.
4. Right-click the OLAP Administrators group in the right-hand window, and then click Properties.
5. Click Add in the OLAP Administrators Properties dialog box.
6. In the Select Users or Groups dialog box, make sure you select the domain in which you created the OLAP Administrators group.
7. Locate the OLAP Administrators group in the list, and then double-click the OLAP Administrators name to add this group.
8. Click OK to close the Select Users or Groups dialog box.
9. Click OK to close the OLAP Administrators Properties dialog box.
10. Close the Computer Management console.

To remove sharing from the MsOLAPRepository$ share on ClusterNode2

1. Open Windows Explorer.
2. Navigate to the C:\Program Files\Microsoft Analysis Services\ Bin folder.
3. Right-click the Bin folder, and then click Sharing.
4. Click to select the Do Not Share This Folder option button.
5. Click OK to close the Bin Properties dialog box.

To move the Analysis Services repository

1. In Windows Explorer, navigate to the Program Files\Microsoft Analysis Services\Bin folder.
2. Copy the Msmdrep.mdb file from the local drive on the cluster to the AnalysisLog folder on the shared disk of the cluster.
3. Close Windows Explorer.

To create a cluster share in the AnalysisLog folder

1. Open the Cluster Administrator console.
2. Open a connection to the cluster.
3. Right-click the Resources folder, and then click New... Resource.
4. In the New Resource dialog box, type the following for the resource name: MsOLAPRepository$.

5. For the description, type **Analysis Services Share**, or something similar that defines it uniquely for you.

6. Change the resource type to File Share.

7. Change the group to be the same group that contains the shared disk in which you want to store the Analysis Services data files.

8. Click Next.

9. In the Possible Owners dialog box, make sure both nodes are listed in the possible owners list.

10. Click Next.

11. In the Available Resources list of the Dependencies dialog box, select the physical disk that contains the OLAP data files.

12. Click Add to move the physical disk to the Resource Dependencies list.

13. Click Next.

14. In the File Share Parameters dialog box, for the share name, type MsOLAPRepository$, or something similar that defines it uniquely for you.

15. Type the path to the AnalysisLog folder you created in the "Create Folder for Query Log" step.

16. Click Permissions to configure permissions for the share.

17. In the Permissions dialog box, click Add.

18. In the Select Users or Groups dialog box, make sure you have selected the domain in which you created the OLAP Administrators group.

19. Locate the OLAP Administrators group in the list, and then double-click the name to add the OLAP Administrators group.

20. Locate the Domain Admins group in the list, and then double-click the name to add the Domain Admins group.

21. Click OK to close the Select Users or Groups dialog box.

22. In the Permissions dialog box, click the Domain Admins group, and then select the Allow checkbox for full control.

23. In the Permissions dialog box, click on the OLAP Administrators group, and then select the Allow checkbox for full control.

24. In the Permissions dialog box, click the Everyone group, and then click Remove to remove the Everyone group from the permissions on the share.

25. Click OK to close the Permissions dialog box.

26. Click Finish to complete the New Resource wizard. The following message should appear: *Cluster resource 'MsOLAPRepository$' created successfully.*

27. Click OK to close the Message dialog box.
28. Locate the MsOLAPRepository$ in the resource list, and then right-click MsOLAPRepository$.
29. Select Bring Online to Make the Cluster Share Available.

Analysis Services reads a number of registry keys to retrieve information about the configuration of the Analysis Server. You must modify some of the registry keys to reflect the fact that the server is running on a cluster. It is always a best practice to backup the registry before any edit.

To modify the registry keys for the Analysis server on Node-2

1. Run the Registry Editor utility (Regedt32.exe).
2. Navigate to the HKEY_LOCAL_MACHINE\SOFTWARE\ Microsoft\OLAP Server\Server Connection Info registry key.

The `RemoteRepositoryConnectionString` value contains the name of the node for the data source. Change the value to the name of the virtual server. For example,

> Provider=Microsoft.Jet.OLEDB.4.0;Data Source=\\
> MyClusterClusterNode2\MsOLAPRepository$\Msmdrep.mdb

becomes

> Provider=Microsoft.Jet.OLEDB.4.0;Data Source=\\
> ClusterServerVirtualName\MsOLAPRepository$\Msmdrep.mdb

The `RepositoryConnectionString` value contains the path in which the binaries for the Analysis Services product were originally installed. Change the `RepositoryConnectionString` value to point to the new location selected in the `MoveAnalysisServicesRepository`. For example,

> Provider=Microsoft.Jet.OLEDB.4.0;Data Source=C:\Program Files\Microsoft Analysis Services\Bin\Msmdrep.mdb

becomes

> Provider=Microsoft.Jet.OLEDB.4.0;Data Source=Q:\
> AnalysisLog\Msmdrep.mdb

assuming Q:\ is the drive where the AnalysisLog directory was created. If you are running SQL Server 2000 Analysis Services Service Pack 3 to modify the `RemoteRepositoryConnectionString`, follow these steps:

1. Click the server name in Analysis Services.
2. Click Modify Repository Connection String.

The Edit Repository Connection String dialog box appears. Now, you can modify the connection string.

To configure Analysis Services service as a generic service

1. Open the Cluster Administrator console. To open the Cluster Administrator console, click Start on the Taskbar, point to Programs, point to Administrative Tools, and then click Cluster Administrator.
2. Open a connection to the cluster.
3. Right-click the Resources folder, and then click New... Resource.
4. In the New Resource dialog box, type **Analysis Services** for the resource name or something similar that defines it uniquely for you.
5. For the description, type **Analysis Services**, or something similar that defines it uniquely for you.
6. Change the resource type to Generic Service.
7. Change the group to be the same group that contains the shared disk in which the data files are located, the cluster IP address, and the name.
8. Click Next.
9. In the Possible Owners dialog box, make sure that both nodes are listed in the Possible Owners list, and then click Next.
10. In the Available Resources list in the Dependencies dialog box, click to select the MsOLAPRepository$ share.
11. Click Add to move the MsOLAPRepository file share to the Resource dependencies list.
12. Click Next.
13. In the Generic Service Parameters dialog box, type the following as the Service Name: **MSSQLServerOLAPService**.
14. In the Start Parameters text box, type **net start MSSQL-ServerOLAPService**.

15. Click Next.
16. In the Registry Replication dialog box, click Add, and then type the following in the Root registry key entry text box: **Software\Microsoft\OLAP Server**.
17. Click OK to close the Registry Key dialog box.
18. Click Finish to complete the New Resource wizard. The following message should appear: *Cluster resource 'Analysis Services' created successfully*.
19. Click OK to close the Message dialog box.
20. Locate, and then right-click Analysis Services in the resource list.
21. Click Bring Online to make the Analysis Server available.
22. Close the Cluster Administrator console.

To manually verify the appropriate registry keys have replicated on each node of the cluster

1. Run the Registry Editor utility (Regedt32.exe).
2. Navigate to the HKEY_LOCAL_MACHINE\SOFTWARE\Microsoft\OLAP Server registry key, and verify the data is identical on each cluster node.

Clustering SQL Server 2000 Analysis Services Troubleshooting and Best Practices

Because Analysis Services is not cluster-aware, some problems can occur if Analysis Services is clustered and you use these outlined steps. Registry replication synchronizes the memory settings for the Analysis Server, which may be a problem if the two nodes in the cluster have different amounts of RAM.

Although it is possible to administer and query the Analysis Server by using the name of the currently active node on the cluster, you should not do this. You must perform all administration and querying by using the cluster server name.

Analysis Manager registers the Analysis Server by using the machine name of the node. You must remove this server registration and then register the cluster server name. Again, all management functions should be administered through the Virtual Server.

Analysis Manager stores all server registrations in the registry. Registry replication synchronizes the registered servers on the two nodes of the cluster. Therefore, you must perform any new server registrations in Analysis Manager on the currently active node of the cluster.

Troubleshooting, Maintenance, and Best Practices

As an administrator of Windows machines, you are probably used to administering services and server resources through the native tools built into Windows, like the Services applet in Control Panel, or the net use command-line utility, and so forth. When administering a clustered set of servers, all management functions should be administered through the Cluster Administrator Console.

When you install Windows 2000 clustering (before you install SQL Server clustering), it is important you specify the proper network cards for the public and private networks. If you do not, and you need to make a change later, you have to uninstall SQL Server and Windows 2000 clustering, and then reinstall them correctly.

The reason for this is because when installing Windows 2000 clustering, you have to be very careful that you select the appropriate network card for the public and private connections for each node. It is easy to get confused. What may be surprising is that a wrong configuration can often work, making you believe that everything is working properly. After you have discovered you have made a mistake, you may be tempted to try and change the assignments using the Cluster Administrator.

Do not do this, as it may appear to work, but it does not, and it causes further problems. Private NICs should have *netbios over tcp/ip* disabled; this is so there is no master browser selection on the local subnet for the private NICs. If this setting is allowed and the NICs attempt to elect a master browser fails, and if this process fails for any reason, the RPC service may fail. The SQL Server service relies on the Cluster service to start and operate. This relates because the Cluster service relies on the RPC service to start. If the RPC service can't start, you are in trouble.

Fragmentation

It is best to refrain from using defragment utilities or any such products on drives that house data files. SQL Server writes data differently than the standard operating system. Data in tables, and dedicated directly to the data file, is written using pointer records to pages on disk. Indexes are written in a very specific, sequential order with space allocation built in for additional padding called a *fill factor*.

If a utility is used that changes the location of pointer records, or individual indexed records on the physical disks, the time it takes to actually find the records you are looking for on disk can more than triple, causing applications to timeout and other major performance problems. A wide variety of opinions exist on how to best deal with fragmentation of database files. Each scenario we have seen is unique. We find that using the database utilities that ship with SQL Server 2000 are best for maintaining this. If dropping and recreating indexes isn't an option for you, try using the DBCC Indexdefrag utility.

Operating System Level-Backup Utilities

Using an operating system level-backup utility to attempt to back up a database in use by the SQL Server 2000 backup engine is not a good option. Many times we have seen a network administrator try and try again to use the top-of-the-line Windows backup utilities to back up the databases on SQL Server, only to watch it fail. Sometimes it doesn't fail, but we have dared them to prove it by doing a restore of the database files. Backup utilities exist out there that have specialized agents for SQL Server and Clustering, and they can ride together to back up Clustered SQL Server installations.

This may be an option that works for your particular scenario. One of the other options is using the good, old-fashioned `dump database` command. Using TSQL commands to back up databases has never let us down. In some large-scale environments, this is a difficult task; nevertheless, it must be done. We have found that Windows backup utilities waste system resources by trying to back up files that are in use by the database engine. With that said, we exclude the actual database data and log files from any Windows backup scheme.

Anti-Virus Software

Thanks must go to the manufacturers of anti-virus software. In the Windows world, keeping a server safe from virus and worm attacks can be quite a difficult task to manage. This wonderful software does not, however, have any business looking at access to the physical database data and log files. Countless amounts of CPU cycles and wasted memory can be eliminated by excluding the physical database data and log files from on-access read and write scans by anti-virus software. The system files, .exe and .dll files, are one thing; but the physical database data and log files are perpetually in use by the database engine. In a world where performance counts, this can be a black hole of wasted resources.

Windows Updates

There's a bug in the system. Problems with an operating system or applications happen. No one is perfect. In the Windows world, a lot of time and energy is spent by some individuals to attempt to gain unauthorized access to production systems. Windows updates are necessary. Which updates are necessary for your organization and clustered servers are generally based on an administrator's comfort in the products he or she is using. Does a clustered installation of SQL Server 2000 need the most recent upgrade for Windows Media Player? We surely don't think so. Please use Windows update, but be selective in the items that are chosen. Always install updates on a test system first, if possible, in an environment as close to the production environment as possible. If, for whatever reason, this is not possible, install updates on a machine that does not own any resources. If there is a problem with a patch or service pack on the system you are working with, installing the patch with services running and applications open is an easy way to lose valuable data.

MBSA

Microsoft Baseline Security Analyzer (MBSA) is a great tool that digs deep into the innards of your operating system and installed applications, and it reports if and where you have security vulnerabilities. This tool is available at: www.microsoft.com/mbsa. This works for clustered installations and can scan the newer operating systems across the network given the correct credentials. What we have found very useful in regards to the MBSA is that it finds outstanding security vulnerabilities that Windows update does not report. It is always a best practice to stay ahead of the curve when dealing with security.

Time-Out

Many items need to be taken into consideration when creating a high availability solution for SQL Server. Adequate planning, a clear vision of what is to be accomplished, the understanding that even in the event of a disaster there will be data loss, and support from management in these scenarios are all necessary components of a successful solution. Choosing whether to scale-out your database solution is based on your individual business needs.

SQL Server supports multiple configurations of failover clustering, including active/passive, active/active, and N+1 configurations. SQL Server further supports a high availability solution by providing different types of database replication. Merge replication, snapshot replication, and transactional replication are the most prominent. Other powerful tools, such as SQL Server Analysis Services, also can be clustered to support high availability. SQL Server supports a wide variety of scalable, flexible solutions to support your business needs.

CHAPTER 10

High Availability, High-Performance Exchange

Introduction

I t's difficult to call Microsoft Exchange a *mail server* anymore. It truly *is* an information exchange system—an information *network*, if you will. What started out many years ago as a mail server has become a means to manage tasks, appointments, calendars, group-think, document sharing, journaling, and more.

Naturally, email is Exchange's forte. In partnership with the venerable client, Outlook, you have a critical combination of technologies many people and corporations trust to be always available, as the very air we breathe.

Large and small organizations are heavily dependent on the Exchange/Outlook couple. Many new handheld phone/PDA devices are now heavily dependent on the availability of Exchange. Fortunately, Exchange is designed to be scaled up and out. As a testament to this high-performance, high availability system, the authors have installed Exchange systems comprising of one or many more clusters, replacing networks comprised of hundreds of mail servers, gateways, post offices, and more.

Implementing a Microsoft Exchange high availability architecture on the Windows Server 2003 platform builds on the previous chapters' information on fault tolerance, scalability, redundancy, load balancing, and so on.

This chapter also assumes, like the others, that you are familiar with the product or application you are going to make highly available. In other words, by the time you are ready to begin your Exchange high-availability project, you should have completed your basic Exchange Architecture and know how mailbox servers (backends) and front-end servers are deployed, as well as have an understanding of namespace partitioning, routing, Outlook Web Access, Active Directory access, DNS, and so on. Like the previous chapters, we are going to stick to making Exchange highly available and focus on high performance.

In the previous chapters, we installed clusters and resources on traditional shared storage platforms. The file and print chapters installed active/passive clusters using shared SCSI arrays, while in the SQL Server chapter, we installed our resources on the disks of an EMC SAN.

In this chapter, we cluster Exchange on an NSI Software GeoCluster platform in an "active/passive-passive/active" cluster where we have Exchange running on one node and SQL Server running on the other. The shared disk resources the cluster service sees are, in fact, disks replicated with Double-Take from node-to-node, while the GeoCluster services fool the cluster service into *thinking* the replicated disks are on shared storage. It really is a remarkable technology.

GeoCluster is an add-on to Microsoft cluster services. As shown in Chapter 6, "Building the Foundations for a Highly Available Architecture," you set up a standard cluster using standard MSCS configuration. The nodes in the cluster still share one storage solution. GeoCluster uses the replication technology provided by its sister product, Double-Take, to provide each node with an identical copy of the data. As a result, you no longer have a single point-of-failure in the shared storage array; thus, the cluster nodes can be separated between buildings or across the country.

NOTE: You cannot install Microsoft Exchange 2003 Standard Edition on a cluster; you must buy the Enterprise Edition for clustering.

Before going into detail, first let's discuss the essential architecture and design for high availability, high-performance Exchange implementations.

Scale-Out Versus Scale-Up with Microsoft Exchange

Exchange high availability topology is very different from File, Print, or even SQL Server HA topology, which was discussed in previous chapters. An Exchange system can be implemented on a single server, or it can be split between two tiers—the front-end servers and the back-end servers.

Your front-end servers (which provide access to the information) are not typically clustered for failover because they consume little storage, and what storage they do consume does not really change. These front-end servers are clustered for load balancing, the subject of the next two chapters. We only briefly touch on the NLB clustering of the front-end servers in this chapter.

The back-end servers—the mailbox servers—are where the jewels are stowed; the email and information exchange consumes disk space (mailboxes) and is always changing. Mailbox servers are clustered for availability and performance rather than load balancing. You typically cluster Exchange mailbox servers in active/passive failover clusters using shared storage; however, we can and do cluster Exchange in active/active configurations.

A single Exchange active/passive backend cluster can handle a huge volume of email. Two high-end servers can easily cope with two or three thousand mailboxes (so Exchange does not really need to scale up or out in any large degree). In fact, there are several humungous implementations in existence today, in the USA, where only three or four distributed A/P clusters (that is, one active mailbox server and one passive) handle mail and information exchange for upwards of 40,000 people.

Now you can also add more nodes to your failover mailbox cluster, but unlike file or SQL Server clusters, Exchange failover clusters are typically implemented as a single active node with one or more passive nodes for automatic failover.

As discussed in Chapters 5, "Preparing the Platform for a High-Performance Network," and 6, a failover can be any server standing by to take over operations in the event the primary active server fails. Your failover server can be online in the cluster, or it can be offline, disconnected from the cluster, but running as a hot spare. Naturally, the time to bring a hot spare online is something you have to consider. Using a hot spare to back up a failed server that is taken out of the cluster is also a good idea.

Keep in mind, however, hot spares often become hot opportunities for pillaging by network engineers. Many hot spares have ended up used for additional services, lab work, and other parts. Then when they are needed to fill the need for which they were originally intended, they are no longer highly available.

Design

In previous chapters, we discussed how shared single storage solutions, common with MSCS, have an inherent architectural limitation—the shared storage solution. In Chapter 3, "Storage for Highly Available Systems," we talked about how a cluster provides redundant hardware for everything except the most important component, the shared storage. You can have a fancy SAN or a high-end SCSI array, but if the hardware in the SAN or shared storage array fails, the cluster fails.

Specifically, here are the two main limitations:

- Cluster nodes must share the same physical storage; this is how Microsoft Cluster Services work, no matter the size or sophistication of your implementation. If the storage technology were to break, none of the nodes would be able to function. We always assume the server will break, the applications will choke, and all will be well because the node will fail over. But if the shared storage fails, then nothing in the cluster can fail over. The entire cluster fails, the shared data becomes unavailable, and your sophisticated solution becomes a fail-nowhere solution. See Figure 10.1.

- With MSCS, the nodes in the cluster are engineered to share the solution; so it is not easy for the nodes to be geographically separated. While the new majority node set quorum in Windows Server 2003 provides for geographical separation of the nodes, you still need third-party software to properly handle the replication of data between the geographically separated nodes. Geographically separated nodes of a cluster, the so-called geo-cluster, or stretch-cluster, enables you to survive geographical disasters. In other words, if your entire building was taken down (or even just the computer room), there would be no service at all because the entire cluster would be affected.

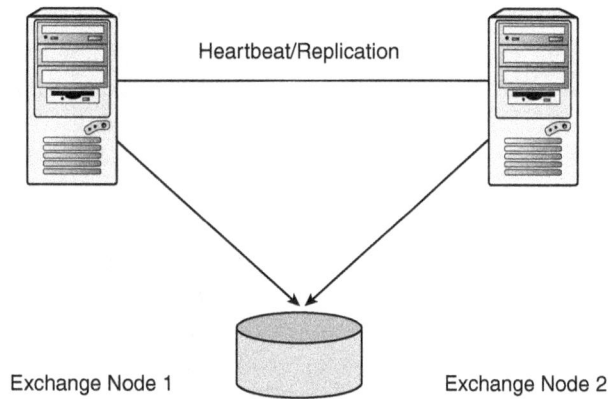

Figure 10.1   Shared storage solution.

One third-party software you can use to address these limitations is NSI's replication technology called *GeoCluster* and *Double-Take*. They can be used to significantly increase the availability of any cluster, but we demonstrate the solution in this chapter with Microsoft Exchange.

GeoCluster on each node of a cluster allows each of the clustered Exchange nodes to have its own copy of the Exchange data. So, any failure of the application or OS (of the active clustered node) would be handled by the cluster. The only difference is the storage would be equally fault-tolerant because an exact copy of it exists in each node. See Figure 10.2.

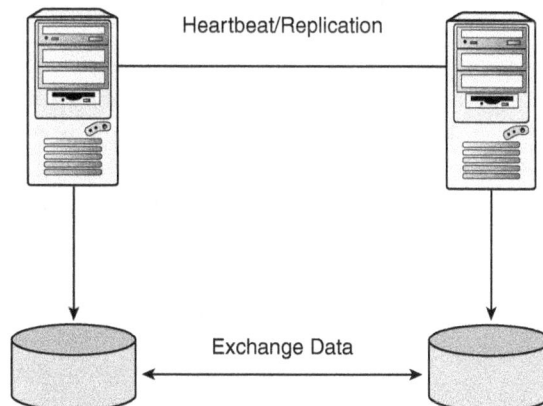

Figure 10.2   Microsoft Exchange on MSCS, with GeoCluster for shared storage.

In addition, to eliminate the potential of a location disaster in which all the nodes of a traditional cluster are down, the GeoClustered nodes can be remote from each other and some distance away. Because each node has its own local copy of the data, the cluster continues to service clients throughout the world, even if the primary nodes in Fort Lauderdale, Florida have been trashed by a hurricane. This is illustrated in Figure 10.3.

In other words, you not only now have *local* high availability, but metropolitan or geographical protection. Your GeoClustered nodes can be across town, across the country, or across the world. Double-Take can replicate the data from the cluster to another platform, anywhere in the world. Double-Take protects traditional MSCS clusters and GeoClustered clusters. This is illustrated in Figure 10.3

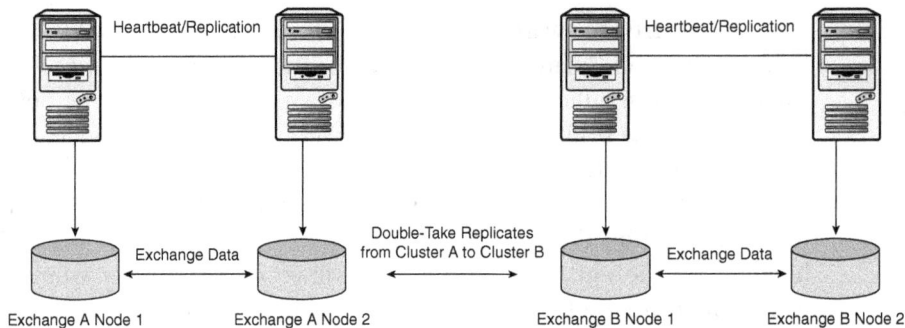

Figure 10.3 Disaster recovery of any cluster (with or without GeoCluster).

Using these tools, the target platform (anywhere in the world) can then be brought online to stand in for a failed production Exchange instance. The failover mailbox cluster design is essentially the same regardless of the number of people to whom you are catering. You either implement one or more failover clusters in a site, or you distribute your Exchange clusters between several sites closest to the population of users who need to access the server.

When you first set out to cluster Exchange, the first item to consider is storage. You cluster on either a SAN or a SCSI disk array for shared storage (see Chapter 3 for storage design and implementation), or you can use local storage replicated across the cluster nodes, which we focus on in this chapter. However, your Exchange server needs access to many more volumes on the storage resource than other cluster implementations, such as file and print.

Exchange generates different types of data, and they are not accessed and managed in the same way. Providing one huge volume for all Exchange data is not considered a best practice for large installations. It is not a big deal for a small company, or even a very busy mail server supporting a small number of high-volume mailboxes, provided of course you have decent server that supports multiple processes, has lots of RAM, and a decent local SCSI storage comprised of RAID-1 and RAID-5 configurations.

Besides the usual quorum resource volume on your cluster, you should also provide a disk for the Exchange transaction logs (which are accessed sequentially by Exchange) and a disk for the databases, which hold the mailboxes. Mailbox databases are accessed randomly. If you study the Exchange database architecture closely, you see it looks a lot like your standard relational database management system. In fact, the next major release of Exchange, some years off, actually uses a DBMS, probably SQL Server 2005.

If you can, implement volumes for the transaction logs on separate arrays from the databases. This helps maximize the performance of your system. You can also go as far as storing the logs for each storage group on a separate disk array. You may not notice an increase in performance with this practice on small SCSI implementations. If your volumes are on a SAN, such as an EMC CX400 or bigger, Exchange does not even notice the difference because the array in these big SANs already provides incredibly high throughput.

If you are going to implement Exchange on smaller arrays, then the rule of thumb is to go for multiple, small RAID volumes, rather than one large disk. Carving out a bunch of logical volumes on a high-capacity RAID-5 array often provides for capacity and growth, and you can witness performance as good as many SAN implementations.

It is also important to size the disks with enough space for online defragmentation (of Exchange databases) or in the event of a restore. In essence, make sure you have enough headroom to work with. If, for example, you calculate needing 36GB, then you likely need to implement 72GB arrays. In a RAID-5 array comprised of three or more disks, the 72GB drives give you about 136GB of working space.

Also activate the Volume Shadow Copy service (see Chapter 3) because this allows you to back up more often than once a day and have access to the restores faster than is possible with traditional tape backup. Volume Shadow Copy service is a marvelous service and, contrary to initial beliefs, it does not affect the performance of your mailbox servers. Of course, you need to implement the service with common sense.

Storage Group Architecture

As you should know, Exchange 2003 server can operate off of up to four storage groups. A storage group requires its own collection of transaction log files, which support up to five databases. A popular debate among Exchange architects is how best to configure the storage groups. The most valid argument is you must configure your storage groups to obtain the best performance from Exchange. The next most important consideration is configuring the storage groups with backup and restore speed in mind.

How the storage group configuration fits into your Exchange High Availability architecture is extremely important. Typically, you would consider keeping the number of databases supported by the cluster to a minimum. This requires fewer resources in the cluster and achieves better performance. Also, make it a rule in the architecture to maximize the total number of databases (you can go as high as five) in each storage group before creating more storage groups.

Again, with disaster recovery in mind, you need to try to decrease the time it takes to back up and restore Exchange considering Exchange, rather than the server, has failed.

Exchange Store Considerations

First, before you do anything, follow a strict naming convention for your storage groups. This is important not only to make life easier when you configure Exchange and the back-end clusters, but also it is important to help you in maintenance, monitoring, troubleshooting, and disaster recovery scenarios. See the sections covering Microsoft Operations Manager in Chapter 13 and the naming convention discussions in Chapters 5 and 6.

Use multiple mailbox stores to increase the reliability and recoverability of your Exchange organization. In a large organization, you spread users across several mailbox stores. In this design, the loss of a store only affects the users who have mailboxes in that store and not the entire organization. You can decide to partition the mailbox stores in various ways. Most architects find it best to partition alphabetically. In other words, the loss of A-H only affects users whose last names begin with the letters that fall between A and H, inclusively. This method would work better than configuring a mailbox on a location basis, such as a building or a campus location, where the loss of the mailbox can take out an entire department or facility. It would be extremely rare to have a location where all users' last names begin with the same letter.

Exchange requires more resources to manage multiple mailbox databases; so, keep this in mind. However, as mentioned earlier, it is easier to recover and restore mailbox A–D than mailbox A–Z.

Next, you need to consider the architecture for your public folder storage. You can use multiple public folder stores, and to handle high-usage traffic, you can place multiple replicas of the same folder on several servers. If you have multiple routing groups, you may want to distribute folders among the routing groups. This provides users with easy access to folders they use most often.

You also need to determine how much data you need for each store. If you accurately project the volumes of your mail, you can appropriately design your storage systems so you do not have to continually expand them—a frustrating and time-consuming exercise when dealing with mailbox clusters.

You also can use the following formula to calculate the amount of data you are able to store on your SAN:

(Number of mailboxes × maximum size of mailbox limit) × adjustment factor

The *adjustment factor* is a value that provides additional space for non-mailbox quotas. This takes into consideration the data in the deleted item retention store and the deleted mailbox retention store.

Always configure quotas. It makes much more accurate assessments of your data store requirements. If you need varying quotas, such as higher limits for the VIP users, you can create separate mailbox databases using multiple system policies with different quota limits. If you have users who need very large mailboxes, you can configure one or more databases that have no quota limits.

Lastly, as you get ready to carve out the disks on the cluster storage you will partition, partition your disks so the following files are located on separate volumes:

- **RAID-1 or RAID-5 Volume:** Windows Server 2003 files, located on the server node's disks.
- **RAID-1 or RAID-5 Volume:** Exchange application files, located on the server node's disks.
- **RAID-5 volume(s):** Exchange database files, located on the cluster's SAN, SCSI arrays, or replicated disks.
- **RAID-5 volume(s):** Exchange transaction log files, located on the cluster's SAN, SCSI arrays, or replicated disks.

Table 10.1 lists the Exchange cluster's hard-disk partitioning design.

Table 10.1   Exchange Cluster Hard-Disk Partitioning Design

Disk	Configuration
Disk 1	Drive C (NTFS): Windows operating system files and swap file
Disk 2	Drive D (NTFS): Exchange files and additional server applications (such as anti-virus software and resource kits)
Disk 3	Drive M (NTFS): Transaction log files for storage group 1
Disk 4	Drive N (NTFS): Database files for storage group 1
Disk 5	Drive O (NTFS): Transaction log files for storage group 2
Disk 6	Drive P (NTFS): Database files for storage group 2

When designing the storage architecture for Exchange, implement it in such a way that ensures reliability. Obviously, RAID-0 is not an option. After you have reliability in hand, then decide if you need performance (typically RAID-1), or if you are looking to optimize capacity (typically RAID-5). For public folder databases, RAID-5 is better than RAID-1 because these databases are usually written once and read multiple times.

If you are unsure how Exchange is performing on your storage, you can run the Microsoft Exchange stress utility occasionally. It is called *Jet-stress* (after the Jet database engine). You can also watch for throughput and stress using performance counters and monitor these resources with Microsoft Operations Manager.

Transaction Log Files

The transaction logs are the most critical component of the storage group. You need to be sure your transaction log configuration is such that you can easily and quickly recover data if the data stores are damaged. This is important even if you only settle for installing the default First Storage Group.

Every transaction that comes into Exchange, such as the creation of a message, is written to a log file and thereafter committed to the store. All stores share a single set of logs, and the logging process ensures every transaction can be recovered if the store is damaged between backups.

You recover the store just as you would recover a SQL Server database. Thus, when you recover a store (database), you first recover the last good copy of the data store, and then you restore the transaction log to restore the most recent log files and recover transactions that were not committed to the server by the last backup.

As long as you have access to the latest backup and the transaction log files since the backup, you can always rebuild the store to the very last message received before the server crashed. Thus, you need to ensure you protect your transaction logs with a sound management plan because if you lose the transaction logs, you lose your data.

SMTP Queue Directory

The SMTP queue directory plays a critical role in the mail delivery process and the Simple Mail Transfer Protocol (SMTP). This folder stores all SMTP messages until they are written to a database or transmitted to another SMTP server or connector. The SMTP queuing process is write-intensive, and it is important you ensure the system can cope with the load and maintain a reasonable message delivery process.

SMTP messages do not remain in the store for a long time. It is possible for the SMTP queue to choke, and this could be due to a backing up of data caused by failure, for some reason, to deliver a message. The storage plan for the SMTP queue should be to optimize for performance ahead of capacity and availability, especially when you have a high volume of mail.

The SMTP messages are stored in the following folder: drive:\ Program Files\Exchsrvr\Mailroot.

By default, this queue is installed on the same partition on which you installed Exchange 2003. However, you can improve the performance of Exchange by moving the Mailroot folder to a different hard disk or partition. It is important to remember the queue must remain available for access regardless of which EVS (Exchange Virtual Server) is using it.

RAID-0 array is not recommended as a storage solution for highly available SMTP queues. With RAID-0, there is a good chance of data loss. RAID-1 is a better solution because it brings redundancy in the mirroring process. It also provides adequate throughput. RAID-0+1, on the other hand, provides both performance and availability for the SMTP queue.

Use the Exchange System Manager to change the location of your Queue directory. To do this, open Exchange System Manager, and click on the Message tab of the SMTP virtual server object.

Exchange Permissions in the Clustering Architecture

With Exchange 2003, all you need for the cluster service account are the default permissions for Exchange in the forest.

These are as follows:

- If the EVS is the first EVS in the organization, then the cluster administrator must be a member of a group that has the Exchange Full Administrator role applied to it at the Exchange organization level. This is easily achieved using an account that is a member of Domain Admins, Schema Admins, and Enterprise Administrator (you need the latter for ForestPrep and Domain-Prep, so you might as well just use this account to stand up your Exchange cluster as well).
- If the EVS is not the first EVS in the organization, then the cluster administrator must use an account that is a member of a group that has the Exchange Full Administrator role applied at the administrative group level.

If your Exchange organization is in native mode, and if the EVS is in a routing group that spans multiple administrative groups, then the cluster administrator must be a member of a group that has been given the Exchange Full Administrator role applied at the administrative group level for all of the administrative groups that the routing group spans.

In other words, if the EVS is in a routing group that spans the First Administrative Group and Second Administrative Group, then the cluster administrator must be given an account that is a member of a group that has the Exchange Full Administrator role for the First Administrative Group. You must also use an account that is a member of a group that has the Exchange Full Administrator role for the Second Administrative Group.

It is important to remember routing groups in Exchange organizations running in native mode can span multiple administrative groups. This is not true for routing groups in Exchange organizations running in mixed mode. In the latter case, they cannot span multiple administrative groups.

If you are implementing a cluster in a dual domain architecture, as described in Chapter 5, and the cluster server is the first Exchange server in the child domain, then you must have Exchange Administrator-Only permissions at the organizational level to specify the server responsible for the Recipient Update Service in the child domain.

Getting Started with Exchange 2003 Clustering

On a cluster, Exchange runs as a virtual server (not as a standalone server) because any node in a cluster can assume control of a virtual server. If the node running the EVS experiences problems, the EVS goes offline for a brief period until another node takes control of the EVS. As you can see in the following steps, you first install Exchange as you would on a standalone server and then use the Exchange bits to create a virtual server. All recommendations for Exchange clustering are for active/passive configurations, although we do touch on the active/active Exchange cluster later in this chapter.

Installing Exchange on the Cluster Nodes

Before we can install Exchange on the nodes, we obviously need to get the cluster up and running. As promised, we are going to set up the cluster using the replicated or mirror disk technology invented by NSI

Software and known as Double-Take and GeoCluster. NSI Software makes Double-Take and GeoCluster available for trials, and if you plan to cluster with GeoCluster, the company gives you telephone support to help you get a lab going. The process of installing a GeoCluster solution is not too difficult. Here are the steps.

To create a cluster with MSCS and GeoCluster, do as follows:

1. On the first node of the soon-to-be cluster, open Cluster Administrator and proceed to create a cluster as described in the previous chapters. The only difference this time around is you need to select the Majority Nodeset for your quorum resource. Cluster Administrator installs your cluster easily and is not concerned about the lack of shared storage. As soon as the node is created, install GeoCluster on the node. Accept the default properties for the GeoCluster installation. Repeat the process for each node of the cluster, joining the node using the Majority Nodeset resource, and then installing GeoCluster.

2. Next, we need to create a new quorum resource for the Geo-Cluster installation. The idea is to create a replicated disk resource using GeoCluster, and it becomes the new quorum resource, replacing the Majority Nodeset quorum. Right-click the Cluster group just created on your new cluster and choose New, then select Resource. From the Resource type drop-down field, choose the GeoCluster Replicated Disk Resource. This resource was added when you installed GeoCluster, and is shown illustrated in Figure 10.4. Click Next to continue with the installation.

3. You now need to choose the possible owners. Select the nodes you joined to your Majority Nodeset cluster, and click Next.

4. The dependencies come next, and you can select the IP Address Resource and Network Name as dependencies, but ignore the Majority Nodeset quorum. Click Next to continue with the installation.

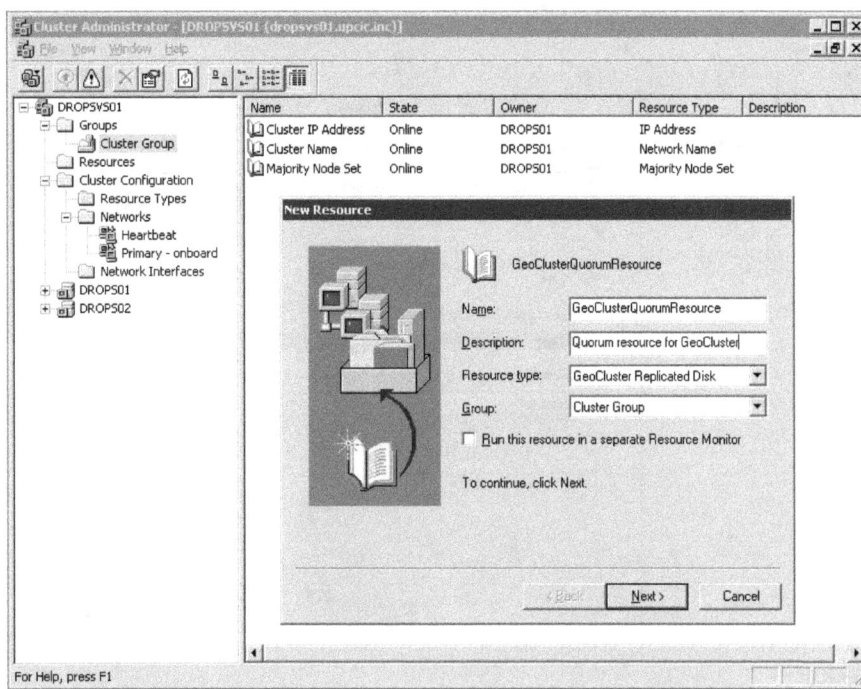

Figure 10.4   Choosing the GeoCluster Replicated Disk Resource.

5. In the next selection, you need to choose a disk that was provided for your new quorum resource. (We carved a 4GB logical
disk out of a huge RAID-5 array, which is on a separate bus,
channel, backplane, and controller on our servers. The disk was
given the Q drive letter.) Choose a disk for your new Quorum
and also select the network you are going to use for the replication of the quorum data, typically the private network between
the cluster nodes. This is shown in Figure 10.5. Click Next to
continue with the installation.

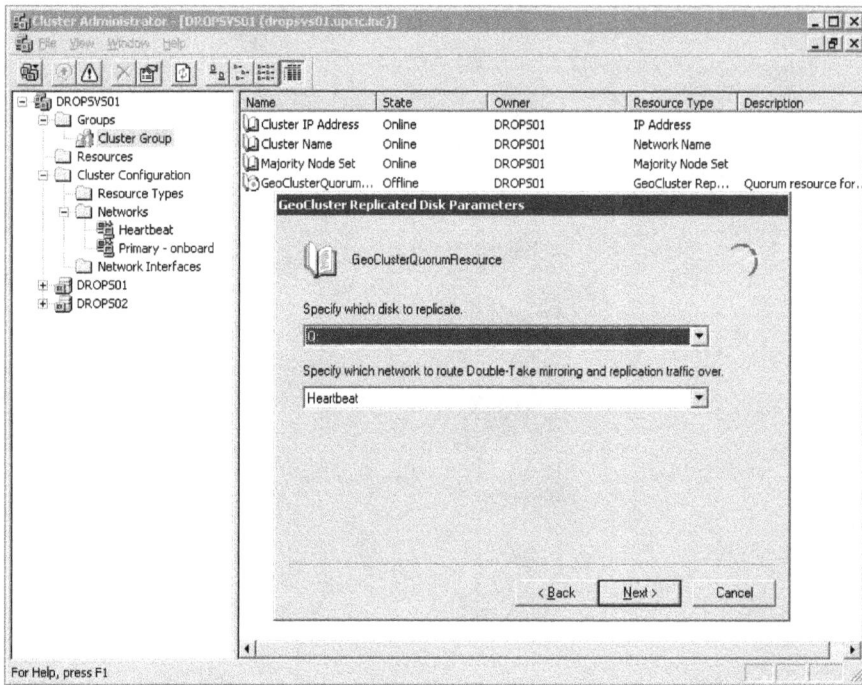

Figure 10.5 Assigning the disk for the GeoCluster Replicated disk resource.

6. Now GeoCluster requires you set up at least three arbitration paths on any additional servers on your network as long as they are not cluster nodes. These arbitration paths are required to assist with the failover of the quorum resource, and without them you are unable to make your GeoCluster replicated disk a quorum resource. You can put the paths on a single server, but you must remember the loss of that target server means you are not able to failover the server (see Figure 10.6). Click Next, and you are done with the creation of the new replicated disk resource. GeoCluster immediately begins replicating the disk to the other nodes in the cluster. It's that easy. Now we need to turn the replicated disk we just created into a traditional quorum.

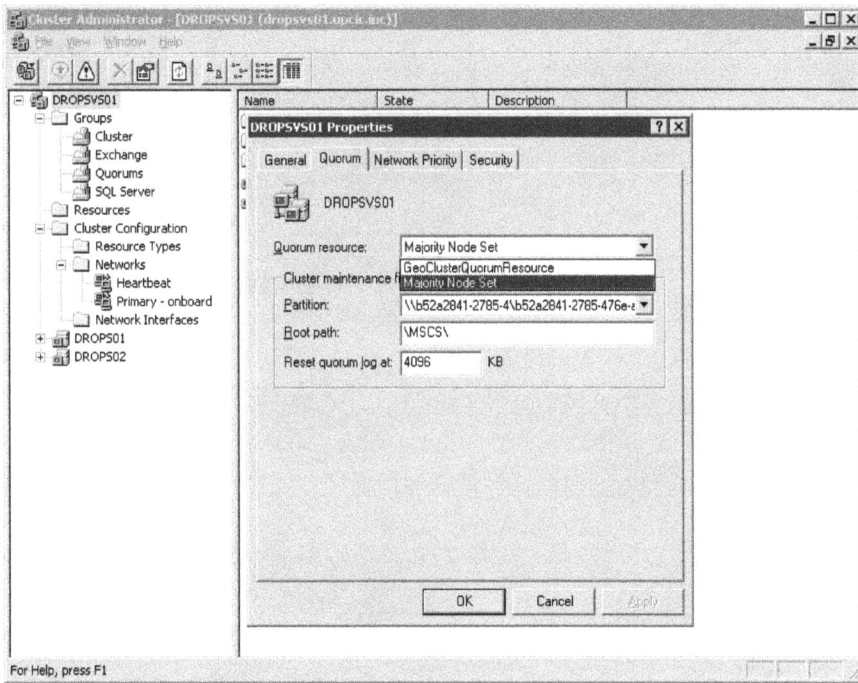

Figure 10.6   Assigning the arbitration paths.

7. To create a new quorum resource, select the name of your cluster in Cluster Administrator, right-click, and select Properties. On the Quorum tab, you see the GeoCluster replicated disk is now recognized by MSCS as being quorum-capable. If you do not see your Q drive in the drop-down list, be patient; replication and the stability of the arbitration paths need to happen. As soon as the disk appears, choose it, and click OK. This is demonstrated in Figure 10.7. You can delete the Majority Nodeset resource as soon as the new quorum is operational.

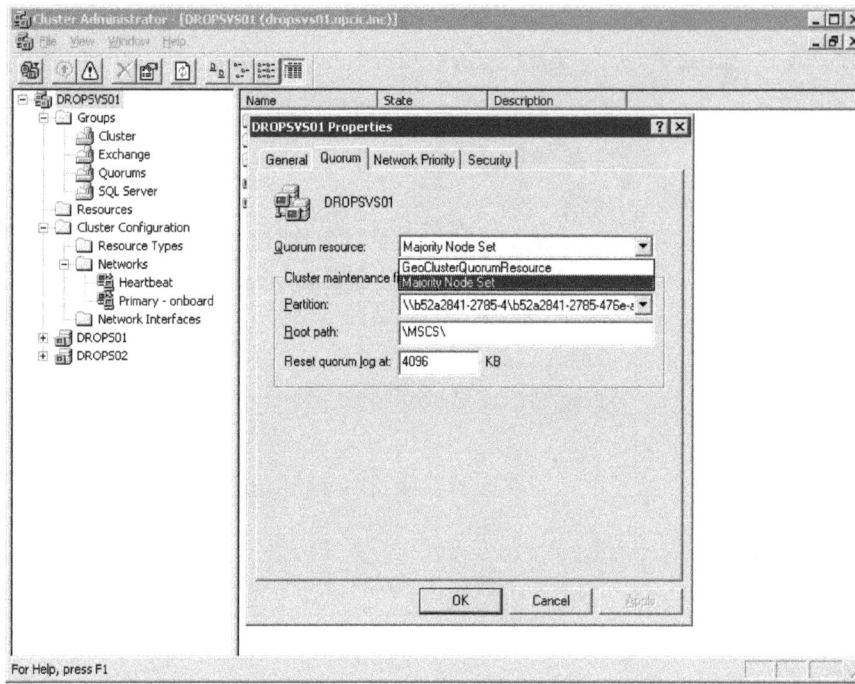

Figure 10.7   Choosing the new quorum resource.

Congratulations, you now have a cluster running without shared-storage, and the nodes can be next to each other in the same rack, or separated by deserts, oceans, or mountain ranges. On this cluster, you can set up additional replicated disks for our Exchange Virtual Servers.

The Exchange Virtual Server

To create an Exchange 2003 cluster, you create a Windows Server 2003 cluster group and then add specific resources to that group. Exchange 2003 clusters create logical servers referred to as Exchange Virtual Servers (EVSs). Unlike a standalone (non-clustered) Exchange 2003 server, an EVS is a cluster group that can be failed over if the primary node running the EVS fails. When one cluster node fails, one of the remaining nodes assumes the responsibilities of the failed EVS. To access this new server, clients can use the same server name.

An EVS is a cluster group that requires, at a minimum, the following resources:

- Static IP address
- Network name
- One or more physical disks for shared storage
- An Exchange 2003 System Attendant resource (the System Attendant resource installs other required Exchange resources)

Client computers connect to an EVS the same way they connect to a standalone Exchange 2003 server. Windows Server 2003 provides the IP address resource, the Network Name resource, and disk resources associated with the EVS. Exchange 2003 provides the System Attendant resource and other required resources. When you create the System Attendant resource, all other required and dependant resources are created. Table 10.2 lists the Exchange 2003 cluster resources and their dependencies.

Table 10.2   Exchange 2003 Cluster Resources and Dependencies

Resource	Description	Dependency
System Attendant	The System Attendant is the fundamental resource that controls the creation and deletion of all the resources in the EVS.	The Network Name resource and the shared disk resources
Exchange Store	This resource provides mailbox and public folder storage for Exchange.	System Attendant
SMTP	This resource handles relay and delivery of e-mail messages.	System Attendant
IMAP4	This is an optional resource that provides access to e-mail messages for IMAP4 clients.	System Attendant
POP3	This is an optional resource that provides access to e-mail messages for POP3 clients.	System Attendant

continues

Table 10.2   Exchange 2003 Cluster Resources and Dependencies

Resource	Description	Dependency
HTTP	This resource provides access to Exchange mailboxes and public folders by means of HTTP (typically Outlook Web Access 2003).	System Attendant
Exchange MS Search Instance	This resource provides content indexing for the EVS.	System Attendant
Routing Service	This resource builds the link state tables.	System Attendant
Message Transfer Agent (MTA)	There can be only one MTA resource per cluster. The MTA is created on the first EVS. All additional EVSs are dependent on this MTA.	System Attendant

As a matter of interest, the NNTP service, a subcomponent of the Windows Server 2003 Internet Information Services (IIS) component, is still a prerequisite for installing Exchange 2003 in a cluster, but it cannot be included as a failover resource, nor is it functional after the EVS is created.

Cluster Groups

When creating groups within the Cluster service, create a separate group for the Microsoft Distributed Transaction Coordinator (MSDTC) resource.

You can create the MSDTC resource in any existing group that contains a Physical Disk resource and a Network Name resource. However, it is not recommended you create the MSDTC resource in the group that contains the quorum disk resource or in a group that contains other program resources (such as Exchange resources).

- To provide fault tolerance for the cluster, create a separate group for the quorum disk resource.

- Assign each group its own set of Physical Disk resources. This allows the transaction log files and the database files to fail over to another node simultaneously.
- Use separate physical disks to store EVS transaction log files and database files. Separate hard disks prevent the failure of a single spindle from affecting more than one group.

Cluster Configurations

Before you configure your Exchange 2003 clusters, you must determine the level of availability expected for your users. After you make this determination, configure your hardware in accordance with the Exchange 2003 cluster that best meets your needs.

Active/Passive Clustering

Active/passive clustering is the recommended cluster configuration for Exchange. In active/passive clustering, an Exchange cluster includes up to eight nodes and can host a maximum of seven EVSs. (Each active node runs an EVS.) All active/passive clusters must have one or more passive nodes. A passive node is a server that has Exchange installed and is configured to run an EVS but remains on standby until a failure occurs.

In active/passive clustering, when one of the EVSs experiences a failure (or is taken offline), a passive node in the cluster takes ownership of the EVS that was running on the failed node. Depending on the current load of the failed node, the EVS usually fails over to another node after a few minutes. As a result, the Exchange resources on your cluster are unavailable to users for only a brief period of time.

In an active/passive cluster, such as an n-node active/1-passive cluster, there are three EVSs: EVS1, EVS2, and EVS3. This configuration can handle a single-node failure. For example, if Node 3 fails, Node 1 still owns EVS1, Node 2 still owns EVS2, and Node 4 takes ownership of EVS3 with all of the storage groups mounted after the failure. However, if a second node fails while Node 3 is still unavailable, the EVS associated with the second failed node remains in a failed state because there is no stand-by node available for failover.

When using an active/active configuration for your Exchange clusters, you are limited to two nodes. If you want more than two nodes, one node must be passive. For example, if you add a node to a two-node active/active cluster, Exchange does not allow you to create a third EVS. In addition, after you install the third node, no cluster node is able to run more than one EVS at a time.

In an active/active cluster, there are only two EVSs: EVS1 and EVS2. This configuration can handle a single node failure and still maintain 100 percent availability after the failure occurs. For example, if Node 2 fails, Node 1, which currently owns EVS1, also takes ownership of EVS2, with all the storage groups mounted. However, if Node 1 fails while Node 2 is still unavailable, the entire cluster is in a failed state because no nodes are available for failover.

If you decide to implement active/active clustering, you must consider the following requirements:

- **Scalability requirements:** To allow for efficient performance after failover, and to help ensure a single node of the active/active cluster can bring the second EVS online, you should make sure the number of concurrent MAPI user connections on each active node does not exceed 1,900. In addition, you should make sure the average CPU load per active node does not exceed 40 percent. For detailed information about how to size the EVSs running in an active/active cluster, as well as how to monitor an active/active configuration, see the Exchange Server 2003 High Availability Guide, which can be downloaded from the Microsoft Web site.

- **Storage group requirements:** As with standalone Exchange servers, each Exchange cluster node is limited to four storage groups. In the event of a failover, for a single node of an active/active cluster to mount all the storage groups within the cluster, you cannot have more than four total storage groups in the entire cluster.

Although a typical cluster topology includes more than two nodes, an easy way to explain the differences between active/passive and active/active clusters is to illustrate a simple two-node cluster topology.

In this example, both cluster nodes are members of the same domain, and both nodes are connected to the public network and a private cluster network. The physical disk resource is the shared disk in the cluster. If only one cluster node owns one EVS, the cluster is active/passive. If both nodes own one or more EVSs, or if either node owns two EVSs, the cluster is active/active.

In active/passive clustering, you can have up to eight nodes in a cluster, and it is required each cluster have one or more passive nodes. In active/active clustering, you can have a maximum of two nodes in a cluster.

Exchange Failover

As part of your cluster deployment planning process, you should understand how the failover process works. There are two scenarios for failover: *planned* and *unplanned*.

In a planned failover:

1. The Exchange administrator uses the Cluster service to move the EVS to another node.
2. All EVS resources go offline.
3. The resources move to the node specified by the Exchange administrator.
4. All EVS resources go online.

In an unplanned failover:

1. One (or several) of the EVS resources fails.
2. During the next IsAlive check, Resource Monitor discovers the resource failure.
3. The Cluster service automatically takes all dependent resources offline.
4. If the failed resource is configured to restart (default setting), the Cluster service attempts to restart the failed resource and all its dependent resources.

The cluster service tries to restart the resource again if the resource is configured to affect the group (default), and the resource has failed a certain number of times (default=3) within a configured time period (default=900 seconds). In the latter case, the Cluster service takes all resources in the EVS offline.

All resources are failed over (moved) to another cluster node. If specified, this is the next node in the Preferred Owners list.

Upon recovery, the Cluster service attempts to bring all resources of the EVS online on the new node. If the same or another resource fails again on the new node, the Cluster service repeats the previous steps and may need to fail over to yet another node (or back to the original node).

If the EVS keeps failing over, the Cluster service fails over the EVS a maximum number of times (default=10) within a specified time period (default=6 hours). After this time, the EVS stays in a failed state.

If failback is configured (default=turned off), the Cluster service either moves the EVS back to the original node immediately when the original node becomes available or at a specified time of day if the original node is available again, depending on the group configuration.

IP Addresses and Network Names

A typical cluster installation includes a public network client computers use to connect to EVSs and a private network for cluster node communication. To make sure you have sufficient static IP addresses available, consider the following requirements:

- Each cluster node has two static IP addresses (the public and private network connection IP addresses of each node) and one NetBIOS name.
- The cluster itself has a static IP address and a NetBIOS name.
- Each EVS has a static IP address and a NetBIOS name.

It is recommended that an <n>-node cluster with <e> EVSs use 2×n + e + 2 IP addresses. The +2 in this equation represents the two additional IP addresses that allow you to locate the quorum disk resource and the Microsoft Distributed Transaction Coordinator (MSDTC) in their own groups (a Windows Server 2003 recommendation). For more information about these recommendations, see the section "Cluster Groups" earlier in this chapter.

For a two-node cluster, the recommended number of static IP addresses is six plus the number of EVSs. For a four-node cluster, the recommended number is ten plus the number of EVSs.

It is recommended you use static IP addresses in any cluster deployment. Using Dynamic Host Configuration Protocol (DHCP) prevents client computers from connecting to the cluster. If the DHCP server fails to renew the IP lease, the entire cluster may fail. It is also recommended you use a private network for cluster communication. A public network connection failure on one node prevents the cluster nodes from communicating with each other. As a result, the failure blocks affected resources from failing over and may even cause the entire cluster to fail.

Creating the MSDTC Group

Before installing an EVS, you must install MSDTC on a server running Windows Server 2003. You should create a separate cluster group containing the Physical Disk, Network Name, and IP Address resources, and then add the MSDTC resource to that cluster group. You can call the group the MSDTC group. This practice ensures a failure of the MSDTC resource or any of its dependencies does not cause the EVS itself to failover.

1. Open the Cluster Administrator and under Groups, create a new cluster group for the MSDTC resource. In this group, create a GeoCluster replicated disk for the MSDTC's Physical Disk resource. You also need to create a Network Name resource and IP Address resource. You do not need a lot of space for the disk if the disk is only for Exchange. A disk of 500 MB to 1 GB will do fine.
2. Now right-click your MSDTC Group, select New, and then click Resource. In the New Resource dialog box, in the Name box, type in a name for your Distributed Transaction Coordinator and a description. Then click Next.
3. Select the MSDTC resource from the Resource drop-down, and then click Next. You now need to select the Possible owners. Select the owners and click Next.
4. Now select both the Physical Disk and Network Name resources you created in Step 1, and then click Add.

The MSDTC resource is now created. Bring it online before creating the EVS.

Creating the EVS

With the previous items in check, you can begin to cluster Exchange for your organization. The previous chapters have set the stage for getting the base clustering services up and running on the server. Return to

Chapter 6 if you need to plan your Exchange cluster from the ground up. Do not forget to create your Exchange cluster's service account. It must have the same permissions on the local server and on the domain as the service accounts we created in the earlier chapters.

Getting an Exchange Virtual Server (EVS) is in many ways identical to creating a SQL Server Virtual Server or SVS. The only real difference between the two cluster solutions is Exchange has many more components to failover, as you will see. But then again, are we just comparing white grapes with red ones. You saw in Chapter 9, "High Availability High-Performance SQL Server Solutions," just how much effort we had to put into clustering SQL Server Analysis Services.

The steps we discuss here assume you are clustering a 2-node active-passive cluster. So, log on to the first Exchange cluster node and run setup on this node. Just do not make the mistake of running setup and both nodes at the same time. It is very easy to start setup on both nodes when you have a dozen servers in a rack and you lose track of which server you are on.

As soon at Setup is complete on both nodes, service pack the nodes as required.

Now let's get cracking with the EVS setup:

1. Gentlefolk, start your Cluster Administrators. You can create the EVS resources from your locally installed Cluster Administrator or directly on the cluster node. It's good practice, however, to do the work remotely. To connect to the cluster, when prompted, specify a cluster name, or browse and select the cluster in which you want to create an EVS. If you are on the cluster node, use a dot (.) to select the local cluster.

2. In the console tree in Cluster Administrator, right-click Groups, select New, and then click Group. The New Group Wizard starts. Type a name for the group in the Name box, and then click Next. This group and all its resources are essentially your EVS.

3. In Preferred Owners, you may select a preferred owner for the EVS group. This is illustrated in Figure 10.8. However, the EVS resource creation can still move forward even if you do not specify a preferred owner at this time.

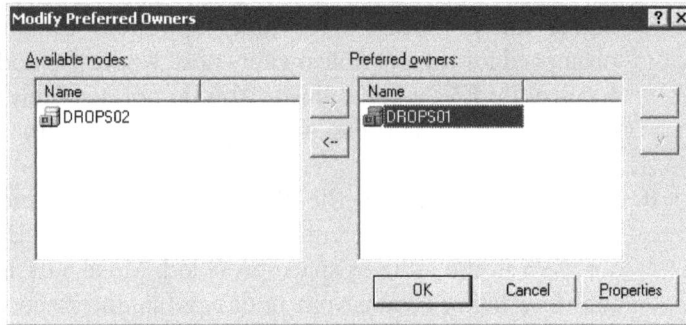

Figure 10.8 The Preferred Owners dialog box.

4. The next step is to create an IP Address Resource. Right-click the EVS group just created and select New, Resource. The New Resource Wizard starts. Here you can enter the name of the IP Address Resource in the Name box. Enter <MyEVSName> IP Address, where MyEVSName is the name of your EVS. This is illustrated in Figure 10.9. We suggest using a name for this resource similar to DREVS01_IP (see Figure 10.9).

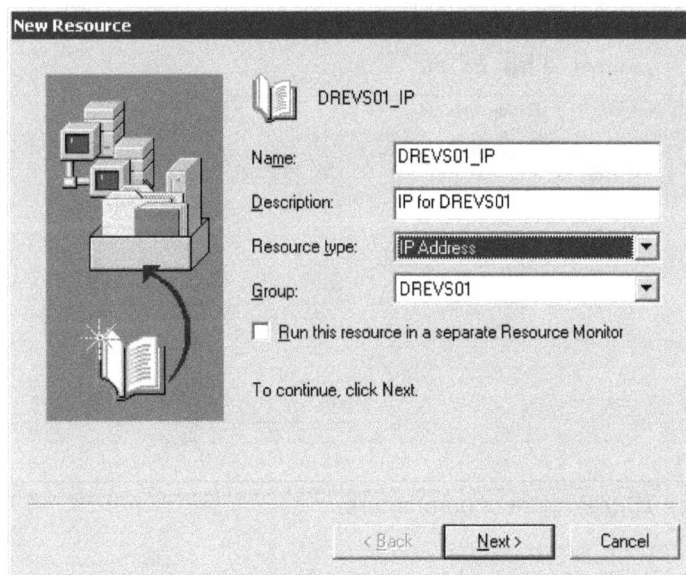

Figure 10.9 The EVS IP Address resource.

5. Select the IP Address resource type from the list. You are prompted for the possible owners next; select the nodes that can receive the EVS upon failover. You do not need any dependencies for the IP address, so simply click Next to add the IP Address.

6. You now are taken to the TCP/IP Address Parameters dialog box. This is shown in Figure 10.10. Type the static IP address of the EVS in the address space provided. Make sure the network interface being used is your node's public interface. Ensure the Enable NetBIOS for this address checkbox is selected. If you do not select NetBIOS for this address, your NetBIOS-based network clients are unable to access cluster services through the provided IP address. As soon as you are sure you have the correct data in this dialog box, click Finish. Bring you new IP Address resource online and ping the address to check it has taken.

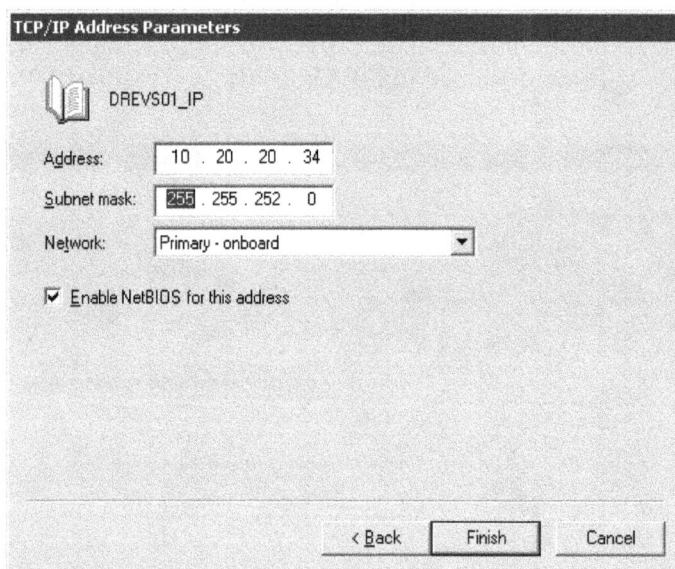

TCP/IP Address Parameters

DREVS01_IP

Address: 10 . 20 . 20 . 34

Subnet mask: 255 . 255 . 252 . 0

Network: Primary - onboard

☑ Enable NetBIOS for this address

< Back   Finish   Cancel

Figure 10.10   TCP/IP Address parameters.

7. Next we need to create a Network Name Resource. Right-click the EVS group, point to New, and then click Resource. When the New Resource Wizard starts, select the Network Name Resource. In the Name box, type the name of your EVS. This

name can be the same name used for the EVS group. See Figure 10.11 where we show DREVS01 as the network name for our server. Click Next to advance the creation of the Network Name Resource.

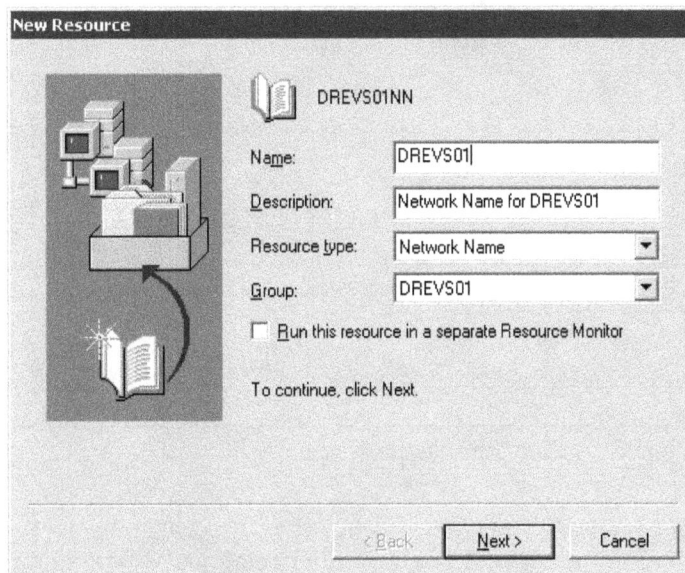

Figure 10.11 EVS Network Name Resource.

8. In Possible Owners, select all the nodes that are candidates for fail-over, and then click Next.

9. The creation of the resource has dependencies. The Network Name obviously depends on the IP Address resource. If you do not select the IP Address Resource, the Cluster Administrator will complain, so don't worry about forgetting this step. Select this resource and then click Add. Click Next when done.

10. Now you can enter the Network Name in the Name box. This name is what identifies the EVS on your network. It is also the EVS name that displays in Exchange System Manager after you have created the System Attendant resource for the EVS. Be sure of the name you are going to add here because after you create it, you cannot rename it. This is illustrated in Figure 10.12.

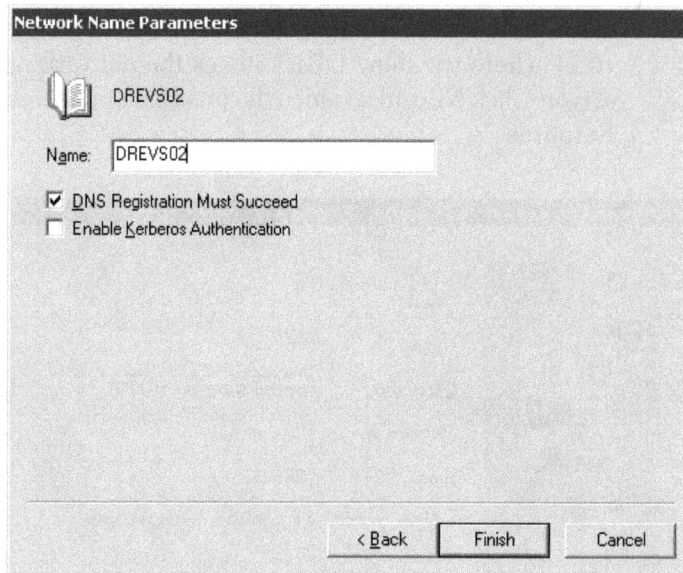

Figure 10.12 EVS creating the Network Name.

11. Before you click Finish, there are a few items on the dialog box to address. In AD implementations where the DNS server accepts dynamic updates, you want the Cluster service to ensure the DNS host record for this network name is updated before the Network Name resource comes online. To achieve this, select the DNS Registration Must Succeed checkbox. Selecting this checkbox ensures network name cannot be registered in DNS dynamically, and the Network Name resource fails.

You can also select the Enable Kerberos Authentication checkbox. This tells clients they can use the Kerberos authentication protocol when making an authenticated connection to the EVS's Network Name resource. Enabling Kerberos at this point can interfere with trials and requires coordination with the AD administrators. Leave it unchecked at present. You can always enable Kerberos connectivity later. See Microsoft Knowledge Base article 302389, "Description of the Properties of the Cluster Network Name Resource in Windows Server 2003" (http://go.microsoft.com/fwlink/?linkid=3052&kbid=302389). If you are satisfied with the parameters provided, click Finish.

12. You are now ready to add a Disk Resource to the EVS. You probably already set up the disk resources for the EVS because disk work usually gets done at the same time as setting up the actual cluster. Simply move the physical disk resource you want to move to the EVS group. Make sure the node on which you create the EVS owns this group, otherwise you have to first move the group to this node. One note of caution when clustering on the Double-Take replicated disk is to make sure the disk is not being accessed on the other node. Unlike true shared storage, the other nodes can see the replicated disk. Follow the recommended precautions to prevent possible damage to the disk.

You are now ready to add the System Attendant Resource to the EVS. At this point in the installation, your EVS looks similar to what you see in Figure 10.13. Note we are going to use one disk for both Exchange Logs and Storage Groups on this cluster because the single disk is sufficient for the type of application (there are about a 100 users on this system, but several mailboxes produce about $500,000 a month in business, and the owners wanted it clustered).

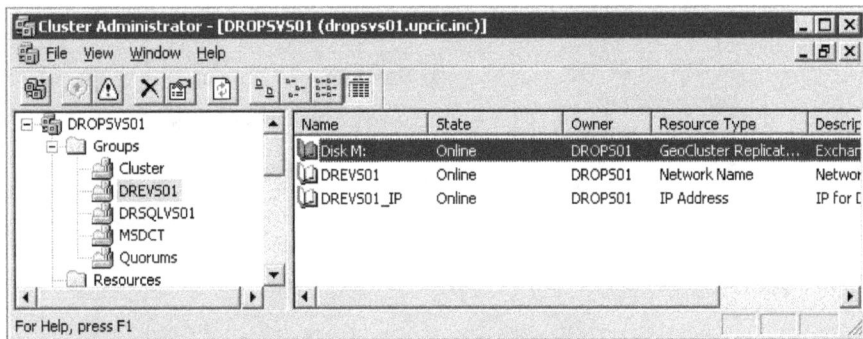

Figure 10.13   EVS ready for System Attendant Resource.

Creating an Exchange 2003 System Attendant Resource

To create an Exchange 2003 System Attendant resource, perform the following tasks:

1. Go back into Cluster Administrator and right-click the EVS group. Select Bring Online if you have not already done so because the base resources need to be up for the addition of the System Attendant Resource. Right-click the EVS group, then select New, Resource. The New Resource Wizard starts. In the Name box, enter the EVS name provided in the previous procedures. This is illustrated in Figure 10.14. Click Next to continue with the installation.

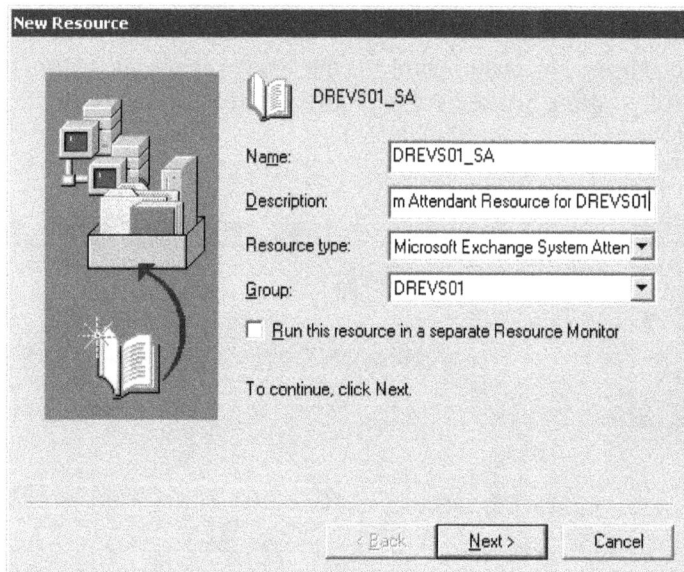

Figure 10.14 EVS System Attendant resource.

2. Select the owners for the resource in the Possible Owners dialog box, and then click Next. You now arrive at the Dependencies dialog box. Under Available resources, select the Network Name resource and the Physical Disk resources for the EVS—in other words, all the disk resources placed in the group for exclusive use of the EVS. You do not need to select the IP Address

resource because the Network Name resource already depends on it. Click Next to set dependencies and move on.

3. The wizard now arrives at the Exchange Administrative Group setup. You need to select the location in the Windows directory where you want to create the EVS. This option is available only when you create the first Exchange Virtual Server in a cluster, but there is not much choice. They must reside in the group specified. In future EVS installs, you will not get this option again. All EVSs must reside in the same administrative group. Simply click Next here and continue onward. This is shown in Figure 10.15.

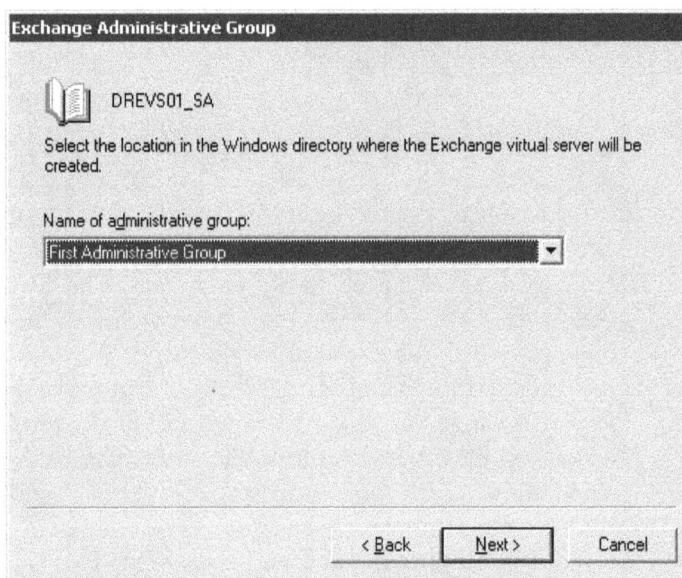

Figure 10.15   EVS First Exchange Administrative Group.

4. At the Exchange Routing Group dialog box, perform the same procedure as before, and click Next to select the routing group in which the EVS is created. This is illustrated in Figure 10.16. Click Next to complete the task. Again, this option is available only when you create the first Exchange Virtual Server in a cluster because all EVSs must reside in the same routing group.

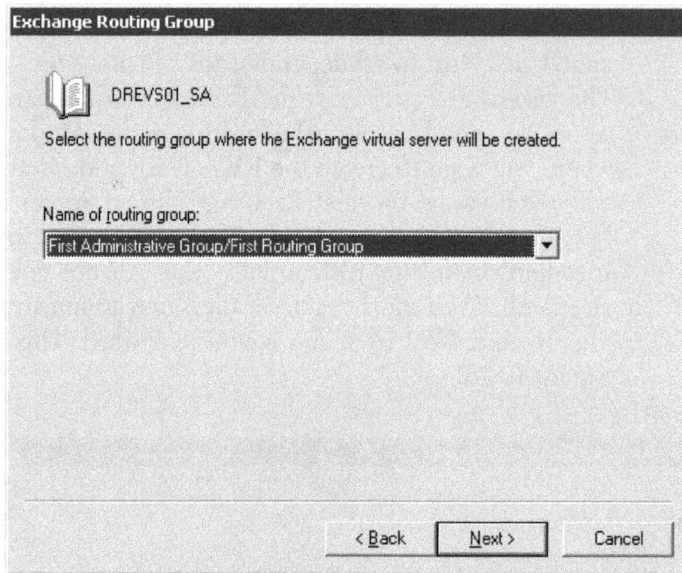

Figure 10.16   EVS First Exchange Administrative Group/First Routing Group.

5. Now we need to install to the data disks. The Data Directory dialog box loads. Here you must enter a path to the data folder, one of the disk resources provided earlier. You must verify this path points to a shared physical disk resource assigned to this EVS. Exchange uses the drive you select here to store the transaction log files, the default public store files, and the mailbox store files, pub1.edb, pub1.stm, priv1.edb, and priv1.stm, respectively. Here we are going to choose our GeoCluster replicated disk. Choose the disk and click Next. This is illustrated in Figure 10.17.

6. You now see the summary of procedures that are undertaken. This procedure actually creates the EVS. After you create the EVS, you cannot rename it. As the dialog box summary indicates, if you want to rename an EVS after it has been created, you must remove it and then re-create it with another name. See "Removing an Exchange Virtual Server" in the Exchange Server 2003 Administration Guide (http://go.microsoft.com/fwlink/ ?linkid=21769). There is nothing left to do now; so if you are sure of the parameters provided, click Finish. That's it. EVS, here we come.

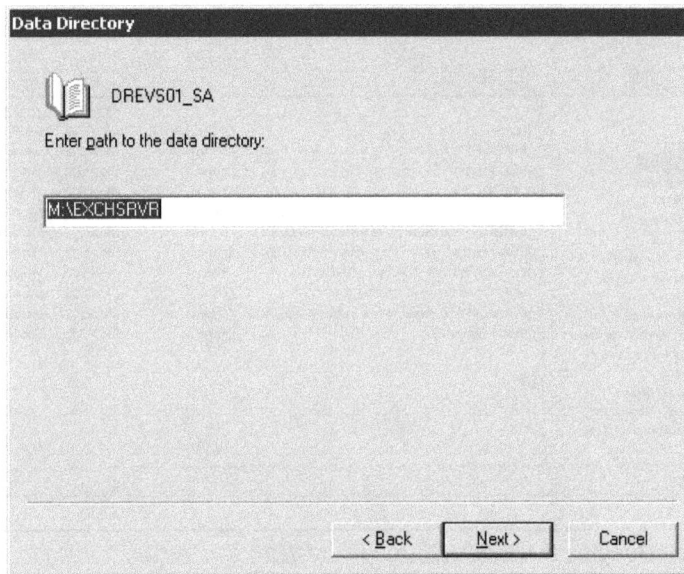

Figure 10.17 Selecting the Data Directory.

You should see a dialog box telling you the EVS was successfully created. All the EVS resources now appear in Exchange System Manager. If the operation failed, you are told soon enough why it failed. If it fails, the New Resource Wizard remains open, so you can go back in the wizard, fix the indicated problems, and then try again.

You can now go into Cluster Administrator, right-click your new EVS, and then click Bring Online. You may not see all resources coming online at the same time. This is shown in Figure 10.18. Replication latency is the reason. Simply wait for replication to occur, and then try bringing the resources online again. As we mentioned earlier, if you are adding online resources to the dependencies list when creating the Exchange System Attendant resource, first ensure the resources you want to add are online. This helps with bringing the entire EVS online quicker.

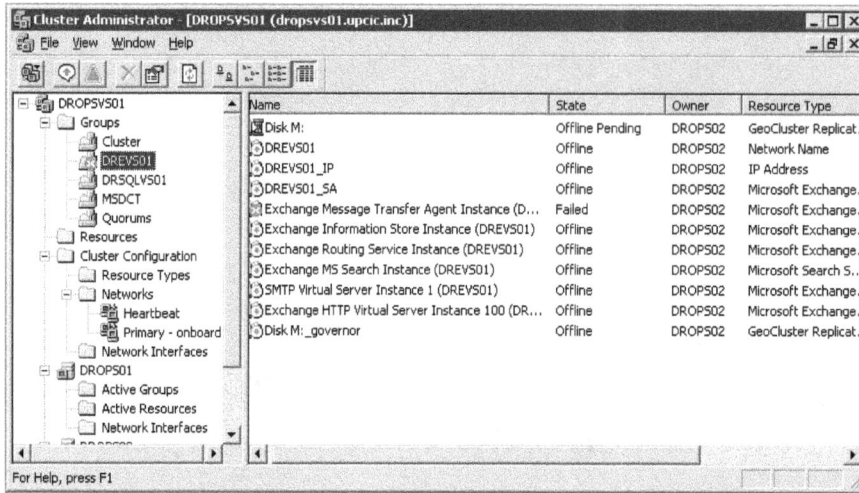

Figure 10.18   Bringing the EVS online.

Notice after you successfully created the Exchange System Attendant resource, it automatically creates the resources it needs for the EVS to work. These resources are

- Exchange Information Store Instance
- Exchange Message Transfer Agent Instance (the Message Transfer Agent Instance resource is created only in the first EVS added to a cluster. All EVS in the cluster share the single Message Transfer Agent Instance resource.)
- Exchange Routing Service Instance
- SMTP Virtual Server Instance
- Exchange HTTP Virtual Server Instance
- Exchange MS Search Instance

NOTE: The Windows IMAP4 and POP3 protocol services are no longer enabled by default on servers running Windows Server 2003. Also, the IMAP4 and POP3 protocol resources are no longer created by default upon creation of an Exchange 2003 Virtual Server. This is done for security reasons. For information about adding IMAP4 and POP3 resources, see "Managing Exchange Clusters" in the Exchange Server 2003 Administration Guide (http://go.microsoft.com/fwlink/?linkid=21769).

Your Exchange implementation is ready for work. You should now perform service pack installation for Exchange 2003. Also, after you have your Exchange cluster fully operational, you can change resource names, group names, and so on so they adhere to your naming conventions. This is especially important if you are installing more than one cluster and multiple Exchange virtual servers.

Configuring a Clustered Back-End Server

A clustered back-end server improves the overall performance and security of your Exchange architecture. Because high performance and availability is the key objective, you should ensure the clustered back-end servers have been properly configured to handle the HTTP requests from the front-end server. You don't need the Enterprise Edition of Microsoft Exchange for a front-end server, the Standard Edition will do fine.

When you configure a clustered back-end server, typically referred to as a mailbox server (MBX), you need to map a front-end Exchange server to the nodes of the cluster. This allows the node to accept proxy requests from any front-end server in the organization. These so-called proxy requests are requests for messaging services from client computers running Microsoft Outlook, Outlook Web Access, Outlook Mobile Access, Microsoft Exchange ActiveSync, POP3, or IMAP4. The requests are sent to the EVS through the front-end server (FES), and all communication between FES and back-end servers goes through TCP port 80. The data stream between the front and backends can be encrypted for maximum security.

Did you notice when you created the EVS, during the installation of the System Attendant resource, Exchange created an HTTP virtual server resource? For a front-end server to use a clustered back-end server, you need to create more HTTP virtual servers on each EVS on your clusters. You have to create one Exchange HTTP virtual server for each front-end. See the Microsoft Exchange 2003 Deployment Guide Microsoft provides for an in-depth discussion of front-end/back-end Exchange architecture.

Time-Out

This chapter covered the essential components of clustering Microsoft Exchange 2003. It is important the System Attendant resource obtains the correct security and permissions it needs to keep the EVS alive. As we are sure you are aware, if you lose the System Attendant, you essentially lose all the resources that depend on it.

CHAPTER 11

Load Balancing

Introduction

In previous chapters, we presented high-availability technology, which is based on the principle of server and data redundancy and virtualization of resources (such as clustered applications, file shares, or printers). Typically, each server functioning as a cluster member is capable of supporting all resources independently of other members. This fact, combined with failover mechanisms, ensures that a server or service failure has no impact on resource availability. Remaining cluster members take control of resources residing previously on the failed server and bring them automatically online, preserving their state and maintaining their availability. In the worst-case scenario, users experience a short delay in application response or file access.

Server clusters, however, are not capable of true load balancing. This is not an issue of technical limitation but rather a direct result of server clustering principles. Load balancing implies having multiple targets across which a load can be distributed, but, by design, there is only one active instance of every resource defined on the server cluster at any given time. To remedy this shortcoming of server clustering, Microsoft provides an alternative solution called *Load Balancing* present in all general-purpose editions of Windows 2003 Server (Standard, Enterprise, and Datacenter) as well as in Windows 2003 Web Server. In this chapter, we take a closer look into its architecture, implementation, and management.

Scale-Out Revisited

Clearly, fault tolerance is not the only issue being addressed by designers of clustering technologies. Another equally important one is scalability, which describes the capability of gracefully handling fluctuations in resource utilization. In the case of server clustering, your primary recourse is investment in hardware powerful enough to handle failure of remaining cluster members and failover of all their resources. This means, however, expensive upgrades of all servers participating in a cluster is needed, which could include installation of multiple processors and gigabytes of memory. This could even require replacement of existing hardware resulting in even higher cost. In addition, each upgrade typically translates into server downtime (unless the components are hot-pluggable). However, even with careful design, there is a limit you are likely to reach at some point. This might be number of processors or amount of memory supported by hardware or software, maximum speed of the I/O bus, or operating system resources. In any case, this process, known as scaling-up, becomes increasingly difficult as demand for server resources grows. In addition, upgrades are likely to lead to the situation where system hardware is underutilized for extended periods of time. When the frequency of incoming requests decreases, this yields a poor return on investment (although, on the other hand, replacing a large number of smaller servers with fewer more powerful ones might help you reduce maintenance cost, lowering at the same rate total cost of ownership, so the scaling-up approach has its advantages).

The answer to the drawbacks of scaling-up is the strategy known as *scaling-out*. Its premise is based on creating a distributed environment where individual servers work together as a virtual unit. If a resource load increases, all that is needed is the addition of another potentially inexpensive server, which typically does not need to have the same specifications as other servers (which is the case with server clustering where not only are all the nodes required to be identical, but they must comply with the restrictive Cluster Hardware Compatibility List). Analogically, if a resource load decreases, you can remove a server without affecting overall resource availability. Both operations usually do not require any downtime. This also simplifies performing maintenance and troubleshooting tasks by temporarily removing individual servers. The main limiting factors of the scaling-up approach are no longer applicable, such as insufficient hardware and operating system resources and disk or network I/O bottlenecks, which restrict the applicability of the scaling-up approach.

Another significant benefit of scaling-out is the role it plays in high availability solutions. Network Load Balancing can serve here as one of the primary examples.

Fault Tolerance and High Availability of NLB

Network Load Balancing (NLB) is an operating system component that brings load balancing functionality into all editions of Windows 2003 Server (Standard, Web, Enterprise, and Datacenter). Just like server clustering, it uses server redundancy and virtualization of resources. What makes the two solutions distinct is duplication of resources. As mentioned before, with server clusters, only a single instance of each resource is active at any time (and this is also true of so-called Active-Active clusters). In the case of Network Load Balancing, there are identical copies of each resource running at the same time on each cluster member. The software component managing operations of the NLB cluster runs on each of its nodes and determines which of them should handle the next request. This is done according to parameters set during NLB cluster configuration and assigned to each node that subsequently joins the cluster. Any change in cluster membership, such as sudden shutdown of one of its nodes or the addition of a new server, is almost immediately detected, so the distribution algorithm can be adjusted and client sessions properly redirected. This mechanism forms the basis for high availability in the Network Load Balancing solution. Single server failure does not significantly impact the availability of a cluster resource as long as other servers with the same resource are still functioning.

On the other hand, Network Load Balancing does not truly qualify as a fault tolerant solution (at least not to the same extent as server clustering). The main reason for this is the lack of a built-in support for failover or failback, which is essential for server cluster operations. In server clustering, the state of each resource is maintained despite node failures, typically by using shared storage where ownership and control can be transferred from one node to another. Because there is no direct equivalent of such a mechanism in NLB, after a member server fails, all of its resources and all user information associated with the user's state are no longer available. A user can connect to another server in the cluster and access an identical copy of the resource, but any node-specific resource data needs to be re-created. This can be remedied to some extent by setting up a back-end data store (preferably in the form of a server cluster) where such data is recorded for each new user connection. If one NLB node fails, other nodes can retrieve recorded data when requests for reconnect are redirected to them.

Note also that while NLB nodes can recognize a server failure and automatically adjust cluster membership, they are not capable of detecting problems with clustered applications or services. You need to employ other solutions, such as Microsoft Operations Manager or third-party server-monitoring products, to provide notifications about such events and develop remediation procedures.

Load Balancing for High Performance

The term high availability does not necessarily mean exclusively minimizing downtime. Frequently, it is used in the context of delivering sufficient performance levels. The ever-increasing pace of our lives is inversely proportionate to our patience. Commercial Internet sites run the risk of losing hundreds of customers with every one-second delay it takes to load web pages into the browser. One of the benefits of Network Load Balancing is its capability to quickly adjust to increased demand for server resources, satisfying most rigid performance requirements.

As the exemplification of the scale-out approach, Network Load Balancing allows the dynamic addition (or removal) of nodes without noticeable impact to cluster operations. This way you can gracefully accommodate fluctuations in demand for cluster resources.

Sharing Server Load

The Network Load Balancing component in Windows 2003 Server monitors incoming network IP packets reaching the designated server's network adapter. It also takes note of source and destination IP addresses; transport layer protocol, such as UDP (User Datagram Protocol); TCP (Transmission Control Protocol); and the corresponding destination port. These values are matched against parameters assigned to the cluster (shared parameters) and individual nodes (host parameters), which are part of NLB configuration. Based on results, a common algorithm determines which cluster node should process the packet. A filtering mechanism is used to discard the packets on all remaining nodes. Even though the algorithm runs independently on each server, it is guaranteed to yield the same outcome; so there is no danger of having two cluster nodes simultaneously responding to the same packet. This approach is more efficient and scalable than the rerouting-based one (used by a number of hardware load balancers).

It is important to realize that cluster node selection does not take into account current server utilization levels but rather characteristics of incoming traffic and parameters specified during cluster configuration only. This fact emphasizes your responsibility as the cluster administrator to ensure that traffic is properly distributed. For example, when adding a less powerful server to a cluster, adjust the percentage of the traffic handled to reflect the different performance characteristics of the cluster members. This topic is further explored in the section "Setup and Configuration of NLB Cluster" later in this chapter. Unfortunately, even such measures do not ensure that utilization will be evenly balanced across all cluster nodes, but that is the best option you have without resorting to specialized and expensive solutions, such as Component Load Balancing, which is included as part of Microsoft Application Center 2000 or MetaFrame XP from Citrix (in the area of thin client technology).

Virtual Servers

The virtualization of resources is one of the mechanisms used by the high availability functionality in Network Load Balancing clusters. This mechanism is based on having one or more IP addresses assigned on each cluster node to a designated network adapter named *cluster network adapter* (this adapter needs to face the client network because it accepts client requests). Typically, you need a separate virtual IP address for every resource (application) with distinct load balancing requirements. Load balancing criteria, which are applied to requests sent to a virtual IP address, are specified by groups of configuration settings known as *port rules* (each of these concepts is covered in more detail in the section "Designing the NLB Cluster" later in this chapter).

Because clients typically communicate with servers using easy-to-remember server names, you should ensure that each IP address is registered with DNS and has a name associated with it. Note that NLB does not automatically register a cluster name with DNS servers, so host and pointer records for each resource need to be manually created within respective DNS zones.

What Cannot Be Scaled

Scalability potentials of the Network Load Balancing-based solutions are limited by a number of factors. In general, these factors can be grouped in two broad categories. The first one includes restrictions inherent to the technology used by NLB. Such requirements have to be satisfied first for NLB to work at all. The second factor deals with NLB component, server application, and resource configuration settings, which might have to be properly adjusted to take advantage of full NLB scalability potentials.

Restrictions in the first category are associated primarily with networking requirements. First and foremost, Network Load Balancing mechanism functions are based on TCP, UDP, and IP parameters, which means the client must communicate with load balanced applications through TCP connections or UDP streams. The underlying network has to be FDDI, Ethernet, or Gigabit Ethernet-based (TokenRing is not supported). Additional conditions need to be satisfied that refer to features supported by server network adapters and interconnecting devices, such as switches and routers. We discuss these in more detail in the "Design Specifications" section later in this chapter.

Among the most common restrictions in the second category are related to maintaining client session state. This results from the fact that the Network Load Balancing model is based on having multiple, identical instances of applications or services operating simultaneously. If these instances are static and non-secure (such as some public Web sites), session state is not relevant. However, with the omnipresence of e-commerce and electronic shopping carts, this is rarely the case.

Two main methods exist for securing session data. The first one involves storing it directly on a node to which a client is connected; the second uses back-end servers (preferably server clustered). In the first case, you need to ensure that the client's requests are processed consistently by the same server, which is possible by manipulating NLB configuration parameters (which we discuss in the "Network Load Balancing Architecture" section later in this chapter). In the second case, you might need to redesign your application to ensure session data can be stored outside of the cluster nodes where an application is installed. For example, when dealing with Web connections, a session-specific identifier can be appended in obfuscated form to URL strings exchanged between the Web client and Web server and used to access a client-specific record stored in a separate database server. We discuss this and other aspects of designing and configuring Web farms in Chapter 12, "Internet Information Server."

A number of applications are stateful, dynamic, and high-volume in nature, such as Microsoft SQL Server or Microsoft Exchange Server. This makes them unsuitable for Network Load Balancing unless you can either make their content static (for example, by creating read-only replicas of SQL Server databases) or modify their architecture (for example, by dividing Exchange Server functionality into two tiers and load balancing access from Outlook Web Access clients to front-end servers while maintaining high availability of the back-end tier with server clusters).

Distribution of traffic provided by Network Load Balancing is based on a randomization algorithm, so it does not perform well if the number of client requests is small. In addition, if resource utilization varies dramatically from one request to another, it is unlikely load balancing will yield any considerable scalability benefits because it is based exclusively on analyzing network characteristics of incoming traffic and does not take into consideration server processing load.

Other restrictions apply to load balancing .NET Remoting and COM+ connections. In both cases, the capability to load balance is limited by the fact that their invocations from the same client are carried over an established TCP connection (assuming one already exists) instead of being distributed across NLB nodes by creating a separate TCP connection for each. This means a single client ends up reusing the same TCP connection. However, connections from multiple clients should be fairly well load balanced. A partial solution to this problem, as far as COM+ connections are concerned, is the use of Application Center 2000 with Component Load Balancing. (This solution is described in more detail in the section "Load Balancing and COM Application Servers" later in this chapter.)

Additionally, Network Load Balancing is not supported on the servers where Microsoft Server cluster component is installed. This is because of incompatibilities between their configurations and the lack of a mutual communication mechanism as well as because of differences in fundamental principles of their designs. Server clustering operates by running unique instances of failover-capable resources; NLB clusters function with multiple instances of the same resource without the capability to failover. NLB traffic directed at server cluster resources does not make sense because only a single instance of such a resource is active at a time. However, if possible, you should separate application functionality into two or more layers with highly available front-end network load balanced servers handling client requests in a distributed fashion and redirecting them to fault-tolerant, back-end cluster servers for processing. We discuss such an approach in more detail in the section "Multi-Tiered Server Farms" later in this chapter.

Selecting NLB Clustering Candidates

Based on scalability restrictions discussed in the previous section, you should already have some idea about the criteria for selecting candidates for NLB clustering. First of all, any shared application or resource needs to be accessed through IP-based communication because the load balancing algorithm works only with TCP and UPD protocols. Its clients should be able to survive server failure without loss of stability and be easily reconnected to another server to reestablish a new session. This implies that the best candidates are stateless (where new client requests are not dependent on prior communication), or relatively static applications easily replicated across multiple servers, or the ones designed to operate in a multi-tier hierarchy with the NLB load balancing tier separate from the one where state information is stored.

As you can expect, Network Load Balancing is most commonly used when clustering applications hosted on Web servers, especially the ones running Internet Information Server 6.0. ADO.NET provides excellent support for multi-tier architecture, simplifying development of disconnected database applications, which do not maintain connections to a database open over an extended period of time. Similarly, Web services and remoting fit well into this type of environment. The capability to load balance Web servers makes NLB applicable to a wide range of products and applications, such as front-end servers providing Outlook Web Access to Microsoft Exchange Server. We discuss various aspects of designing and configuring Web farms in Chapter 12.

A variety of other Microsoft technologies exist, not necessarily falling into the application category, that scale as well as IIS 6.0. Among the most popular candidates are resources accessed through such protocols as FTP or Telnet—providing Streaming Media or Message

Queuing services—as well as servers running Terminal Services (providing access to Windows 2003-based applications in combination with Session Directory service), LDAP Directory Services, VPN (operating as part of Routing and Remote Access Server component accessible through PPTP and L2TP protocols), or Internet Security and Acceleration software (delivering security, VPN, Network Address Translation, and Web Caching features).

It is also possible to load balance NetBIOS traffic (although you need to carefully consider locking and data synchronization issues when allowing access to multiple copies of shares across NLB cluster nodes). This requires NLB nodes to have at least two network adapters with the clustered one having the primary IP address. This results from the fact that NetBIOS sessions can access remote shares only by connecting to the primary IP address of the server that hosts them. In addition, you need to set the value of the DisableStrictNameChecking entry (of REG_DWORD type) stored in the HKEY_LOCAL_MACHINE\ System\CurrentControlSet\Services\LanmanServer\Parameters registry key to **1**, and follow this change by restarting the Server service on each NLB cluster node. This solution is documented in the KB article "Connecting to SMB Share on a Windows 2000-Based Server May Not Work with an Alias Name" (`http://go.microsoft.com/fwlink/?LinkId=18382`).

Network Load Balancing Architecture

The core of NLB functionality is implemented as an NDIS packet filter driver called WLBS.SYS, which operates, from the architectural point of view, above the network adapter driver and below the IP network layer. This placement enables the NLB driver to monitor all IP-related traffic and determine its parameters, such as source and destination IP address, or transport layer protocol and its port, which are subsequently used by the load balancing algorithm. Only packets sent to one of the virtual IP addresses that are supposed to be handled locally according to the load balancing rules are passed to the higher networking layers for further processing (all remaining packets targeting that virtual IP address are discarded because they are processed by another cluster node). This optimizes utilization of the local resources. This driver needs to be loaded on every server that participates in the NLB cluster.

The architecture of the NLB cluster is based on a number of shared elements. All cluster members that provide access to the same service or resource must have the same virtual IP address representing this resource assigned to their cluster network adapter (at the very least, they share the same cluster virtual IP address assigned to it during the initial NLB setup). The same identically configured resource needs to be present on every node. Cluster network adapters share the same auto-generated virtual MAC address (unicast or multicast, depending on the option selected when the cluster is created). The common IP and MAC addresses are used to deliver incoming client traffic to all nodes

The nodes also share a common network infrastructure, which distributes every client request to each of the nodes. This is typically done by connecting the nodes to the same hub, switch, or, preferably, a set of redundant switches. All nodes are configured with the same set of rules running a common algorithm that uses them to determine one node responsible for processing a particular request. Because the outcome of the algorithm is identical across all nodes, only one of them responds while all remaining ones ignore it. This scenario repeats for every incoming IP packet.

An NLB cluster usually has multiple rules defined, each consisting of a set of criteria, which are matched against the characteristics of a network request to determine whether a rule should be applied (such as source and target IP addresses, transport layer protocol, and sequential range of destination ports); it also has configuration parameters, which affect load balancing behavior (such as filtering mode, affinity, load weight, and handling priority). For a rule to be considered (and, effectively, for the load balancing algorithm to apply), an IP packet must target one of the NLB cluster virtual IP addresses as well as a TCP or UDP port within the range included in the port rule definitions. Depending on the filtering mode (disabled, single, or multiple), an IP packet can be blocked, handled by a designated node (one with the highest handling priority, which is a value between 1 and 32, unique to each member server), or distributed in the load balanced fashion. The load distribution is affected by the load weight parameter, which is an integer between 1 and 100 you associate with every node. This number is used to calculate the weighted average. To obtain it, the weight load value for a particular node is divided by the sum of weight loads for all nodes and multiplied by 100. This yields a percentage of overall traffic handled by selected node (provided the multiple filtering mode is used). All described parameters are rule-specific, which means a server can have two different load weight parameters for two separate rules. Finally, the affinity parameter affects how subsequent requests from the same client or group of clients are handled. With no affinity, statistical algorithm used by NLB ensures that TCP connections from the same IP address and source port number are processed by the same cluster node, unless the cluster membership (through the addition or removal of a cluster member) or the load weight parameters change. This means a single client might have simultaneous connections to multiple cluster nodes as long as these connections originate from different ports. Single affinity causes every packet originating from a particular IP address to be processed by the same cluster member, regardless of the source port (as with no affinity, this is subject to changes in cluster membership). Class C affinity also disregards the source port but redirects all requests from the same class C subnet, rather than an individual IP address, to the same node. Choice of affinity is made based on application characteristics. If an application session runs over multiple, simultaneous TCP connections, then single or class C affinity should be used. Otherwise, if the application does not rely on having a multi-connection session processed by the same target server, no affinity is the preferred choice because this offers the most evenly load-balanced traffic.

NLB nodes exchange heartbeat network messages between themselves periodically (by default every 1 second, although this interval is configurable) using the cluster network adapter. If five consecutive messages from any one of them are not received (this value is also configurable), the convergence process is initiated. Convergence is triggered by some administrative changes, such as adding or removing a cluster node or port rule modifications. Its duration is typically no longer than 10 seconds.

Controlling NLB Heartbeat Parameters

You can control parameters of the NLB heartbeat messages by modifying entries under the registry key HKEY_LOCAL_MACHINE\SYSTEM\Current-ControlSet\Services\WLBS\Parameters\Interface\Adapter-GUID, where the Adapter-GUID designates the GUID of the clustered network adapter.

AliveMsgPeriod of REG_DWORD typesets the interval between messages. Its default value is 1000 (decimal) milliseconds and can range from 100 to 10000.

continues

AliveMsgTolerance of REG_DWORD typesets maximum number of messages that can be missed before convergence is initiated. Its default value is 5 and can range from 5 to 100.

For these changes to take effect, you need to restart cluster nodes.

Designing the NLB Cluster

Design of the NLB cluster should start with identifying applications and services that can benefit from load balancing. Decisions should be based on the criteria outlined in the previous sections "What Cannot Be Scaled" and "Selecting NLB Clustering Candidates." If this process yields multiple results, you might need to consider their ability to coexist on the same nodes. This might not be a problem when dealing with a mix of IIS 6.0 Web applications, but combining Terminal Services, Routing and Remote Access services, or Internet Security and Acceleration server software on the same node is not recommended. In general, you should evaluate performance, security, and management implications to make your design decision. This process yields a list of applications that can work together and which would be installed on all nodes within the same NLB cluster. Each set typically requires a separate cluster. You should also take note of applications that expect session coherency and initiate multiple TCP/IP connections targeting different ports because this information is needed when defining NLB port rules.

After the first stage of the design is completed, you need to review core (rather than application-specific) requirements of the NLB cluster. During this process you need to keep in mind the hardware and software requirements of cluster members, the configuration of network infrastructure, and setting the NLB cluster shared and individual host parameters, as well as port rules.

Design Specifications

As indicated at the beginning of this section, we start by analyzing hardware and software requirements of cluster members. Choice of operating system does not introduce any restrictions because the NLB component is available on Windows 2003 Server Standard, Enterprise, Datacenter, and Web Editions. In addition, within the same cluster, you can mix different implementations of Microsoft load balancing solutions, including Windows 2000 Server NLB (provided as part of Advanced and Datacenter Editions) and Windows NT 4.0-based Windows Load Balancing Services. The maximum number of nodes in the NLB cluster is 32, although there are ways to network load balance traffic beyond this limit. For example, you can use the *DNS Round Robin* mechanism to distribute client requests across multiple, identically configured NLB clusters. Depending on the application or a service you selected as the candidate for load balancing, you might need to perform additional installation or configuration tasks (such as installation of Internet Information Server 6.0, Routing and Remote Access Server, or Terminal Server components).

While in general Network Load Balancing does not need to operate in the Active Directory environment, you might find that in certain scenarios this is not the case. For example, when load balancing access to Terminal Services, cluster nodes need to belong to the Windows 2003 Active Directory domain to take advantage of Session Directory. In addition, the Session Directory service has to operate on Windows 2003 Enterprise or Datacenter Edition server.

Analysis of network infrastructure is an important part of the NLB cluster design. The path between clients and load balanced servers should not constitute a bottleneck or a single point of failure. In addition, your network design should guarantee proper management capabilities and a sufficient level of security.

Each cluster member requires at least one network adapter used for load balancing client requests. Because all cluster adapters share the same IP address, they need to be attached to the same physical or virtual subnet. This might require changes to your networking gear in case your current equipment does not support VLANs. The network path between your clients and the NLB cluster should be fully redundant, which implies two independent switch and router paths. Dual switch configuration can be accomplished by splitting the cluster subnet into two parts, each managed separately by one of them. Each switch can be connected through separate uplinks to a pair of routers with failover capability (for example, an active/standby pair connected together through router links and communicating using Cisco's Hot Standby Routing Protocol or Virtual Router Protocol); switches can also be connected by dual crossover cables. This type of design creates two fully redundant paths between cluster nodes and routed networks. If clients are external, then the design should also include separate, redundant firewalls or Internet Security and Acceleration (ISA) servers.

In addition, you need to designate a management adapter, which is used for monitoring and content management (maintaining data across all cluster nodes in consistent state). Even if this is the same network adapter as in the cluster, you need to assign it a dedicated IP address on each node (different from the shared one). Traffic directed to this IP address is not load balanced. Both cluster and dedicated IP addresses need to be statically assigned. An additional adapter might be necessary, depending on the application or service (for example, in case of ISA or VPN servers), but, in general, it is always recommended because it enables you to separate client requests from management and content replication traffic.

Carefully consider whether network adapter teaming can be used. This is a popular solution offered by hardware vendors. Network teaming provides network adapter driver-based load balancing and failover capabilities and is implemented using two separate network cards (or dual-port adapter) connected to the same network segment. Because teaming, like NLB, relies on virtualizing MAC addressing, you need to evaluate whether there are any incompatibility issues between them, especially when operating in unicast mode. For more information, refer to the Microsoft Knowledge Base article Q278431 at `http://support.microsoft.com/default.aspx?scid=kb;en-us;278431`.

For illustration purposes, we will follow the design process with an example involving configuration and installation of three Web servers: NAUSNYCWEB01, NAUSNYCWEB02, and NAUSNYCWEB03, forming a single NLB cluster NAUSNYCWEBVS01. Assuming our sample three-server configuration uses dual network adapters per node, we have the following settings, shown in Table 11.1.

Table 11.1 Web Server NLB Cluster IP Configuration

Server Name	Cluster IP Address	Dedicated IP Address
NAUSNYCWEB01	10.10.100.20	10.10.100.12
NAUSNYCWEB02	10.10.100.20	10.10.100.14
NAUSNYCWEB03	10.10.100.20	10.10.100.16

The next decision that affects your network infrastructure is the choice between unicast and multicast mode of NLB cluster operations. The purpose of this step is assignment of a uniform MAC address associated with each virtual IP address. After all, the frames targeting this IP address need to reach every one of the cluster nodes. In unicast mode, NLB overrides the MAC address hard-coded into the cluster network adapter with a virtual one derived from the cluster IP address (to guarantee its uniqueness across multiple clusters). Multicast mode creates a multicast MAC address, which is used by each node in addition to individual MAC addresses of cluster network adapters.

Having the same MAC address assigned to multiple network adapters is not something you typically see on the network. Under normal circumstances, this situation might cause a problem on a switch, which records MAC addresses included in frames entering its ports (these addresses are then used to deliver frames to the right destination). If the frames leaving NLB nodes contain a unicast MAC address, its mapping to ports on the switch might not reflect cluster membership, disrupting proper functioning of the load-balancing algorithm. To avoid such problems, it is possible to prevent NLB nodes from including cluster MAC address in outgoing packets through registry changes. This is accomplished by setting the MaskSourceMAC entry of REG_ DWORD type under the key HKEY_LOCAL_MACHINE\SYSTEM\ CurrentControlSet\Services\WLBS\Parameters\Interface\AdapterGUID (where Adapter-GUID is the GUID assigned to the clustered network adapter) to **1**, which generates a substitute MAC address, replacing the cluster address. This modification is not needed (and the MaskSourceMAC entry should be set to **0**) if clustered network adapters are connected to a hub. The main drawback of this method is switch flooding, which denotes a situation in which a switch, not aware of the MAC address to which client requests should be sent, relays them to all of its ports. While this is the desired effect if a separate switch is used for cluster network adapters, it might cause network bandwidth issues if the same switch is shared with other, non-clustered systems because they all receive client traffic, which is not intended for them. This can be mitigated in one of three ways—by creating a separate VLAN for all cluster adapters from the same cluster, by using dedicated switches for each set of cluster adapters, or by connecting all of them to a hub, which in turn plugs into a single port on a switch. The first workaround requires

VLAN-capable switches; the second one typically results in an inefficient use of switches; and the last one introduces a single point of failure.

Another potential solution to the "switch flooding" problem is use of multicast mode, as long as your networking gear supports multicasting. In this case, you can either create mapping between the cluster multicast MAC address and switch ports connected to cluster adapters through static entries in the Content Addressable Memory on the switch, or you can enable the Internet Group Multicasting Protocol feature, which advertises the multicast MAC address assigned to cluster adapters to the switch. This way, the switch can forward client traffic to the relevant ports only, avoiding polluting ports used by non-clustered systems.

One of the negative side effects of unicast mode with a single network adapter is the inability to establish direct communication between two cluster hosts. This can be resolved either by adding the second network adapter to each node (with dedicated IP assigned to it) or by switching to multicast mode. On the other hand, unicast mode is compatible with all routers and switches, while multicast mode can cause problems with entries in the ARP cache on routers facing cluster network adapters. Routed traffic needs to eventually resolve IP addresses to corresponding MAC addresses. Some routers, however, do not properly handle ARP frames where a unicast IP address is mapped to a multicast MAC address. You might also encounter a problem with some routers if the MaskSourceMAC entry is enabled (set to 1) because some routers cannot properly process packets that contain one MAC address (substitute) in the Ethernet frame and another (cluster MAC address) in the ARP header. As a workaround, static ARP entries can be created on the routers.

Connecting cluster adapters to a hub rather than a switch is not advisable. While a hub serves the same role as a switch when it comes to inbound cluster traffic (because both propagate packets to all ports), this is not the case with outbound responses to clients. The switch relays them to a single port, while the hub treats them the same way as inbound traffic and sends them to all ports. Installing separate network adapters on each cluster node, connecting them to a switch, and using them exclusively for outbound traffic can resolve this issue. This requires modifications to the IP configuration parameters on cluster nodes (either by altering the default gateway or modifying the IP routing table). The need for additional switches combined with increased complexity of this setup makes it a less desirable alternative.

The general recommendation is to use dual network adapters with cluster adapters connected to a dual, redundant, multicast-, or VLAN-capable switches facing the client network. This prevents contention between client network requests and other types of traffic (management, content updates, heartbeat, and cluster convergence). If the switch supports multicasting, then you can set your NLB configuration to the multicast mode with IGMP enabled, preventing switch flooding. On the other hand, if your network infrastructure does not support multicasting, but has VLAN capability, then you can use the unicast option, isolating switch ports connected to the cluster adapter into separate VLANs. Multicasting might cause increased CPU utilization with some network adapter types, so unicast tends to be a more reliable and stable choice.

After network infrastructure-related decisions are made, it is time to look into cluster and host parameters. In the first category, there are characteristics common to all nodes, such as cluster IP address configuration (already established), cluster fully qualified domain name (resolving to the cluster IP address), cluster operation mode (unicast or multicast), and remote control settings. The second set of parameters covers host priority, dedicated IP address configuration, and initial host state.

Because we have already described the process of selecting cluster IP address and operation mode, let's review the remaining cluster parameters. The cluster fully qualified domain name should resolve to the cluster IP address; however, its registration is not performed automatically following initial cluster setup. Remember to create appropriate entries (host and pointer records) on your DNS servers ahead of deployment.

Remote control provides the capability to perform administrative tasks through the command line utility NLB.EXE; however, the more powerful and easy-to-use GUI-based Network Load Balancing Manager should be your primary management interface. Avoid enabling remote control due to security implications (by default, this setting is disabled). Using it creates a potential vulnerability to denial of service or data integrity attacks. If remote control is necessary, choose a strong remote control password and block UDP ports 1717 and 2504 on your firewall.

The purpose of the dedicated IP address has been described earlier in this section. The second host-specific NLB parameter—host priority—is a unique integer between 1 and 32 assigned to every cluster node (the lower numeric value represents higher priority). The value of host priority is relevant in a couple of scenarios. The host with highest priority handles the convergence process and decides when it is complete.

Initial host state determines when and how NLB becomes operational on a particular host. It can take one of three values—Started, Stopped, and Suspended. The Started option causes automatic startup of NLB, which is the right setting provided the load balanced services or applications are already available at that point. Otherwise, clients might be redirected to a node that cannot respond properly to their requests. This is frequently the case if application or service startup is longer than the NLB component. To prevent such situations, you can set the initial host state to Stopped and use either scripting or management software (such as Microsoft Operations Manager) to initiate NLB startup after the operational status of hosted applications or services has been verified. Finally, Suspended initial host state is typically used during node maintenance. Its purpose is to prevent the node from accepting any commands other than Resume, which means that attempts to start it (or execute any command other than Resume) will fail.

Table 11.2 presents cluster and host parameters for our sample NLB cluster.

Table 11.2   Web Server NLB Cluster and Host Parameters

Server Name	Server Type	Parameters
NAUSNYCWEBVS01	Virtual Cluster	Cluster Parameters Cluster IP address: 10.10.200.20 FQDN: nausnycwebvs01.mydomain.inc Operation mode: Unicast Remote control settings: Disabled
NAUSNYCWEB01	Cluster Node	Host Parameters Dedicated IP address 10.10.100.12 Host Priority: 1 Initial host state: Started
NAUSNYCWEB02	Cluster Node	Host Parameters Dedicated IP address 10.10.100.14 Host Priority: 2 Initial host state: Started

Server Name	Server Type	Parameters
NAUSNYCWEB03	Cluster Node	Host Parameters Dedicated IP address 10.10.100.16 Host Priority: 3 Initial host state: Started

Port Rules

To complete the design process, we need to specify parameters that determine the load balancing mechanism. These parameters are grouped together forming port rules, shared across cluster nodes. While initial setup of Network Load Balancing automatically creates a default port rule, which might be suitable in some scenarios, it is likely you will need to alter it and create some additional ones.

Whenever a client packet reaches cluster nodes, the NLB component on each node compares the packet's destination IP address, transport layer protocol (TCP or UDP), and destination port against IP address, transport layer protocol (TCP or UDP), and port range defined in all of the cluster port rules. If there is a match on all three values, the remaining parameters of the port rule are analyzed, which, in turn, triggers the desired load balancing action. These remaining parameters are *filtering mode, affinity*, and *distribution method*.

The cluster IP address of the port rule needs to correspond to one of the clustered IP addresses. There is also the all-inclusive option of setting this value to All (used by the default rule created at the initial setup of the NLB component).

Port range is determined by the From and To values, which implies each port rule needs to cover a consecutive range of port numbers. This means, for example, to load balance FTP-related traffic, you need to define two port rules—one covering the TCP ports from 20 to 21, the other ranging from 1024 to 65535. On the other hand, when setting up a port rule for a non-secure Web site using the default HTTP port, you need to set both From and To values to 80. Each port range can apply to TCP, UDP, or both.

Filtering mode determines how many cluster nodes participate in the processing of client requests targeting particular cluster IP address, transport protocol, and port range. It can take one of three values. The Disable option filters out client responses, effectively blocking them from reaching any of the nodes. The single host option forces processing by the node with the highest handling priority (lowest numeric value between 1 and 32) assigned to it (this is different from the host priority value because it is applied on a per port rule basis). Multiple hosts is the only option providing load balancing functionality by distributing client requests across cluster nodes.

With the multiple host filtering mode selected, two additional parameters can affect the distribution of incoming traffic matching parameters defined in the same port rule.

The first one is *affinity*, which controls what parameters are considered for the statistical mapping algorithm. This algorithm determines which cluster node is selected for processing a current packet. Affinity can be set to None, which ensures all TCP connections from a specific source IP address and source port are processed by the same node (unless the cluster membership or properties change in the meantime because these types of events also alter the statistical mapping algorithm); affinity can also be set to Single, which works similarly but does not take into consideration port information, or it can be set to class C, which also ignores source port number but extends the range of source IPs handled by the same cluster node to all IP addresses within the same class C subnet. No affinity is applicable in situations where multiple connections from the same client originating from different ports can be handled by multiple hosts. This also might be useful if multiple clients connect from behind a single client-side proxy. In this case, incoming communication originates from the same IP address but different ports; hence, affinity set to none results in a well-balanced load. It also can be used if communication is stateless (static Web pages) or where session information is stored outside of the cluster nodes. If these conditions are not satisfied, the remaining two types should be used (although in either case, it is recommended to store session-related data outside of cluster nodes). Class C affinity could be considered a special case of the single affinity, useful in situations where users reside behind a farm of client-side proxy servers; so their requests arrive with different source IP addresses. This works as long as proxy servers belong to the same class C network. If they extend beyond the range of a single class C network (which might be the case with large enterprises or megaproxy services) and you need to maintain session affinity, you will need to employ another solution. Solutions include the modified cookie-based approach implemented in the Microsoft Application Center 2000 (which forwards client requests to the appropriate server based on its identifier included in the session cookie) or redesigning your application so it stores session information outside of the cluster node where the session was initiated.

The second parameter applicable when multiple host filtering mode is selected is load weight. This setting, which is an integer between 0 and 100, is used to calculate the percentage of traffic each of the nodes will be handling. The calculation is based on the weighted average, which means that for a given node, its load weight is divided by the sum of load weights for all nodes and then multiplied by 100. For example, if three nodes had values set to 10, 30, and 40, respectively, then the first one would be handling $(10 / 80) \times 100\% = 12.5\%$ of the total traffic that matches individual port rule criteria; the second one would be $(30 / 80) \times 100\% = 37.5\%$; and the third one would be $(40 / 80) \times 100\% = 50\%$. The values should reflect the level of system resources available on each node when compared with others; so in our case, the assumption is that the second node can handle three times as many requests as the first one, which, in turn is four times less powerful compared to the third node. Note that you can set the load weight value to **0** if you want to exclude a specific server from processing client traffic matching a specific port rule.

Let's assume in our example that we have a well-designed application that handles session coherency properly by storing session information in a back-end SQL Server database. This allows us to use the settings presented in Table 11.3.

Table 11.3 Web Server NLB Port Rule Parameters

Server Name	Parameters
NAUSNYCWEBVS01	Web Server Port Rule Cluster IP Address: 10.10.200.20 Port Range: From 80 to 80 Protocols: TCP Filtering Mode: Multiple host Affinity: None
NAUSNYCWEB01	Web Server Port Rule Cluster IP Address: 10.10.200.20 Port Range: From 80 to 80 Protocols: TCP

continues

Table 11.3   Web Server NLB Port Rule Parameters

Server Name	Parameters
NAUSNYCWEB01	Filtering Mode: Multiple host Affinity: None Load Weight: 10
NAUSNYCWEB02	Web Server Port Rule Cluster IP Address: 10.10.200.20 Port Range: From 80 to 80 Protocols: TCP Filtering Mode: Multiple host Affinity: None Load Weight: 30
NAUSNYCWEB03	Web Server Port Rule Cluster IP Address: 10.10.200.20 Port Range: From 80 to 80 Protocols: TCP Filtering Mode: Multiple host Affinity: None Load Weight: 40

Our sample configuration creates a single virtual Web site hosted on three servers. Note that we could assign another cluster IP address and fully qualified name to set up another Web site (or another type of service or application), which, from the client point of view, would appear as a separate entity. While this is obviously also possible in a non-clustered configuration, in our case, we can define separate load balancing rules for both sites if they behave differently (for example, to accommodate legacy applications, which store session information locally on a cluster node).

Setup and Configuration of the NLB Cluster

The Network Load Balancing driver is included in all editions of Windows 2003 Server, and it does not need to be separately installed. It appears in the list of networking components in the Network Connection Properties dialog box. You can activate it by simply enabling the checkbox next to its name (at that point, you are prompted for a number of configuration parameters); however, this is not the method you should use.

While it is possible to create and manage a NLB cluster by configuring cluster and host parameters individually on every node, it is strongly recommended to use Network Load Balancing Manager. This utility has a number of built-in safety checks, preventing misconfiguration errors. You can use it for the initial setup of a cluster and all of its operations afterward.

NLB Manager appears in the Windows 2003 Server Administrative Tools menu. Unlike most other management utilities, it is not implemented as the Microsoft Management Console snap-in but as an executable NLBMGR.EXE. Its interface consists of three window panes—the top left presents the list of Network Load Balancing clusters, which you can connect to by selecting the appropriate option either in the Cluster top menu or in the context-sensitive menu of the Network Load Balancing Clusters top level node. The same menu provides an option to create a new cluster—which is the option we will explore further shortly. This pane corresponds to a tree pane of a standard MMC console. The top-right pane displays content of the node selected on the left, functioning as the details pane. The bottom portion of the window displays notification messages generated in real time, informing about the cluster status and results of management operations. You also have an option of enabling logging to a text file from the Options menu.

Assuming you followed the instructions regarding network infrastructure, hardware configuration of cluster member servers, operating system installation, and manual registration of A and PTR records on your DNS server (according to the information from Table 11.2), you can start the procedure of creating a new NLB cluster using the following steps:

1. Launch Network Load Balancing Manager from the Administrative Tools menu on a Windows 2003 Server system, which has an existing connection to the computer that will be configured as the first node of the NLB cluster.
2. Select New Cluster item from either the Cluster menu or context-sensitive menu of Network Load Balancing Clusters node. This brings up the Cluster Parameters dialog box, prompting you for Cluster IP Configuration, Subnet Mask, Full Internet Name, Cluster Operation Mode, and remote control settings.
3. Provide information where applicable according to the settings specified in Table 11.2, as shown in the dialog box in Figure 11.1, and click Next.

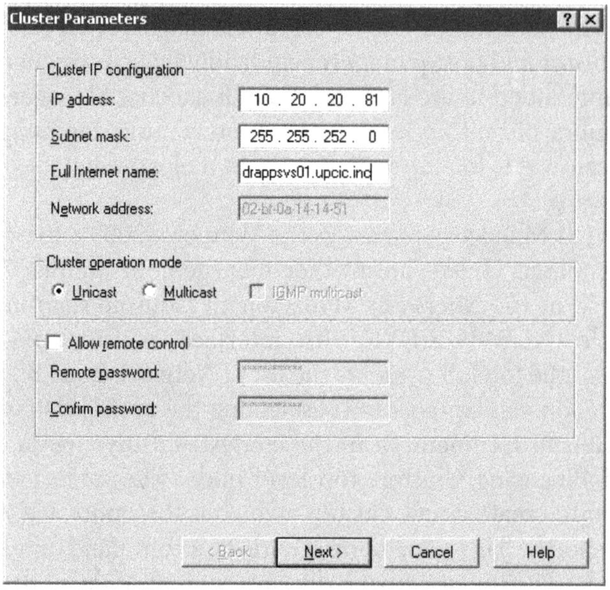

Figure 11.1   Creating a new NLB cluster using Network Load Balancing Manager.

4. In the Cluster IP address box, you have the option to type in additional cluster IP addresses. Because our design involves setting up a single cluster only, go to the next page by clicking Next.

5. The next dialog box labeled Port Rules allows you to add, edit, and remove port rules. You need to start by removing the existing default port rule (otherwise, you would not be able to define any new ones because the default rule covers all IP addresses, ports, and transport layer protocols). Highlight the default rule; click first on Remove, and then on Add. This brings up the Add/Edit Port Rule dialog box.

6. In the dialog box, provide the IP address used by the virtual Web server (in our case, this is the same as the Cluster IP address), Port Range, Protocols, and Filtering Mode, according to the content of the first row in Table 11.3, as shown in the dialog box in Figure 11.2. After you click OK, the new rule should appear in the Port Rules dialog box. Click Next to display the Connect page.

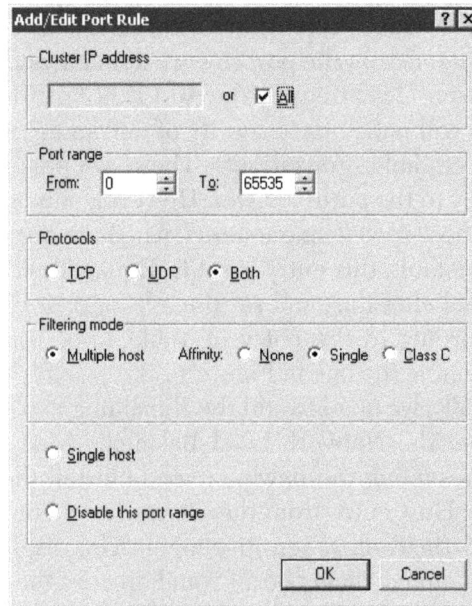

Figure 11.2   Defining a new port rule using Network Load Balancing Manager.

7. The Connect dialog box enables you to specify the name or IP address of a server that will become a member of the new cluster. Type in the information from Table 11.2, and click Connect. This should display network adapters on the target server. Select the cluster adapter and click Next.

8. In the Host Parameters dialog box that follows, you need to choose the host priority, confirm the selection of the dedicated IP address, and set the initial host state according to the information in Table 11.2. Click Finish and observe messages appearing in the bottom windowpane, making sure there are no error messages. After a few seconds, the update should be complete and a new cluster with the first node should appear in the top-left windowpane.

9. Note that we have not yet set host-specific values for our port rule contained in the lower rows in Table 11.3 (in particular, the Load weight). To accomplish this, you need to select the node representing the member server in the top-left windowpane and select either Properties from the Host top menu or Host Properties from the context-sensitive menu. This displays the Host Properties dialog box.

10. In the Host Properties dialog box, select the Port Rules tab, single-click on the port rule we defined, and finally click the Edit button. This brings up the Add/Edit Port Rule dialog box.

11. You will notice the majority of entries are already filled out and not editable (grayed out). These are port rule parameters that apply to the entire cluster. However, you have option of modifying host-specific parameters, which, in our case, is Load weight. By default, this entry is set to Equal. To change it, uncheck the Equal checkbox and set the appropriate value for Load weight according to the entry in Table 11.3. Your dialog box should resemble the one in Figure 11.3.

12. Finally, we need to add the remaining two servers to the cluster. From the Network Load Balancing Manager, select the node representing the newly created cluster, then choose either the Add Host entry from the Cluster menu or Add Host to Cluster from the context-sensitive menu. This displays the already familiar Connect dialog box. From here, use the procedure described in steps 7–11. This completes the process of setting up the NLB cluster. To remove a cluster member, you can simply click on it in the left windowpane and select Delete from the Host top-level menu or Delete Host from the context-sensitive menu.

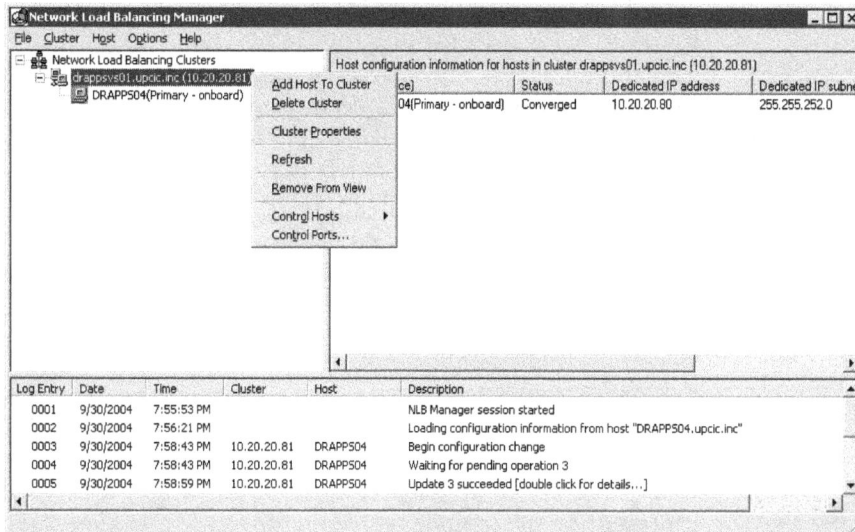

Figure 11.3 Defining host-specific parameters in the Add/Edit Port Rule dialog box.

From the same interface, you can perform a range of other administrative tasks. We cover them in the section "Administering the NLB Cluster" later in this chapter.

Example NLB Cluster: IIS

Without a doubt, Network Load Balancing is used most commonly with Web-based applications. The architectural and configuration details specific to Internet Information Server 6.0 on the Windows 2003 Server platform are discussed in the IIS Cluster Design Specs section of Chapter 12.

Example NLB Cluster: Terminal Services

Windows Server 2003 Terminal Services is Microsoft's offer in the area of Thin Computing. Its main purpose is to allow multiple users to interactively access Windows desktop applications executing on remote servers. Lightweight Remote Desktop Protocol is used to send the keystrokes and mouse movements from the local computer to the remote server and bring back screen scrapes of the interactive server session. Since the original release of Windows NT 4.0 Terminal Server, this basic functionality has been extended by redirecting serial and parallel ports, clipboard, sound, and local disks. Another significant enhancement included in the Windows Server 2003 platform is support for load balancing of Terminal Servers with Session Directory.

You could install the Terminal Services component in application mode (which is required for true application sharing) on a Windows 2000-based Network Load Balancing cluster. Setting a virtual IP address with properly configured port rules results in the load-balanced distribution of RDP connections from clients. However, Thin Client technology presents a new challenge. Because user applications are running on the server, it is possible for a user session to be temporarily disconnected (either intentionally or accidentally) without affecting their state. When dealing with a single Terminal Server system, a user can easily reconnect to the same session and access applications at a later time; however, in a load-balanced cluster environment, this might be problematic if a user tries to resume the session at a new location where the source IP address is different from the original one. Session Directory resolves this issue.

Session Directory is implemented as a service present on any Windows 2003 Enterprise and Datacenter server (although you should consider setting it up as a resource on a highly available server cluster). The service keeps track of all Terminal Server sessions established with computers that are members of the local group called "Session Directory Computers" and have appropriate Terminal Services Configuration settings. A user's connection request is redirected to cluster node using the load balancing algorithm, which then prompts the user for credentials. After they are verified, the node queries the Session Directory server to see if the logged-on user has an existing session. If this is the case, the Session Directory server responds with the unique (rather than virtual) IP address of a node hosting the session, which is then used to automatically redirect the user request.

Setup of a Session Directory environment consists of three main steps. The first step deals with the Session Directory Server and includes enabling the Session Directory service (which is disabled by default), setting its startup mode to Automatic, and adding computer accounts of clustered member servers to its local "Session Directory Computers" group. This ensures the server only accepts queries from authorized computers, which are members of the load balanced cluster. The second step required you to install the Terminal Services component from the Add or Remove Programs in the Control Panel on each cluster member server (this is required because, by default, RDP functionality is restricted to two remote desktops and one console connection). The third step involves the configuration of Terminal Server properties on every cluster node. This can be handled using either one of two methods.

The easier method, from the implementation and maintenance perspective, uses Windows 2003 group policies. The most efficient way to apply them is to place computer accounts of all clustered Terminal Servers in the same Organizational Unit and create a new (or use an existing) group policy and modify three settings in the Computer Configuration > Administrative Templates > Windows Components > Terminal Services > Session Directory folder:

- Enable Join Session Directory entry.
- Enable Session Directory Server entry and set its name to the name of the previously configured server hosting the Session Directory Service.

- Set Session Directory Cluster Name to the name of the Terminal Server cluster.

You can use group filtering or create multiple Organizational Units if you have multiple Terminal Server clusters. For each cluster, you could create a separate group policy with a distinct Cluster Name entry (the remaining two entries would stay the same). This way, you can use a single Session Directory computer to handle clients connecting to multiple NLB Terminal Services clusters.

The alternative method, which is more time-consuming and cumbersome to manage but is slightly more versatile, requires manual changes to the Terminal Services Configuration tool for each clustered Terminal Server. Select the Server Settings in the tree pane of the console and double-click on the Session Directory entry in the Details pane (note that this entry appears only if you have installed the Terminal Services component from the Add or Remove Programs applet in the Control Panel). From the displayed dialog box, check the "Join Session Directory" checkbox and provide names of the cluster and Session Directory server. As with the first method, multiple clusters can be configured with the same Session Directory server. You also have the ability to specify the network adapter to which user traffic should be redirected (which is not possible with the first method).

An additional option available with both methods is IP address Redirection. With Network Load Balancing clusters, this setting always should be enabled. As we explained earlier in this section, Session Directory provides NLB clients with the unique IP address of servers hosting their existing sessions; so they can reconnect directly with them (hence, IP address redirection is enabled). This, however, might not be possible with other load balancing solutions. In such cases, the checkbox should be unchecked, which causes the Session Directory server performing redirection to use routing tokens. *Routing token* is a network packet that is sent back to a user (instead of the IP address used in Network Load Balancing clusters) after the initial login to one of the nodes if it turns out that this user already has an existing connection elsewhere. Routing token contains embedded information about the IP address and port to which the client should be redirected that is used subsequently by the load balancer.

Some additional Terminal Server settings should be used in combination with NLB clustering and Session Directory. Because the premise of this solution is to allow reconnection to previously established sessions, you need to ensure that broken connections are not terminated. This is controlled by RDP-Tcp connection session settings. You can configure them on each node of the cluster using the following steps:

1. Launch the Terminal Services Configuration MMC snap-in located in the Administrative Tools menu group.
2. Select the Connections folder in the tree pane and double-click on the RDP-Tcp connection in the details pane.
3. Choose the Sessions tab on the RDP-Tcp Properties dialog box.
4. Turn on the Override User Settings option and select the desired value from the End a Disconnected Session list box.

Alternatively, you can set this value through group policies using the Set Time Limit for Disconnected Sessions entry located in the Computer Configuration > Administrative Templates > Windows Components > Terminal Services > Sessions folder.

With Session Directory server in place, your Network Load Balancing Terminal Server cluster port rule is likely to take on the values (RDP protocol uses TCP port 3389) presented in Table 11.4.

Table 11.4 Port Rule for Terminal Server Cluster with Session Directory Services

Parameter	Value
Port range	3389 to 3389
Protocols	TCP
Filtering mode	Affinity: None Multiple hosts Load weight: dependent on performance characteristics of cluster nodes

Load Balancing and COM Application Servers

Besides the two generic clustering solutions—server clustering geared towards high availability for back-end, stateful, powerful solutions and Network Load Balancing intended for front-end, stateless, lightweight applications and services—there is another type of clustering, which, unlike the other two, is not implemented as the operating system component. Component Load Balancing, available as part of Microsoft Application Center 2000, was designed to deliver scalability and high availability to the middle tier in the three-tier architecture of COM+–based applications.

COM+ is a technology introduced in the Windows 2000 platform providing packaged functionality in the form of COM+ components, which can be used in a distributed environment. Components are implemented as small programs that deliver specific functions and can easily interact with other programs. In addition to their reusability and distributed nature, they also have a number of other attractive features, such as transactional support, which allows them to operate as part of larger transaction-based systems; built-in security with multiple access levels; good performance enhanced by support for concurrency (simultaneous execution by multiple programs); and pooling (keeping invoked COM+ components active to avoid their activation and deactivation, which are expensive in terms of resource utilization). COM+ greatly simplifies software development, replacing complex programs running on one system with a number of smaller, easily reusable ones operating on multiple computers.

While COM+ is being replaced with significantly improved .NET technology, it is still used by a fairly large number of legacy applications. Typically, such applications would implement a front-end interface using Active Server Pages running on Internet Information Server (accessible through Web browsers), code business logic invoked by this interface as a collection of custom COM+ components, and use Microsoft SQL Server database as a data store.

To scale-out this application, COM+ components can be placed directly on the Web servers running identically configured ASP-based applications in the front-end tier clustered with Network Load Balancing. Client requests would be load balanced according to the port rules defined for the Web application traffic. However, Network Load Balancing, as we already explained, does not take into consideration resource utilization levels on cluster nodes. This means that unbalanced COM+ invocations would likely result in the mix of overloaded and underutilized servers. Component Load Balancing was designed to resolve this issue.

Improved load balancing architecture is based on separation between network load balanced Web application servers forming the first tier and COM+ components installed on the second tier. Component Load Balancing software running on the Web servers keeps track of the servers hosting COM+ components by periodically sending them heartbeat network packets. Length of response delay is used to evaluate processing load of each server, which determines which one is least utilized. This server is then used as a target for incoming COM+ component activation requests. Because this process is repeated within small time intervals, servers in the second tier remain evenly utilized, complementing the Network Load Balancing of the Web servers in the first tier. In addition, failure of any server is quickly detected, causing new requests to be distributed between remaining ones.

Multi-Tiered Server Farms

Combining different clustering solutions can provide additional high availability, performance, and load balancing benefits. Because each cluster type has distinct characteristics and requirements, you can easily determine their role and placement in a multi-tier design.

Clustering front-end servers is best handled with Network Load Balancing. This applies not only to Terminal or Web servers, which we discuss in more detail in Chapter 12, but also to network edge services, such as ISA servers, which combine firewall, Web Proxy and caching, and Virtual Private Network (VPN) functionality.

ISA Server 2000 needs to be installed and identically configured on every Windows 2003 Server cluster node. You can set it up in either stand-alone or Enterprise mode (note that the latter requires Active Directory schema updates). In addition, you should also install ISA Server 2000 Service Pack 1 and the latest hot fixes (most notably, ISAHF255.EXE). Use VPN Server Wizard to enable Routing and Remote Access Service and set up packet filters controlling the flow of PPTP and L2TP/IPSec traffic (both mechanisms are supported in combination with NLB on Windows 2003 Server platform). By default, the filters allow inbound VPN connections targeting the primary IP address bound to the external interface of cluster nodes. Because this is different from the cluster IP address used by VPN clients, the following modifications are required:

1. Launch the ISA Management console.
2. Locate the cluster member under Servers and Arrays node in the tree pane. Drill down through the Access Policy node to the IP Packet Filters subfolder. After you select it, you see a list of filters in the details pane.

3. You have two pairs of filters for L2TP and PPTP—Allow L2TP protocol IKE packets, Allow L2TP protocol packets, Allow PPTP protocol packets (client), and Allow PPTP protocol packets (server). For each of them, modify the IP address to which the filter applies. This is done by selecting This ISA Server's External IP Address option on the Local Computer tab of each filter's Properties dialog box and typing in the cluster virtual IP address.

4. Repeat steps 2 and 3 for each of the remaining cluster nodes.

Note that support for VPN clients also involves providing name resolution and IP address assignment methods (typically through DNS and DHCP). Remember also that NLB port rules controlling PPTP and L2TP traffic must be configured with Single or Class C affinity mode.

Middle-tier servers usually implement business logic in the form of COM+ components, which can be load balanced with the help of Component Load Balancing, as explained in the previous section.

Back-end servers forming the third tier are intended for storing data and session state. Because synchronization between them might be difficult, their high-availability is accomplished through server clustering.

NLB Cluster Management

Windows 2003 Server Network Load Balancing cluster configuration and management should be performed using Network Load Balancing Manager, available from the Administrative Tools menu. This saves you additional work when setting NLB components individually on each member server (through the Network Load Balancing item listed in the Properties dialog box of the clustered network connection) and protects you from accidental misconfiguration errors. Cluster shared parameters and port rules are automatically replicated to every node. Similarly, host parameter assignments can be applied from a single interface to each of the nodes. As we already discussed earlier in this chapter in the section "Setup and Configuration of NLB," the lower portion of the tool's graphical interface displays the status messages informing you about cluster status and the result of interactively administered changes. Use of the NLB.EXE command line utility is discouraged due to its security implications. If you feel strongly about using it, then at the very least, you should limit its use to trusted computers on your internal network only and ensure that access to NLB cluster from the Internet has been secured by firewall blocking UDP ports 1717 and 2504.

Administering the NLB Cluster

In this section, we review the most common tasks related to managing the NLB cluster using Network Load Balancing Manager. We already presented steps required to create a cluster, add and remove its nodes, and define port rules in the section "Setup and Configuration of NLB Cluster" earlier in this chapter. Now let's take a look at others which are node-related, such as stopping, starting, suspending, resuming, and draining, as well as the ones controlling network traffic characteristics, such as enabling or disabling connectivity on individual ports. Note that management of NLB Cluster operations requires local Administrator's privileges on each of the cluster nodes.

In general, each of the node-related commands can be executed for individual or all cluster member servers. In the first case, you should first select the target server from the NLB Manager interface and then use the Control Host option on the top-level Host menu or the context-sensitive menu. Equivalent cluster commands are available from the top-level Cluster menu or the context-sensitive menu after selecting the cluster node. In either case, the second level menu gives you five options—Start, Stop, Drainstop, Suspend, and Resume.

Issuing the Stop command stops node or cluster operations and closes all existing connections. If the command is issued against a single node, the convergence process is initiated to redirect client traffic to remaining operational nodes. Executing the Start command can restart the stopped node or cluster. If you want to disconnect all current clients from a specific node or cluster in a more graceful manner, you can use the Drainstop command, which prevents any new connections and triggers the Stop command once the last client disconnects. Suspend is similar to Stop in that it terminates all cluster operations and existing connections, but, in addition, it ensures that no other command can be executed against the cluster or node until Resume is issued. To make the cluster or node operational again, you need to follow Resume with the Start command.

You can perform similar actions on a per-port rule basis with the Enable, Disable, and Drain commands for individual hosts and entire clusters using the Control Ports menu option from the Host or Cluster top-level menus (or context-sensitive menus) after selecting the target node or cluster, respectively. In either case, you are presented with the Control Ports dialog box from which you can select the relevant rule, and click one of the three command buttons corresponding to the three available port rule actions. The end result is similar to host and cluster-level operations, effectively starting or stopping traffic controlled by selected rule, or preventing any new connections, which match rule criteria.

Node- and cluster-specific administrative actions trigger the convergence process, which typically affects statistical mapping of future client connections but, in general, should not disrupt their existing sessions with clustered servers (with exception of events that directly affect a node hosting these sessions). These actions include addition, removal, stopping, starting, suspending, and resuming of cluster nodes, as well as changing host properties, such as host priority or load weight. Remember that, as we mentioned earlier, adding or removing cluster nodes or modifying load weight might affect existing sessions if they rely on affinity to maintain session state (this does not, however, apply to L2TP and IPSec sessions, which remain preserved even if membership or load-weight parameters change).

Probably the most annoying feature of the NLB Manager is its inability to store console settings. This means that every time you launch it, you need to provide names or IP addresses of clusters and hosts to which you want to connect. Fortunately, you have an option of storing their list into a text file, which you can subsequently load (using the Save Host List... and Load Host List... options in the File menu).

Troubleshooting

Problems with Network Load Balancing clusters typically result from misconfiguration of cluster or host parameters. Most of the time, they can be avoided by ensuring that Network Load Balancing Manager is the only tool used for cluster management. In addition, NLB has a number of automatic built-in mechanisms that attempt to minimize the impact on existing client connections. For example, if an incorrectly configured server is in the process of joining a cluster, it is prevented from accepting any traffic until the error is corrected (and during this time, the cluster remains in a converging state. To correct the situation, you can stop the new host with the Stop command (using either NLB Manager or by running NLB.EXE from the command prompt).

Information useful in troubleshooting can be found from a number of sources. NLB-specific information, warning, and error events are recorded in the Windows System Event Log. This, however, does not include notifications about activities initiated through NLB Manager. You can view them interactively through the console or record them in a text file. This is done by selecting the Log Settings option in the Options menu, marking the Enable Logging checkbox in the Log Settings dialog box, and specifying the name and location of the log file. In your quest for resolution to NLB problems, you can also employ System and Network Monitors.

Disaster Recovery

Because the primary purpose of Network Load Balancing is to provide distribution of client requests across multiple instances of stateless applications, the recovery in case of a site-wide disaster, affecting all cluster members, would simply involve reinstallation of the application and re-creation of the cluster with the same cluster and host parameters, as well as with the same set of port rules.

If you have full server backup, you can use it to restore each of the servers. Another more time-consuming option relies on recording cluster configuration. This can be easily done using the NLB.EXE command line utility. NLB.EXE executed with the PARAMS ALL option displays all of the cluster and local host parameters, including all of it port rules. You can dump the output of the command to a text file and save it for future reference. It is also possible to back up cluster settings by creating a VBScript code interacting with the Windows Management Instrumentation object model.

Time-Out

This chapter introduced Network Load Balancing as a form of clustering that aims to fan out connections to multiple servers, all of which are able to service inbound requests. The idea behind the NLB cluster is to allow a collection of identically configured servers to act as a single server. As far as the client is concerned, it connects to a single resource and is not aware of any particular server that takes the request. Servers may be added to or taken away from the cluster without interrupting services on the remaining members.

We saw the difference between the NLB cluster server and the fail-over cluster server is that any of the involved NLB cluster nodes can service the request, as opposed to the fail-over cluster in which only one server can be active in the cluster.

You typically would use NLB cluster Web servers, such as IIS 6.0 on Windows Server 2003 (all editions) or the Web Server edition. In Chapter 12, we will use the design we started with in this chapter and implement an IIS server farm.

Internet Information Server

Introduction

Over the last few years, Microsoft started focusing its attention on Internet-related technologies, from both Web client and server perspectives. While Internet Explorer started dominating Windows desktops, Internet Information Server, introduced in the Windows NT 4.0 Option Pack and built into later operating systems, gained popularity on the server side.

Its initial versions fell short when compared to similar offerings from other vendors in terms of scalability and reliability, but with the release of the Windows 2003 Server platform and Internet Information Services 6.0 (IIS 6.0), Microsoft finally managed to deliver an enterprise-class solution. High availability features have been incorporated into the core operating system and its optional components, which enables you to take advantage of synergies between them. In this chapter, we discuss how the scalability features of the Microsoft Web server can be further enhanced by combining them with clustering technologies discussed earlier in the book.

IIS 6.0 and the Dedicated Web Server

The Windows 2003 Server platform, like its recent predecessors (Windows 2000 and Windows XP operating systems), includes Internet Information Services components, which you can install easily through the

Add or Remove Programs applet in the Control Panel. Such an option makes it convenient to include Web server functionality whenever needed, but sharing it with other types of services should be carefully considered. Using dedicated systems to function as Web servers is preferred, due to their unique set of security, scalability, and performance requirements. While it is possible to satisfy these requirements with general purpose Windows 2003 Servers, a fairly complex and time-consuming configuration might be necessary. In addition, with the majority of services turned off, paying the price of a full-featured operating system is cost-inefficient. Microsoft decided to address these issues by offering its Web server solution as a separate, competitively priced, lightweight, and specialized product in the form of Windows 2003 Server Web Edition. IIS 6.0 runs as its core, enhanced further by ASP.NET and the Microsoft .NET Framework, with non-essential components either disabled or not present.

Even though Microsoft imposed some restrictions on functionality and scalability in Windows 2003 Web Server to make its reduced pricing justified, it is unlikely this would constitute a problem in most typical deployment scenarios. From a hardware perspective, the Web Server supports a dual processor in a symmetric multiprocessing configuration and up to 2GB of memory. While it is limited only to ten inbound Server Message Block (SMB) connections, they are typically used only for content management, not for communication with Web clients. Because its sole purpose is to run IIS 6.0, it cannot be promoted to a Windows 2003 domain controller or host a range of processor-intensive applications, such as Microsoft SQL Server; Universal Description, Discovery, and Integration (UDDI); and Terminal Services (however, you can access it through Remote Desktop sessions for management purposes).

The new version of IIS has very significant design changes, providing improvements in areas of fault tolerance, manageability, scalability, and security. Just like its predecessors, IIS 6.0 is capable of delivering a wide variety of services, ranging from serving static and dynamic Web pages by accepting HTTP requests and processing them depending on the content (through World Wide Web Publishing service), hosting FTP sites (through FTP service), handling discussion groups (through Network News Transfer Protocol [NNTP]) to sending and routing e-mails with Simple Mail Transfer Protocol (SMTP). However, its visibility and importance has drastically increased. IIS 6.0 is an essential component of several key Microsoft products, such as Exchange Server 2003 (it must be installed to set up Outlook Web Access), Systems Management

Server 2003, SharePoint Team Services, or BizTalk Server 2004, just to name a few.

Secure by Default

Be aware that, unlike in Windows 2000 Server, the IIS component is not automatically installed. This decision has been made to increase the default security level of the operating system. For the same reason, manual installation results in "locked-down" configuration, which only enables serving static Web content (through HTML pages). Dynamically generated pages, using technologies such as CGI, ASP, or ASP.NET, must be explicitly enabled to be properly processed.

Among the most important differences from the architectural standpoint is the unique implementation of a module responsible for listening to incoming Hypertext Transfer Protocol (HTTP) requests from Web clients and their initial processing. Unlike earlier versions where this module was operating in the user mode using Windows Socket APIs, which we're using for this purpose, IIS 6.0 relies on the HTTP.sys module residing in the protected kernel mode. If a client's request is valid, the module first checks for a cached response (in case the same request has been handled before), and if no match is found, the module redirects the request to a queue associated with a target Web application running in user mode. After the request is processed by the application, HTTP.sys sends the result back to the client. This is beneficial for a number of reasons. Cached responses can be used immediately without context switches between user and kernel mode, which speeds up processing and minimizes utilization of system resources. In addition, by storing requests in separate queues, temporary problems, such as high traffic volume or Web application stability issues, can remain undetected by clients. Placement of the HTTP.sys in kernel also isolates it from third-party code, which otherwise could negatively affect its operations.

If Web communication is encrypted with Secure Socket Layers, HTTP.sys employs a separate component, HTTPFilter, running in user mode to decrypt client requests (and, subsequently, encrypt server replies). In such a case, HTTPFilter becomes responsible for redirecting traffic to the appropriate application queue. Note that applying encryption utilizes a considerably larger amount of system resources, and, therefore, it should be used only in situations where content needs to remain confidential and authentication is required.

The details of the queuing process and Web application operations depend on the isolation mode in which the Web Server functions. With IIS 6.0, you have two options—*IIS 5.0 isolation mode* and *worker process isolation mode* (they are exclusive, which means you can not run both on the same server simultaneously).

IIS 5.0 isolation mode exists solely for the purpose of compatibility with older applications that cannot run in worker process isolation mode. If a Web application needs to be separated from others (because of its design caveats or instability and performance problems), it can run in a separate process space provided by individual instances of DLLHost.exe. While this serves the purpose, providing a sufficient level of protection, it also results in a negative impact on performance (due to increased resource utilization). If a Web application is capable of sharing process space with others, it can be configured to execute within the same process as Inetinfo.exe, shared also by FTP, SMTP, and NNTP services (which is referred to as *low isolation*), or it can be configured to share process space with others outside of Inetinfo.exe (known as *medium isolation*). In IIS 5.0 isolation mode, all applications use the same queue for communication with the HTTP.sys module (which creates a performance and scalability bottleneck). This design is illustrated in Figure 12.1.

Worker process isolation mode, whose architecture is shown in Figure 12.2, is the recommended choice because of its enhanced functionality, robustness, and security. In this mode, each Web application runs as one or more worker processes hosted by W3wp.exe, separate from HTTP.sys listener, World Wide Web Publishing service, or Web Administrative services. This offers a higher level of isolation without a performance penalty incurred by a DLLHost.exe-based implementation (Web applications are loaded in-process with W3wp.exe). HTTP.sys communicates with applications through multiple queues, which eliminates the performance and scalability bottleneck. Worker processes are initialized on an as-needed basis, contributing to lower resource utilization. In addition, stability is improved because an application failure does not have a negative impact on other applications, the World Wide Web Publishing and IIS Admin services, or the HTTP.sys component. You can perform typical maintenance tasks, such as application upgrades, debugging, or troubleshooting, without affecting client access to other Web resources residing on the same server. In the past, some of these procedures would have required restarting the Web services or even rebooting the server.

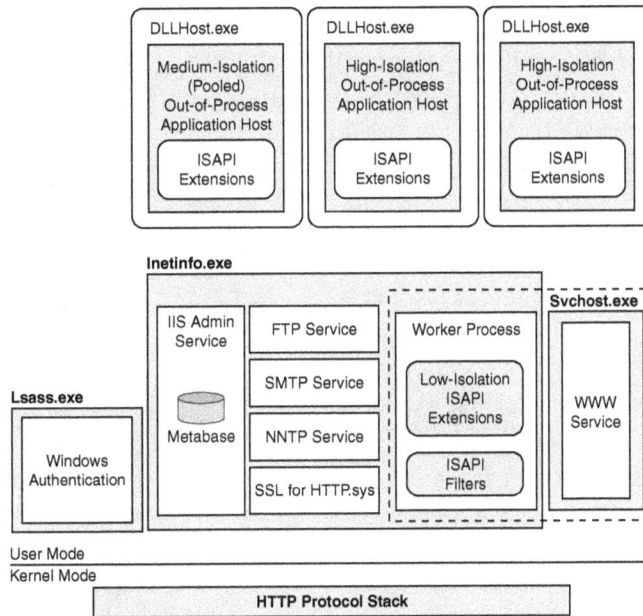

Figure 12.1   Architecture of IIS 5.0 isolation mode.

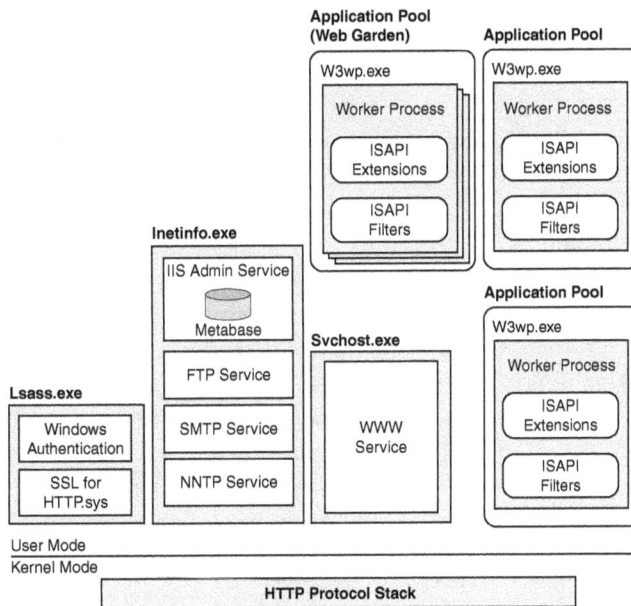

Figure 12.2   Architecture of worker process isolation mode.

While most legacy applications can execute in worker process isolation mode without additional modifications, some exceptions apply. In particular, this applies to those that require Read Raw Data Filters or those with built-in dependencies on IIS 5.0 components (such as Inetinfo.exe or DLLHost.exe).

Worker process isolation mode makes available a number of new high-availability features, such as application pools, health detection, and worker process recycling. Application pools host Web applications and are typically serviced by individual worker processes (however, it is possible to configure an application pool with multiple worker processing, creating a so-called Web garden, which we discuss shortly). Each application pool has an individual request queue through which the HTTP.sys component routes client traffic.

Each pool forms an operational, security, and administrative boundary, ensuring isolation of worker processes, identity, and management settings between different Web applications. Each pool can function in the security context of a separate user account, which determines its privileges and permissions. This is, by default, a NetworkService account, with a much lower level of privileges than the LocalSystem account automatically assigned to processes running in IIS 5.0 isolation mode.

The status of application pools can be detected through monitoring conducted by the World Wide Web Publishing service. Threshold levels and corrective actions are configurable through the IIS Manager administrative interface on a per-application pool basis. Worker processes can be automatically restarted (recycled), which helps mitigate problems resulting from external conditions, such as a temporary increase in client load, as well as the ones inherent to applications, such as memory leaks. In general, it is possible to configure restart to happen automatically based on elapsed or scheduled time (enabled by default and set to 29 hours), number of requests (disabled by default), virtual memory threshold (recommended setting is 70 percent of available virtual memory), used memory threshold (typically configured at 60 percent of total physical memory), or interactively, on demand. Health monitoring involves such methods as pinging worker processes or checking the values of parameters indicating application pool problems, such as extended application startup or shutdown times (both configured by default to 90 seconds) or an extensive number of application restarts, which implies frequent failure of worker processes (known as rapid-fail condition).

Using ping for monitoring purposes is based on the premise that a delay in response is indicative of the application state. After the threshold is reached, worker process restart is triggered. However, frequent process restarts indicate problems with its underlying application and are detrimental to performance and perceived availability. To protect your server against this issue, you can use the rapid-fail protection feature, which keeps track of the number of failures within a specific amount of time. If the configurable limit is reached, the application shuts down permanently and needs to be restarted manually. The default setting of five failures within the five-minute interval should be sufficient in most scenarios.

You can also fine-tune performance by setting timeouts for idle worker processes (enabled and set to 20 minutes by default) or assigning limits to the request queue (assigned the default value of 4000 requests). Cutting down on the number of worker processes residing in memory or ensuring that the number of requests awaiting processing does not get too high (which might happen as the result of denial of service attacks) contributes to the amount of available resources. At the same rate, you need to avoid setting both values too low, as this might also negatively affect performance and availability (by underestimating the queue length limit, legitimate client requests might be returned with the HTTP "503: Service Unavailable" error).

Another way to improve performance is to implement processor affinity on multiprocessor systems. This way, you tend to increase the frequency of CPU cache hits because requests targeting specific application pools are always handled by the same processor.

Besides having definite benefits, automatic recycling of worker processes also has some disadvantages. Each restart causes in-process data to be lost. This is a problem if the application state is maintained within the worker process (to prevent such loss, session data should be maintained outside of the application pool, for example, in a SQL Server database; we discuss such a setup in more detail later in this chapter). In addition, performance is negatively affected because the application pool cache needs to be cleared and subsequently re-created. Recycling also creates problems with applications that have long startup times. Availability of application pools can be further increased by assigning multiple worker processes to them in the configuration known as a Web garden (where the number of processes is controlled with the Max-Processes metabase property and can be altered using the Maximum

Number of Worker Processes entry in the Web garden section on the Performance tab of the Application Pool Properties dialog box). This way, a busy process does not block new requests from being processed. Note that Web gardens are different from Web farms, which operate as a group of independent physical servers, providing an additional level of fault tolerance, and whose design and implementation are covered later in this chapter.

Improved scalability and availability result from changes to the way IIS configuration information is stored. Binary metabase, used in previous versions, has been replaced by two XML-formatted text files. The first one, MBSchema.xml, defines the format of metabase attributes; the second, MetaBase.xml, contains actual configuration settings. IIS Admin component also maintains a memory resident copy, initialized when the World Wide Publishing service starts, which makes it possible to apply configuration changes dynamically (without the need for restarting the Web server). These changes are periodically flushed to the respective XML files. Using text, rather than binary format, simplifies editing (configuration files can be easily modified with any text editor, provided that direct Metabase edits are enabled), but it also allows for easier rollbacks or restores. Changes to metabase can be easily tracked because, by default, they are maintained by storing older versions in the %SystemRoot%\System32\inetsrv\history folder. Number of backup copies is determined by the MaxHistoryFiles metabase property. You can access the most recent versions of the metabase from the IIS Manager MMC console by selecting All Tasks > Backup\Restore Configuration from the top Action menu item or from the context-sensitive menu of the computer icon representing target server. Available backups are listed in the Previous Backups list box.

Scale-Out Versus Scale-Up IIS

Internet Information Services 6.0 operating in the worker process isolation mode can handle a large number of high-volume Web applications; however, specifics depend on server hardware, its configuration, and the type of services provided to your clients. While Windows 2003 Web Server Edition supports only two processors, you can install IIS 6.0 components on Enterprise or even Datacenter servers and take advantage of processor affinity and increased throughput on systems with up to 32

CPUs. HTTP.sys kernel mode driver can be configured to take advantage of a cache size of up to 64GB. It is also possible to run IIS on 64-bit versions of the Windows 2003 Server, which eliminates architectural limits imposed by the x86 processor design. New Web service features, presented at the beginning of this chapter—such as application pools with individual request queues, health monitoring, Web gardens, on-demand creation of worker processes, and their recycling—further enhance scalability and fault tolerance characteristics.

However, the scaling-up approach has its limitations. You can mitigate vulnerability by duplicating components on multiple levels (processor, memory, hard disks, power supplies, fans, worker processes and their queues, and so forth); however, your server still remains a single point of failure. Effectively, server uptime can be affected not only by human error or problems exceeding the level of redundancy you provided, but it can also be affected by common maintenance tasks, such as hardware or software upgrades. This might not be acceptable in situations where Web applications deliver mission-critical tasks, such as e-commerce or financial transaction processing.

To satisfy the needs of the most demanding environments, you have to look into scaling out your infrastructure into Web farms consisting of a number of identically configured servers. This yields a number of potential benefits. Scalability and availability levels are increased; so multiple instances of the same application can run simultaneously and accept client requests in a load-balanced fashion. At the same rate, you are no longer bound by single server hardware limitations. With every new server added to the farm, you accomplish linear improvement, which rarely can be done with hardware component duplication. You can dynamically increase or decrease the number of servers according to the fluctuations in client traffic and processing load without affecting application availability.

We already presented the functionality of IIS 6.0 relating to its scaling up capabilities (although some of it, such as application pools, can be considered a scaling out approach implemented within server boundaries). While this functionality is useful when scaling out, to create a Web farm, you also need to employ some type of load balancing solution. An overwhelming number of solutions are available on the market, but, in general, they fall into a few distinct categories.

Round Robin DNS

The simplest solution involves redirecting client requests with round robin DNS. The load balancing mechanism is based on the fact that a single DNS name can have multiple IP addresses assigned to it. When a Web client contacts a DNS server requesting translation from a target fully qualified name (which designates a Web site) into its IP address, the DNS server responds with all of them. With the round robin option active, the order of these entries changes with every reply. More specifically, if the first one contains all IP addresses corresponding to the requested name in a particular order, the next shifts all of them forward by one, which results in the first entry becoming the second, the second landing on the third spot, and so forth, and the last one appearing at the front of the list. In effect, connections from different clients to a Web site represented by a single name (but multiple IP addresses) should be evenly spread out across all physical servers where copies of the Web site reside.

DNS round robin is very straightforward and inexpensive to implement (no additional hardware or software is needed), but it has several major drawbacks. DNS server does not check the status of computers referenced by the IP addresses it distributes; so, it can potentially redirect a client's request to one that is overloaded or not functioning. This results in random, difficult-to-troubleshoot connectivity problems. Another drawback relates to the ability of the DNS client and server to cache recent query results. While both can be disabled, doing so affects overall performance by forcing the DNS client and server to query all requests, delaying generation of responses. These two issues make the DNS round robin solution not suitable for mission-critical applications.

Load Balancing

Two main types of enterprise-level load balancers exist, and they are grouped based on the layer of the OSI networking model they use. This can be either application-specific information, which qualifies them as Application (Layer 7) load balancers, or TCP/IP characteristics, which makes them dependent on Network and Transport (3 and 4) layers. Numerous vendors exist that integrate load balancing features into their switch offerings.

Load balancing switches are, in essence, traditional network switches with a built-in intelligence managing load balancing algorithm.

This algorithm bases its operations on information from Layer 4 (more commonly) or Layer 7 (less commonly, due to the performance implications and increased management complexity). The goal is to provide load balancing at the core-wire speed, close to the one at which switching takes place. Integrating load balancing functionality into a switch minimizes the number of network devices to administer and simplifies the architecture and failover scenarios. On the other hand, because a hardware load balancer becomes a single point of failure in your infrastructure, you need to ensure its high availability by configuring a secondary backup unit, preferably with a hot, stateful failover capability and automatic synchronization mechanism.

Higher-end switches, from vendors such as Foundry Networks, Radware, or F5 Networks, in addition to scalability and high-availability, are also capable of serving as VPN devices or IDS/IDP (Intrusion Detection/Intrusion Prevention and Detection) systems. They also can perform in-depth analysis of application layer information, such as XML content, and use it for traffic redirection (for example, by introducing custom XML tags). By including such performance enhancements as SSL acceleration, which encrypts incoming and decrypts outgoing communication, they offload highly processor-intensive tasks from Web servers. Higher-end switches offer elaborate target server health checking features (some of them are agent-based) and support a variety of session persistence mechanisms, based on such parameters as source IP addresses, SSL sessions, or cookies. On the downside, their power and versatility are reflected by high cost.

Microsoft Network Load Balancing, which we described in Chapter 11, "Load Balancing," is an example of a software-based Layer 4 solution. Several main differences distance it from hardware-based products. First of all, it operates as part of the Windows 2003 operating system (it is included as a built-in component in every edition, including Windows 2003 Web server). More importantly, its load balancing algorithm is based on a different set of principles. Client traffic reaches every server in a farm (which eliminates the bottleneck created by hardware-based load balancers and makes its architecture more scaleable), but only one of them is responsible for processing the traffic (all the others discard it). The selection of the processing server is made with a deterministic algorithm using set of parameters shared across all nodes, which guarantees a single outcome.

Layer 7 load balancers operate by checking characteristics of application layer protocols. This might involve HTTP or Secure Sockets Layer (SSL) parameters, including cookie information (cookies are small text files used during Web communication to keep track of a client's preferences or identity). An example of a product with such capabilities is Microsoft Application Center 2000, discussed in more detail in Chapter 11. Entries contained in the cookie could provide information requesting redirection to a specific server or load balanced distribution if no affinity is required. Note that use of affinity is strongly recommended when load balancing SSL sessions. This is because SSL sessions rely on a Session ID established between an individual Web client and a specific Web server. Such an identifier needs to be recreated if the target Web server changes. Even though this process is transparent to users, it results in increased utilization of server resources and communication delays.

It is possible to mix different load balancing solutions to enhance their strengths or remove their limitations. For example, because Microsoft Network Load Balancing is limited to 32 servers per cluster, you can combine it with DNS round robin to load balance larger farms. Similarly, failure of the entire site, hosting a mission-critical Web application, can be mitigated by using an independent load balancing mechanism capable of handling intersite traffic (Microsoft NLB cannot be used for this purpose because it requires all servers to have network adapters located on the same subnet).

Note that the concept of scaling out might need to be applied on multiple levels, depending on the type of resources and services provided to clients. For example, it is recommended to load balance Web applications using COM+ components by creating a three-tier hierarchy, with Web servers providing a client interface occupying the front end, the COM+ layer implementing business logic positioned in the middle, and a data store residing in the back end. The Web farm can be scaled-out with Network Load Balancing, Microsoft Application Center 2000 can provide Component Load Balancing for servers hosting COM+ components, and availability of the back-end server can be increased with Microsoft server clusters.

Alternatively, data served by a Web farm can be copied across multiple locations using a variety of replication technologies, incorporated into a Distributed File System, and referenced through virtual directories. We discuss topics relating to data replication mechanisms later in this chapter in the section "IIS Storage."

Scalability of your Web farm can be evaluated with Microsoft Web Capacity Analysis Tool (WCAT) provided as part of the IIS 6.0 Resource Kit. This handy utility is extremely useful in load simulation tests against different types of client traffic.

NLB for IIS

As we pointed out in the previous section, one way to increase scalability and high-availability of Web servers is to employ the Microsoft Network Load Balancing solution, available as a built-in component of Windows 2003 Server. Improvements to IIS 6.0, presented in the previous section, can contribute to additional scalability and availability of a load-balanced Web farm if used properly. Such a farm can serve local ASP or ASP.NET applications, or it can function as an entry point to back-end applications, such as Windows SharePoint Services, Windows Rights Management Services, or Exchange 2003 Server.

In general, the impact of IIS 6.0 scalability features on the behavior of Layer 3 and 4 load balancers (such as Microsoft Network Load Balancing) differs from the impact on Layer 7 load balancers. In the case of the former, a number of different critical conditions, such as an application pool failure or exceeding configurable safety limits (CPU utilization threshold or HTTP.sys queue length), terminate the connection, while the latter behave in a more sophisticated manner by sending a 503 HTTP Error (Service Unavailable) to its clients, which causes connection retries after a short waiting period (by that time, the application pool should be available).

To ensure the Windows 2003 Server Web component works properly with Network Load Balancing, set the IIS Metabase LoadBalancer-Capabilities property to **1** (and assign a value of **2** if you are using the Layer 7 load balancer). This can be accomplished with the following sample script, executed on the server hosting the IIS 6.0 components (in this example, the value of **1** is applied to the LoadBalancerCapabilities of the DefaultAppPool application pool):

```
Set oIISPrv = GetObject("winmgmts:/root/MicrosoftIISv2")
Set oAppPoolSettings = _ oIISPrv.Get("IIsApplicationPoolSetting=
➥'W3SVC/AppPools/DefaultAppPool'")
oAppPoolSettings.LoadBalancerCapabilities=1
oAppPoolSettings.Put_()
```

Before you start looking into specifics regarding planning and configuration of Network Load Balancing with IIS 6.0, you should review the content of Chapter 11, which discusses its generic principles, network dependencies, and configuration procedures. All of these are applicable in this particular case because the underlying technology and operating system remain the same. In the next section, we focus on specifics relevant to load balancing Web applications running on a Windows 2003 Server.

Planning and Configuration

Planning and configuration of a load-balanced Web server farm needs to be considered in two separate contexts. The first context deals with Network Load Balancing technology, which has an impact on network infrastructure, placement of Windows 2003 servers, and cluster configuration details. The second context is specific to IIS 6.0 and its two modes of operation. Because the first of these processes has already been described in Chapter 11, we start by describing issues relating to the second.

Note that it is not possible to operate separate Web applications within the same instance of the IIS in different isolation modes. This means, as part of your planning stage, you need to evaluate which applications are capable of executing in worker process isolation mode. In case it turns out some of them are dependent on IIS 5.0 features, you might want to separate these applications from others (which might require a separate farm).

Next, for those compatible with worker isolation process mode, define a set of application pools. Because each pool can be configured with distinct parameters, base your definition on criteria such as level of criticality, stability, or unique security requirements. Placing a troublesome application in its designated pool isolates its failures from others. Similarly, server vulnerability can be minimized by ensuring its applications operate using non-privileged accounts. It is common to separate static and dynamic content sites in separate application pools.

Besides defining application pools, you need to analyze how your applications deal with session state. HTTP by its nature is connectionless—which creates a problem with stateful applications, where user-specific data needs to be preserved during communication exchanges with a Web server (this is very common in e-commerce scenarios). Such data is typically stored as part of the application-specific session state and maintained for the duration of the session in the form of cookies.

Unfortunately, there is no automatic mechanism that allows members of an NLB cluster to exchange session state data. At the same rate, NLB as a Layer 4 balancer does not possess the capability to analyze the content of a cookie and redirect requests to the server that issued it. This means without additional provisions, a load-balanced client can be redirected to a server that does not have its session information. To resolve this dilemma, the following approaches can be used:

- Configure NLB with single or class C affinity, which forces requests from the same client to the same server. The class C affinity option is used in case clients reside behind a farm of load-balanced proxy servers (which means requests from the same client might actually arrive at the NLB Web Server farm with a different source IP address). Note, however, this solution still has significant drawbacks. If state information is stored directly on a Web server, then Web application or server failure results in a loss of session data and forces the client to reload the same set of pages. The same problem might surface as the result of other types of events, such as recycling of worker processes (if session data is maintained in-process).
- Session state can be stored on a separate server (for example, in a database) or on a Web client (through client-side cookies). A session-specific identifier can be appended, in obfuscated form, to URL strings exchanged between a Web client and Web server and used to access an appropriate database record.

The first of these two methods does not require any modifications to application configuration. The second method requires you to make changes. For legacy ASP applications, you can enable session state by modifying the value assigned to the AspAllowSessionState metabase property (this is typically done through graphical interface by selecting the Enable Session State checkbox on the Options tab of an Application configuration dialog box in IIS Manager); however, keep in mind this results in session data being stored locally on the Web server. ASP.NET is much more flexible in this aspect, and it lets you easily maintain session state in one of two ways:

- **In-process:** Session state is contained in the same worker process as the corresponding ASP.NET application. This implies session state is local to the server (so it cannot be obtained if a client request is redirected to another server in a load-balanced Web farm), and it is lost if a worker process is recycled (or if a Web application or server fails). However, this method offers the best performance.
- **Out-of-process:** Session state is contained in a separate process on the same Web server or another server (including an SQL Server database). The increased reliability of this method comes at the cost of performance because out-of-process is always slower.

Deciding which of these two methods to use for maintaining session state depends on the mode attribute of the <sessionState> section in the appropriate .config file (Machine.config file for all Web applications or Web.config for individual ones). The mode attribute can take one of the following values:

- **InProc:** Representing in-process configuration, which is the default mode. This might be suitable for Web gardens, where multiple worker processes serving a single Web application have their own copies of session information, but it cannot be used to share session information across multiple Web servers.
- **StateServer:** First type of out-of-process configuration, where session data is stored outside of the worker process on a local or remote server. The session state is maintained by the ASP.NET state Windows service (aspnet_state.exe). This can be used in scenarios involving Web farms. Note that in this case, however, the server storing session data constitutes a single point of failure. The configuration parameters in the <sessionState> section include the stateConnectionString attribute, which contains the server name and port.

- **SQLServer:** Second type of out-of-process configuration, where session data is stored in an SQL Server database, also applicable to situations in which Web farms are used. The sqlConnection attribute of the <sessionState> section designates, in this case, the SQL ODBC connection string, providing location and authentication information for connecting to the SQL Server database.

For out-of-process methods (StateServer and SQLServer), a session identifier can be transferred between the Web server and client either with cookies or URL strings. The choice is determined by the value of the cookieless attribute included in the <sessionState> section of the relevant .config file. As previously discussed, only the two out-of-process methods ensure session data can be maintained in the load-balanced configuration.

When using StateServer and SQLServer session state modes, you need to make sure the application paths of load-balanced Web sites on all cluster nodes are identical (otherwise, session state might be lost if a client connects to a different server). These paths have the format LM\W3SVC\x (the notation is case-sensitive), where x is an integer designating an individual Web site that needs to match on every server. While you can modify this number manually, it is easier to use Moveinstance.vbs script, included in the Microsoft Knowledge Base article Q325056, which describes this problem and its resolution.

For the basic steps involved in configuration of the Network Load Balancing cluster, refer to Chapter 11 where you find detailed information about setting up cluster and host parameters. It is likely (because this is the operating system default with Windows 2003 Server) you will also need to install the IIS 6.0 component. This can be part of an unattended server installation, or it can be done through the Add or Remove Programs applet in the Control Panel. It is also possible to use one of the Manage Your Server wizards by following these steps:

1. Start by clicking the Add or Remove a Role option in the Manage Your Server wizard (available in the Administrative Tools menu).
2. You are prompted to complete preliminary steps, such as installation of modems or network cards, attaching cabling, and having the Windows 2003 Server setup CD available. This is

followed by a page that lists the available types of Server Roles. One of them is an Application Server (IIS, ASP.NET). Make sure this option is selected, and click Next.

3. You are presented with Application Server options, giving you a chance to select additional components, such as FrontPage Server Extensions and ASP.NET. FrontPage Server Extensions simplify publishing Web content from Microsoft development programs, such as FrontPage or Visual Studio; however, they are not supported by Network Load Balancing; so make sure you do *not* select this option. ASP.NET is needed if your Web server is hosting an ASP.NET Web application. Considering the growing popularity of the .NET platform, it is likely this is your choice.

4. Continuing with the wizard, your ASP.NET selection results in the installation of IIS 6.0, the configuration of COM+ for remote transactions, the configuration of Microsoft Distributed Transaction Coordinator (DTC) for remote access, and the enabling of ASP.NET. You are prompted for the source files; so make sure you have a Windows 2003 installation CD handy.

This also automatically enables ASP.NET Web Service Extensions (which you can verify by accessing the Web Services Extensions node in the IIS Manager console).

The isolation mode is configurable from the Services tab on the Web Sites folder Properties dialog box in the IIS Manager console (switching from one to the other requires a restart of IIS). To set IIS 6.0 to IIS 5.0 Isolation mode, do the following:

1. In the Internet Information Services Manager MMC snap-in, open the Properties dialog box of the Web Sites folder on your server. This is illustrated in Figure 12.3.

2. Select the Service tab.

3. Check the Run WWW Service in IIS 5.0 Isolation Mode checkbox in the Isolation mode section.

4. Click OK.

5. You are prompted to accept the change and restart the IIS service. Click Yes to continue.

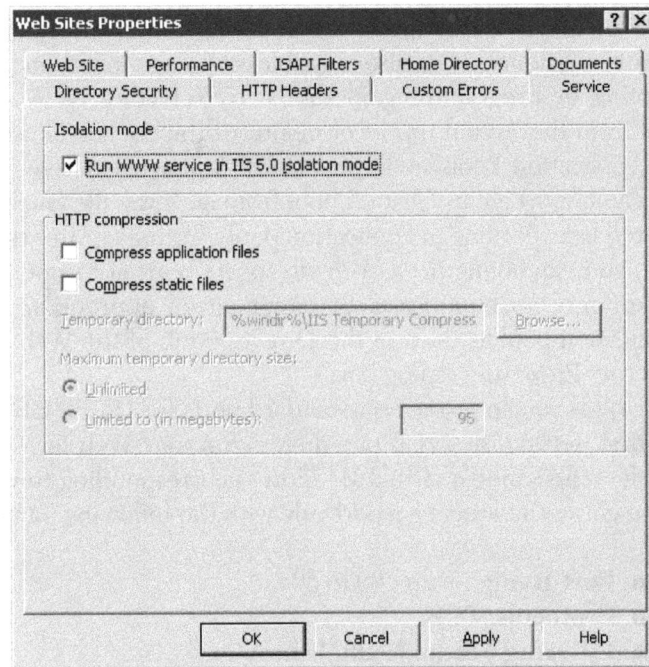

Figure 12.3 Web Sites properties.

After the Web server operates in the IIS 5.0 isolation mode, you can designate which applications run with low, medium, or high isolation. This is done from the Home Directory tab of the Web site or virtual directory Properties dialog box. The Application Protection list box in the Application settings section gives you three options to choose from—Low (IIS Process), Medium (Pooled), and High (Isolated).

To configure Internet Information Services 6.0 in the worker process isolation mode (note this effectively disables the IIS 5.0 Isolation Mode because both of them cannot coexist):

1. In the Internet Information Services Manager MMC snap-in, open the Properties dialog box of the Web Sites on your server.
2. Click the Service tab.
3. Uncheck the Run WWW Service in IIS 5.0 Isolation Mode checkbox in the Isolation mode section.
4. Click OK.
5. You are prompted to accept the change and restart the IIS service. Click Yes to continue.

Creation of application pools also can be handled with the IIS Manager console (although it is also possible with command-line utilities and scripting or programming methods) by selecting New > Application Pool from the Action top-level menu (or the context-sensitive menu of the Application Pools node) in the IIS Manager console. Alternatively, you can import an application pool from an XML file (such a file can be created by exporting an application pool's settings). After the pool is created, you can configure a Web site or its portion to operate within its worker process boundaries by assigning an appropriate value in the Application pool list box on the Directory tab of the Web site or virtual directory Properties dialog box.

Unless you are using non-standard ports for HTTP intranet communication, setting the NLB parameters for your Web farm should be as simple as assigning a virtual IP address corresponding to your Web site to the cluster and setting a port rule with the following parameters:

- **Port Range:** From 80 to 80
- **Protocols:** TCP
- **Filtering Mode:** Multiple host

Standard HTTP port 80 (TCP) is used by Web Services and SOAP communication. Affinity settings depend on whether session coherency is required, and if so, how you handle its storage. With ASP applications, you most likely need to set it to Single or Class C. The load weight parameter for each host should reflect its processing capacity.

If you are using SSL traffic, your configuration is more complex because you also need to obtain and install certificates identifying your Web site on every cluster member. In addition, as indicated before, when using SSL sessions in a load-balanced Web farm, you should configure the clustering affinity parameter to single or class C. This forces all TCP connections from the same client to be processed by the same Web server. By consistently pointing the same client to the same server, regardless of ports used, negotiation of SSL Session ID takes place only once during the initial connection.

IIS Storage

The decision determining how the storage of a load-balanced IIS 6.0 farm should be handled is critical to its proper operation. If copies of Web applications and their data residing on load-balanced Web servers are relatively static, they can be easily replicated across cluster nodes (Microsoft Application Center 2000 helps manage and monitor this process, including the deployment of updates from staging servers). However, this is rarely the case these days. Most Web content is interactive, not only delivering information to the Web client but also accepting their updates. Synchronizing highly dynamic content across all nodes in real time tends to be difficult and introduces a potential for issues with data inconsistency.

The most common solution to this problem is redirecting IIS 6.0 Web site content to a Distributed File System structure (this is done by selecting the A Share Located on Another Computer option on the Home Directory tab of the Web Site Properties dialog box and specifying the name of the DFS replica), which is maintained outside of the Web farm on back-end, frequently clustered file servers. DFS replicas can, in turn, be synchronized using a number of different methods, such as Windows 2003 native File Replication Service (FRS), or the third-party products previously discussed in the book.

File Replication Service operates on the file level, which is the reason for its main limitations—it does not apply to open files (a file needs to be closed before it can be copied); it is very inefficient (it always copies the entire file, regardless of the amount of changes—synchronization is triggered by differences in file modification timestamps), and it does not provide any bandwidth throttling mechanism (so, a large file copy can saturate all available bandwidth).

If back-end data is maintained in multiple SQL Server databases, you can synchronize them using native mechanisms available in SQL Server 2000, such as transactional or merge replication, and through log shipping.

Another, usually much more expensive possibility, is *hardware-based replication*. In this case, data copy to remote locations is handled by a disk controller, which performs two, instead of one, data writes. This can be done either synchronously or asynchronously. Software-based replication products also exist (such as Double-Take from NSI Software or Veritas Storage Replicator) that operate in a similar manner, although they are implemented as filter drivers. They function by intercepting I/O write requests issued by the operating system, before they reach the File System level, and sending out a duplicate to a remote system. For more information on these two methods, refer to Chapter 3, "Storage for Highly Available Systems." Both mechanisms are much more efficient than whole-file replication and are not application-dependent, like SQL Server synchronization.

FTP Service

File Transfer Protocol Service offers two basic features—the capability to download and upload files. Unlike its less reliable counterpart, TFTP (Trivial File Transfer Protocol), which uses connectionless User Datagram Protocol (UDP), FTP relies on the acknowledgement-based nature of Transmission Control Protocol (TCP).

FTP can be easily deployed across multiple Network Load Balanced Web servers. Its implementation consists of two basic steps—assignment of NLB-specific parameters (including the virtual IP address of the FTP site and port rules covering the range of FTP ports) and the setup of storage with appropriate directory structure and replication mechanisms.

If an FTP site is supposed to provide upload capabilities, then you might want to consider designating one server in the farm as the target. In our example, this is NAUSNYCFTP01, with NAUSNYCFTP02 and NAUSNYCFTP03 as the failover hosts (in case the primary fails). This can be accomplished by creating a designated FTP upload virtual cluster (NAUSNYCFTPVS01, in our case), assigning a unique virtual IP address to it (10.10.200.50), and configuring it with the port rule parameters presented in Table 12.1.

Table 12.1 FTP Upload Cluster Port Rule Parameters

Server Name	Parameters
NAUSNYCFTPVS01	Web Server Port Rule Virtual IP Address: 10.10.200.50 Port Range: From 20 to 21 Protocols: TCP Filtering Mode: Single host
NAUSNYCFTP01	Web Server Port Rule Virtual IP Address: 10.10.200.50 Port Range: From 20 to 21 Protocols: TCP Filtering Mode: Single host Handling Priority: 1

Server Name	Parameters
NAUSNYCFTP02	Web Server Port Rule Virtual IP Address: 10.10.200.50 Port Range: From 20 to 21 Protocols: TCP Filtering Mode: Single host Handling Priority: 2
NAUSNYCFTP03	Web Server Port Rule Virtual IP Address: 10.10.200.50 Port Range: From 20 to 21 Protocols: TCP Filtering Mode: Single host Handling Priority: 3

Because FTP uses two ranges of TCP ports, you also need to define the second port rule, covering the range from 1024 to 65535 with identical values of Cluster IP Address, Protocols, Filtering Mode, and Handling Priority parameters.

You could use the same NLB cluster to provide download capabilities with different port rules (assuming that either the proper synchronization mechanism is in place or you pointed virtual directories to the same location), as long as you define a separate virtual IP address for this purpose. This can be accomplished by creating a designated FTP download virtual cluster (NAUSNYCFTPVS02, in our case), assigning a unique virtual IP address to it (10.10.200.60), and configuring it with the port rule parameters presented in Table 12.2.

Table 12.2   FTP Upload Cluster Port Rule Parameters

Server Name	Parameters
NAUSNYCFTPVS02	Web Server Port Rule Virtual IP Address: 10.10.200.60 Port Range: From 20 to 21 Protocols: TCP Filtering Mode: Single host

continues

Table 12.2 FTP Upload Cluster Port Rule Parameters (continued)

Server Name	Parameters
NAUSNYCFTP01	Web Server Port Rule Virtual IP Address: 10.10.200.60 Port Range: From 20 to 21 Protocols: TCP Filtering Mode: Multiple host Affinity: Single Load Weight: 10
NAUSNYCFTP02	Web Server Port Rule Virtual IP Address: 10.10.200.60 Port Range: From 20 to 21 Protocols: TCP Filtering Mode: Multiple host Affinity: Single Load Weight: 10
NAUSNYCFTP03	Web Server Port Rule Virtual IP Address: 10.10.200.60 Port Range: From 20 to 21 Protocols: TCP Filtering Mode: Multiple host Affinity: Single Load Weight: 10

As before, you also need to define the second port rule, covering the range from 1024 to 65535 with identical values of Cluster IP Address, Protocols, Filtering Mode, and Handling Priority parameters.

An alternative solution is based on pointing the FTP site directory to a DFS replica, synchronized with methods described in the previous section. NTFS permissioning and FTP user isolation can be used to secure multiuser access. FTP user isolation uses functionality built into IIS 6.0 FTP implementation, which automatically redirects individual clients at the logon time to FTP subfolders that match their usernames.

Troubleshooting

Problems with load-balanced Web applications can be difficult to troubleshoot because they might be triggered by a variety of conditions, and yet they exhibit fairly similar symptoms.

Regardless of the symptoms, you typically employ a number of similar monitoring and auditing tools to analyze the Web farm and application status. Among the most popular ones are Windows Event Log Viewer, System and Network Monitor, as well as Network Load Balancing and Internet Information Services Manager consoles. Key performance counters relevant in Web farm health monitoring include the following:

- **Processor: % Processor Time (_Total):** Expresses processor time for all processors. Consistently high values might indicate the need for scaling up or out.
- **System: Processor Queue Length:** Should not exceed the level of two or more per CPU sustained for more than 5 minutes.
- **Physical Disk: Avg. Disk Queue Length:** Should not exceed two per drive over a period longer than five minutes.
- **Memory: Pages/Sec:** Helps tracking paging activity. High values might suggest a memory upgrade or better load distribution across the NLB cluster.
- **ASP.NET: Request Wait Time:** Reflects the most recent Web client request wait time in the kernel queue; so you want to ensure it is as low as possible (average value should be close to 0 milliseconds).
- **ASP.NET: Requests Queued:** Linear growth is a sign of the server approaching its processing capacity. After the queue limits are reached, client requests are returned with an HTTP 503 Error.
- **ASP.NET: Requests Rejected:** A value other than 0 is typically the result of the request queue reaching its capacity and it should be further investigated.
- **ASP.NET: Worker Process Restarts:** Indicates serious application problems.
- **ASP.NET Applications, Error Total:** Constitutes a sign of application problems if greater than zero.

Log Parser, included as part of the IIS 6.0 Resource Kit, is a handy utility simplifying analysis of IIS logs as well as standard operating system and application events accessible through Windows Event Viewer. Typically, you use it to monitor client request response times and HTTP error messages.

In case of application pool problems, you can enable debugging, which stops automatic behavior associated with worker process isolation functionality. Instead, a lack of response to a ping within a defined interval triggers a custom action, such as a notification message sent to the administrative team of memory dump of the worker process space. It is also possible to "orphan" a failing or troublesome process, which permits troubleshooting it in isolation from other worker processes within the same application pool.

Network Load Balancing supports logging, helpful in troubleshooting issues triggered by its activities. To enable it, check the Log Settings entry box from the Options menu in the NLB Manager administrative console.

Maintaining the IIS Server Cluster

Your maintenance plan should involve monitoring the cluster status with tools such as Microsoft Operations Manager (or other enterprise class products, such as HP OpenView or CA Unicenter). Through their agents, you are able to analyze event logs and respond to critical events through automated and customizable actions.

Network Load Balancing has the capability to automatically exclude a failed server from the cluster. This determination, however, is made based on a lack of response to heartbeat signals sent periodically to each node and might not detect performance or stability issues at the application level. If IIS 6.0 operates in worker process isolation mode, you can rely on the self-healing capabilities of application pools. Otherwise, with IIS 5.0 isolation mode, you can resort to tools such as HTTP Monitor (HTTPMon.exe) included with the Windows 2000 Resource Kit, which oversees Web activity by reviewing HTTP traffic. Among the tests it can run are checks for status code against target Web sites. By analyzing the result, HTTPMon can determine, for example, if the site is not responding (indicated by HTTP 500 Errors) and triggers the removal of an unstable server from the cluster.

Disaster Recovery

As previously mentioned, Metabase in IIS 6.0 supports automatic configuration versioning and history. Changes to metabase are kept track of, and up to 10 previous versions are maintained in the %SystemRoot%\ System32\inetsrv\history folder. These copies can be used for rollback or restore. Configuration of the application pools or Web sites can be exported and imported using XML files. These capabilities can be used to store the configuration of the entire IIS 6.0 installation for the purposes of disaster recovery.

IIS 6.0 also includes a number of Visual Basic Script files residing in the %Windir%\System32 directory, which simplify automation of management tasks. In particular, IIsBack.vbs backs up or restores Metabase, and IIsCnfg.vbs exports or imports IIS 6.0 or the individual Web site configuration to an XML file.

In general, Web farms should be stateless, which means users data should be stored on clustered back-end servers. If this condition is satisfied, disaster recovery procedures involve reinstallation of the operating system with the IIS 6.0 component and restoration of the Metabase and Web site's configuration.

Best Practices

Configure your load-balanced servers with dual network adapters. This offers separation between client traffic (potentially insecure) and the demilitarized zone (DMZ) or internal network. Make sure you disable the "Client for Microsoft Networks," "File and printer sharing for Microsoft networks," and NetBIOS components on the front-end adapter (the one that has the virtual IP address of the Web site and Network Load Balancing activated). The same components are typically enabled on the back-end adapter to enable management and content replication.

With dual network adapters, using NLB unicast mode is recommended because it is compatible with virtually any router or switch. While multicast mode has its benefits, it might cause problems with some of your networking gear.

To secure your configuration, disable the NLB remote control feature and use NLB Manager or Windows Management Instrumentation as your exclusive management tool. NLB remote control decreases security, making the cluster vulnerable to denial of service attacks and data tampering. NLB Manager, on the other hand, is much more secure and has built-in safety mechanisms, which ensure cluster and host parameters, as well as port rules, are consistent across all nodes.

You might want to consider setting the initial host state to Stopped. While this forces you to come up with another automated mechanism to start the service (or do it manually), it gives you a chance to ensure the Web application is fully operational before client requests are redirected to it through the load balancing algorithm.

Keep in mind having the same server participating simultaneously in a Server and a Network Load Balancing cluster is *not* supported.

Try to use the IIS 6.0 worker process isolation mode, which offers advantages in the area of stability, scalability, performance, and security. While this is application-independent, it should work in most scenarios with both traditional ASP Web sites and those implemented through ASP.NET.

Time-Out

We have reached the end of a host of chapters dealing with high-performance, high availability Windows Server 2003. Each chapter covered the performance monitoring and troubleshooting aspects of the server or service.

In Chapter 13, "Looking for Trouble: Setting Up Performance Monitoring and Alerts," we focus on troubleshooting, performance monitoring, and alerts. We also slightly delve into Microsoft Operations Manager configuration.

Looking for Trouble: Setting Up Performance Monitoring and Alerts

Introduction

The previous 12 chapters have dealt mainly with the architecture, design, and implementation of high availability and high-performance services of Windows Server 2003. Does this mean our job is now done, systems are redundant, and they will stay up all the time? Can we go home and work on the shrimp boat? Not so fast.

While we may have implemented systems to provide maximum uptime, this does not mean there won't be failures. On the contrary, you must assume there will be failures, and now you need a plan for what to do when the failures occur. With the disaster recovery plan in hand and a list of what-ifs pinned to the wall, it is critical you engineer a system to alert you to impending doom, so you have enough time to react and mitigate against the failure, if not completely prevent it.

As with many different problems in life, if you know about a problem about to happen, and catch it early, you can limit the amount of damage and get out of harm's way. Most network and systems disasters occur because something unrelated to the actual system failed and caused a ripple effect. If you "nip the problem in the bud," so to speak, you can save yourself a lot of wasted time and aggravation,

To illustrate the point, a certain story comes to mind. Back in 1999, a computer virus called Melissa shut down many systems across the world and caused billions in damage. Our network of 30,000 users serviced a major food distribution subsidiary that was connected to the parent company's network.

We realized something big was about to go down when some of us in the 400-strong IT department started getting numerous identical emails professing love and peace on earth. Our IT director wasted no time. He rushed into the network room and shut down the main router, essentially decapitating the network. This stopped the attack in its tracks, and we spent the rest of the day cleaning out a few hundred Exchange mail-boxes.

On the contrary, the IT director at the parent company, worrying about losing business, kept his routers up for a few hours longer, which caused the collapse of all his servers, the loss of all mailboxes, and many days of downtime.

What you need is a constant flow of data and metrics concerning the health of your systems, so you can preempt outages and take the neces-sary action to circumvent the outage. This chapter is devoted to such a reporting and monitoring service.

We begin with a discussion of the Windows event system, how and what events are reported to the event system, and how to constantly be informed of any events that might pose a threat to the system. Thus, we cover performance monitoring, and, of course, Microsoft Operations Manager.

This chapter does not cover the various tools you use to troubleshoot problems after you have been notified of them, such as Network Moni-tor. You can use many tools to fix problems that occur, but they are beyond the scope of this chapter. In other words, this chapter deals with system information, not fixing a system that is down.

Understanding the Windows Server 2003 Monitoring Systems

We have learned that high availability services, like clustering and load balancing, are only available in the Enterprise and Datacenter versions of the Windows Server 2003 operating system. However, the perfor-mance tools, system monitoring tools, event management systems, and so on are available to all versions of the OS.

We also have discussed that high availability systems cannot be created without the supporting infrastructure systems. Clusters and their applications need the DNS services, Active Directory, the NTFS file system, and so on. These systems depend on the servers and the network. The network depends on routers and switches. All services on the network are so interrelated with each other and so dependent on each other that, to ensure you being properly informed of the condition of the network, you really need to be monitoring everything.

For example, on any Active Directory network with more than one domain controller, you need to be constantly monitoring the File Replication System (FRS). Without it, domain controllers cannot share data, replicate changes in group policy, log in scripts, and so on. If FRS breaks and an important update never arrives at a certain DC, this can cause a cluster to fail, and you end up with a much bigger problem than the original loss of FRS.

The Windows Server 2003 monitoring tools are not simple and you need to know how they work before they can be of use to you. The tools include the following:

- Event Viewer
- Task Manager
- System Monitor
- Quality of Service
- Windows Management Interface
- SNMP

In addition, a separate Microsoft product called Microsoft Operations Manager may be used to consolidate the alerts and monitors on the Windows Server 2003 monitoring tools. MOM is discussed in the second part of this chapter.

Windows Server 2003 monitors or analyzes storage, memory, networks and processing, and so on. However, instead of just monitoring these subsystems, you need to be analytical. You should not be monitoring the memory itself, or disk usage itself, but rather how the various sub-systems, software, and hardware components use these resources. It is less important to know 100MB of RAM were used between x time and y time and more important to know what used the RAM at a certain time and why so much was used. Set a baseline for usage, and then set alerts to tell you the usage has breached the baseline.

You probably know what a memory leak is. It means an application is stealing RAM somewhere. RAM is stolen because some part of a program that used the memory for a process has not released the memory after it has used it. As long as the bug or badly written software keeps *stealing* the memory, your server will eventually run out of memory and suffer. First it pages out memory requirements to the hard disks, but eventually performance is so poor that even if the server does not crash, the applications will probably cease to offer any service.

It helps to know which application is responsible for the memory loss. System monitoring does this for you, so you can take the necessary steps to fix the problem, like simply shutting down the offending service, or checking with the manufacturer to see if a patch is available.

So many software components, services, and threads of functionality exist in the operating system; it is literally impossible to monitor tens of thousands of instances of storage, memory, network, or processor usage. Thus, you need to be very selective about what you are watching and obtain adequate notifications. The system monitoring, event tools, and Microsoft Operations Manager (MOM) let you do this. Let's first talk about the operating system's event reporting architecture.

Event Viewer

According to Microsoft documentation, any event occurring in the operating system signifies an occurrence of something in the OS or in an application that must be reported to the administrators of the system.

These events are recorded in *event logs* and are viewable by the event viewer. The event logs and the event viewer are critical tools because they let you identify problems and troubleshoot issues. For example, there are many reasons why the FRS stops working, and the numerous events posted into the event logs about FRS failure let you determine why the service has stalled and whether you need to rebuild the FRS databases, fix a network issue, or restart a service.

The event log also lets you monitor security events—such as logon and logoff, invaluable in network protection—and monitor DNS, Active Directory, applications, and so on. The event viewer on a DC lets you monitor the following six event groups:

- System logs
- Security logs
- Application logs

- DNS Server logs
- File Replication Service logs (only available on a DC)
- Directory Service logs (only available on a DC)

The *System log* logs events such as starting and stopping of services, subsystem functionality, printing, DHCP Server events, driver events, and any events applying to the system.

The *Security log* logs audited events related to the security systems of the operating system. By *audited*, we mean you determine which events in the security system you want audited, and these are reported to the event viewer. These auditable events include file system access, password changes, account lockouts, and so on. Besides the basic auditable events reported by default in the system, you need to specify what to audit and how the events are logged to the event logs and viewed in event viewer. Auditing is initially set up in Group Policy objects and by setting SACLs on Active Directory objects. See Chapter 5, "Preparing the Platform for a High-Performance Network," for more information on setting up Security event logs.

The *Application log* logs events in applications that include certain application-layer services, such virus scans, remote access events, network events, and so on. The Application log is also typically used by independent software vendors (ISVs) as a place for posting events.

The remaining logs are found on domain controller, DNS Servers, or file servers with replication and are dedicated to these services respectfully. The DNS Server log posts events related to name resolution and the workings of the DNS Service, and the File Replication Service is dedicated to the critical FRS system (which can get a little flaky at times).Events posted into the logs can vary in severity, and the information that is attached to the messages varies as well. In other words, an event can tell you a critical error has occurred (accompanied by the now famous *red cherry* bullet with an X through it) or just provide warnings and information messages (signified with an exclamation icon). Each event has the following information attached to it:

- **Data and Time:** The data and exact time the event occurred.
- **Source:** The source of the event, such as a driver, service, or application, which tells you what process or application posted the event.

- **Category:** The source also provides a category for the event, such as logon/logoff for security logs, object access, and so on.
- **Event:** This is the event itself, which provides an event ID allowing you to track the event in a knowledge base, reference document, or online. A well-designed event hierarchy in an application or system categorizes event IDs according to severity or processing states.
- **User:** The user property identifies the user associated with the process that caused the event. In security events, it is critical to know which user account was logged as the source of the event. For example, if you see multiple Administrator events occurring, you know an attack is likely underway on the network, and a hacker is targeting the Administrator account. You know this because you are a wise network administrator who never uses the Administrator account, except to create the first domain controller.
- **Computer:** The property identifies the computer instrumental in causing the event. In security logs, you see the computer associated with the user account. If the computer name in the log does not correspond with any computer in your domain, then you can be sure you have an attack underway. Pay attention to the previous list because you will need to know how to use them when configuring alerts in MOM, which is described later in this chapter.

The Event Viewer MMC is a snap-in that lets you view and manage the event logs. You can sort the logs and filter the events according to your needs. As mentioned in Chapter 5, if you need to set event log properties, such as event log size, you should do this using Group Policy to keep your settings consistent across all servers and classes of servers.

As the crucible of event information on the Windows Server platform, it is crucial, as a developer, that you post all your application events, serious or just informational, to the event log. Gone are the days of creating text files and posting error information into them. If you are writing an application only you will use, then go ahead and write your events and errors to a custom event log, but if you plan to market a product, it needs to use the event log. One of the key reasons for this is the event log enables remote viewing of the event from any Event Viewer MMC on the network. The other key reason is the event logs are accessed by event monitoring systems, such as Microsoft Operations Manager, discussed later in this chapter.

In addition to custom event posting into the event log, the operating system also comes equipped with various tools for monitoring and event raising. We look at these now with readying the system for monitoring under the watchful eye of MOM in mind.

Exploring System and Performance Monitoring Objects

Windows Server 2003 includes numbers built-in software objects for monitoring associated with various services, applications, and processes. These objects are able to collect data in various places, and then log an event associated with the data you are collecting.

You have two key methods for collecting system information in Windows Server 2003. First, you can access registry functions that force the release of performance data. These functions call performance counter DLLs in the operating system. Second, you can collect information through the Windows Management Infrastructure.

In Windows 2000, Microsoft introduced a new technology for recovering performance data. This technology uses managed object files (MOFs), which correspond to or are connected to various facilities and resources in the system.

There are too many MOFs to talk about in the limited space of this book, but you can look them up in the *Performance Counters Reference* for Windows Server 2003, which is accessible online at Microsoft (it is part of the Windows Server 2003 Deployment Kit). This guide is an indispensable resource for administrators of high availability and high-performance systems.

The PerfMon objects include the operating system's base services, such as the services that gather data about memory, Paging File functionality, and Physical Disk usage. There are also objects that gather data on the operating system's advanced services, such as Active Directory, .NET Framework, IIS and the FTP service, DNS, WINS, and so forth.

To fully understand how to work with these objects, you should be familiar with performance data and analysis terms. Performance monitor is a three-legged stool, comprised of throughput, queues, and response time. If you fully understand these concepts, you are able to broaden your scope of analysis and perform calculations to report transfer rate, access time, latency, tolerance, thresholds, bottlenecks, and so on. Then you can decide how you want information on these metrics posted and how you are alerted to thresholds and bottlenecks as they are reached.

Rate and Throughput

Throughput is not a difficult concept to grasp. It is simply the amount of work done in a unit of time. If you are able to catch 10 fish per hour, you could say your catch rate is 10 fish per hour, assessed over a period of x hours, as long as the rate remains constant. However, if the rate of catches varies, we cannot calculate the throughput. We say throughput increases as the number of components increases, or the available resources are reduced. In our fish example, throughput increases if you are able to catch more fish, in less time, with the same piece of bait. The slowest point in the system sets the throughput for the system as a whole.

Understanding the Work Queue

If you ask your partner to help you catch more fish by having him provide you with bait, at a moment's notice, on a number of fishing rods (to reduce the time taken to bait and prepare a hook), and suddenly the fish don't bite, then the number of baited hooks on waiting rods is going to pile up. This also happens in information systems when working threads and processes begin to back up, one behind the other, in a queue. When such a queue develops on the system, a bottleneck has occurred.

Bottlenecks can bring a network and its services to a standstill. No system has unlimited bandwidth to handle parallel processes. There is no such system that can use an unlimited number of processes. Some scientists have tried to raise the bar of parallel processing by trying to join all the computers in the world together is a single system. However, there would be bottlenecks at the system-level; so even if you were able to eliminate the queues at the processor-level, bottlenecks would arise at the network-level. You strive to monitor for bottlenecks on your system, to determine if flaws are the cause, or if there are more sinister reasons why the bottleneck has occurred.

Queues become bogged down if a request for resources is not evenly spread over the unit of time. Getting back to the fishing story, if you are able to catch a fish at the constant rate of one per hour, you probably will easily use every piece of bait and rod set for you. But if the fish spend eight hours not eating, and then they suddenly get a craving for shrimp-on-a-hook, a bottleneck will occur.

If queues and bottlenecks on your systems are allowed to overload, the systems become unresponsive. Requests for processor, disks, and memory choke. When requesting services are not satisfied, the bottleneck problem begins to compound, and the system response time begins to increase.

Response Time

Response time tells us how much time is needed to complete a task. Thus, it is considered a measure of performance. Response time increases as the load increases. Take a Microsoft Exchange system, for example. If it has insufficient memory or processing power, it is unable to process a large volume of email that comes flying at it. As mentioned in Chapter 10, "High Availability, High-Performance Exchange," if you do not adequately cater to Exchange with the right disk partitioning or provide high throughput hard disks, Exchange begins to slowly choke under the queues and bottlenecks that begin to form on the system.

If the response time on the Exchange server is unsatisfactory, you either have to move a bunch of mailboxes off the server, work with less data, or increase the resources, such as better hard disks, extra CPUs, and more memory.

You can calculate the response time of a system by dividing the queue length over the resource throughput. Response time, queues, and throughput data is reported on and calculated by the Windows Server 2003 monitoring technology.

How Performance Objects Work

The performance monitoring objects do their magic using processes called *performance counters*. The counters are what perform the actual analysis and hand off the data collection to the monitoring objects. For example, hard disk performance counters can assess transfer rate while processor counters assess processor time.

To gain access to the data a counter produces, you first have to create the performance counter object. This is done by calling a create function from a user interface or other process—a process that is hidden from most system administrators—that creates counters in Performance Monitor. As soon as the counter is created, its methods, or functions, begin the data collection and store the data in various ways. They can stream the data out to disk or store it in files or in RAM. The presentation components access the data for you and present it in a form conducive to analysis.

The objects are created in various ways. Some objects can be created as needed, as many as needed. Others only can be created once. This means that, depending on the object, your analysis software can create at least one copy of the performance object and analyze the counter information it generates. Other objects can be instantiated more than once. You can also instantiate an object for a local computer's services, and you can create an object that operates on a remote computer.

There are two methods of data collection you can use. First, you can create objects to sample data. In other words, data is collected periodically and not when a certain event occurs. This is important because data collection places a burden on resources; it requires systems resources, such as processor time and memory.

For your analysis to be less intrusive on the system and less of a load, sample data periodically. The downside of the sampling route is you may miss data that fell outside the sampling period. This could lead to inaccuracies and the data may be misleading.

You also can do event tracing. With event tracing, you can collect data as certain events occur. This means you can open a sampling window when a certain event begins to occur. You can, for example, place a trace on a certain event that happens in an application. You would then *watch* the application and system state when it executes a certain function and monitor what transpires during the execution of a function.

Event tracing is not without its limitations. It consumes more resources than sampling. If you plan to event trace, do so for short periods where the objective of the trace is to troubleshoot. Don't simply trace for the sake of tracing.

The counters are able to provide data in one of two ways: They can perform instantaneous counting or average counting. The instantaneous counter reports data as it happens. Thus, it is a snapshot, a capture at a certain moment in time. The counter does not compute snapshot data it receives, it just reports it. Average counting computes data for you. Average counting reports stuff like bits-per second, or pages-per-second, and so forth.

Other counters are able to report percentages, difference, and so forth.

System Monitoring Tools

You have two primary monitoring tools on the Windows Server 2003 operating system—the Performance Console and Task Manager. Task

Manager is an on-systems instant access portal to systems activity, such as memory usage, processor activity, process activity, and resource consumption. Task Manager is very helpful for immediate reporting of system problems, but it cannot do much more than say you have a problem.

Performance Console, on the other hand, provides you with performance analysis and is used to troubleshoot and analyze bottlenecks. Performance Console also can be used to establish regular monitoring regimens as ongoing server health analysis and report what it finds as alerts.

Performance Console is really two tools in one: the System Monitor and Performance Logs and Alerts.

Working with the Performance Console and the System Monitor

The Performance Console encompasses the System Monitor and Performance Logs and Alerts. The Performance Monitor, which is often referred to as *perfmon* from its Windows NT ancestor, is usually found on the Administrative Tools menu as Performance. The console loads in an MMC snap-in, and you can execute it from the Run console, Task Manager, or at the command line by executing perfmon.msc.

The System Monitor is also available as an ActiveX control, namely sysmon.ocx. This control can be loaded into OLE-compliant applications, such as Microsoft Word or Visio, and even an HTML page on a Web site. It also can be wrapped in the .NET Framework. You can program against the OCX in your applications and set up interfaces and processes specifically created for performance monitoring and analysis.

When you run the Performance Console, it starts with a blank System Monitor graph that gets loaded into the console tree.

System Monitor

System Monitor enables you to create graphs, histograms (bar charts), and text reports of performance counter data. It lets you monitor data for diagnostics on a short-term basis. The System Monitor has the following features:

- It is hosted in MMC, which means you can run it against any system from any system. In other words, you can use it on a workstation and monitor a remote processor.

- A toolbar enables you to copy and paste counters, purge or clear counters, add counters, and so forth.
- You have the ability to easily manipulate the interface to control how counter values are displayed. You can do things such as vary the line style and width, and you can change the color of the lines. The chart window is also highly configurable, allowing you to do things like change the color of the chart and manipulate the chart window.
- The monitor provides legends that indicate selected counters and associated data, such as the name of the computer you are monitoring, the objects themselves, and their instances.

How to Use System Monitor

You can access and configure the monitor from its toolbar or by using its shortcut menu. You can also access the shortcut menu by right-clicking in the blank-graph area and selecting one of the options presented. The toolbar is the default option.

From the toolbar, you can configure the type of display you wish to view by clicking the View Chart, View Histogram, or View Report buttons. The same information is available in chart, histogram, or report format.

Differences in the view formats exist, however. Use the histograms and the charts if you want to view multiple counters. Be aware, though, each counter displays only a single value in the chart.

These can be used to track current activity, or you can use them to view the graphs as they change. Use the report if you want to view multiple values. For real-time data, click on the View Current Activity button. Another option allows you to select the View Log File Data button, which lets you access data from the completed running logs.

To get the flow of data moving, you first have to select the counters in which you are interested. The toolbar includes Add, Delete, and the New Counter Set buttons that can be used to start the process. The toolbar also can be used to select new counters. Clicking the Add counters button loads the dialog box, as illustrated in Figure 13.1.

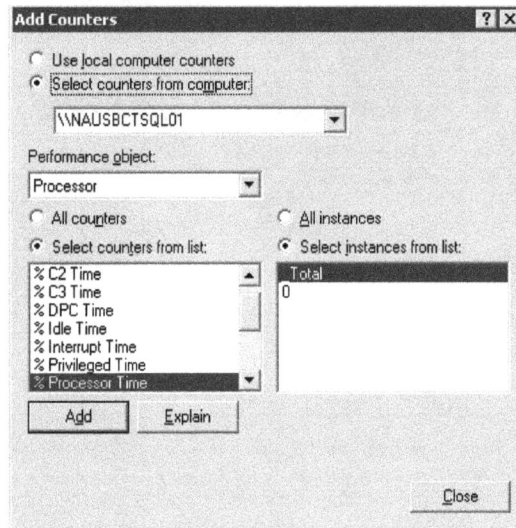

Figure 13.1   Add Counters.

The Add Counters dialog box lets you to select the computer you want to monitor. It then lets you select the performance objects and counters with which to do the job. For convenience, you have an Explain button that, when clicked, lets you learn more about the individual counters selected.

The Clear Display option lets you update the display, and you can also freeze the display with the Freeze Display button. The Freeze Display button suspends data collection while the Update Data button resumes collection.

To make the reporting stand out, you can click the Highlight button, which highlights the line or bar for a selected counter. It makes the selected counter more visible by putting it against a white or black background.

Displays also can be exported to places like the Clipboard. You can also export the display into the running display.

The Properties button lets you access to settings to control fonts, colors, and the like. When you click the Properties button, the System Monitor Properties dialog box loads, as illustrated in Figure 13.2.

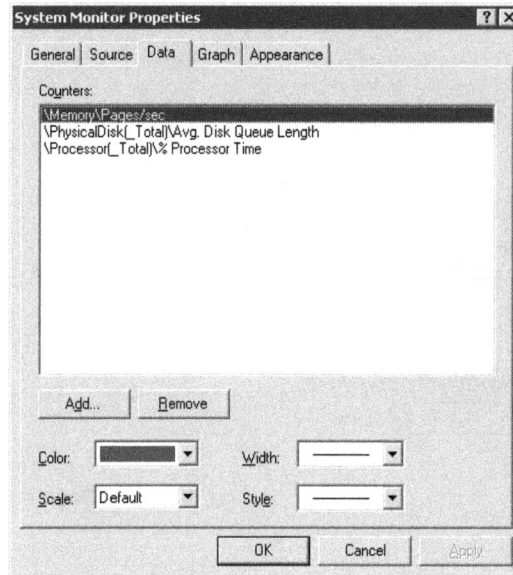

Figure 13.2   System Monitor properties.

There are several ways you can save data from the monitor. Besides the Clipboard option described previously, you can add the control, as discussed earlier, to a host application. You can also preserve the look and feel of the display and save the display to HTML. To do this, right-click the pane and select the option to save to the HTML file.

It is also possible to export the log data as comma-separated (CSV) or tab-separated (.tsv) format, and then import the data in a spreadsheet and write it to a database, where you can report on it using SQL Server Reporting or Crystal Reports.

From the Add Counters dialog box, you also can select exactly the counters and instances you wish to monitor from a list. However, the more you need to monitor, the more system resources you use. To keep the monitoring impact low, when you have a large amount of monitors and counters working, you can redirect the data to log files and then read the log file data in the display offline. Or, better yet, strive to use fewer counters and instances. You can also load two instances of System Monitor into the Performance consoles, which makes it easier to compare data from different sources.

Performance Logs and Alerts

There are two types of performance related logs available on the Windows Server 2003 platform: counter logs and trace logs. You can use these logs for advanced performance analysis and also for periodic record keeping.

Of bigger interest to us here is the alerting mechanism. The Performance Logs and Alerts tree is shown in Figure 13.3. You start the tools in the same fashion as described earlier.

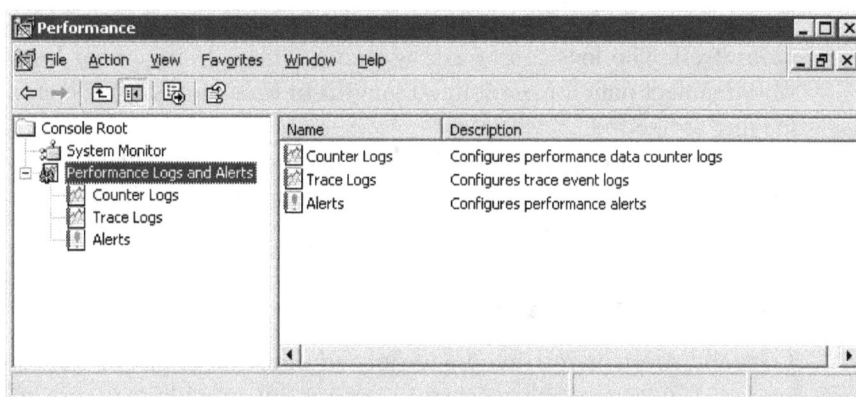

Figure 13.3   The Performance Logs and Alerts tree.

Counter logs record data you have sampled off hardware and system services based on performance objects provided by the operating system. The service makes use of counters in the same way System Monitor does. The data is obtained from the operating system when the update interval elapses.

The trace logs mechanism collects the event traces. Trace logs let you measure the performance associated with events related to aspects of the systems, such as memory, storage file I/O, and the like. Whenever an event occurs, its data is piped to the logs. The data captured is analyzed from the start of the event to the end of the event. This is in contrast to the sampling activity of the system monitor.

The alert system triggers an alert on a defined counter. It can then send a network message, execute a program, or start a log based on the event. You can use this system to monitor your server or network. For example, you can easily monitor activity considered suspect and define an alert to let you know when the event occurs. One popular use of the system is to watch a *honey pot*, a deliberate baiting of a network or system resource, that would attract a hacker. The alert can trigger a notification event when the honey pot is attacked.

Another good use of the alert service is you can instruct it to report to the event log when a particular resource drops below or exceeds predefined values, thresholds, or baselines.

Besides being able to view the counter logs in System Monitor or saved to CSV and TSV files, where they can be viewed in a spreadsheet or report software, you can also configure the logs to be circular. This means when the log file reaches a predetermined size, it begins to overwrite itself. The logs can be configured as linear. Using linear logs, you would collect data for predefined lengths of time, and start and stop the logging as needed.

The files also can be saved to various formats and, like the System Monitor, you can import the entire control OCX into a custom application or Web page.

Using Logs and Alerts

Logs and Alerts is restricted and only administrators have Full Control access. You can enable access to groups by providing access to the registry subkey HKEY_CURRENT_MACHINE\SYSTEM\CurrentControlSet\Services\SysmonLog\Log_Queries. In addition, running or configuring the service is also only available to administrators. The entire monitoring facility can be opened to group membership through Group Policy.

You can start using the Logs and Alerts application by right-clicking the details pane and selecting the New Log Settings option from the Contact menu. You are asked to name the log or alert and then you can define its properties.

When you choose the Properties option, the Counter Log Properties or Trace Log Properties dialog box loads. This is illustrated in Figure 13.4 and Figure 13.5, respectively.

To begin setting up the alert system, you would first need to configure counters for the alerts, the sample interval, and the alert threshold. You then need to decide what action must be taken when the event occurs. As discussed, the action can be one of many actions, but with Microsoft Operations Manager waiting to see the events, in this case, we simply instruct the system to write to the event log.

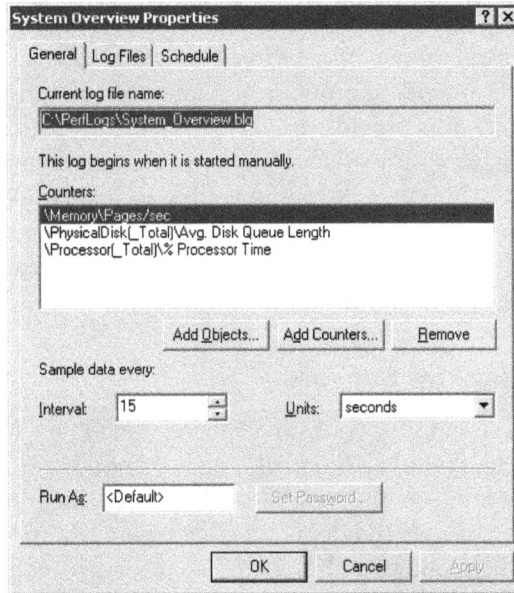

Figure 13.4   The Counter Log properties.

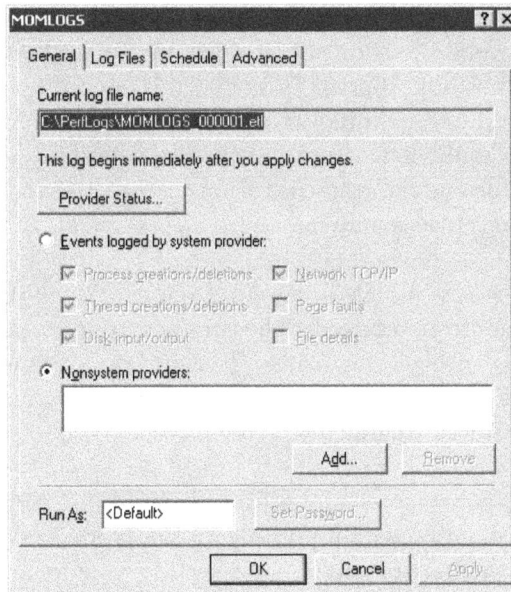

Figure 13.5   The Trace Log properties.

If you plan to configure Counter Logs, then you need to set the counter log counters and provide them with their sample intervals. You also need to provide a number of parameters if you plan to write to log files. You need to provide a file type, size, and path and any automatic naming parameters needed. Finally, for counter logs you need to specify them as SCV files or TSV files, text files, or binary linear or circular files.

You can configure Counter logs to start automatically. However, if the log file is configured to stop manually, it will not automatically restart. This holds true for Trace Logs as well.

Monitoring the Servers

How can you monitor your server if you don't know how it's supposed to perform when times are good? If you have nothing to compare it against, no data that reflects the baseline or metric considered a healthy system, you will not be able to adequately determine whether a system's performance is beginning to slip. Thus, you need to collect a considerable amount of data during normal operations and then use that data later when you compare additionally collected data against it.

Collect data over several weeks, even months, and then use that data to establish a baseline against which to base future analysis. It makes no sense to say a system is running *normally* when you have no data that can confirm whether it is or not. It does not help either to assert that just because a machine appears to be idle, it is operating normally. And there might actually be nothing wrong with the machine, in which case, the idle state should alert you to investigate why there is no activity. If you expect traffic and the traffic does not materialize, you need to start looking in various places, network interfaces, services, and hard disks, and so on.

As long as you have a baseline, you can be alerted to performance that appears to be unusual. The memory counter on a mail server, for example, is an ideal mechanism to alert you to unusual activity on the server. If Exchange is under attack, the memory counter can be used to post an alert that an attack is taking place.

Take notes of periods of low usage, average usage, and high or peak usage. If your servers are providing real-time communications, they should be monitored continuously for this type of information.

As we demonstrate in the next section, you do not need to bog down your servers with continued data collection. Gather data in the early life of the server and then at certain times during its service. Then configure the Alert system to fire events into the event log when data begins to signal behavior that deviates from what you consider the norm.

Monitoring for Bottlenecks

Table 13.1 lists some thresholds for a minimum set of system counters.

Table 13.1 System Counters

Item	Resource	Object	Counter	Threshold
1	Disk	LogicalDisk	% Free space	15%
2	Disk	LogicalDisk	% Disk Time	80%
3	Disk	Physical Disk	Disk Reads/sec, Disk Writes/sec	See manufacturer's recommendations
4	Disk	Physical Disk	Current Disk Length Queue	Number of spindles, plus 2
5	Memory	Memory	Available Bytes	4MB minimum
6	Memory	Memory	Pages/sec	20 per second
7	Network	Network Segment	% Network Utilization	30%
8	Paging File	Paging File	% Usage	More than 70%
9	Processor	Processor	% processor time	85%
10	Processor	Processor	Interrupts/sec	1500/sec
11	Server	Server	Total bytes	
12	Server	Server	Work item shortages	3
13	Server	Server work queues	Queue length	4
14	Multiple Processors	System Processor	Queue length	2

The values in Table 13.1 are recommended for minimum performance monitoring. Your options may not be exactly the same, but what you have here is enough for you to start establishing a baseline. The following notes offer guidance and correspond with some of the options listed in Table 13.1:

- **LogicalDisk:** We list a threshold of 15 percent; this may be too low depending on what the machine is being used for. Technology such as disk quotas may cause the threshold to suddenly increase; so you need to take issues like this into account. We configure alerts when the threshold is exceeded.
- **LogicalDisk:** The value indicated for Disk Time must be considered a usage period. In other words, the disk should not be used more than 90 percent of the time. Before you settle on the value, see what the disk manufacturer suggests. If work caused the disk time to exceed recommended values, the disk may fail. Don't be surprised if the disk overheats and crashes if it exceeds 100 percent.
- **PhysicalDisk:** Examine your disk for transfer rate information. Set up the system to alert you if the monitor reports rates are exceeding this. This information also tells you whether the disks should be upgraded to faster technology (15,000 RPM instead of 10,000 RPM, for example).
- **PhysicalDisk:** Here we talk about the number of spindles, which is a snapshot. Observe this value over several intervals. You can also use the Avg. Disk Queue Length.
- **Memory:** If you run out of RAM, paging activity begins to increase and system response begins to wane to the point that the OS reports it is low on resources. Watch memory closely.
- **Network:** The Network value depends on the type of network you are running, which is likely to be Ethernet. An Ethernet network's typical threshold should be around 30 percent.
- **Paging File:** The paging file is a complex piece of technology and its behavior can vary according to the nature of your hardware and the number and type of applications you have running. Before you investigate this counter, you should first become familiar with how paging works (the same goes for the other counters, some of them more so than others).
- **Processor:** Task Manager is the application most administrators reach to check out what the processor is doing. It's a great tool for observing Processor Time and which applications are monopolizing the CPU. If you see processor usage hitting the 85 percent

and higher mark, you have a cause for concern. Instead of logging onto the server every day to check out the health of the CPU, this counter should be programmed to alert you to excessive CPU usage. It also points the way if you need to upgrade the CPU or additional processors. The server work queues are another snap-shot counter that may signify a processor bottleneck. You should observe this counter over several intervals.

■ **Server:** This counter plays an important role in server health. Watching this counter can tell you if you have a hardware prob-lem somewhere. It reports interrupt activity. Thus, any increase in interrupts may point to disk controllers, network interface cards, and so on. The server counter also lets you sum the total Bytes/sec for all servers, and if the value is equal to the maximum transfer rate for the network, you have some data that points to possible segmenting you need to do.

Let's now look at the workload of specific servers types.

Understanding Your Server's Workload

It is useful to categorize your servers according to the key roles they play. While we like to think the days of server failures are over, they aren't. If you are catering to a medium to large enterprise, you typically dedicate a server to this function. Exchange has its own server as does SQL Server, and most certainly your domain controllers should be left to be domain controllers and nothing else.

Smaller companies that cannot afford multiple servers may find a DC can easily double as a file server, a firewall server, SQL Server, and so forth. Have a look at any small implementation of Windows Small Busi-ness Server 2003, and you'll find it running just about every Microsoft server product available, even IIS for the company Web site.

Application servers are your typical standard application servers and terminal service servers that host multiple user connections or user ses-sions. A terminal server service can be very demanding and require con-stant performance monitoring. This is especially true of servers in which multiple copies of memory-intensive applications, such as Microsoft Word, are opened by a large number of users. Memory and CPU can come under heavy workload and, thus, objects to monitor include cache, memory, processors, and the system.

Backup servers constantly read from the network and can create bottlenecks on the network. They also tend to suffer from extensive CPU usage. You should monitor not only the backup server's systems, but also the remote server's Processor and Network Segment objects during the backup window.

Database servers impact disks and CPU. You need fast hard disks for database servers, dedicated SCSI disk controller cards, and you should monitor objects such as the PhysicalDisk, LogicalDisk, Processor, and System.

The most important server to watch on a network is the domain controller. Domain controllers consume many different resources, including CPUs, disks, memory, and networks. Monitor Memory, CPU, System, Network Segment, Network Interface, and the protocol counter objects, such as TCP, UDP, IP, NBT, connection, and so forth. You should also monitor Active Directory's NTDS service objects and the Site Server LDAP service objects. Monitoring WINS and DNS also helps issue alerts that may point to an attack.

Domain controllers are the prime target of hackers aiming to trash your network with denial of service (DOS) attacks. They'll go after DNS and WINS, which if corrupted can render the directory service inoperable. It's critical that you always monitor the networking services on the DC.

File and Print Servers are constantly accessed by users. They can consume too much hard disk space and network resources, which impact their performance. Keep Memory, Network Segment, Physical Disk, and Logical Disk objects in check. You should also monitor the PrintQueue object to troubleshoot spooling. Look for heavy queue usage. If you get an alert that the print queue has passed what you consider normal for hourly spooled jobs, it's a sign of trouble at the printer (such as toner shortage, paper jams, loss of network to printer, and so on).

As mentioned in the previous chapter, Exchange needs high performance disks and disk volume topology. Exchange also uses CPU, disks, and memory the heaviest. Monitor the memory collection, Cache, Processor, System, PhysicalDisk and LogicalDisk objects. Exchange puts a number of its own objects on to the server dedicated to Exchange health monitoring.

Internet Information Server (IIS) consumes extensive disk, cache, and network components and, thus, you should monitor the Cache, Network Segment, PhysicalDisk, and LogicalDisk objects.

Performance Monitoring Tips

As mentioned earlier, performance monitoring places some overhead on your servers, and you should be aware that too much monitoring could impact a server. The last thing you want to observe in the data that points to excessive resource consumptions is that the *monitoring* is the key reason the server is unresponsive.

System Monitor is demanding. If you need to do some serious analysis, export data to the logs instead of displaying graphs. You can then export the data to SQL Server or some other data format and report on the data offline.

Use only the number of counters deemed essential for the analysis at hand. Counters may be costly and can increase overhead as mentioned earlier. See the *Performance Counters Reference* for Windows Server 2003 in the Windows Server 2003 Deployment Kit. Counter overhead data is available in this document.

Be aware the very narrow data collection intervals also place a strain on resources. If you are unsure of the interval, the rule of thumb is a ten-minute interval.

You should also monitor during peak usage periods to obtain the best assessment of resource usage. Monitoring an idle system just makes no sense. Take care not to impact resources the server needs for serving your customers.

One final recommendation is to monitor remotely if possible. With remote monitoring, you would set up an architecture for centralized data collection. This might involve setting up an analysis server or a report server onto which you can drop your monitoring logs and run analysis applications. Consider making the monitoring server part of your MOM infrastructure (this is discussed next). Be mindful, again, that too much downloading of *heavy* data to a monitoring machine can impact the network.

Invest in a fast external USB hard disk drive that you can attach to a monitored server. Instead of pulling the files across the network, you can save the data to the external drive and then move it to the monitoring server. The instant recognition of the USB external disk makes it perfect for moving logs from source to target servers.

Microsoft Operations Manager

If you have spent some part of your MIS life managing servers, configuring counters and alerts, scavenging event logs and the task manager, and so on, you must have wished a product was available that could automatically do everything we have discussed in the first part of this chapter and in previous chapters. There is such a product. It is called Microsoft Operations Manager (MOM).

MOM is just one of several products that comprises Microsoft's collection of system and operations management products. Not satisfied to let the likes of IBM (with its Tivoli enterprise management system), HP (with OpenManage), and so on dominate the systems management market, Microsoft set out long before Windows 2000 to create products specializing in the systems and operations management of its own operating systems.

Microsoft's operations and systems management sojourn started in the 1990s with the advent of Systems Management Server (SMS). SMS is Microsoft's Change Management and Configuration Management product. SMS is responsible for remote management, licensing, hardware inventory, software distribution, remote control, and reporting.

For many years, SMS carried the reputation of being one of Microsoft's most complex products to master. It also lagged years behind the advent of Active Directory and Windows 2000. This allowed Microsoft to lose much of the systems management market share to its competitors.

However, with the purchase of the MOM code from NetIQ Corporation, when it was little more than a log "scraper," the advent of SMS 2003, MOM 2000, and MOM 2005, Microsoft has taken back much of the market share it lost in the 1990s. It's not because its recent products are superior; it has more to do with the Microsoft Solutions Framework (MSF) and Microsoft Operations Framework (MOF), discussed in Chapter 1, "The World of High-Performance, High Availability Windows Computing," which provides a holistic framework that Microsoft Certified Professionals are comfortable operating in. When it comes to system and operations management, it is, in fact, far better to use Microsoft's own products.

Both MOM and SMS are going to be integrated into one systems and operations management product called *System Center 2005*. A comprehensive discussion of SMS is beyond the scope of this book. We are primarily interested in MOM, however, as the key tool to monitor system performance and operations management. To make sure our high-performance and highly available systems remain operating and available, we need to use a high-performance and highly available operations management tool.

MOM's central task in your operations arsenal is to provide comprehensive event management, monitoring and alerting, reporting, and operational trend analysis. The software has the capability to consolidate events and analyze the data in such a way it can be configured to report to you, in real-time, which events are of critical importance to you. You configure MOM to respond to these events by contacting you, the help desk, or IT staff by phone, email, page, fax, and so on. You can also configure MOM to resolve the event automatically.

For the record, MOM 2005 provides the following services:

- **Distributed event management:** MOM captures a wide variety of system and application events from Windows-based computers that are distributed throughout an enterprise IT environment and collects them in a central database.
- **Performance monitoring:** You can configure MOM to monitor key performance thresholds. You can monitor performance trends by using a predefined set of rules or customized rules. Additionally, you can set thresholds that generate alerts and actions in response to performance changes.
- **Enterprise-class scalability:** MOM manages events for networks of all sizes, from small-business networks to enterprise networks. By using a three-tier architecture, you can design systems running MOM that can handle hundreds of millions of events per day, with full redundancy and workload distribution.
- **Mission-critical availability:** MOM provides mission-critical availability of the servers and of the MOM database itself. You can eliminate single points of failure by using MOM database clustering and redundant DCAMs.
- **Global systems support:** MOM can monitor localized servers and applications.
- **Interoperability:** MOM with WMI can collect a wide range of events and performance data from any Windows 2000-based system.
- **SNMP:** You can configure MOM to monitor SNMP event data (traps) for any specified devices. Additionally, you can set MOM to generate SNMP trap messages. MOM can deliver such traps to

a third-party SNMP management console. This lets MOM send data into third-party management systems, including network and enterprise management frameworks.

- **Shades of X:** Further, you can use the Syslog protocol to have MOM monitor live event streams generated by UNIX-based systems and by many network devices.

MOM was once called the killer log scraper of all time. But it is now a lot more sophisticated. In fact, it is essential for any IT team minding a shop of cluster servers, load-balanced servers, and servers running the likes of Exchange, SQL Server, ISA Server, and so on. MOM pulls data as server events log them. The data is transferred to consolidation services and finally makes its way into one or more SQL Server databases on the network.

In addition to the basic event monitoring tools, MOM also provides the following features:

- Allowing non-English environments to be managed through improved international language support.
- Improving performance and scalability to let you monitor twice as many servers as before.
- Providing support for installing the MOM database on a SQL Server Cluster.
- Adding updates to Microsoft Exchange 2000 and Active Directory Management Pack modules.
- Adding new Management Packs modules for Microsoft .NET Framework, Network Load Balancing, and Server Clusters.
- Server Status Monitor (SSM).
- New testing and debugging tools that let you test scripts prior to production use.
- A data warehousing process and tool.

MOM SDK2 includes documentation and samples for two-way connectors, integrations of user-interface views, creation of management packs, and better support for managing third-party platforms.

Back in Chapters 4, "Highly Available Networks" and 5 "Preparing the Platform for a High-Performance Network," and in several places in this book, we mentioned how critical it is you come up with a formal nomenclature and naming convention document for your entire architecture (see the section "Naming Conventions" in Chapter 5). This document should be used like a data dictionary and it is critical you name all your services according to this document, primarily for MOM.

In other words, as you can see from the example shown, name all your primary onboard network interface cards on your servers as *primary–onboard* or something similar. Heartbeat or private networks for clusters can have names like *heartbeat*. Now when MOM reports an event, it can tell you the *primary–onboard* NIC on server01 has failed. And you know exactly what that means. If the heartbeat NIC failed and the message you received is *network interface 1 card on blah blah blah failed*, how would you know if it's just the private NIC or what users need to connect to?

Do the same thing for all your cluster resources. Should a group on a certain cluster fail over, then you know exactly which group on what cluster has failed over. In previous chapters, we told you what you needed to set up on the various servers with respect to MOM. Now let's look at a minimum MOM installation to cater to your immediate needs.

MOM Rapid Fire Deployment

Let's be quite clear: You need to install and test MOM in a lab before you attempt to deploy it into production. Of course, you need to do this with all your new systems, but if you think you can wing it with MOM to save time, forget it. You are almost certainly going to end up pulling the solution out by the roots and starting again from the beginning. Also, MOM installs bits on all your machines on the network. As with SMS 2003, you need to be careful not to compromise existing operations.

There are many different ways to get MOM going in your organization, and, until you know what it does and how it does it in the lab, you will not be able to plan an enterprise-wide deployment. This chapter is designed to help you get a basic MOM installation going in the lab and then from there design a system for production. We'll also show you how MOM can be used to report on the event architecture. Anything more advanced on this comprehensive tool is beyond the scope of this book. First, let's get an understanding of what MOM is made of.

MOM comprises a number of user interfaces referred to as *consoles*. The consoles are all accessible from the MOM Administrator Console, MOM's interactive dashboard. These consoles provide a window to the various configuration groups, installation options, agent options, alerting, operator setup, and more.

Central to MOM management are configuration groups. These are comprised of the following components:

- **MOM Database:** Microsoft SQL Server is the database that stores all configuration and monitoring data for MOM.
- **MOM DCAM**: This is the central MOM server. DCAM stands for *data consolidator*.
- **MOM Agents:** Agents are processes that run on the monitored server that gather the data to send to the DCAM.
- **MOM Administrator console:** This is the main MOM user interface.
- **Active monitoring agents:** Based on the rule-sets that are defined by the administrators at a central console, MOM agents provide a high degree of active monitoring. These local agents filter, collect, and consolidate event data. They can trigger actions locally. This architecture minimizes the traffic MOM creates on the network, and it allows critical data to flow freely to administrators.

In the remainder of this chapter, we are going to create a single management group for MOM. You can create and alter management groups after you have installed MOM. In fact, the process of installing MOM requires the setup of a default management group.

So what's in a MOM management group? They comprise the MOM database, one or more MOM Management Servers, the MOM Administrator console and MOM Operator console, the managed computers—that have agents on them—the MOM Reporting console, and the MOM Web console. You can set up all these components or you can install them on a single computer. It all depends on the architecture and the size of the installation. The components can be installed on multiple machines.

For larger shops, you want to install the MOM database, Management Servers, and System Center 2005 Reporting on several computers. When the MOM components are spread out over several computers, you obtain better performance. There is also a big debate raging in the IT community about installing MOM directly on a SQL Server, which implies it should be dedicated to the MOM data. But we eschew this.

The network is fast enough and the SQL Server system is easily able to cope with the queries to the server. However, you cannot install the first MOM bits to any remote SQL Server. You have to run Setup on a SQL Server and select to only install the database. Then you can install bits to other servers and simply point the MOM installation to your new SQL Server MOM database.

If you have a formal data tier in your architecture, such as the SQL Server clusters and SAN given as an example in Chapter 9, "High Availability, High-Performance SQL Server Solutions," then there is no reason to spend more money on additional SQL Server installations.

In the remainder of this chapter, we demonstrate installing MOM on two Management Servers, which provides for the much-vaunted agent failover. In other words agents can report to either server if the primary server is lost. This way, you lessen the risk of losing important event data. As part of the lab, however, you can create a single management group with a single Management Server, which does not provide for failover.

Verifying Software and Hardware Requirements

First, from your new designated MOM server, you can run the Prerequisite Checker in MOM Setup to check the hardware and software prerequisites and to create a report that lists what your computer requires to run MOM 2005.

The checker checks whether the computer can host a MOM component or agent and ensures all the software requirements are met. If your server does not have the required software, you can either remove the server from the deployment plan or install the required software. If you do not have SQL Server Service Pack 3 (SP3), the checker has cause to complain. Also, you need to have the SQL Server agent running in Auto startup configuration for the agent checker to give you a pass.

As discussed in Chapter 6, make sure the new server you plan to install has been fully patched with the appropriate security updates, hotfixes, and service packs. You should install a Windows Update Server (WUS) or SMS server in your lab to do this for you. Under no circumstance should you install a new operating system exposed to the Internet without first locking down and patching up your server.

The checker also ensures your server hosts a certain MOM component or agent and ensures the minimum hardware requirements can be met. If the server fails the hardware test, you can fix the problems identified and then recheck the server. You need to be sure the server has sufficient disk space on the server. If you can, use a dedicated computer for the production MOM database. You can test the MOM architecture on a multi-purpose server in the lab, but you should use dedicated servers out in production.

MOM Service Accounts

Service accounts are the next step to take. MOM uses two principle service accounts. You should not use the same account for both service accounts, and it is our recommendation you stay away from multi-use Domain Administrator accounts and the Local System account. The two principle service accounts are

- **MOM Management Server Action account (MSA):** You can create this account in your Service Accounts OU as mom.msa.sa. This is the account MOM uses to automatically install agents on servers and to run the discovery processes prior to agent installation. This account enables a Management Server to communicate with and to run actions on agentless-managed computers. It is also used to collect data from the registry and event logs of agentless-managed computers and on the local computer on which the Management Server is installed.
- **Data Access Server (DAS) account:** Create this account as mom.dsa.sa. This is the account that obtains centralized access to the MOM database.

Treat your MOM security accounts with the utmost respect and protect them from compromise. Remember these accounts have deep access to all your servers, especially domain controllers. Incidentally, Microsoft publishes a Microsoft Operations Manager 2005 Security Guide, which you should read. It provides much more information on the security accounts than we have space for in this book.

MOM Database Sizing

The next step you need to do is calculate the size of the MOM database. It's critical you decide now what the size should be because, after you install MOM, you cannot (easily) change the database size. If you have a small site of, say, 20 servers, then a database of between 5 and 7GB is more than enough. Also, the database size depends on a number of issues. For example, if you are upgrading or migrating from MOM 2000, the database sizing requirements you were met with when MOM first emerged have not changed. MOM database size depends on the following items:

- The number of computers MOM monitors. The more computers, the more data, the bigger the database.
- The number of events, alerts, and performance data MOM collects. If you gather just about every squeak on a server, you'll need a database so big MOM will not even start up.
- The type and number of Management Packs to be installed. The more management packs, the more data you are reporting on.
- The rate and frequency you are grooming the MOM database. Like all databases, if you neglect them, you'll end up with transaction logs resembling the trans-Siberian railway.

MOM can support databases up to 30GB in size, but you don't really want to go that big. Use a smaller size if possible. The reason for going smaller is performance. Databases larger than 15GB can be less responsive to events and alerts than smaller databases. We are not saying SQL Server cannot easily cope with very large MOM databases; it's just a best practice to keep your database size below 15GB because a smaller database can respond more quickly to events and alerts.

MOM automatically sets the size of the SQL Server log file (SDF) to 20 percent of the size of the database file (MDF) when you first install it. In other words, if you specify the database file size should be 2GB, MOM automatically sets the log file to 400MB. Leave MOM to set the default log file size. If you set a database to 7GB, MOM makes the log about 1.2GB.

Determining the database size is another reason we design our MOM system in the lab first. In a lab environment, we are able to estimate the database size we might need for a given number of managed computers.

Incidentally, the MOM 2000 SP1 shipped with a "Performance and Sizing" whitepaper. While the paper is aimed at MOM 2000, the underlying architecture is very much the same and you should read before settling on the final database size. By the time you get to read this chapter, Microsoft probably will have updated this whitepaper for MOM 2005.

It is also important to ensure your SQL Server implementation is sound. While this is not the forum to discuss best practices for SQL Server, you should not install a MOM SQL Server database on the same volume as the operating system. You do not want to install the database and log files for MOM on the same drive as the Windows Server 2003 paging file.

Follow best practices for installing SQL Server on high-performance volumes, either locally on the server on RAID-5 or RAID-10 arrays, or on RAID-5 or RAID-10 volumes on your SAN. Read Chapter 9, which covers SQL Server best practices. Also, for maximum availability of your MOM databases, there is no harm attaching them to your SQL Server cluster.

Design

Ready one or two MOM servers, join them to the Active Directory domain, and name them DRMOM01 and DRMOM02 or something similar. These servers are your Management Servers that host the main MOM monitoring and management components.

The MOM Administrator console and the MOM Operator console can be installed on either one of the aforementioned Management Servers, or both. You can also install the consoles on a management workstation, which is highly recommended.

At this point, your SQL Server also is ready to receive the MOM databases, as are the test servers that receive MOM monitoring agents as part of the discovery process. The design and architecture is illustrated in Figure 13.6.

The MOM database, the Management Servers, and the managed computers all become part of a single management group, which you can call HQ or DR or a much longer label. You should also include your workstations with the MOM Administrator consoles in this group, as well as the MOM Operator console and the System Center 2005 Data Warehouse.

The default MOM management packs described earlier in this chapter are also installed as part of the setup. But the installation of the management packs occurs after the management servers have completed installation. After the MOM Management Servers are in place, you have to import additional Management Packs from the MOM 2005 distribution CD. Management packs should, if possible, be imported only after the computer discovery process has run and you have deployed agents, and, if desired, you installed System Center 2005 Reporting.

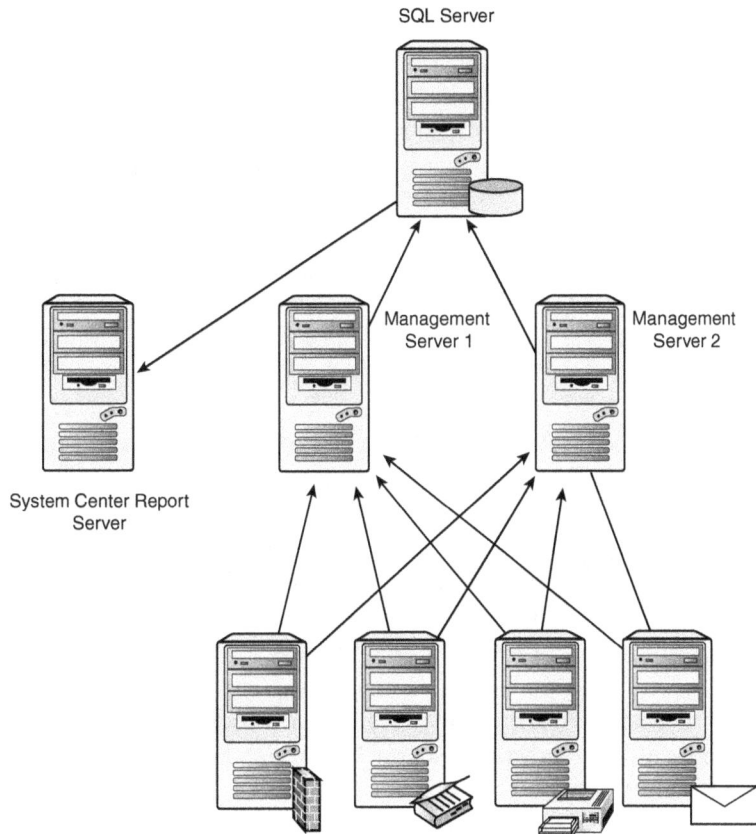

Figure 13.6   Microsoft Operations Manager architecture and design.

SQL Server Notes

Before you install MOM, consider the following SQL Server configuration data. Limit the amount of memory SQL Server uses by configuring the memory to be static, instead of dynamic. See Chapter 9 for more specifics on how to do this. The idea, of course, is to limit SQL Server from using too much system memory. SQL Server can cause page faults and reduce the performance of the operating system on which SQL Server depends if you just let it consume all available memory on the server.

You can monitor the MOM server itself for paging file issues, memory, and performance using the counters discussed in the first part of this chapter. We show you this after the installation described here completes. If MOM alerts its own server may be headed for trouble, you are able to intervene and reduce the demand on memory or install additional memory if needed. There is one caveat to what we just described. The action may result in reduced MOM performance; so you should watch memory usage on the MOM server carefully.

To calculate the fixed amount of memory you should use, subtract the memory required by your operating system and any other critical services or SQL Server instances running on the server from your total available RAM. The remainder can be set for the fixed memory setting.

To configure SQL Server memory, do as follows:

1. Open SQL Server Enterprise Manager.
2. Expand Microsoft SQL Servers, and then expand SQL Server Group.
3. Right-click the server to be configured, and then click Properties.
4. Select the Memory tab and click Use a Fixed Memory Size (MB). You are able to move the slider control to specify the amount of RAM you want to allocate for SQL Server.

After you have the memory requirements (both RAM and database size) fixed, you are ready to install the MOM databases.

Installing MOM Databases

To install the MOM database, do as follows:

1. Log onto the designated MOM server as a server administrator, close all open applications, insert the MOM 2005 CD, and double-click setup.exe. The Microsoft Operations Manager 2005 Setup Resources dialog box loads. This dialog box is illustrated in Figure 13.7.
2. Click Install Microsoft Operations Manager 2005. This action starts the MOM 2005 Setup Wizard. On the Installation Options page, click Custom.
3. Next, the Custom dialog box loads. Now expand all components except the MOM 2005 Database, which is not yet available.

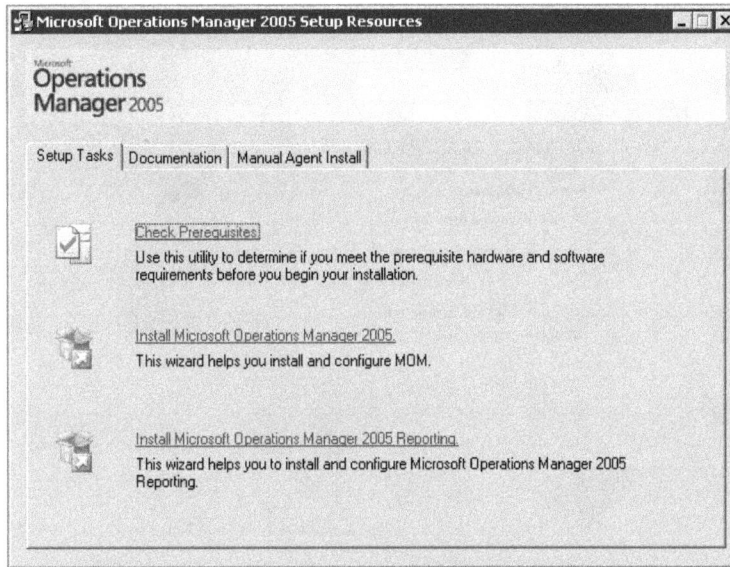

Figure 13.7   Microsoft Operations Manager 2005 Setup Resources.

The Prerequisite Check page loads and indicates whether you have met all the requirements for installing the MOM database, as discussed earlier in this section. The Prerequisite Check is available on the Setup Resources page as well. See Figure 13.8.

4. On the SQL Server Database Instance page, shown in Figure 13.9, click the server instance on the SQL or MSDE Service Instance list on which you want to install the MOM database. Setup automatically starts the MSSQLSERVER and SQLSERVERAGENT services when you install and uninstall MOM on a server with SQL Server locally installed. If you are gong to remove MOM from the server after setup, MOM needs to stop and restart the Windows Management Instrumentation service.

By default, the MOM 2005 Setup Wizard installs the data file and log file on the same hard disk drive. Follow the guidelines discussed earlier in this chapter for installing the data file and log file on different hard disk drives.

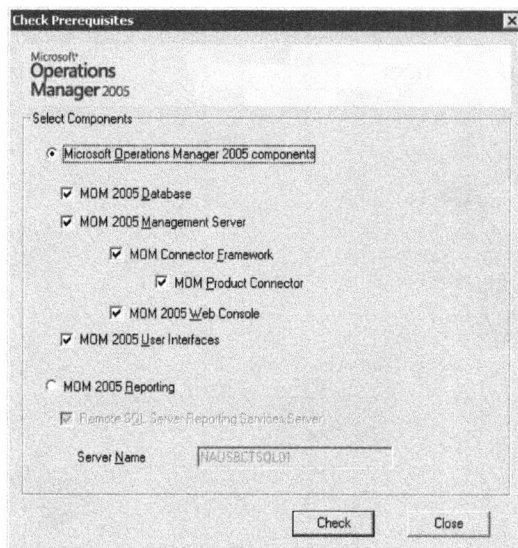

Figure 13.8   Check Prerequisites.

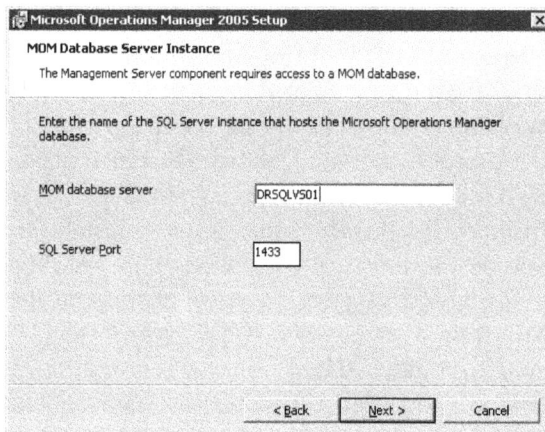

Figure 13.9   Selecting the SQL Server for MOM.

5. Specify the size of the MOM database. This is an important step. Make sure you enter the correct options, as shown in Figure 13.10.

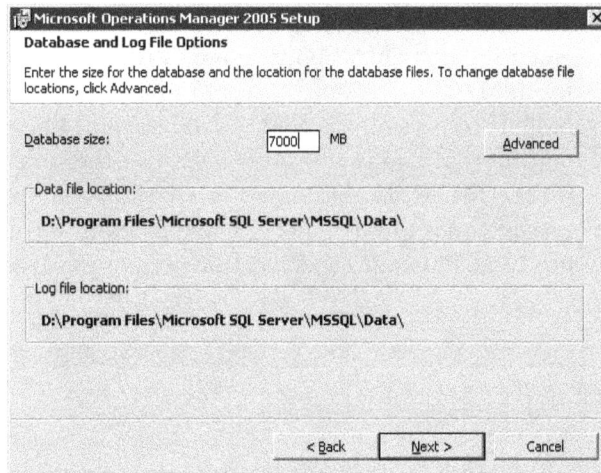

Figure 13.10   Database size.

6. On the Management Group Name page, shown in Figure 13.11, type the name you want to use for the management group. Keep it simple. If the MOM server is going to be keeping an eye on the server in the main office, call it HQ, or something similar.

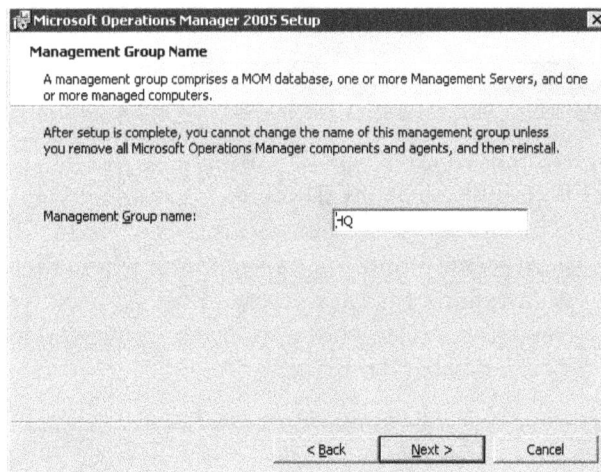

Figure 13.11   Specifying the Management Group Name.

7. Your next page is the Data Access Server (DAS) Account page. Enter the domain account you want Management Servers to use for the DAS to log onto and communicate with the MOM database. If you install the MOM database and Management Server on different computers, you must use the same DAS Account for the MOM database and for all Management Servers in the management group. This is a requirement for installation. Figure 13.12 illustrates specification of the service accounts.

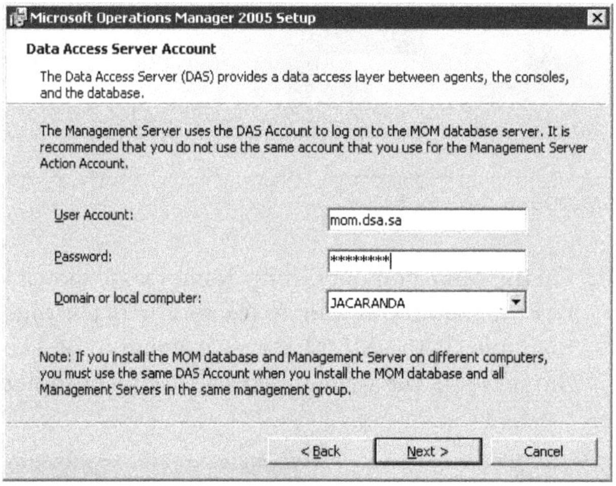

Figure 13.12   Specifying service accounts.

8. On the MOM Error Reporting page, select the Enable Error Reporting checkbox. This is an optional setting, and you also can automatically send service error reports to Microsoft. MOM stores error reports on the computer where they occur. You can store reports for later access. The next time you log onto the computer, a dialog box appears and gives you a chance to send the accumulated reports.

9. The last important pages require you to tell MOM about your environment. This page is called the Active Directory Configuration page, and it is shown in Figure 13.13. On this page, select the appropriate option for your environment for this management group. You need to select if all computers on your network are in Active Directory domains that trust each other. MOM uses mutual authentication for all communication between Management Servers and agents within the management group.

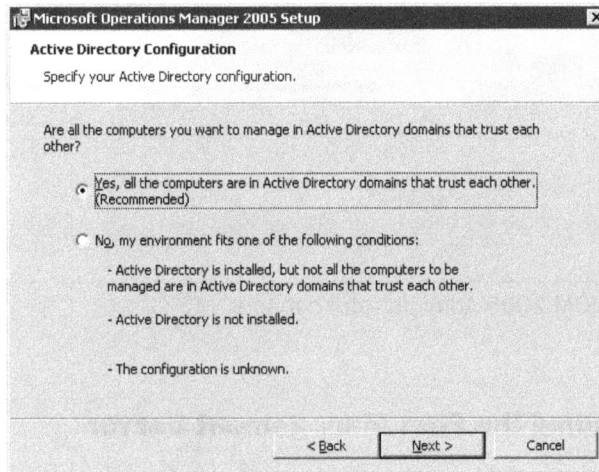

Figure 13.13   Active Directory Configuration.

10. On the Ready to Install page, click Install.

You are now ready to install the first of the management servers, and you have access to the first MOM 2005 Administrator Console, as shown in Figure 13.14.

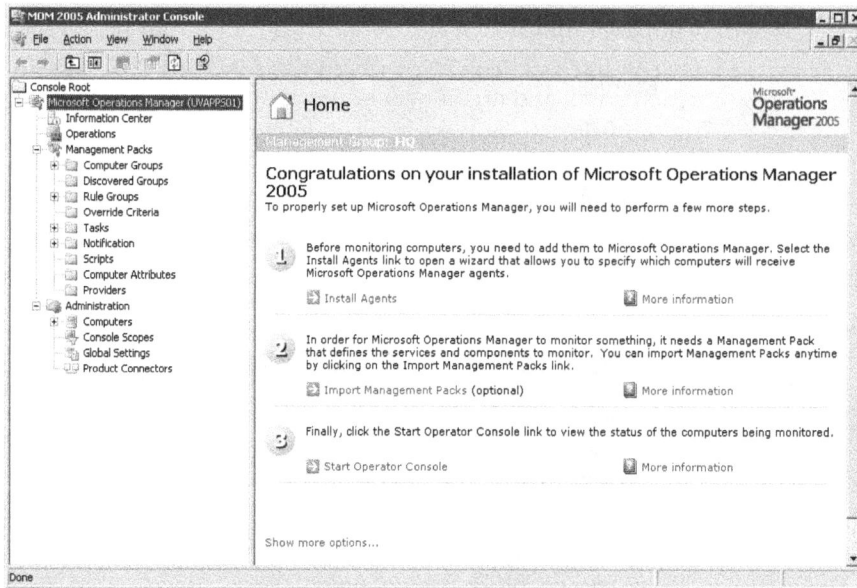

Figure 13.14   MOM 2005 Administrator console.

Installing the First Management Server

From the first Management Server, log on and double-click Setup again on the MOM 2005 CD.

1. In the Microsoft Operations Manager 2005 Setup Resources dialog box, click Install Microsoft Operations Manager 2005 to start the MOM 2005 Setup Wizard.
2. On the Installation Options page, select Custom.
3. On the Custom Setup page, expand the MOM 2005 Database, and then click This Component Will Not Be Available.
4. If you do not want to install the MOM Administrator console and the MOM Operator console on the same computer, expand the MOM 2005 User Interfaces, and then click This Component Will Not Be Available.

If you want to install the MOM 2005 Web console, expand MOM 2005 Web Console, and then click This Component Will Be Installed on Local Hard Drive. You can only install the Web console on a Management Server.

Do not install the Microsoft Connector Framework or the MOM Product Connector under the MOM 2005 Management Server component at this time. These components are required only for tiered management groups and, by default, they are not installed.

After the base installation procedures, you can then select the database server. Type the name of the SQL Server instance on which the MOM database is installed on the MOM Database Server Instance page.

MOM attempts to connect to the SQL Server with OLE DB. It uses SQL Server port 1433 by default. You can use a different SQL Server port, so long as you specify your custom port value on this page.

After selecting the databases you are prompted for the service accounts. Enter a domain account that you want the Management Server to use to communicate with, run responses on, and perform actions on managed computers. Next is the Data Access Server Account page. Here you enter the account you want MOM to use for the DAS to communicate with the database.

You must use the same DAS account you used to install the MOM database, however, you should use different accounts for the MSA and the DAS service accounts.

After you have performed the initial install, you are able to install an additional nine Management Servers in the same management group, all sharing the same MOM database.

When you install additional Management Servers, ensure you

1. Select the option This Component Will Not Be Available for the MOM 2005 Database.
2. Point the installation to the same MOM database you used for the first Management Server.
3. Use the same Data Access Server account you used for the MOM database and the first Management Server. You can, however, use a different MOM Management Server Action account for each Management Server.

Installing the MOM Administrator and MOM Operator Consoles

The first thing to note about installing MOM is you cannot install the consoles on the same computer as the MOM database. Thus, when you install MOM for the first time, you first install the database on the database server and only install the database.

Second, before you install the consoles, set your display resolution to at least 1024×768, with 24-bit color or higher. This lets you see as much detail as possible in what can be very busy console trees.

To install the MOM Administrator console and the MOM Operator console, do the following:

1. Log on to the MOM server using an account with administrative credentials on the local computer. This account can be a Domain Admin account or a server admin account that is a member of the local Administrators group.
2. Close all open applications, such as Explorer and Computer Management, after you have located the MOM 2005 product CD and double-clicked setup.exe. The Microsoft Operations Manager 2005 Setup Resources dialog box now loads. Click Install Microsoft Operations Manager 2005 to start the MOM 2005 Setup Wizard.
3. The first page to load is the Installation Options page. Click Custom here, and then click Next. The Custom Setup page loads. Now expand all components except the MOM 2005 User Interfaces and click OK. The Prerequisite Check page loads with errors and warnings if you have issues to address. Otherwise, if it does not load, your system has met the requirements.
4. Next, on the Management Server page, enter the name of the Management Server to which you want the consoles to initially connect. Finally, on the Ready to Install page, click Install.

The MOM Administrator Console and the Operator Console are now ready for duty.

Discovering Computers and Deploying Agents

Now that you have your MOM database in place and the MOM console is up and running, you can begin to deploy agents. You use the Administrator Console to select computers you want MOM to discover and manage. But before MOM can take these servers under her wing, you first need to install agents on the servers.

NOTE: If you plan to have more than one Management Server in your management group, then you must first determine which Management Server will be the primary MOM host for each managed computer.

When you hear us talk about load balancing MOM, we are not talking about load balancing in the traditional sense, or like the NLB discussed in the previous two chapters. MOM does not actually support any software-based or hardware-based load balancing. But a MOM environment can consist of multiple Management Servers within a specific management group. The load balancing you can do here is limited to how you balance the workload between the servers. In other words, you load balance by distributing the number of managed computers across the Management Servers. You can also balance workload by creating multiple management groups.

Let's look at an example. Let's say our MOM management group contains two Management Servers, one in the HQ site and one in the DR site. We can then use one Management Server as the primary host for all the computers in HQ. The other Management Server can be the primary host for the servers in the DR site. Now you have effectively load balanced (albeit crudely) between the two Management Servers in the organization. The agents can be redirected to a second Management Server in the event their primary server is unavailable.

So let's now deploy agents to the servers. Open the MOM 2005 Administrator Console and click the root node in the console tree. The home page of your first management group loads in the right-hand detail pane. The first open lets you install agents to the computers. You can either browse for the servers or search for them according to search criteria. Until you are up-to-speed with MOM and have experience installing agents to the machines and wiring them up to MOM, browse for a single server and start working with that server. This is illustrated in Figure 13.15.

After you begin the process, you are prompted by MOM to enter the accounts used for the agent installation. Choose to install the agents with the Management Server Action (MSA) account we set up earlier. You are asked for an Agent Action Account; simply choose the Local System Account for this, if it has permission to install, or use a domain account with the capability to install software to the server. This account can be either a Domain Admin account or an account you explicitly add to the Administrators group of the server. You need to supply a password for an account other than Local System. Accept the remaining defaults, and then click Finish to install the agent to the server. Also make sure the logon domain controller adjacent to the MOM server has an updated copy of the catalog, or it might not recognize credentials until the installation is complete.

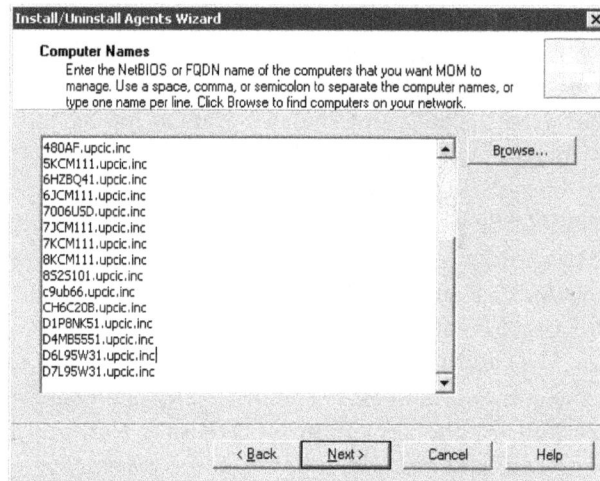

Figure 13.15   Deploying agents to computers.

Agent Failover

A primary Management Server you provide for a managed computer is the Management Server you use to install an agent on a server. If you add additional Management Servers and an agent cannot communicate with its primary Management Server, it automatically fails over to another Management Server in the same management group. This is useful for redundancy. If a primary server is offline, then a secondary can still receive data and communicate with the agent.

The best part of the agent failover process is you do not need to configure anything for agent failover. MOM automatically configures each additional Management Server as a redundant Management Server for the others in the management group. You also have the option of manually configuring which specific Management Servers should function as a redundant host for a primary Management Server.

To manually configure redundant Management Servers for agent failover:

1. In the MOM Administrator console, expand Administration, expand Computers, and then click MOM Management Servers.
2. In the details pane, right-click the Management Server you want to configure agent failover for, and then click Properties.
3. In the Management Server Properties dialog box, click the Failover tab.
4. In the Management Servers list, select or clear the checkboxes to specify which Management Servers you want to be redundant hosts for the Management Server you are configuring.

When you use the Add Computer wizard to add computers to the additional Management Servers, ensure you specify the correct Management Server on the Select MOM Management Server page. This determines the primary Management Server for the computer.

Installing System Center 2005 Reporting

MOM 2005 has made significant strides in the area of reporting on system state monitoring and alerts. The report component is part of the quest of Microsoft to deliver an end-to-end operations and administration product that will be known as System Center 2005. If you manage or direct operations in your enterprise, then the System Center reports will become part of your life every day, several times a day. The MOM Reporting console is part of SQL Server 2000 Reporting Services, a recent addition to the SQL Server product line.

System Center 2005 ships with the installation CD, so it's easy to install as part of setup. However, if you plan to install the reporting component, make sure to do it before you import MOM 2005 Management Packs because these include the MOM reports, which do not get installed if the reporting component is omitted. You have to re-import the reports after installing Microsoft System Center 2005 Reporting if you leave System Center until last, or return to it at a later installation. It is unlikely you'll not install reports in the initial setup because reporting is so critical to operations management.

The database is installed as part of the deal, and a base scheduled job handles the process of transferring data from the MOM database to the System Center 2005 Reporting database. The interface for the reporting process is the MOM Reporting console. From the console, you can run and view MOM reports based on queries from the System Center 2005 Reporting database.

You have the option of installing System Center 2005 Reporting on the same computer as the MOM database, or you can install it on a separate computer. We recommend you set up a dedicated server for all your reporting, especially in a large network environment, and install System Center 2005 Reporting on that dedicated computer as well. SQL Server Reporting Services is a very popular product and, if your shop has a significant data tier, you'll likely have more than one Reporting Services server for the System Center.

Importing MOM 2005 Management Packs

As mentioned earlier, the Management Packs are the essence of MOM. With the Management Pack, you set up the rules and actions to take with respect to how a certain system operates. Within the pack, you can set up how MOM should monitor a system and what it monitors. After you have a pack working for your environment, in the lab, you can export it to the MOM production environment.

Before we work with a pack, let's first review installing the packs. With all of MOM, including reports, installed, your last important task is to install the MOM Management Pack. The MOM Management Pack is automatically installed when you run setup. This task should be scheduled after you have installed all the agents within a specific management group; however, you can import, reimport, and update Management Packs, even custom ones, at any time after the installation.

Before you go rushing into installing Management Packs, there are some guidelines to consider:

- For a new installation, install the agents and make sure the agent process is working well before importing Management Packs. The exception to this guidline is the MOM Management Pack, which is installed on the MOM server as part of the installation process.
- As mentioned earlier, install the MOM Reporting console before installing Management Packs.

- Take your time with each management pack. Install a Management Pack, and then evaluate the effect it will have on your network. You need to stabilize the volume of data the pack's rules will generate. If you install all the Management Packs at the same time without first evaluating their rules and the amount of data generated, you can flood the network and your servers with too much data.
- Get to know each Management Pack and the data it generates in a lab. You can test the pack in the lab and, when comfortable with its operation, you can migrate it into production. Remember to overwrite any existing Management Pack already in production; otherwise, you'll end up with more packs than you intended. If you decide not to overwrite the pack, you can delete a Management Pack from the production environment.

To import a Management Pack

1. Go to the MOM Administrator Console, expand the tree in the left pane, and then select Management Packs.
2. The Import/Export Management Packs option now appears in the details pane. Click it to launch the Management Pack Wizard, which guides you through the installation. This is illustrated in Figure 13.16.

You can also right-click the Management Pack item in the tree and select Import/Export Management Pack.

NOTE: Management Packs can be customized and built from the ground up for any Microsoft OS application. Even the vendors, such as Dell Computers, provide management packs for MOM customized for their platforms and software.

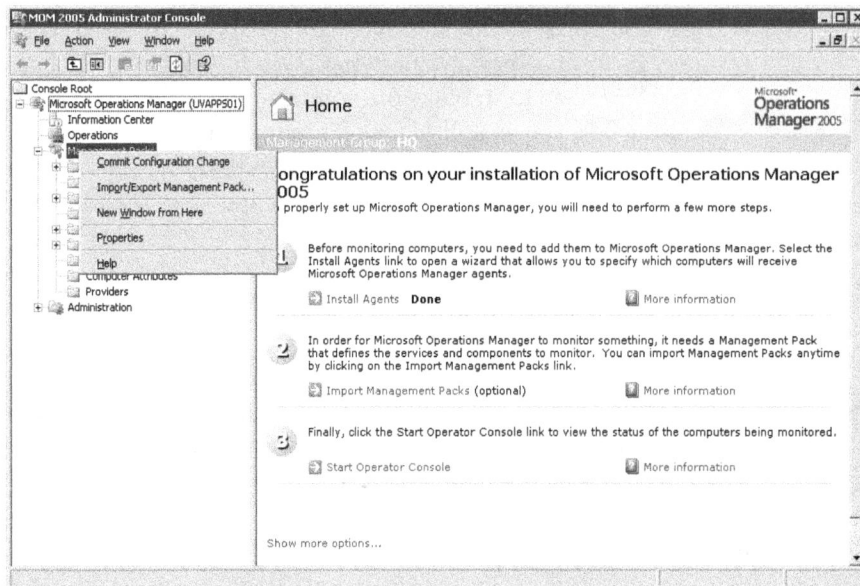

Figure 13.16 Importing Management Packs.

Management Pack Management

If you are new to MOM, we suggest you do not install any new Management Packs until you are familiar with the process of importing, exporting, and configuring rule groups (the stuff management packs are made of). The best place to start learning about the packs is in the lab. MOM 2005 support is illustrated in Figure 13.17 and shows the following components:

- **Event Rules:** Event rules dictate how MOM responds when an event occurs. These rules specify actions. Actions alert to operators or some respond to an event. The rules essentially filter events and they can also detect missing events, such as informational events you may want to know about.
- **Alert Rules:** Alert rules dictate how MOM finds and responds to alerts. The alert rule can be used to specify what alerts properties MOM should look for. MOM can search for an alert source or an event severity level. You can also program how MOM should respond to an alert, which we show you shortly.

■ **Performance Rules:** Performance rules dictate how MOM processes performance counter data and Windows Management Instrumentation (WMI) numeric data. You can create measuring rules, rules based on performance counters, and threshold rules (when a particular WMI value or performance counter crosses a defined threshold).

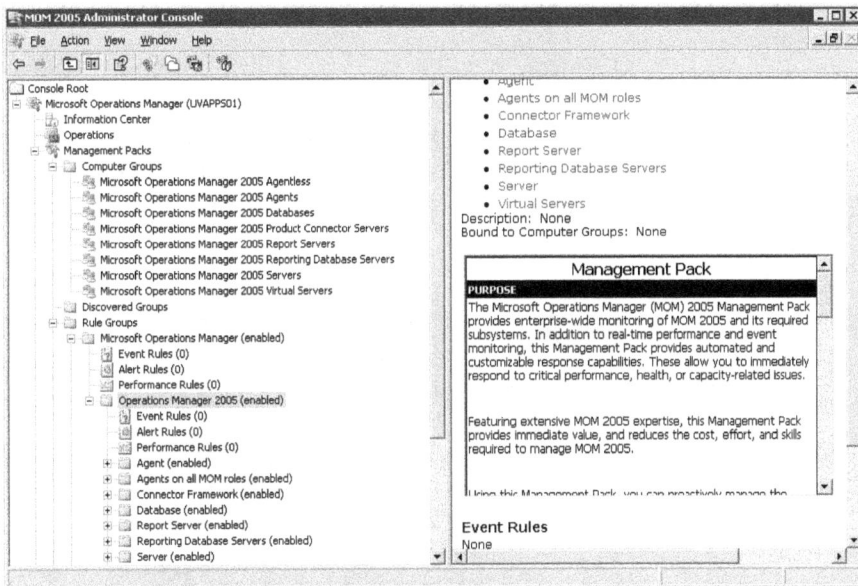

Figure 13.17   MOM 2005 Management Packs.

The MOM Management Pack, which was installed by default, contains rules for both MOM 2000 and MOM 2005. Have a look at the rule groups for MOM 2005. If you expand the MOM rule groups, you notice you can create any number of rule groups under a parent rule group and, thus, keep an entire collection of rule groups tailored to a particular product or service. If you browse through rule groups and investigate the Event Rules, Alert Rules, and Performance Rules, you begin to understand how these Management Packs work. If you are familiar with MOM 2000, you will soon realize MOM 2005 is a much more cohesive and streamlined product.

By now you begin to see how the first part of this chapter, which covered Performance Console and the alert architecture, ties in with the second part of this chapter on MOM. Performance Console and alerts go down to the lower layers of the operating system and applications and generate the objects and data for you to access. MOM handles how data is found, filtered, and acted on. To bring the two worlds together, let's create our own rule group.

To create a rule group, do the following:

1. Expand Management Packs down to Rule Groups, right-click on Rule Groups, and select Create Rule Group. The Rule Group Properties–General dialog box loads. Enter a name and description for the rule, and uncheck the Enabled checkbox. This is illustrated in Figure 13.18. Click Next to advance to the Rule Group Wizard.

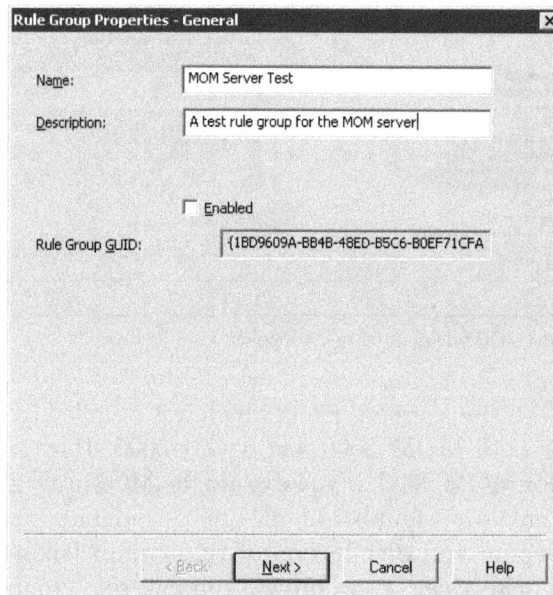

Figure 13.18 Creating a test rule group for the MOM server.

2. Next, you are given the opportunity to add some knowledge your company may have about the events and data that is going to be the focus of the rule group. Enter this information into the edit

control, as shown in Figure 13.19. MOM gives you a little editor you can use to format your knowledge for presentation.

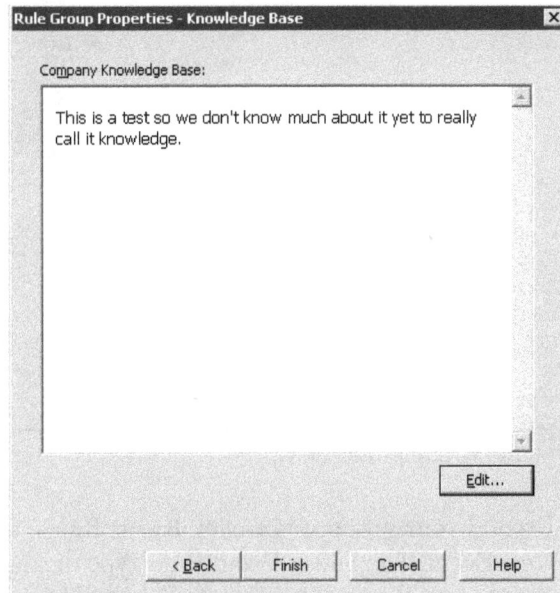

Figure 13.19   Adding to the knowledge base.

3. Click Finish after you have entered the data, and MOM immediately asks you if you want to deploy the Rule Group to a specific group of computers. Click Yes, and the wizard grows a new page for the computer groups. Because this is a new installation, we only have one group to monitor. Click Add, and then select Microsoft Operations Manager 2005 Servers from the list. This group's Properties dialog box now loads, as shown in Figure 13.20. Choose the Included Computers tab, and add your MOM Server as shown here. As you can see, the properties dialog box has a lot to show and, for the sake of time, space, and trees, we do not go into it further. Click Apply and OK until you are back at the Rule Group wizard we started the exercise with. Then click Apply, and then finish the wizard. You now see the new rule group you created under the Rule Groups node.

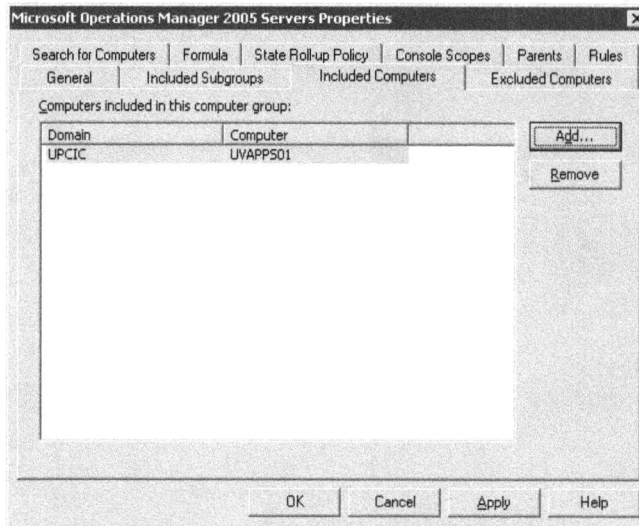

Figure 13.20   Computer Group properties.

4. Expand your group, right-click Event Rules, and select Create
   New Event. The Select Event Rule Type dialog box loads. Select
   Alert on or Respond to Event (Event) from the dialog box, as
   shown in Figure 13.21. Then click Next.

5. You now arrive at the Event Rule Properties–Data Provider wizard. From the drop-down control, select Application from the
   Provider Name list. This refers to the Application log. You can
   choose any event log provided on the platform, such as System
   or DNS. This is shown in Figure 13.22. (Notice you can click
   New to create your own event classification, which is where you
   can track custom application events.) Click Next to continue
   with the event setup.

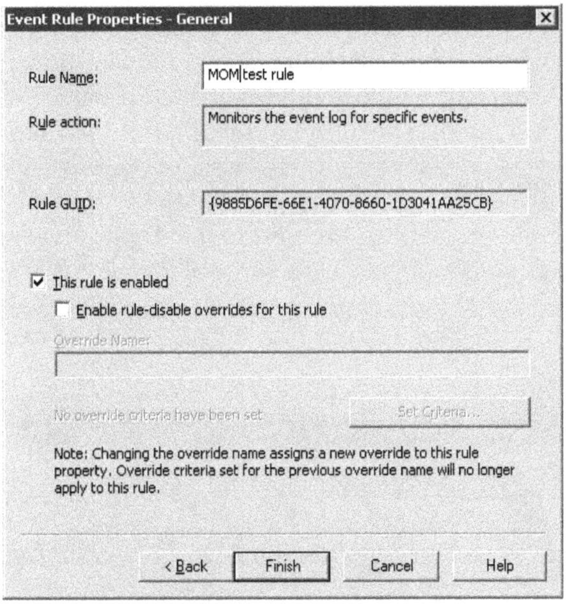

Figure 13.21 Creating a new event rule.

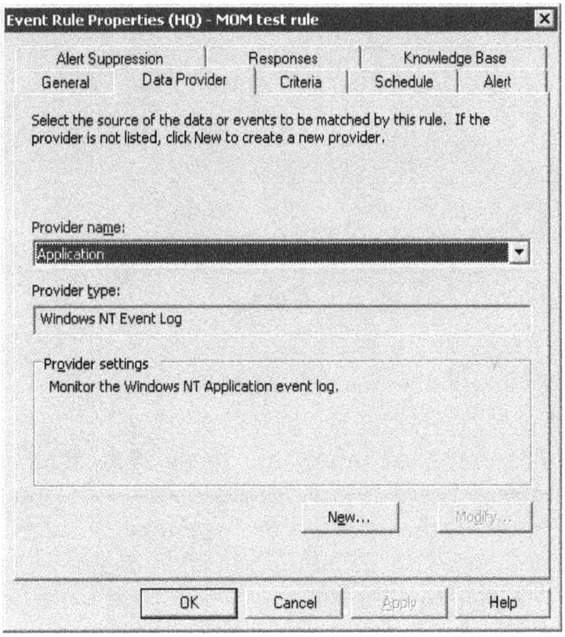

Figure 13.22 Event Rule Properties, Data Provider selection.

6. Next, select the properties of the event to monitor. Now this is where it becomes interesting. You can trace an alert or event from any source you have created using the Performance console, as described in the first part of this chapter. The example here acts on an alert that warns of excessive disk usage posted to the event log. We have created the alert in the Peformance console, and it posts the alert to the Application log, which is where custom alerts go. The source of the alert is SystmonLog and the event ID we are going to look for is 2037. This is shown in Figure 13.23.

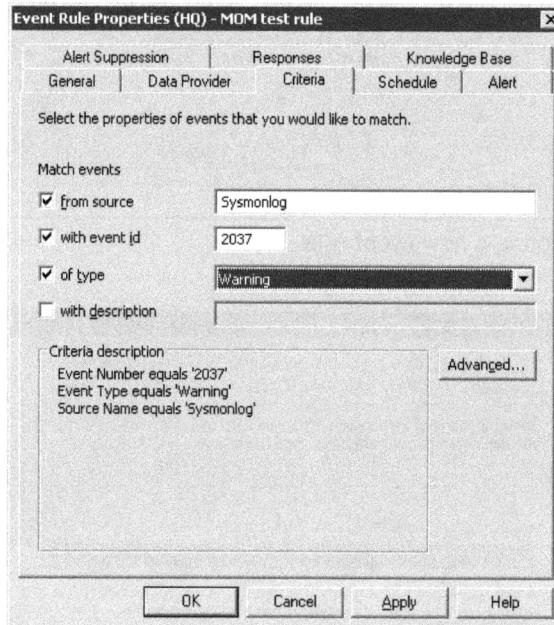

Figure 13.23 Event Rule Properties, Criteria selection.

7. Clicking Next brings you to the Schedule option. Choose to Always Process Data (no schedule needed now), and click Next. You are asked if you want to generate an alert. There's no point at this stage in generating an additional alert, unless you want to override the original alert. Click Next to accept the defaults on this page, and continue with the wizard. Accept Alert Suppression defaults on the next page, and click Next again.

8. Now you can Define a response to the alert in the Responses page of the wizard. This dialog box is shown in Figure 13.24. As you can see, you have a lot of options of what MOM can do if a match is found. You can even transfer a file somewhere. In the example shown, we have chosen to execute a script (and we won't go into what the script does, save to say that if MOM traps the event ID, the operator must immediately call our vendor and order new hard disks).

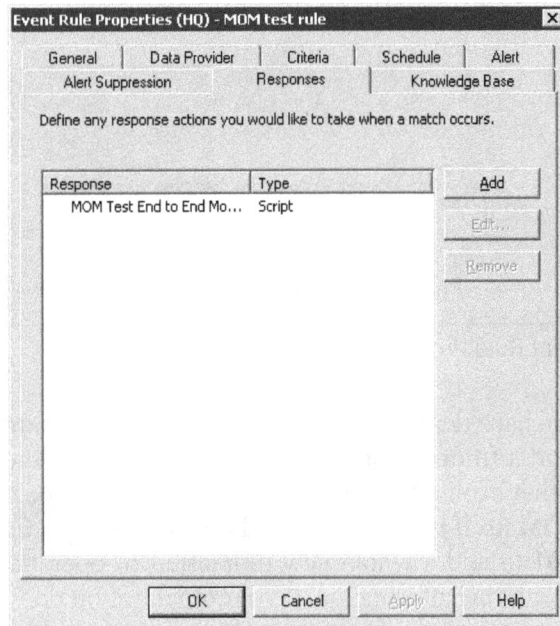

Figure 13.24 Event Rule Properties, Responses.

9. You have another chance to add more knowledge, this time as it applies to the specific alert rule we have created. We won't go into that here. Click Next to arrive at the Finish page. This is where you give your rule a name, as shown in Figure 13.25. Click Finish. We now have an event rule that will fire and alert us based on data generated by a performance counter created in the Performance console.

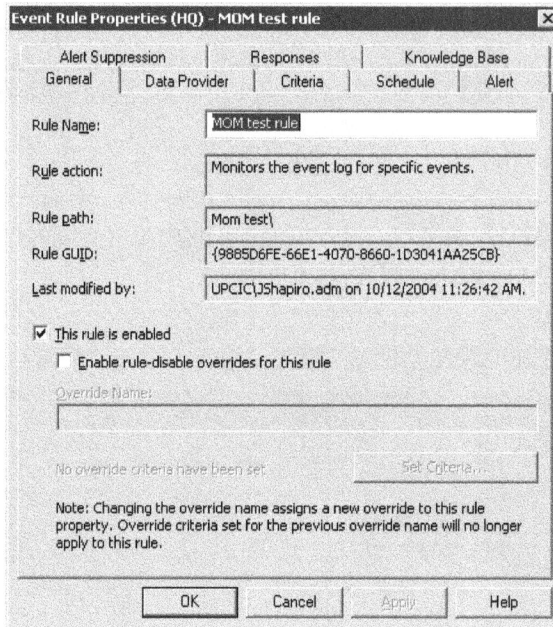

Figure 13.25   Event Rule Properties, Rule Name.

After you have deployed your Management Pack (your rule group), you can export it from the lab and import it into production.

Further exploration of MOM is beyond the scope of this chapter. In fact, MOM itself is worth a whole book. But you get the idea how to set up MOM to add a whole new dimension to operations management. Armed with this information, if your organization does its own software development or in-house programming, you should have the engineers post errors and application events to the OS logs so that the operations management team can monitor these systems easier and more closely.

Time-Out

We spent a lot of time in this chapter covering the basics of monitoring your servers and setting up a proactive alert notification and reporting system for your operations management. You can go back to the previous chapters and spend time setting up MOM agents on all of your servers and setting up the alerts you want MOM to catch.

Now is the time to do your Q&A and validation, and make sure labeling and naming conventions are consistent across your enterprise, so MOM reports data to you that makes sense and that you can act upon without further investigation.

Index

Q-R

informIT

Register
Your Book

at www.awprofessional.com/register

You may be eligible to receive:

- Advance notice of forthcoming editions of the book
- Related book recommendations
- Chapter excerpts and supplements of forthcoming titles
- Information about special contests and promotions throughout the year
- Notices and reminders about author appearances, tradeshows, and online chats with special guests

Contact us

If you are interested in writing a book or reviewing manuscripts prior to publication, please write to us at:

Editorial Department
Addison-Wesley Professional
75 Arlington Street, Suite 300
Boston, MA 02116 USA
Email: AWPro@aw.com

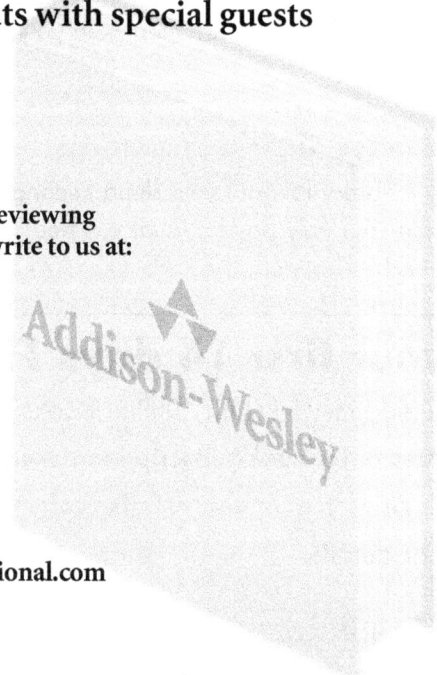

Visit us on the Web: http://www.awprofessional.com

www.ingramcontent.com/pod-product-compliance
Lightning Source LLC
Chambersburg PA
CBHW080120220326
41598CB00032B/4898